Study Guide

Amy Fowler

GLEITMAN
Basic Psychology
Third Edition

JOHN JONIDES
UNIVERSITY OF MICHIGAN

PAUL ROZIN
UNIVERSITY OF PENNSYLVANIA

W · W · NORTON & COMPANY · NEW·YORK · LONDON

Permission and credits, constituting an extension of the copyright page, are located on pages 279–280.

W. W. Norton & Company, Inc., 500 Fifth Avenue,
New York, N.Y. 10110
W. W. Norton & Company Ltd., 10 Coptic Street,
London WC1A 1PU

ISBN 0-393-96165-6

3 4 5 6 7 8 9 0

CONTENTS

ACKNOWLEDGMENTS

The authors would like to thank Caroline Arnold, Jason Fabozzi, Elizabeth Gross, Georgia Larounis, Jennifer Lerner, Laura Lowery, Maureen Markwith, Linda Millman, Deborah Reyher, Nathan Witthoft, and Barbara Zeeff for their contributions and valuable suggestions.

In the course of developing the sections entitled "Investigating Psychological Phenomena" for each chapter, we have had occasion to seek the advice of colleagues and students who have particular expertise in the areas in question. We would like to acknowledge the help of Lyn Abramson, Henry Gleitman, Aaron Katcher, Charles G. Morris, Lorraine Nadelman, Harriet Oster, Christopher Peterson, Martin E. P. Seligman, W. John Smith, Marjorie Speers, and Edward Stricker. We also thank Walter Love and Jeannie Morrow for special assistance in field testing a number of the activities that we have included.

Finally, we thank Donald Fusting for his encouragement and advice throughout the development of the text. We are also extremely grateful to Cathy Wick and Sandy Lifland, both of whom reviewed the entire manuscript with great care, suggesting many improvements and clarifications.

The authors are listed in alphabetical order on the title page.

TO THE STUDENT

This study guide is designed to help you to understand and apply the material presented in *Basic Psychology*, Third Edition, by Henry Gleitman. Each chapter in the study guide corresponds to one in the textbook. There are four sections in each study guide chapter: Learning Objectives, Programmed Exercises, Self-Test, and Investigating Psychological Phenomena. The first three sections will help you determine the essential ideas of the chapter, as well as give you experience with possible test questions. The fourth section, Investigating Psychological Phenomena, allows you to extend your knowledge of some issues raised in the text. This section will also give you a feeling for how the data used by psychologists are collected, and how theories are tested in psychology. Let us briefly review the function of each of these sections.

LEARNING OBJECTIVES

We have provided an outline of the key issues discussed in each chapter. Each entry in the outline refers to a basic fact, theory, or relationship that you should have learned from the chapter. These entries are listed in order of occurrence in the chapter and are arranged under the same headings used in the chapter. It may be useful to read the learning objectives before reading the chapter, as well as after. They will help to orient you to the major issues, or the "big picture," of the chapter.

PROGRAMMED EXERCISES

For each chapter of the text, we have provided fill-in-the-blank questions. These questions test your basic knowledge of the key words and concepts of the chapter. These questions are very straightforward and can be looked up and verified in the text. So that you will know whether you are correct, the answer has been provided on the right side of the page. Be sure to cover that side of the page with your hand or a piece of paper as you do the exercises.

To facilitate locating the answers in the text, the programmed exercises are also arranged under the major headings of the textbook, and they follow the order of presentation in the text. This allows you to see which fact or theory pertains to which major point of the chapter.

SELF-TEST

For each chapter in the text, we have prepared a self-test composed of multiple-choice questions. They also follow the order of the text. In general, these questions are more difficult than the fill-ins, though both types of questions cover the range of materials presented in the text. The multiple choices sometimes highlight subtle distinctions, ask for some amount of integration, or test your ability to apply some of the material in the text.

Since multiple-choice questions are commonly used in examinations, and since they can also be very instructive, we will spend some time in this section discussing how to answer them. We will also describe and illustrate some different types of multiple-choice questions used in this study guide.

First, some basic strategies: Most multiple-choice questions on examinations, and in this study guide, have four or five choices. On most examinations there is a penalty of $-1/3$ point for wrong answers of four-choice questions and $-1/4$ point for wrong answers on five-choice questions. This would mean that wild guessing should net a score of zero. But if you can eliminate even one choice, it pays to guess among the remaining alternatives.

Read each question carefully. Try to understand the *point* of the question. Read through the alternatives. The answer may be obvious to you. If not, try to eliminate some of the choices. You may be able to eliminate choices on the following grounds:

1. The choice is inherently inconsistent, illogical, or actual nonsense (e.g., word salad: a bunch of usually relevant terms combined in a meaningless way).

2. The choice makes sense and may even be true, but it is not an *answer* to the question.

3. On the basis of your knowledge, the choice is just the wrong answer to the question.

Get used to sorting out sense from nonsense and relevant from irrelevant answers. These skills will stand you in good stead in many of your activities outside of this course. Work with the remaining choices (if more than one choice remains), and do the best you can to determine the best fit between the question and the answer.

We will illustrate a number of different types of multiple-choice questions, all represented in this study guide. For each example we will indicate the correct answer and add comments on some of the incorrect choices.

Straight factual questions. Many multiple-choice questions simply ask for your knowledge of facts: names, definitions, and basic concepts.

1. The Prime Minister of Great Britain at the end of World War II was:
   a. Neville Chamberlain
   b. Winston Churchill
   c. Harold Wilson
   d. Sir D. Winter
   e. Anthony Eden

Comment: This is a very straightforward question. You know it or you don't. The answer is *b*, Winston Churchill. The other names were selected to make the question somewhat difficult: Three of the other choices were prime ministers of Great Britain at the beginning or after the war, and one, Sir D. Winter, is a fictitious name.

2. The best way to describe inflation is:
   a. increase in the gross national product not accompanied by increased unemployment
   b. a general increase in prices
   c. a decrease in the money supply
   d. a decrease in the value of the monetary system, when associated with a gross national product
   e. another form of recession

Comment: This question is more difficult than 1. This is in part because the choices are more difficult. The correct answer is *b*. Answers *a, c,* and *e* are just wrong. Though *a* is consistent with inflation, it does not define it. Item *d* is inherently wrong, that is, it is nonsense. What does it mean to decrease the value of the monetary *system* as opposed to money? And everything is associated with some gross national product. Keep your eyes open for nonsense. There is a lot of it in the world.

Evaluating evidence for a theory. In this type of question you are asked to judge whether particular results (real or hypothetical) support a particular theory (or which theory would be supported or opposed by a particular result). The theory and/or results may have been presented in the text, or they may be introduced in the question. The question tests both your knowledge of the materials and your progress in understanding how to evaluate evidence. This type of question is often formulated in the negative—"Which of the following would be evidence against theory X?"—simply because it is usually easier to come up with results supporting major theories than results opposing them. We will assume, for the next sample question, that you have read in some text or other that Yentzel claimed that the crime rate increases as population mass and density increase. (Yentzel is a fictitious name.)

3. Which of the following would be evidence against Yentzel's theory? (Note: We assume that New York is larger than Philadelphia, which is larger than Tucson.)
   a. Philadelphia has a crime rate higher than Tucson.
   b. a few cities with increasing population also have increasing crime rates
   c. a few cities with decreasing population have an increase in crime rate
   d. Philadelphia has a lower crime rate than New York
   e. the ratio of murders to robberies is lower in New York than in Tucson

Comment: The correct answer is *c*, because this result is opposite to what would be predicted by Yentzel's theory. Answers *a, b,* and *c* are supporting evidence for the theory. Answer *e* is irrelevant: The theory says nothing about the types of crime, and *e* says nothing about the overall crime rate. (Note another clue to the right answer: *b* and *c* are opposites, so it is likely that one is evidence against the theory. However, clever exam writers know about this and sometimes put in opposites that are irrelevant to the question to keep you on your toes.)

Extending a principle or theory to a new situation. This type of question tests your understanding of a principle, theory, or concept by asking you to apply it to a situation other than those presented in the text.

4. If the saying "a stitch in time saves nine" were applied to medicine, one would recommend:
   a. reducing the amount of sewing in surgery
   b. increasing the cost of medical insurance
   c. increasing the frequency of checkups
   d. increasing the number of physicians

e. making prescription drugs available over the counter

Comment: The correct answer is *c*. To answer the question one must understand the saying and translate it into medical terms. This translation would be something like: Medical precautions can lead to avoidance of major illnesses. Alternative *a* is irrelevant to the *real* meaning of the saying and simply alludes to the *literal* meaning. Answer *b* would not lead, in any direct way, to avoidance of illness. But *b* is a sort of correct answer, since one might assume that increasing the cost of medical insurance would lead to increased coverage. However, the answer says increasing the cost, not the amount of insurance. Answer *c* relates directly to the saying: More checkups should lead to earlier discovery of illnesses that might prove harmful if allowed to develop. While *d* might well cut down the rate of illnesses, it is not a direct way of arriving at prevention. Lastly, *e* is irrelevant to the issue raised in the saying.

Relating different ideas or facts, or integrating materials. This type of question often involves materials from different sections of a chapter or perhaps from different chapters (we have refrained from the latter, since we don't know the order in which you will be reading the chapters in the book).

5. The President of the United States is related to the electoral college as a U.S. Senator is related to:*
a. his own college faculty
b. the voters of his state
c. the members of the House of Representatives
d. the state of his electors
e. the state of his voters

Comment: The correct answer is *b*. The electoral college is the group of people who actually elect the president. The voters of a senator's state are the people who elect the senator. Item *a* is totally wrong and simply a play on the word college. Item *c* is factually wrong. Item *d* is wrong and doesn't make too much sense, and item *e* is a reversal of the correct answer and has no relation to the question.

INVESTIGATING PSYCHOLOGICAL PHENOMENA

For each chapter of the text, we have presented one or two activities or experiments. These activities build upon concepts or theories presented in the chapter and

*This type of relation is often stated as "President of the U.S.; electoral college::U.S. Senator: _____."

extend and deepen your knowledge and understanding of these concepts or theories.

The activities give you an opportunity to understand something about the progress of psychology as a science. While the text emphasizes our current understanding of psychology, the activities emphasize the process through which we arrive at this understanding. How is the theory tested? How do psychologists get data to describe basic relations or test theories? How do they analyze the data? We hope to give you a feeling for how progress is made, while at the same time indicating the problems and difficulties associated with the serious study of something as complex as the human mind.

We have attempted to provide you with a variety of activities. Some emphasize the generation or testing of theories, others data collection or analysis. We have tried to cover the major methods of data collection used by psychologists: Among all the activities are included examples of the experiment, the questionnaire, direct observation, and the interview. In many cases we provide data from studies we have done with introductory psychology students as a base for comparison with the data you collect. In each activity in which you collect data, we guide you through some analysis of the data and get you to try to interpret the data and relate it to issues raised in the text. If your instructor wishes to include the activities as part of the course, he or she may ask you to tear out the report (data) sheet pages and hand them in. These sheets are duplicated at the end of the book in Appendix B. Otherwise, you may consider these activities as a less formal extension of your education in psychology.

We have tried out all of these activities on undergraduate students like yourselves. We have only included studies that work out for the great majority of students. Of course, with people as variable as they are, all the studies that you do on one or a few students will not show the same results. But we expect that most of you will get most of the predicted results.

Many of the most important phenomena in psychology cannot be included in these activities because they must be measured under controlled conditions, which you could not easily arrange. Some involve expensive equipment, like timers that can time thousandths of a second, or panels of lights and switches. Some important relations are not striking enough to be seen in one or a few subjects. We have tried to find, for each chapter, at least one activity that can be appreciated within the limits that you will be working under. We require no equipment other than pencil, paper, some sort of second indicator (stopwatch, digital watch with second indicator, or a watch with a second hand), and materials presented within this study guide. We have limited the time demands on you for any activity to less than one hour. In all but a few cases, we have limited the number of subjects to a very few. At the beginning of each activity, we indicate the equipment involved and the time demands it will make on you and the subjects.

These activities are designed to be both educational and entertaining. We hope that you find that they meet these goals.

Introduction

Learning Objectives

THE SCOPE OF PSYCHOLOGY

1. Give examples of psychological phenomena.

   Electrically triggered images
2. Explain what experiments on electrical stimulation of the brain tell us about the relationship between psychology and physiology.

   Ambiguous sights and sounds
3. Be able to explain what determines the interpretation of an ambiguous stimulus.

   The perceptual world of infants
4. Explain how the study of infants suggests that some abilities may be innate.

   Displays
5. Describe how social interaction in animals differs from that in humans. Describe how it differs from one animal to another. Give an example to prove each point.

   Complex social behavior in humans
6. Be aware of the characteristics of social interactions in humans.

A SCIENCE OF MANY FACES

7. Discuss the range of phenomena studied by psychologists.
8. List several of psychology's approaches to the study of the individual. List several fields that have contributed to the development of psychology.

THE TASK OF PSYCHOLOGY

9. Explain what the main purpose of psychology is and what it is not.

Programmed Exercises

THE SCOPE OF PSYCHOLOGY

1. Psychology involves not only the study of the mind, but also the

   study of _behavior_.   behavior
2. Electrical stimulation of the brain sometimes results in reports of

   sensations.   sensations
3. _Context_ is an important determinant of how we perceive an   Context
   ambiguous figure.
4. The study of perceptual skills in infants using the visual cliff

   shows us that some skills are _learned_ while others are   learned

   innate .   innate

1

5. In animals, many social interactions depend largely on _innate_ forms of communication.

                                                           innate

6. Many types of animal communication are based on signals called _displays_

                                                           displays

7. The behavior of panicky crowds is determined not only by each individual, but also by individuals' _social_ interactions.

                                                           social (group)

A SCIENCE OF MANY FACES

8. Psychology can be studied from perspectives emphasizing _action_ (overt behavior), _cognition_ (human knowledge), _social behavior_ (the influence of others on individual action), _development_ (growth), and _individual_ differences (how people are alike or different).

                                                           action, cognition

social behavior

development, individual

THE TASK OF PSYCHOLOGY

9. Psychology, like other sciences, seeks _general_ principles to explain its phenomena, rather than concentrating on individual events.

                                                           general

Self-Test

1. Psychology is the:
   a. science of the mind.
   b. science of behavior.
   c. both of the above
   d. neither of the above

2. When the brain is stimulated electrically:
   a. visual experience may occur.
   b. previous memories may be blocked.
   c. new memories are blocked.
   d. none of the above

3. If we are first shown a picture of a rat, and then the ambiguous figure below, we will most likely see:

   a. the man.
   b. the rat.
   c. the rat or the man, depending on other factors.
   d. neither the rat nor the man.

4. The visual cliff results suggest that:
   a. perceptual skills are learned.
   b. perceptual skills are innate.
   c. perceptual skills could be innate.
   d. none of the above

5. Psychology consists of the study of
   a. action.
   b. cognition.
   c. social processes.
   d. individual differences.
   e. all of the above

Answer Key for Self-Test

1. c p. 1   4. c p. 3
2. a p. 2   5. d p. 6
3. b p. 2

INTRODUCTION

Investigating Psychological Phenomena

THE CONSISTENCY OF DREAMS

Equipment: None
Number of subjects: One, yourself
Time per subject: Ten to twenty minutes
Time for experimenter: Ten to twenty minutes

Although the introduction is intended as a general overview of psychology, it also provides an opportunity to illustrate how a particular psychological phenomenon can be studied scientifically. Professor Gleitman provides several examples of the sorts of studies that can be illuminating about phenomena, studies such as the electrical stimulation of the brain, investigation of the perception of ambiguous stimuli, and depth perception in infants. These examples illustrate the wide array of investigations that psychologists carry out in order to understand the phenomena of mind and behavior. Let us provide yet one more example, one drawn from the study of dreams (a topic to be discussed later in the text). The technique we illustrate involves collecting ratings or categorizations of various stimuli.

One of the fundamental issues in dream research concerns the extent to which dreams represent the realization of basic problems, wishes, needs, or areas of concern to the dreamer. Some (such as the famous psychologist Sigmund Freud, whose work will be discussed in Chapter 10) believe that factors such as these are the primary determinants of the content of dreams. That is, they believe that dreams are primarily constructed out of the fundamental urges of the dreamer. This position suggests that the dreams of any one person ought to be identifiably more similar to one another than the dreams of several people are to each other. This position thus poses the question: Is there consistency in a dreamer's dreams?

To test this idea, nine dream reports have been transcribed below. These reports were collected from three individuals, with three reports collected per individual. Your task is to select which three dreams were produced by each of the three individuals sampled.

There are several criteria that you could use to classify the dreams. One caution: You might think to use the language characteristics, that is, the use of certain consistent phrases, but don't be led astray by such a strategy. Language characteristics would not be appropriate criteria, since the purpose is to assess whether there is evidence of consistency in dream *content*. So you should concentrate on the content of the dreams as a basis for classification.

DREAM 1

A girl and I were being chased through a wood. We entered a log cabin. We were hiding when two people came in after us. One of the men who entered was tall with a thick dark beard. He looked like a typical backwoodsman. His assistant, by contrast, was short and fat. I decided to outsmart them. I crawled into a back room and began to make some noise. I stood on a box holding a milk bottle in my hand. The man entered. I hit him over the head several times, but the bottle did not break and he only laughed. The next thing I knew, the man was pointing a two-barrelled shotgun at me. I noticed that the ends of the barrels seemed magnified. He shot me in the lower right stomach. I looked down at the hole, saw the blood, and felt very weak. Then I was driving in my car by some railroad tracks. The wheels of my car became stuck on the tracks; my car would only move backward. I saw a train approaching rapidly and somehow managed to move off the tracks. I watched a huge train go past. My car continued moving in reverse. I had to keep the car moving perfectly straight, which was a very difficult task, and the train only missed me by inches. As I sped backward, I noticed a fence alongside the tracks; I saw a spot where the fence had been pushed down. I got out, picked up my car, and climbed over the fence. As I did this, I noticed two wounds, the one from the shotgun and a similar mark on the other side of my body. I began to look for a girl, not sure if I was looking for the one who had been with me in the cabin. I searched through a series of backyards, hiding behind bushes. I felt guilty about something. I found the girl I was looking for; she helped me attempt an escape. She led me back over to the fence, which was on a hill above the tracks. I started to climb the fence, which resembled a baseball backstop, but I was too weak from my wounds to be successful. The girl climbed on ahead and offered to hold my shirt as I climbed. Suddenly, two men on the railroad tracks below caught my eye. They were shooting at me with a bow and arrow. I told the girl not to worry; I thought I would be safe because the wind would deflect the arrows. Three or four of the arrows missed, but I was finally hit on my left front pocket. Luckily, the arrow had pierced my wallet instead of going into my leg. (In real life I keep my wallet in another pocket.)

DREAM 2

New York was being attacked by Germans. My mother told me not to worry. She told me that the last time the Germans attacked, only three persons who were in a cemetery had been killed. I went to warn my grandmother, who was at my uncle's basement apartment. My aunt was standing outside of the building. She also told me not to worry; she said she would wait outside for me. I walked down two flights of stairs. Strangely, the walls were made of dirt. I saw several of my relatives. Suddenly, I heard a loud noise. Water poured out of one of the walls. My uncle and cousin were covered with dirt. I dug them out just before they would have suffocated. I left with my grandmother. Then, things changed to a cemetery; I saw people walking behind a coffin. I was looking down from an aerial view. (I have had this kind of dream once before, several years ago.)

DREAM 3

I was with a group of people in the church I attended as a child. I knew most of the people there. I saw Paul Newman among the group. Guns appeared from somewhere; everyone grabbed one. Two groups formed; shooting started. I watched Newman fight a burly man. It seemed I became Newman—I could hear and feel everything he felt and heard. We threw "ourself" out into the open to try for a clear shot, but had no time to shoot before we were shot by the burly man. We felt the searing pain; I was sure death was imminent. Suddenly, the pain cleared. We shot the burly man, killing him. The fighting ended. We went inside, once again having our own identities. I saw Newman shaking his head, saying that it was only supposed to have been a game.

DREAM 4

I was on a highway, walking instead of driving. There were no cars, and everyone was walking, but I felt as if I were in a car. I saw someone I knew; we started talking. I got off at the exit to the beach. I walked up a circular ramp. The end of the ramp resembled a manhole. I had a bathing suit on under my clothes, but I had no towel. I started looking for one. I found two that looked as if they did not belong to anyone, so I took them. A woman approached me while I was lying on the sand. She said they were her towels. I told her I had taken them by mistake; she said she was going to call the police. I stayed; the police never came.

DREAM 5

I was in a restaurant or a cafeteria. I picked up some food. I thought it was a dessert and expected it to be sweet and delicious. Instead, I found that it tasted terrible. I thought someone had substituted salt for sugar in the recipe. I felt as though the salty taste grew and grew; I was now alone in a vast, dry wasteland with

no relief in sight. (I woke up with the taste of salt still parching my mouth.)

DREAM 6

First, I was seated on the top bunk of my bed. I was with some friends. Then I found myself walking around piles of boards. My house had been destroyed—either it had collapsed or burned down—and my belongings were covered with rubble. Then I was outside the house digging a ditch longer than it was deep. Building materials lay nearby. While I dug, I got dirt in my hair. I wanted a hat, so I went to the part of the house where the boards were. After finding a hat, I started out of the rubble. Some of the boards fell out of place; they knocked my father's car, our dog, and a chair over a steep cliff. I did not look over the cliff. I could hear my father's car smash into pieces. Then I saw a large field below the cliff. The dog and the chair also broke into pieces. The pieces began moving end over end to the other side of the field. When they stopped rolling, they were reassembled. I felt very unhappy about all this. I returned to the ditch and saw my father. I told him not to worry as he would soon be getting a company car. Then things changed and I was driving in my convertible with three friends. We had a case of beer with us. The road was covered with snow, although it was only snowing lightly at that moment. We stopped at a house where I walked around to the yard. It was twenty-three minutes to six, and I had to be home at five, but I felt that I could not tell my friends this. I saw my roommate swinging on a pole in the backyard. He said he wanted to swing up onto a window ledge. I offered to help; he refused my offer. Eventually we both got up on the ledge. I looked in through the window. A lady was in the kitchen. By now it was almost six, so I jumped down from the ledge, saying I had to go. I was alone.

DREAM 7

I was in a room I am familiar with but cannot now identify. A girl I work with was also there. The room made me think of Patricia Hearst; perhaps she had lived there. I thought she might be close by. I searched for clues. I wanted to find the clue that would solve the kidnapping case. I found something small lying on the floor; it was thin and cylindrical with screwlike threads at one end. I felt that this might be the clue to the kidnapping that I was looking for, but when I showed it to the girl she said it was something of hers. She took it.

DREAM 8

My brother and I were standing on a patio waiting for something. Four or five large jet planes passed the yard. The planes were a few feet above the ground. As my brother went to get a better look, another plane came by and snatched him up. He was strapped into a seat like a baby's car seat. Next, I was inside a house. I was handed a tube about a foot long. The tube was clear; it had white caps at either end. Something was inside – something red and jellylike. It reminded me of lobster. I was shocked when they told me it was my brother. I wanted to let him out of the tube; I was also afraid of what might happen. The organism was fighting violently; it was my brother. A strange-looking person entered the room then. He said he was my brother. I thought the person was wearing a disguise. I grabbed him; we started to fight. Somehow I was convinced it was my brother. I said, "I hate to do this, but it's for your own good." Next I found myself walking with two friends towards a building. I had books in my hand. I then noticed that all of the lights in the town were off, so that there was no sense in continuing to go where I had intended. I crossed the bridge and left my friends, telling them I was going back for something. I returned to the patio. People were coming towards me. My brother was standing beside me. A group of girls I knew walked out of the building; I then recognized it to be a movie theater. I walked over to one of the girls, who said that she had seen an "awfully strange movie." I was very relieved that everything that had just happened to me was only a movie and that my brother was safe beside me.

DREAM 9

I was going to school in Paris. I did not feel that I was really in Paris, however. I received a letter from a friend. He had just spent two weeks in Lorraine. He thought I should also travel. I decided to go to Geneva.

Write your answers in the spaces below:

Dreamer A _____ _____ _____

Dreamer B _____ _____ _____

Dreamer C _____ _____ _____

After you have made your judgments, check the correct answers on the bottom of this page. How correct were you? Based on your results, what would you conclude about the consistency of people's dreams? What is the implication of these conclusions for a theory of dreams? You may want to come back to these results after you have read Chapter 10, which provides much more detail about the topic of dreams. In Chapter 10, you will discover that certain theories of dreams claim that the overt content of a dream may be different from its true (but hidden) meaning. Certain events in dreams are supposed to symbolize other events that are not directly present. Once you have read this section, you should return to these nine dreams to check whether you might be able to discover some "latent" content in them that could provide a new basis for your judgments.

ANSWERS TO DREAM EXPERIMENT

Dreamer A _____ 8,6,1

Dreamer B _____ 9,4,2

Dreamer C _____ 7,5,3

Biological Bases of Behavior

Learning Objectives

THE ORGANISM AS MACHINE

Descartes and the reflex concept

1. Be familiar with Descartes's conception of the reflex, and how, in part, it still forms the basis of animal and human action.

The basic nervous functions: reception, integration, reaction

2. Be able to describe fully the action sequence: reception, integration, reaction.
3. Review what function the following serve: receptors, afferent nerves, efferent nerves, effectors, interneurons.

NERVE CELLS AND NERVE INPULSE

The neuron

4. Explain what dendrites, the axon, the synapse, the myelin sheath, and the nodes of Ranvier are.
5. Explain what purpose the sensory neurons and motor neurons serve.
6. Be able to describe the electrical activity of the neuron; know the difference between resting potential and action potential.

The electrical activity of the neuron

7. Describe the action potential.
8. Define the all-or-none law.
9. Explain what effect stimulus intensity has on the number of neurons stimulated and on the frequency of impulses.

INTERACTION AMONG NERVE CELLS

The reflex

10. Describe the reflex arc.

Inferring the synapse

11. Describe how Sherrington inferred the existence of the synapse. Describe spatial and temporal summation.
12. Be able to explain central excitatory state, inhibition, and disinhibition.

The synaptic mechanism

13. Describe Loewi's classic demonstration of the existence of neurotransmitters.
14. Know the anatomy of the synaptic mechanism (pre- and postsynaptic neurons, synaptic gaps, synaptic vesicles, and neurotransmitters) and the way that neural excitation (the nerve impulse) is transmitted across the synapse.
15. Be able to explain how inhibition and excitation occur at synapses and how the postsynaptic neuron integrates the various inhibitory and excitatory effects on it.
16. Explain the basic differences between action potentials and synaptic transmission.
17. Know what a neurotransmitter is. Know what the lock-and-key model is.
18. Explain what drugs called agonists and antagonists are and the different ways in which they can exert their effects.
19. Describe the effects of some major neurotransmitters (acetylcholine and dopamine) and how these effects are modified by the drugs curare and chlorpromazine (respectively).
20. Indicate the way in which dopamine has been proposed to be involved in schizophrenia.
21. Know what the endorphins are and how they are related to the perception of pain.

INTERACTION THROUGH THE BLOODSTREAM: THE ENDOCRINE SYSTEM

22. Explain the mode of action of the endocrine system, and know the similarities and differences

between the types of interaction and transmission in the nervous and endocrine systems.

THE MAIN STRUCTURES OF THE NERVOUS SYSTEM

The peripheral nervous system

23. Be able to distinguish the peripheral from the central nervous system and the somatic from the autonomic nervous system.

The central nervous system

24. Describe the basic anatomy of the brain, including the functions of the hindbrain, midbrain, and forebrain.
25. Know the structure of the cerebral cortex, including the four lobes, the basal ganglia, and the limbic system.

THE CEREBRAL CORTEX

Projection areas

26. Describe the function of projection areas of the brain, and indicate what determines how much space in these areas is devoted to different parts of the body.

Association areas

27. Explain what association areas are.
28. Explain how PET and CAT scans operate.
29. Define apraxia and agnosia.

30. Distinguish receptive and expressive aphasias in terms of site of brain damage and type of symptoms.

One brain or two?

31. Explain the meaning of lateralization.
32. Describe what research on people with split brains tells us about the differences between the cerebral hemispheres.
33. Be able to explain how measures of brain blood flow indicate which hemisphere of normal people is more activated.
34. Explain the two modes of mental functioning that some believe are associated with the right and left hemispheres.

Recovery from brain injury

35. Describe how recovery of damaged neurons, collateral sprouting, and substitution of function allow for recovery from the loss of nerve cells in cerebral lesions.
36. Explain why brain grafts in rats hold promise for the treatment of Alzheimer's disease.

SOME PROBLEMS IN LOCALIZING BRAIN FUNCTION

37. Describe the problems, in both our understanding of behavior and of the organization of the nervous system, that make it difficult to assign psychological functions to particular parts of the brain.

Programmed Exercises

THE ORGANISM AS MACHINE

1. The conception of man as a machine can be traced to the great French philosopher _Descartes_.

   Descartes

2. According to Descartes, excitation from the senses leads to muscle contraction in what we now call a _reflex_ .

   reflex

3. The three basic components of an action sequence are _reception_ , _integration_, and _reaction_.

   reception, integration, reaction

4. Nerves that connect receptors to the central nervous system are called _afferent_ nerves.

   afferent (sensory)

5. Nerves carrying excitation from the central nervous system to muscles and glands are called _efferent_ nerves.

   efferent (motor)

6. Afferent neurons usually produce effects in efferent neurons via _inter_ neurons.

   inter-

NERVE CELL AND NERVE IMPULSE

7. The basic building block of the nervous system is the nerve cell,

   or _neuron_ .   neuron

8. The basic unit of nervous function is the _nerve___impulse._   nerve impulse

9. Label the following diagram of the neuron.

   A. _Dendrites_   B. _cell___Body_   dendrites, ~~cell body~~

   C. _Axon_   D. _Myelin__sheath_   ~~axon, myelin sheath~~

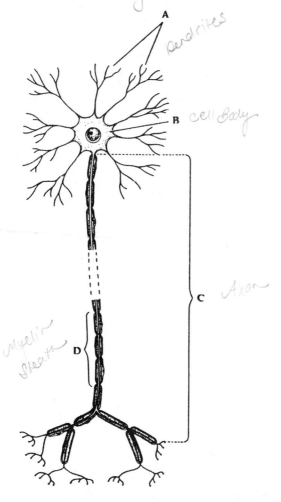

10. The gap between the axon terminals of one neuron and the

    dendritic processes of another is called the _synapse._   synapse

11. Receptor cells _transduce_ stimulus energy into nerve impulses.   transduce

12. The axons of _motor___neurons_ terminate in effector cells and   motor neurons

    activate the _motor___neurons_ .   skeletal musculature (muscles)

13. In complex organisms, the vast majority of neurons are neither

    sensory nor motor, but rather _interneurons_   interneurons

14. The fine wire or tube that allows investigators to record electrical activity in neurons is called a _microelectrode_   microelectrode

15. The device used to record nerve impulses on a fluorescent screen is called an _oscilloscope_   oscilloscope

16. The _Resting_ _potential_ of the neuron is about –70 millivolts.   resting potential

17. The reversal of polarization that passes along a nerve fiber when it is stimulated is called the _action potential_   action potential

18. When the cell membrane is depolarized past a certain _threshold_ value, the _action potential_ results.   threshold

action potential
(or nerve impulse)

19. The _all_-_or_-_none_ law states that the size of the action potential and its speed are independent of the intensity of the stimulus, provided the stimulus is above threshold intensity.   all-or-none

20. The above-mentioned law does not apply to the stimulation of nerves since there is much variation in the _thresholds_ of the neurons in the nerve.   thresholds

21. Stimulus _intensity_ is conveyed by both increases in the number of neurons firing and by increases in individual neurons' _frequency_ of firing.   intensity

frequency

INTERACTION AMONG NERVE CELLS

22. The fact that a chicken may run around for a while after its head has been cut off shows that some movements and reflexes are controlled by the _Spinal cord_ .   spinal cord

23. The _reflex arc_ is the pathway that leads from stimulus to response.   reflex arc

24. The existence of the synapse was inferred from evidence at the level of _behavior_ by the great English physiologist _Sherrington_.   behavior, (Sir Charles) Sherrington

25. Subthreshold stimulation, when applied a few times in rapid succession, may lead to a response. This illustrates the phenomenon of _temporal summation_   temporal summation

26. According to Sherrington, temporal summation occurs because of integration at the _synapse_, which is accomplished by "storage" of excitation from previous stimulation. This results in an increase in the _central excitatory state_ .   synapse

central excitatory state

27. Subthreshold stimulation at two adjacent points, when applied simultaneously, may lead to a response. This illustrates the phenomenon of _spatial summation_   spatial summation

28. Sherrington observed that when a flexor muscle contracts, the corresponding extensor relaxes. This is an example of _reciprocal inhibition_   reciprocal inhibition

29. Whether a neuron fires or not is determined by the net result of its integration of _excitatory_ and _inhibitory_ stimulation.

excitatory, inhibitory

30. An increase in the strength of a reflex when higher brain centers are removed is called _disinhibition_

disinhibition

31. Loewi's classic experiment showed that stimulation of the vagus nerve to the heart caused release of a _neurotransmitter_ which we now call _acetylcholine_.

neurotransmitter

acetylcholine

32. Electrical activity is transmitted across the synapse by neuro-transmitters, from the _presynaptic_ neuron to the _postsynaptic_ neuron.

presynaptic, postsynaptic

33. The synaptic vesicles contain chemical substances called _neurotransmitters_

neurotransmitters

34. Label this diagram of a synapse.

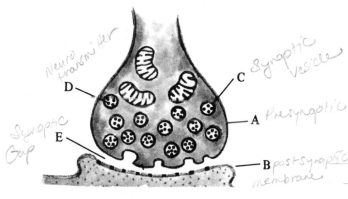

A. presynaptic membrane
B. postsynaptic membrane
C. synaptic vesicle
D. neurotransmitter
E. synaptic gap

35. The activity of the postsynaptic neuron results from the summation of _inhibitory_ and _excitatory_ inputs. These are produced by _neurotransmitters_ liberated by firing of the presynaptic neuron.

inhibitory, excitatory

neurotransmitters

36. While action potentials are all-or-none, synaptic potentials are _graded_.

graded

37. Inhibitory neurotransmitters _increase_ the nerve's resting potential, while excitatory neurotransmitters _decrease_ it.

increase

decrease

38. Neurotransmitters are disposed of by breakdown by enzymes and _reuptake_ by the presynaptic cell.

reuptake

39. Acetylcholine, dopamine, and norepinephrine are all _neurotransmitters_.

neurotransmitters

40. The idea that neurotransmitters only affect the postsynaptic membrane if their shape fits the shape of the certain receptor sites on that membrane is called the _lock_ - _&_ - _key_ model.

lock-and-key

41. Drugs that enhance a transmitter's activity are called _agonists_.

agonists

Drugs that impede transmitter activity are called _antagonists_.

antagonists

42. Curare and chlorpromazine are _drugs_ that affect synaptic transmission.

drugs

43. The action of the neurotransmitter _acetylcholine_, which causes muscles to contract, is blocked by the drug _curare_.

acetylcholine

curare

44. The arousing effects of the neurotransmitter _dopamine_ are blocked by the drug _chlorpromazine_, which is used to treat the major mental disorder _schizophrenia_.

dopamine

chlorpromazine

schizophrenia

45. Neurotransmitters similar to the drug morphine that seem to reduce pain are called _endorphins_.

endorphins

46. A drug, _nalaxone_, that blocks the effect of endorphins also blocks the lessening of pain produced by the Chinese technique of _acupuncture_.

nalaxone

acupuncture

INTERACTION THROUGH THE BLOODSTREAM: THE ENDOCRINE SYSTEM

47. The _endocrine_ glands secrete _hormones_ into the bloodstream.

endocrine, hormones

48. _Hormones_ are chemical messengers that are distributed indiscriminately throughout the body, while _neurotransmitters_ exert their effects in a very limited area.

Hormones

neurotransmitters

THE MAIN STRUCTURES OF THE NERVOUS SYSTEM

49. The brain and spinal cord together comprise the _central nervous system_.

central

nervous system

50. The two divisions of the peripheral nervous system are the _somatic_ and the _autonomic_.

somatic, autonomic

51. The portion of the hindbrain concerned with controlling some critical body processes, such as respiration and heartbeat, is called the _medulla_.

medulla

52. The portion of the hindbrain that controls bodily balance and motor coordination is called the _cerebellum_.

cerebellum

53. The general activating system that extends from the hindbrain through the midbrain and into the forebrain is called the _reticular formation_.

reticular formation

54. The _hypothalamus_ is a part of the forebrain involved in the control of behavior patterns that stem from basic biological urges such as feeding.

hypothalamus

55. Label the four major lobes of the human cerebral cortex.

A. _____   C. _____

B. _____   D. _____

A. frontal

B. parietal

C. occipital

D. temporal

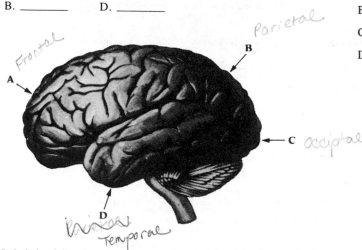

56. Label the following structures on the sketch of the human brain.

A. _____

B. _____

C. _____

D. _____

A. medulla (hindbrain)

B. cerebellum

C. cerebral cortex

D. corpus callosum

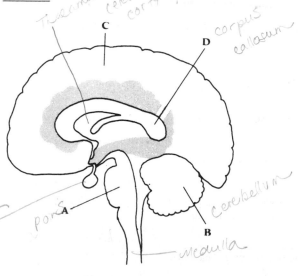

57. A part of the cerebral cortex involved in large muscle movements

is called the _basal ganglia_.

basal ganglia

58. An older portion of the cerebral hemispheres with particular importance in the mediation of emotional and motivational

activities is called the _limbic system_.

limbic system

THE CEREBRAL CORTEX

59. Excitation of the left _motor   projection area_ will lead to   motor projection area
    movements of the right side of the body.   (motor homunculus)

60. In man, the greatest amount of cortical space for motor functions
    is assigned to the _fingers_ and _tongue_.   fingers, tongue

61. Each portion of the body surface is represented in the sensory
    homunculus, located in the _somatosensory area_ of the _parietal_   somatosensory area, parietal
    lobes.

62. The projection areas for vision and hearing are located in the
    temporal and _occipital_ lobes, respectively.   occipital, temporal

63. The portion of the cerebral cortex that is part of neither the motor
    nor sensory areas is described as the _association area_ .   association areas

64. When there is damage to neural tissue, we describe it,
    technically, as a _lesion_ .   lesion

65. It is now possible to make precise representations of brain
    structure with the aim of localizing lesions. When this technique
    involves computer reconstruction of brain structures based on
    multiple X-ray exposures, it is called a _cat_ scan.   CAT

66. When the picture of the brain is based on representation of the
    level of metabolic activity in different areas of the brain, it is
    called a _pet_ scan.   PET

67. _Apraxia_ is a serious disturbance in the organization of voluntary   Apraxia
    action.

68. A disorganization of aspects of the sensory world, without loss
    of basic sensory capacities, is termed _agnosia_.   agnosia

69. A patient with a primary disorder in the expression of speech
    can be described as suffering from language apraxia, or an
    expressive aphasia. This disorder is commonly caused by   expressive aphasia
    lesions in _Broca's area_ .   Broca's area

70. In right-handed persons, aphasia usually results from lesions in
    the _left_ hemisphere.   left

71. A language defect reflected primarily by an inability to
    comprehend language, or a language agnosia, is described as a
    receptive aphasia. The lesions responsible for this disorder   receptive aphasia
    commonly occur in _wernicke's area_ .   Wernicke's area

72. The asymmetry of function in the human cerebral hemispheres is
    described as _lateralization_   lateralization (of function)

73. In terms of differences in function between left and right cerebral
    hemispheres, left-handers are generally less _lateralized_ than right- lateralized
    handers.

74. A right-hander who, following a stroke, has great difficulty with spatial representation, maps, and the perception of complex

   forms, probably has a lesion in the _right_ hemisphere.   right

75. A split-brain patient is someone whose _corpus callosum_ has been surgically severed.   corpus callosum

76. A right-handed split-brain patient would probably not be able to

   name a common object placed in his _left_ hand.   left

77. rCBF studies show that more _blood_ goes to the left as opposed to the right hemisphere of normal subjects when they are speaking or solving a verbal task.   blood

78. Many psychologists believe that _verbal_ and _spatial_ processes represent radically different modes of thought which reflect different clusters of intellectual functioning.   verbal, spatial

79. Recovery from loss of cerebral nerve cells can occur by the

   processes of recovery of _damaged neurons_ , _collateral_   damaged neurons, collateral

   Sprouting, and _substitution of_ _function_   sprouting, substitution of function

80. Brain _transplants_ involving fetal brain tissue of rats have had some success and hold the promise to replace acetylcholine-   transplants

   secreting cells lost in _Alzheimer's_ disease.   Alzheimer's

SOME PROBLEMS IN LOCALIZING BRAIN FUNCTION

81. To understand the relation between the brain and pathological

   function, we must understand something about the _behavior_   behavior

   itself, as well as the _anatomy_ of the brain.   anatomy

Self-Test

1. Which of the following commonly obeserved characteristics of human or animal behavior goes counter to Descartes's reflex notion?
   a. the withdrawal response upon touching a hot object
   b. the appearance of a behavior (e.g., running) in the absence of any obvious stimulus
   c. the existence of nerves connecting receptors and effectors to the brain
   d. the repeatability of reflexes
   e. none of the above

2. By viewing animal behavior as the result of a machine's responding to external stimuli, Descartes made the claim that:
   a. animal behavior is governed by physical laws and is therefore predictable.

   b. animal behavior can only be understood in terms of the hierarchical organization of the nervous system.
   c. animals must have souls.
   d. neither humans nor animals have free will.
   e. introductory psychology is *the* fundamental science.

3. The course of excitation through the nervous system following a stimulus is:
   a. interneuron, efferent nerve, afferent nerve.
   b. efferent nerve, interneuron, afferent nerve.
   c. afferent nerve, interneuron, efferent nerve.
   d. integration, reception, reaction.
   e. action, reaction, integration.

4. The tripartite view of an action sequence—reception, conduction and integration, reaction—

is clearly represented by the sequence of:
a. afferent nerve, efferent nerve, interneuron.
b. axon, cell body, dendrites.
c. push, fall, hurt.
d. axon, interneuron, dendrite.
e. none of the above

5. Under normal circumstances the path of excitation in the neuron would follow the sequence:
a. dendrite → cell body → axon → synapse.
b. axon → dendrite → synapse → cell body.
c. dendrite → cell body → synapse → axon.
d. dendrite → axon → cell body → synapse.
e. synapse → dendrite → axon → cell body.

6. Which of the following is *not* part of an individual neuron?
a. axon
b. myelin sheath
c. synapse
d. dendrite
e. cell body

7. Receptors:
a. are always a specialized part of sensory neurons.
b. transduce physical stimuli into neural impulses.
c. are responsible for the conduction of optic stimuli.
d. a and b
e. b and c

8. Which of the following properties are characteristic of interneurons?
a. They usually show much branching of dendrites.
b. They perform the integration function of the action sequence.
c. They comprise the majority of neurons.
d. all of the above
e. none of the above

9. When graphed over time, the complex electrical event known as the action potential looks something like:

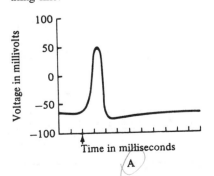

A

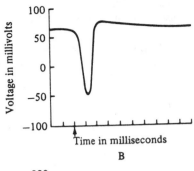

B

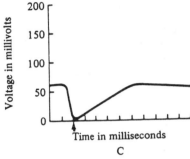

C

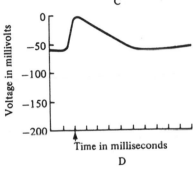

D

10. The all-or-none law states that:
a. the threshold of a single neuron is a property which alternates between two extreme values but never has any of the values in between.
b. reflexes cannot involve just the spinal cord; the entire nervous system must respond by generating a central excitatory state.
c. an axon terminal releases a chemical substance, called a neurotransmitter, when an action potential arrives.
d. the frequency of spikes in an individual nerve fiber increases with the number of action potentials per unit time.
e. once a stimulus exceeds the threshold of an individual neuron, further increases in stimulation intensity make no difference in the height and form of the action potential generated.

11. The all-or-none action potential is:
    a. accompanied by depolarization of the nerve membrane.
    b. initiated by an adequate stimulus.
    c. propagated from one part of the membrane to neighboring parts.
    d. all of the above
    e. none of the above

12. How can the nervous system represent increases in the intensity of a *stimulus*?
    a. by an increase in the size of the action potential in every neuron fired by the stimulus
    b. by an increase in the number of neurons being fired by the stimulus
    c. by an increase in the frequency of firing in the neurons fired by the stimulus
    d. b and c
    e. a and c

13. Sherrington used a spinal animal in order to:
    a. eliminate inhibition.
    b. simplify the system he was studying.
    c. take advantage of brain modulation of neural activity in the spinal cord.
    d. study the irreversibility of conduction.
    e. cut expenses.

14. Hormones and neurotransmitters are both:
    a. secreted only by endocrine glands.
    b. secreted into the bloodstream.
    c. chemical messengers.
    d. all of the above
    e. none of the above

15. Many neurons fire action potentials at a moderate rate even when they are not receiving synaptic excitation from presynaptic neurons. This is called spontaneous activity. Which plot indicates what would happen to the firing rate of such a neuron if it was first exposed to synaptic inhibition and then synaptic excitation?

16. From his observations of temporal and spatial summation in reflexes, Sherrington inferred the existence of:
    a. receptors.
    b. inhibition.
    c. the synapse.
    d. disinhibition.
    e. the simple reflex.

17. A subthreshold stimulus will evoke a spinal reflex if it is repeated within a reasonable interval, say 1/2 second. This temporal summation is caused by:
    a. increased frequency of neural firing.
    b. enhanced central excitatory state.
    c. the spinal cord.
    d. the release of neurotransmitters from motor neurons to interneurons.
    e. inhibition.

18. Consider this example: Brief strong stimulation of a receptor produces no movement, but a longer period of stimulation causes a particular muscle to stop contracting. These results could most easily be explained by the principles of:
    a. excitation and inhibition.
    b. inhibition and disinhibition.
    c. all-or-none law and inhibition.
    d. temporal summation, spatial summation, and the all-or-none law.
    e. inhibition and temporal summation.

19. The phenomenon of disinhibition:
    a. exists only in insects.
    b. depends on reflex interaction, especially in the spinal cord.
    c. reveals the presence of inhibition.
    d. takes place entirely within a single neuron.
    e. all of the above

20. Sherrington reported that the time (reflex latency) between stimulation of a reflex and the reflex

response was much longer than the time it would take for an action potential to go from the receptor to the muscle. This "delay" could be accounted for in terms of:
a. inhibition.
b. excitation.
c. the time for disinhibition to occur.
d. the time for depolarization of the axon membrane.
e. the time for the neurotransmitter to cross the synaptic gap and stimulate the post-synaptic neuron.

21. Axon conduction resembles synaptic transmission in that:
a. both involve neurotransmitters.
b. both are about the same speed.
c. both are all-or-none.
d. all of the above
e. none of the above

22. The lock-and-key model accounts for:
a. the existence of neurotransmitters.
b. the summation of excitation and inhibition in postsynaptic neurons.
c. the fact that specific neurotransmitters stimulate specific postsynaptic neurons.
d. the release of neurotransmitters from synaptic vesicles.
e. the all-or-none law.

23. Chlorpromazine and curare have in common the fact that they:
a. block the action of specific neurotransmitters.
b. enhance the action of specific neurotransmitters.
c. produce postsynaptic inhibition.
d. produce postsynaptic excitation.
e. relieve the symptoms of schizophrenia.

24. A new drug is found to increase arousal. All but one of the following are possible modes of action of that drug. Which is *not*?
a. blocks reuptake of dopamine
b. increases availability of norepinephrine precursors
c. blocks the enzyme that breaks down dopamine at the synapse
d. mimics the effect of norepinephrine
e. blocks the postsynaptic receptor for norepinephrine

25. The relation between acetylcholine and curare is like the relation between:
a. acetylcholine and dopamine.
b. horse and rider.

c. endorphins and naloxone.
d. endorphins and placebo.
e. dopamine and placebo.

26. A dentist finds that when she gives her patient what is actually a sugar pill, and tells the patient that it will relieve his pain, all of the patient's pain disappears. This is an example of:
a. an effect of naloxone.
b. a placebo effect.
c. an endocrine effect.
d. the all-or-none law.
e. synaptic interaction.

27. In which of the following sequences are the main divisions of the central nervous system arranged in ascending order?
a. peripheral, somatic, autonomic
b. cerebellum, integration centers, transmission tracts
c. spinal cord, autonomic system, brain
d. spinal cord, motor areas, sensory areas
e. spinal cord, brain stem, cerebral hemispheres

28. Match the structure on the left with its associated function on the right.

i. medulla	a. sleep
ii. cerebellum	b. respiration and heartbeat
iii. reticular formation	c. basic biological urges
iv. hypothalamus	d. balance and motor coordination

i. ___B___

ii. ___D___

iii. ___A___

iv. ___C___

29. The lobes of the cerebral hemisphere are:
a. frontal, parietal, occipital, temporal.
b. hindbrain, midbrain, forebrain.
c. limbic system, corpus callosum, cerebral cortex.
d. each cerebral hemisphere is a single lobe of the cerebral cortex
e. none of the above

30. Which of the following statements is *not* true of the limbic system?
a. It is a subcortical structure.
b. It is anatomically associated with the hypothalamus.
c. It is present on both sides of the brain.
d. It is involved in the control of emotional and motivational activities.

e. It integrates the functions of the cerebral hemispheres.

31. What part of an elephant might you expect to have a particularly large representation in the motor homunculus?
    a. the ears
    b. the front legs
    c. the back legs
    d. the trunk
    e. the eyes

32. Following a stroke, a patient shows grossly diminishing sensitivity to touch and other stimulation in the right hand and arm. The probable site of the lesion is:
    a. the motor homunculus.
    b. the left somatosensory area.
    c. the right somatosensory area.
    d. the left frontal area.
    e. the right frontal area.

33. A disorder in the organization of voluntary movement is called:
    a. agnosia.
    b. aphasia.
    c. apraxia.
    d. amenorrhea.
    e. none of the above

34. A person exhibiting "psychic blindness," or the inability to coordinate the separate details of the visual world into a whole, suffers from:
    a. visual agnosia.
    b. receptive aphasia.
    c. a lesion in Broca's area.
    d. a lesion in Wernicke's area.
    e. visual apraxia.

35. Apraxia, expressive aphasia, and receptive aphasia have in common:
    a. lesions in the same brain area.
    b. that basic sensory and motor functions are intact.
    c. some deficit in voluntary motor function.
    d. a and b
    e. a and c

36. Damage in a left-handed person in the language center often has less drastic consequences than in a right-handed person because:
    a. left-handers are slower to develop language functions.
    b. recovery is more rapid in the left hemisphere in left-handers.
    c. the hemispheres are not as functionally lateralized in left-handers.
    d. highly developed visual-spatial abilities

compensate for language loss.
    e. a and d

37. Afferent input from the right hand projects primarily to the left hemisphere while the left hand projects primarily to the right hemisphere. In an average right-handed, split-brain patient, which hand would the subject have to use to handle an unseen object in order to name it?
    a. the left hand
    b. the right hand
    c. neither hand could do it
    d. both hands could do it equally well
    e. a split-brain patient cannot name any objects

38. A right-handed subject has lost the entire projection area of his left occipital cortex, as shown below, but is otherwise normal. Which of the following deficits would you expect?

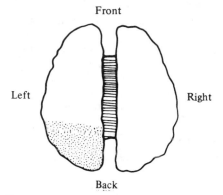

Front

Left   Right

Back

    a. loss of the right side of his visual field
    b. loss of the left side of his visual field
    c. inability to produce speech despite ability to understand it
    d. inability to understand speech despite the ability to produce it
    e. inability to read

39. The same subject referred to in the previous question suffers an additional defect: His corpus callosum is completely cut. What is the extent of his deficit?
    a. inability to produce or understand speech
    b. inability to produce speech despite understanding it
    c. inability to understand speech despite the ability to produce it
    d. inability to read
    e. visual agnosia

40. In which of the following tasks would you expect superior performance from the left hemisphere of a right-hander?

a. matching paint colors
b. recognizing faces
c. remembering a series of movements to be performed in a specific order
d. drawing the floor plan of a familiar house
e. all of the above

41. Recovery from cerebral damage occurs in a number of ways. Which of the following actually involves addition of new nerve cells to the damaged brain?
a. transplantation of fetal nerve tissue
b. collateral sprouting
c. substitution of function
d. all of the above
e. none of the above

42. Localizing psychological functions in specific parts of the brain is difficult because:
a. many psychological functions are represented in more than one part of the brain.
b. we are not certain as to what meaningful psychological functions are.
c. we have no way of determining what part of the brain is damaged.
d. a and b
e. all of the above

Answer Key for Self-Test

Investigating Psychological Phenomena

SPEED OF THE NERVE IMPULSE: THE USE OF REACTION TIME IN THE MEASUREMENT OF A PSYCHOLOGICAL PROCESS

Equipment: A stopwatch that indicates seconds
Number of subjects: Five
Time per subject: Fifteen minutes (all subjects are involved at the same time)
Time for experimenter: Twenty-five minutes

One of the great stumbling blocks to advances in theory about psychological processes was the belief that thought, and hence nervous impulses, occurred instantaneously or nearly so. In fact the German physiologist Johannes P. Müller (1801–1858) once estimated that the speed of the nerve impulse was eleven million miles per second. Naturally, this claim that nerve impulses travel at an immeasurably fast rate discouraged scientific research on the physiology of the nervous system and encouraged mystical or dualistic interpretation of mind. It also discouraged study of the speed of various mental activities, research that is today an important cornerstone of the field of cognitive psychology.

In 1850, Herman Ludwig Ferdinand von Helmholtz (1821–1894) succeeded in measuring the speed of the nerve impulse and found it to be much slower than previously believed, between fifty and one hundred meters per second in humans. This finding was followed by intensive investigation of the nervous system within the framework of the physical and biological sciences. It also opened the door to the use of reaction time as a tool in the study of thought processes. This experiment is an attempt to familarize you with the general logic used by a psychologist who is interested in measuring the speed of a psychological event that cannot be directly observed. To accomplish this, you must first understand the experiment that Helmholtz performed and also how his experimental technique can be applied to the measurement of the speed of the nerve impulse in humans.

Helmholtz's technique was quite simple. He first dissected out a muscle and an attached nerve fiber from a frog's leg. The experiment then consisted of stimulating the nerve at various distances from the muscle and measuring the length of time between nerve stimulation and muscle contraction. First, he electrically stimulated the nerve close to the point at which it was attached to the muscle, then he stimulated the nerve farther from this point of attachment. He found that the second reaction time (that is, the time between stimulation and contraction) was longer than the first. To obtain an estimate of nerve impulse speed, he used a simple bit of reasoning: The difference in time between the two measurements must correspond to the time it takes the impulse to travel the distance between the two points of stimulation (see the figure below). Hence, the distance between the points of stimulation divided by the time *difference* between the conditions of stimulating close to the muscle versus stimulating farther away should yield an estimate of nerve impulse speed. This is how he obtained his estimate of fifty to one hundred meters per second. Let A and B be two points of stimulation, M be the point at which the nerve is connected to the muscle, t_A be the time to contraction from stimulation at A, and t_B the time to contraction from stimulation at B:

nerve   A   B   M(muscle)

Then $\dfrac{\text{(A to M)} - \text{(B to M)}}{t_A - t_B}$ = speed of nerve impulse.

Happily, Helmholtz's estimate can be demonstrated in humans without resorting to dissection. You might suppose that the simplest way to do this would be to perform the following sort of experiment: Stimulate someone on the ankle (by pinching him, for example) and have him respond by pushing a button as soon as he feels the stimulation. With a good timer, you could then measure the time between stimulation and depression of the button. To estimate nerve conduction time, you would then measure the total distance between ankle and brain, and between brain and finger, and divide this number by the subject's reaction time. But there are complications which make this procedure unsuitable. Part of the reaction time, for example, would be due to the length of time it took the subject to decide to press the button, a figure which would obviously include more than simply nerve impulse time. From the point of view of processes in the nervous system, the reaction time includes the time to cross synapses as well as axon conduction time. In short, total reaction time is a confounded measure.

Thus, the experiment must be made more complicated. Using Helmholtz's logic, one could measure not only the time between ankle stimulation and response, but also between, say, upper arm stimulation and response. The ankle condition should result in a longer reaction time than the upper arm condition. The difference between these reaction times corresponds to the time it takes for the nerve impulse to travel a distance equal to the difference between the ankle and the finger, and the upper arm and the finger. Notice that this difference excludes any time due to such things as decision-making processes. So the nerve conduction time can be estimated by subtracting the distance between the upper arm and the brain from the distance between the ankle and the brain (the distance from the brain to the finger is constant) and dividing by the reaction time difference.

In practice, the reaction time for either stimulating the ankle or stimulating the upper arm is quite small, and hence a clock that measures time in hundredths of a second would be needed to measure it. This problem can be solved by adding together the reaction time of several people; after obtaining the total time, simply dividing this by the number of people would give the average individual time. This general mass reaction time technique will be used to measure the speed of the nerve impulse. Perform the nerve impulse speed experiment in the following way:

Get five people to participate. Have them form a circle with each person very loosely clasping the ankle of his neighbor to the right. Tell each person to squeeze the ankle he is holding when he feels his ankle squeezed. Be sure the subjects' eyes are closed during all trials. You can then start the experiment by squeezing one person's ankle and simultaneously noting the time on a second hand of a watch. Now watch the ankle that you squeezed. When you see it squeezed for the fifth time (excluding your initial squeeze) note the time that elapsed. Repeat this procedure for a total of five times, each time recording the time in the spaces provided in part I of the answer sheet on the next page (record results to an accuracy of .1 second).

Next have each person in the circle release the ankle he is holding and grasp the upper arm, *just below the shoulder* of the person to the right. You run another five trials exactly as you did for the ankle trials, each time recording the time in part II of the answer sheet.

You will probably note that the total reaction time dropped within each set of five trials. Why? Hopefully, the last two to three trials yielded about the same values.

These ten trials serve as practice: The group of five subjects and the measurer "learn" in some general way, to do this task efficiently. Having completed practice, you are now ready to begin the measurement of the speed of the nerve impulse. Run four more trials as before, the first and fourth with ankle stimulation, the second and third with upper arm. This will generate two ankle and two upper arm mass reaction times (record these in part III of the data sheet).

Each reaction time represents the sum of twenty-five reaction times (five subjects, five times each). Obtain the average individual reaction time by dividing the total reaction times by twenty-five. Now average the two ankle reaction times and, separately, the two upper arm reaction times. Subtract the average arm time from the average ankle time. This is the amount of time it takes the impulse to go the extra distance from the ankle to the level of the shoulder. To calculate the speed of the nerve impulse, you must estimate the magnitude of this distance (in meters).

Measure the distance for the third tallest person in your group of five subjects. Measure the distance from the ankle to the base of the neck and from the upper arm to the base of the neck. Take the difference between the numbers, divide by the time difference, and you will have an estimate of the speed of the nerve impulse. How does it compare with Helmholtz's estimate? (Helmholtz estimated a speed of from 50 to 100 meters per second. Modern measurements range from 6 to 122 meters per second, depending on the type of nerve fiber). *(If your instructor collects the data, fill out the report sheet in Appendix B.)*

FURTHER EXPERIMENTS

Now that you have calculated an estimate of the speed of the nerve impulse, you might want to test whether some fairly common variables will affect this speed. Consider fatigue for instance. If a person is tired, does his nerve impulse speed slow down? To test this, design your own experiment, using the same measurement technique you used to get your main estimate of nerve impulse speed. To test whether fatigue has an effect, measure the speed both at a time when subjects are well rested and at a time when the same subjects are tired (for example, in the morning and at night, or before and after exercise). Does fatigue affect nerve impulse speed? Note, by the way, that given the way the estimate is obtained, it is possible to find that fatigue may well slow down reaction time in general, yet have no effect on the speed of the nerve impulse.

Can you come up with other variables which you think might affect (speed up or slow down) nerve impulse speed? If so, design experiments to test your hypotheses.

Report Sheet

Practice   Time in seconds*

Part I   Trial 1 ankle = _____

           Trial 2 ankle = _____

           Trial 3 ankle = _____

           Trial 4 ankle = _____

           Trial 5 ankle = _____

Part II   Trial 1 upper arm = _____

           Trial 2 upper arm = _____

           Trial 3 upper arm = _____

           Trial 4 upper arm = _____

           Trial 5 upper arm = _____

Test

Part III   Trial 1 ankle time =   _____

           $\div 25 =$ _____ (a)

           Trial 2 upper arm time = _____

           $\div 25 =$ _____ (b)

           Trial 3 upper arm time = _____

           $\div 25 =$ _____ (c)

           Trial 4 anklc time =   _____

           $\div 25 =$ _____ (d)

$\dfrac{a + d}{2} =$ _____ (average ankle time)

$\dfrac{b + c}{2} =$ _____ (average upper arm time)

Average ankle time – average upper arm time = _____ (difference 1)

(1) Distance of ankle to base of neck (for third tallest person) = _____

(2) Distance of upper arm to base of neck (for third tallest person) = _____

      Distance 1 – distance 2 = _____ (difference 2)

$\dfrac{\text{difference 2}}{\text{difference 1}} =$ (speed of nerve impulse)

*Record time accurate to .1 second.

CHAPTER 2

Motivation

Learning Objectives

MOTIVATION AS DIRECTION

1. Explain whether directed action can be reconciled with Descartes's notion of humans and animals as reflex machines.

Control systems
2. Describe the action of negative and positive feedback systems. Give examples of negative and positive feedback systems from modern technology.

SELF-REGULATION

Homeostasis
3. Define homeostasis.

Temperature regulation
4. Know how reflexes and behavior function to maintain body temperature.
5. Describe the way the two branches of the autonomic nervous system function in temperature regulation and the role of the hypothalamus.

THIRST

6. Describe how the brain is informed about the body's need for water.

HUNGER

The signals for feeding
7. Give the evidence indicating that animals regulate calorie (energy) intake.
8. Indicate the internal and external signals that influence hunger and satiety.

Hypothalamic control centers
9. Describe the role of the hypothalamus in feeding.
10. Explain the dual-center theory. How do the phe-

nomena of aphagia and hyperphagia support this theory?
11. Show how the idea of a setpoint helps account for the regulation of temperature and food intake, and how it accounts for the behavior of hyperphagic rats.

Obesity
12. Indicate bodily factors that may contribute to obesity, and review genetic evidence that establishes a role for bodily factors.
13. List the behavioral factors that may be involved in obesity. Describe the externality hypothesis and the restrained-eating hypothesis.
14. Explain restrained eating in terms of setpoint.
15. Explain whether overweight is a disorder. Consider its health and social consequences, and decide which are more important.

Anorexia and bulimia
16. Describe the symptoms and possible causes of anorexia nervosa and bulimia.

FEAR AND RAGE

Threat and the autonomic nervous system
17. List the functions of the parasympathetic and sympathetic systems.
18. Describe the emergency reaction. Explain what role the sympathetic arousal system plays in the flight-or-fight response. Understand the biological survival value of the emergency reaction.
19. Describe how fear and rage responses are organized in the central nervous system. Explain the role of the limbic system.

Disruptive effects of autonomic arousal
20. Describe the immediate disruptive effects of sympathetic arousal and possible long-term effects on health.

SLEEP AND WAKING

Waking

21. Describe the action of the reticular activating system. Where is it located? How do brain lesion and stimulation studies demonstrate that it is involved with wakefulness?

Sleep

22. Be able to describe the stages of sleep and the two kinds of sleep.

23. Explain the relation between REM sleep and dreaming.

24. Discuss whether dreaming has a function, and if so, what it might be.

WHAT DIFFERENT MOTIVES HAVE IN COMMON

Level of stimulation

25. Describe Hull's theory of drive reduction. Be able to criticize this theory.

26. Explain what is meant by optimal arousal level and its relationship to drive reduction. What is the evidence for an optimal arousal level above zero?

Drugs and addiction

27. Explain how drugs can be used to manipulate arousal. Give examples of depressant and stimulant drugs, and contrast the effects of these two types of drugs.

28. Describe drug addiction and the phenomena of tolerance and withdrawal.

29. Describe the opponent process theory of motivation. How do studies of drug addiction support this theory? What are some problems with it?

The biology of reward

30. Review what studies of electrical stimulation of the brain tell us about motivation.

31. Indicate the evidence that the priming function of brain stimulation differs from the rewarding function.

The nature of motives

32. Indicate how the biological basis for motives interacts with individual experience (learning).

Programmed Exercises

MOTIVATION AS DIRECTION

1. In _positive_ _feedback_ systems, the feedback strengthens the initial behavior.

   positive feedback

2. In a _negative_ _feedback_ system, the feedback stops, or even reverses, the original behavior.

   negative feedback

3. _Servomechanisms_ are man-made devices which operate according to the principles of negative feedback.

   Servomechanisms

SELF-REGULATION

4. The maintenance of a stable equilibrium in the body is called

   homeostasis

   homeostasis

5. Vasoconstriction is a form of _reflexive_ response to _decreases_ in body temperature.

   reflexive, decreases

6. The autonomic nervous system sends its commands to _glands_

   glands

   and _smooth_ _muscle_.

   smooth muscles

7. The _sympathetic_ and _parasympathetic_ divisions of the autonomic nervous system work in opposite directions to control temperature.

   sympathetic, parasympathetic

   The _sympathetic_ division acts to generate heat, to counteract low temperatures.

   sympathetic

8. The activation of the divisions of the autonomic nervous system

   is determined by _receptors_ located in the part of the brain that

   (thermo)receptors

   controls these divisions, the _hypothalamus_

   hypothalamus

THIRST

9. The brain detects the body's need for water based on information

   on both the _volume_ and _concentration_ of blood and body fluids.   volume, concentration

HUNGER

10. The fact that animals increase intake of foods that are diluted
    with non-nutritive substances suggests that they regulate

    calories.   calories (energy)

11. Receptors sensitive to the metabolic state (energy need) of the

    organism have been postulated to exist in the _brain_ and   brain

    liver .   liver

12. Satiety signals also originate in the gastrointestinal system, from

    nutrient receptors in the _stomach_ , and as a result of a release   stomach

    of _CCK_ when food passes into the duodenum.   CCK

13. The human infant has a few innate preferences, including an

    avoidance of _bitter_ tastes and an attraction to _sweet_   bitter, sweet
    tastes.

14. The dual-center theory is supported by the fact that lesions in the

    lateral hypothalamus produce _aphagia_, while lesions in the   aphagia

    ventromedial hypothalamus produce _hyperaphagia_.   hyperaphagia

15. According to dual-center theory, "on" and "off" feeding centers

    in the hypothalamus are mutually _inhibitory_.   inhibitory

16. The fact that hyperphagic rats gain weight and then maintain
    themselves at the new, higher weight suggests that they are

    regulating their body weight around an elevated _setpoint_ .   setpoint

17. The high resemblance in obesity and body distribution of fat in

    twins for a _generic_ determinant of obesity.   twins, generic

18. Recent studies suggest that some obesity may be caused by
    bodily factors. Excess feeding early in life and genetic factors

    may influence the _#_ of _fat_ cells in the body.   number, fat

19. According to the _externality hypothesis_, obese people are relatively   externality hypothesis
    unresponsive to their own internal hunger signals and more
    susceptible to signals from the outside, like taste.

20. According to the _restrained_-_eating hypothesis_, externality is a   restrained-eating hypothesis
    feature of people who go on diets.

21. Obese people may have, on the average, higher _setpoints_ than   setpoints
    the rest of the population.

22. A justification of getting treatment for obesity is that thinner

    people are more attractive, and hence are more _socially_   socially

    successful. There are probably also _health_ benefits for not   health (medical)
    being obese.

23. _Anorexia nervosa_ is an eating disorder characterized by extreme and self-imposed underweight.   Anorexia nervosa

24. _Bulimia_ is an eating disorder characterized by repeated binge and purge bouts.   Bulimia

FEAR AND RAGE

25. The parasympathetic system handles the _vegetative_ functions of the body.   vegetative

26. The sympathetic system has an _activating_ function.   activating

27. Sympathetic action is supported or amplified by the secretion of the hormone _adrenaline_ (or _epinephrine_).   adrenaline, epinephrine

28. The emergency reaction results from activation of the _sympathetic_ nervous system.   sympathetic

29. Decreased electrical resistance of the skin, or the _galvanic_ _skin response_, is sometimes used as an index of auto-nomic arousal.   galvanic

    skin response

30. The portion of the brain that governs the autonomic system and is responsible for the control of emotional reactions is called the _limbic_ sysem.   limbic

31. _Autonomic_ arousal can have disruptive effects which, if main-tained, can compromise health.   Autonomic

SLEEP AND WAKING

32. The arousal of the brain is the function of the _reticular_ _activating_ system.   reticular

    activating

33. The reticular activating system can be aroused either by _sensory_ stimulation or internally, via connections with the _cortex_ .   sensory

    cortex

34. The record of the voltage changes occurring in the brain over time is called the _EEG_ ( ). _Electroencephalogram_   electroencephalogram (EEG)

35. An EEG associated with waking relaxation shows _alpha_ waves.   alpha

36. Rapid eye movements (REM), a waking EEG, relaxed muscles, and low sensitivity to external stimulation all characterize _active_ (also called _REM_) sleep.   active (REM)

37. The average person dreams (exhibits REM sleep) for about _1 1/2_ hour(s) each night.   one-and-a-half

38. Dreaming typically occurs during _Rem_ sleep.   active (REM)

39. According to _Freud_ , dreams have a function of allowing expression of unacceptable wishes in a disguised form.   Freud

WHAT DIFFERENT MOTIVES HAVE IN COMMON

40. Hull believed that all built-in rewards produce some decrease in

    tension, or _drive_ _reduction_.   drive reduction

41. The fact that animals will learn to press a lever to engage in

    sexually arousing behavior argues for an _optimal_ _level_   optimal level

    of _arousal_ that is greater than zero.   arousal

42. Alcohol, barbiturates and opiates are examples of _depressant_   depressant
    drugs.

43. Amphetamine and cocaine are examples of _stimulant_ drugs.   stimulant

44. Addiction is associated with decreased sensitivity to a drug. This

    effect is called _tolerance_   tolerance

45. Addiction is also characterized by effects opposite to a drug's

    effects when the drug is discontinued. This is called _withdrawal_.   withdrawal

46. According to _opponent-process_ theory, withdrawal symptoms   opponent-process
    can be explained as a result of action by the nervous system to
    neutralize the effects of the drug.

47. Hot peppers produce unpleasant pain in people who try them for
    the first time. Yet many come to like the "burn" after many

    experiences. This could be accounted for by _opponent-process_   opponent-process

    theory , which might hold that the body counteracts this pain   theory
    by generating pleasure internally.

48. Rats will learn to press a lever if it is followed by _electrical_   electrical

    stimulation of certain _pleasure_ _centers_ in the brain.   stimulation, pleasure centers

49. Rats are more likely to press a lever to stimulate their brain
    electrically if their brain has recently been stimulated. This

    is called a _priming_ effect, and is an example of _positive_   priming, positive
    feedback.

Self-Test

1. Motivated behavior presents a serious problem to
   some machine models of behavior, because:
   a. motivated behavior involves a whole set of
      different reactions, any of which may lead
      toward the same goal.
   b. motivated behavior involves direction, and
      this assumes a type of feedback that cannot
      be incorporated into machines.
   c. motivated behavior assumes the operation
      of at least one type of servomechanism.
   d. all of the above
   e. none of the above

2. In human sexual behavior, sexual foreplay seems
   gradually to increase sexual arousal of the part-

   ners. This would be an example of:
   a. homeostasis.
   b. negative feedback.
   c. a servomechanism.
   d. positive feedback.
   e. none of the above

3. Which of the following is a reflexive thermoregulatory response to high temperature?
   a. shivering
   b. constriction of the blood vessels in the skin
   c. sweating
   d. turning on a fan
   e. moving to a colder place

4. The word pair reflexive-voluntary represents a

relationship paralleled by which of the following pairs?

a. homeostasis-whole organism
b. vasoconstriction-vasodilation
c. sweating-panting
d. vasoconstriction-building a shelter
e. none of the above

5. A dog is in a room comfortably heated to 75°F. His hypothalamus is cooled experimentally. As a result:

a. he will shiver and his body temperature will go up.
b. he will shiver and his body temperature will go down.
c. he will pant and his body temperature will go up.
d. he will pant and his body temperature will go down.
e. there will be no change in temperature, as his skin temperature remains unchanged.

6. A rat's hypothalamus is cooled, and it learns to settle down over a warm air current in one part of its cage. This behavior illustrates:

a. the operation of hypothalamic thermo-receptors.
b. the mobilization of voluntary behavior by the hypothalamic thermoregulatory system.
c. that directly manipulating hypothalamic temperature can cause an animal to make a response that is inappropriate to its actual body temperature.
d. all of the above
e. none of the above

7. Maintenance of the body's water supply is affected by all except:

a. regulation of the volume and concentration of body fluids.
b. changes in reabsorption of water and minerals by the kidneys.
c. drinking in response to signals from internal receptors.
d. a substance secreted by the kidneys and sensed in the hypothalamus.
e. level of activity in the cerebellum.

8. In both thermoregulation and thirst:

a. receptors in the hypothalamus sense important aspects of bodily needs.
b. homeostasis occurs.
c. there is both reflexive and voluntary control.
d. all of the above
e. none of the above

9. When rats are given a great deal of exercise, their intake of food increases, that is, they eat a larger amount of food. Rats also decrease their intake of a food if it is enriched, so that it contains more calories per gram. These findings suggest that:

a. stomach fullness must be critical in regulating the rat's food intake.
b. the rat is regulating the volume of food consumed.
c. the rat is regulating the caloric or energy value of the food consumed.
d. all of the above
e. a and c

10. Which of the following statements best summarizes the way that internal and external signals influence food intake?

a. Signals from various internal structures (brain receptors, liver, etc.) determine the amount eaten; external factors have almost no effect.
b. Metabolic information from receptors in the brain controls about half of food intake, and external stimulation the other half.
c. Metabolic information from receptors in the liver, brain, and possibly other locations interacts with external stimulation to determine the amount eaten.
d. Palatability is the main determinant of amount eaten, as shown by the experiments in which ice cream was diluted with quinine.
e. Hypothalamic receptors for internal and external events have a dual role in maintaining caloric intake.

11. Initiation of eating is most likely to be associated with:

a. high blood glucose.
b. excitation of the lateral hypothalamus.
c. inhibition of the lateral hypothalamus.
d. high liver glycogen.
e. excitation of the ventromedial hypothalamus.

12. Dual-center theory makes all but one of the following assumptions or predictions. Which assumption is not a necessary part of the theory?

a. Information from internal and external receptors is integrated in the hypothalamus.
b. The relation between the two hypothalamic feeding centers is one of mutual inhibition.
c. The liver is the primary source of information concerning the metabolic state of the organism.
d. Damage to the "on" center should produce aphagia.

e. Damage to the "off" center should produce hyperphagia.

13. Two rats (or people) differ greatly in weight and fatness, but each of them holds its weight rather constant over a period of months. These results suggest that the two differ in:
    a. setpoint.
    b. stomach size.
    c. ability to regulate body weight.
    d. ability to regulate food intake.
    e. size of hypothalamus.

14. Which one of the following has *not* been suggested as a cause of obesity?
    a. damage to the lateral region of the hypothalamus
    b. an excessive number of fat cells
    c. a high setpoint
    d. overresponsiveness to palatability of food
    e. none of the above

15. The figure below provides support for:

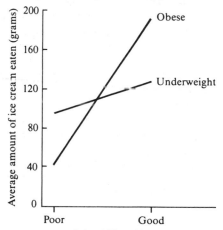

Palatability of ice cream

    a. the dual-center theory of feeding.
    b. the idea that obese people are metabolically different from underweight people.
    c. the drive-reduction theory of motivation.
    d. the externality hypothesis.
    e. all of the above

16. The results in the figure for question 18 can also be explained by the restrained-eating hypothesis, since:
    a. not eating is disinhibited because of the high palatability of the food.
    b. good palatability ice cream is not restrained.
    c. highly palatable ice cream is more fattening than ice cream of poor palatability.
    d. ice cream is external to the eater.
    e. obese subjects have a higher setpoint than

underweight subjects only when ice cream is palatable.

17. When dieters break their diets, they often go on an eating binge. This can be accounted for as:
    a. dropping of setpoint.
    b. raising of setpoint.
    c. externality.
    d. activation of the ventromedial hypothalamus.
    e. disinhibition.

18. The externality and restrained-eating hypotheses make many similar predictions. Which of the following outcomes supports restrained eating as opposed to externality?
    a. Overweight people eat relatively more of tasty foods.
    b. Most overweight people do not differ from normal-weight people in hormones or number of fat cells.
    c. Most overweight people have higher setpoints than normal-weight people.
    d. Overweight people who are not dieting are not as influenced by external cues as those who are dieting.
    e. all of the above

19. Which of the following best describes the relations among externality, restrained eating, and setpoint.
    a. People with higher setpoints are likely to be both more external and restrained eaters.
    b. Anyone with a high setpoint will be external and a restrained eater.
    c. Restrained eating probably causes a higher setpoint, which in turn leads to externality.
    d. a and c
    e. none of the above

20. A major distinction between anorexia nervosa and bulimia is that:
    a. females predominate only in anorexia nervosa.
    b. only anorexics are well below normal weight.
    c. only bulimia is commonly found in people in the 15–25 year age range.
    d. all of the above
    e. none of the above

21. The sympathetic branch of the autonomic nervous system is responsible for which of the following?
    a. decreased heart rate
    b. crying after a sad movie
    c. vegetative functions, such as digestion
    d. emptying of the colon and bladder
    e. none of the above

22. The responses of a cat about to do battle with a dog are mediated by:
    a. the parasympathetic system.
    b. the sympathetic system.
    c. vegetative functions.
    d. the galvanic skin response.
    e. b and c

23. Which of the following is *not* associated with activity of the sympathetic system?
    a. the emergency reaction
    b. epinephrine
    c. secretion by the adrenal medulla
    d. increased heart rate
    e. secretion of digestive enzymes

24. The shaded area of this cross-section of the brain represents a part of the brain that is involved in motivation and emotion. It is called the:
    a. hypothalamus.
    b. limbic system.
    c. cerebellum.
    d. pituitary gland.
    e. corpus callosum.

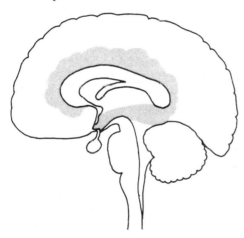

25. The sympathetic system is to the reticular activating system as:
    a. diffuse is to focused.
    b. excitation is to inhibition.
    c. body arousal is to brain arousal.
    d. vasoconstriction is to vasodilatation.
    e. none of the above

26. The involvement of the reticular activating system in wakefulness is demonstrated by all but one of the following results. Which result does not clearly support the RAS-wakefulness linkage?
    a. Stimulation of the RAS leads to wakefulness.
    b. Removal of the RAS leads to somnolence.
    c. External stimuli can arouse an animal even when the direct sensory pathways to the cortex are destroyed.
    d. Transmitter substances are involved in the operation of the RAS.
    e. none of the above

27. Active sleep is considered a paradoxical condition because:
    a. behaviorally the person seems to be sleeping, but his brain waves show a pattern of activity usually associated with a waking EEG.
    b. it occurs at unexpected times, e.g., in a noisy environment or during the day.
    c. the person is easily roused, yet his EEG consists of slow, large amplitude, synchronous waves.
    d. all of the above
    e. a and b

28. Which of the following pairings represents a contrast between active sleep and quiet sleep?
    a. rapid eye movements — no rapid eye movements
    b. dreaming — lack of dreaming
    c. EEG waking activity — EEG slow waves
    d. all of the above
    e. a and c

29. When subjects are awakened after fifteen minutes of REM they relate longer dreams than when they are awakened after five minutes of REM. This result is evidence that:
    a. dreams are not only better remembered during REM, but actually unfold during REM.
    b. dreams are rarely influenced by external sensory stimulation.
    c. as dreams progress, they are related to memories of waking life.
    d. dreams are mediated by the cerebral cortex and the RAS.
    e. all of the above

30. The fact that non-nutritive saccharin serves as a reward for rats and that solving a puzzle seems to be its own reward for monkeys and humans suggests that:
    a. drive reduction is not the only mechanism of reward.
    b. Hull's conception of reward was correct.
    c. drive reduction does not depend on electrical stimulation of the brain.
    d. organisms seek to diminish their arousal levels.
    e. a and d

31. The mechanical puzzle is used to demonstrate that monkeys:
    a. will be motivated by drive reduction.
    b. will perform some acts as ends in themselves.
    c. will only work for drive reduction.
    d. can be stimulated.
    e. none of the above

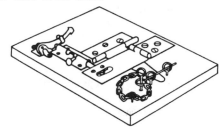

32. Suppose a person is drowsy and inactive much of the time. Which of the following drugs is most likely to reverse these effects?
    a. alcohol
    b. barbiturates
    c. opiates
    d. cocaine
    e. heroin

33. A person addicted to a specific euphoria-producing drug suddenly stops using this drug. He goes into a deep depression. This reaction is an example of:
    a. the effects of tolerance.
    b. the effects of addiction.
    c. a withdrawal symptom.
    d. drive reduction.
    e. a and c

34. Withdrawal results from the same forces that produce tolerance to drugs, according to:
    a. opponent-process theory.
    b. optimal arousal theory.
    c. studies on electrical stimulation of the brain.
    d. drive-reduction theory.
    e. b and d

35. According to the opponent-process theory account of tolerance and withdrawal, the effects of opiate withdrawal should be most like the effects of:
    a. alcohol.
    b. barbiturates.
    c. amphetamines.
    d. cocaine.
    e. c and d

36. According to which formulation is pleasure simply the absence of pain?
    a. opponent-process theory
    b. Hull's theory of drive reduction

c. the externality hypothesis
d. the dual-center theory
e. none of the above

37. Food sometimes tastes better after the first few bites, and then gradually becomes less tasty as we consume substantial amounts. This sequence can be accounted for as:
    a. an effect of brain stimulation.
    b. priming.
    c. positive feedback followed by negative feedback.
    d. opponent processes, in which endorphins are secreted more and more during a meal.
    e. an instance of drive-reduction theory.

38. Which of the following can be considered a homeostatic motive?
    a. hunger
    b. sex
    c. curiosity
    d. a and b
    e. none of the above

Answer Key for Self-Test

Investigating Psychological Phenomena

EFFECTS OF MENTAL PROCESSES ON AUTONOMIC ACTIVITY

Equipment: Stopwatch or watch with second indicator
Number of subjects: Three
Time per subject: Ten minutes
Time for experimenter: Forty minutes

As part of its role in the control of bodily functions, the autonomic nervous system (ANS) controls heart rate. In this way it can influence the rate of delivery of oxygen and nutrients to the cells of the body. In times when the body is stressed, increased heart rate (and other changes) increases the delivery of nutrients to cells, as well as increasing the rate of disposal of waste products. The changes in heart rate are produced directly by nerve impulses sent to the heart. They are also produced indirectly by stimulation, through autonomic pathways, of the release of epinephrine (adrenaline) and related substances from the adrenal glands.

Arousal of the sympathetic system, and hence increased heart rate, occurs when the organism is undergoing physical exertion. But it can also be produced by mental events. Such a pathway would allow an organism to mobilize its physiological resources in anticipation of physical stress. On the other hand, it also allows for high and ultimately damaging levels of sympathetic arousal based on chronic anxiety or mental tension.

In this study we will demonstrate the effectiveness of the link between mental activity and heart rate through the sympathetic nervous system. Subjects will be asked to increase their heart rate by thinking either about a strenuous physical activity or something that is mentally exciting.

Make sure that your subject is seated comfortably, has been relaxing for at least ten minutes, and did not engage in any strenuous exercise in the last half hour. Before reading the instructions make sure you can find the subject's pulse on his or her wrist. The unit of recording for heart rate will be a thirty-second interval. You will record the number of beats every thirty seconds on the data sheet below. Allow fifteen seconds to pass between each thirty-second interval of recording so that you will have enough time to record the pulse and give the instruction. If you have an instruction to give the subject (e.g., "Relax," "Increase Mental"), give the instruction as soon as you have recorded the pulse rate, but wait the full fifteen seconds before counting heartbeats.

Instructions to read to the subject:

This is a short, ten-minute experiment to determine whether you can control the rate of beating of your heart. When I say "Begin," you should close your eyes and relax while I take your pulse. After a minute I will say "Increase physical activity," and you should try to increase your heart rate by thinking about some physical activity in which you are personally engaged and which requires a lot of exertion. After I record your pulse I will say, "Relax," and you should stop trying to increase your heart rate and relax again. I will take your pulse for another minute and then I will say "Increase, mental." This time you should try to increase your heart rate by thinking of something that is exciting but that does not involve a lot of physical activity. This could be a fearful experience that you have had, the excitement from watching a sports event, preexamination anxiety, and so on. Following this one-minute episode I will say, "Relax," and you should stop trying to increase your heart rate and relax. I will take your pulse for one final minute. Before you begin the experiment decide on each image you will think about for the physical activity and the mental activity. After you have decided, stop thinking about the images until I give you the instruction during the actual experiment.

Give the subject a few minutes to decide on the images and then to stop thinking about them before you begin the experiment. Wait one minute after the subject has selected the two images to allow any excitation that this may have produced to go away.

DATA FROM THREE SUBJECTS (A, B, AND C)

Instruction and time	A	B	C
"Begin and Relax"			
00:00–0:30			
0:45–1:15			
"Increase, physical activity"			
1:30–2:00			
2:15–2:45			
"Relax"			
3:00–3:30			
3:45–4:15			
"Increase, mental"			
4:30–5:00			
5:15–5:45			
"Relax"			
6:00–6:30			
6:45–7:15			

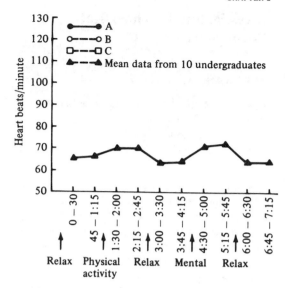

List for each subject the basic situation that they imagined in the "increase" minutes.

	Physical	Mental
A	_____	_____
B	_____	_____
C	_____	_____

Plot the data for each subject on the graph below. Use a different symbol for each subject, and connect the symbols for each subject by lines. Since heart rate is usually expressed as beats per minute, double each of the numbers you have recorded (since you recorded beats per thirty seconds) before plotting. We have plotted the results from ten undergraduates (mean). In our study nine of the ten undergraduates showed the increased heart rate effect.

Do all of your subjects show an ability to increase heart rate by mental activity? Which procedure, thinking of physical activity or something mentally exciting, is more effective? (*If your instructor collects the data, fill out the report sheet in Appendix B.*)

FURTHER PROJECTS

Lowering heart rate is much more difficult than raising it. You might see if you can get some subjects to do that.

Some people have great difficulty in raising their heart rate. If one of your subjects is such a person, you could try to get an increase by having the subject *talk* about physical activity or something exciting during a one-minute period.

You could also explore whether certain kinds of "exciting thoughts" (e.g., fear, excitement of a spectator at a sporting event) are more effective in raising heart rate.

CHAPTER 3

Learning

Learning Objectives

1. Describe the point of view of behavior theorists.

HABITUATION

2. Define habituation and discuss its adaptive significance.

CLASSICAL CONDITIONING

Pavlov and the conditioned reflex

3. Explain the basic procedure (paradigm) of classical conditioning, and define conditioned and unconditioned stimuli and responses.
4. Distinguish between conditioned and unconditioned reflexes (associations) and habituation.

The major phenomena of classical conditioning

5. Distinguish between response amplitude and response latency.
6. Draw a curve to represent the acquisition and extinction of a conditioned response.
7. Be able to define: reinforcement, higher-order conditioning, extinction, and spontaneous recovery.
8. Describe generalization and discrimination, and contrast the two processes.

Extensions of classical conditioning

9. Indicate how classical conditioning can account for acquired fears and phobias, and describe how conditioned fear is measured.

INSTRUMENTAL CONDITIONING

10. Review the major similarities and differences between classical conditioning and instrumental conditioning.

Thorndike and the law of effect

11. Explain the law of effect and indicate the evidence that supports it.

Skinner and operant behavior

12. List the additions and modifications Skinner proposed to Thorndike's view of instrumental conditioning.

The major phenomena of instrumental conditioning

13. Explain how the phenomena of instrumental conditioning parallel those of classical conditioning.
14. Define negative and positive reinforcers, and indicate their relation to appetitive and aversive stimuli.
15. Describe the processes of generalization, discrimination, and shaping in instrumental conditioning.
16. Give examples of conditioned and primary reinforcers, and describe how a conditioned reinforcer can be produced or eliminated.
17. Describe the effect of delay of reinforcement.
18. Define and describe schedules of reinforcement and their properties, and indicate the effect of the schedules on resistance to extinction.
19. Indicate the ways in which aversive stimuli influence learning, by describing punishment, escape, and avoidance learning.
20. Explain why avoidance learning presents a problem for behavior theory and why it is hard to extinguish.

COGNITIVE LEARNING

21. Compare behavior theory with cognitive learning theory, contrasting learning of responses to learning of cognitions (representations).

A cognitive view of classical conditioning

22. Discuss the effects of different times of onset of the conditioned and unconditioned stimulus. State the most effective CS-US interval, and explain why this is adaptive.

23. Distinguish contiguity and contingency, and explain the studies that indicate that contingency is a critical factor in the formation of conditioned responses.
24. Explain the analogy between scientific thinking (the amateur scientist) and classical conditioning.
25. Define blocking, and show how it relates to the "amateur scientist" view.

A cognitive view of instrumental conditioning

26. Review the evidence supporting the position that what is learned in instrumental conditioning is act-outcome associations, as opposed to the strengthening of specific responses. Describe latent learning.
27. Explain the role of contingency in instrumental conditioning and its relation to learned helplessness.
28. Describe the proposed relation between learned helplessness and the functioning of the immune system.

Biological constraints on learning

29. Review the basic criticism of behavior theory that is described as biological constraints. In what sense can animals and humans learn arbitrary relationships?
30. Define the equipotentiality principle, and discuss the evidence against it. Describe belongingness or preparedness.
31. Describe the phenomenon of taste aversion learning, and indicate why it illustrates biological constraints.

32. Discuss the sense in which humans can be considered both intellectual generalists and specialists.

COMPLEX COGNITIONS IN ANIMALS

Cognitive maps

33. Explain what cognitive maps are and what the evidence is that animals have them.

Insightful behavior

34. Describe the phenomenon of insight in animals, and indicate why it presents problems for behavior theory.
35. Review how we determine whether insight or trial and error is a better way of describing a particular learned behavior. Define the role of transfer in making this distinction.
36. Distinguish between generalization and transfer.
37. Explain what a higher-order relationship is, and illustrate this with results from matching to sample and same-different symbol studies.

TAKING STOCK

38. Evaluate the strengths and shortcomings of behavior theory.

Programmed Exercises

1. _Behavior theorists_ believe that a few simple laws of learning can account for most of human and animal behavior.

Behavior theorists

HABITUATION

2. _Habituation_ is a decline in the tendency to respond to stimuli that have become familiar due to repeated exposure.

Habituation

CLASSICAL CONDITIONING

3. Unlike habituation, classical conditioning involves the formation of _associations_ between events.

associations

4. _Classical conditioning_ was first demonstrated in the laboratory by Ivan Pavlov.

Classical conditioning

5. After classical conditioning, the salivation of a dog upon presentation of a previously neutral bell would be called a(n) _conditioned response_. The previously neutral bell is now called a(n) _cond stimulus_.

conditioned response (CR)

conditioned stimulus (CS)

6. In Pavlov's laboratory, food in the mouth was a(n) _unconditioned_ _stimulus_, and the salivation it produced was a(n) _unconditioned_ _response_.

unconditioned
stimulus (US), unconditioned
response (UR)

7. Salivation to meat powder in the mouth is a(n) _unconditioned_ _reflex_ . Salivation to a tone paired with meat powder in the mouth is a(n) _conditioned_ _reflex_ .

unconditioned
reflex (response)
conditioned reflex (response)

8. According to Pavlov, when the CS is followed by the US, the connection between them is _reinforced_.

reinforced

9. Response strength in classical conditioning can be measured as the amount of response, that is, the response _amplitude_, or the time from onset of CS to the onset of the CR, called the _latency_.

amplitude
latency

10. A light is paired with shock. Subsequently, a tone paired with the light comes to elicit fear. This is an example of _higher_-_order_ _conditioning_.

higher- (second-)
order conditioning

11. If after a CR has been established, the CS is presented but not followed by the US, the result will be _extinction_ of the CR.

extinction

12. If time is allowed to pass, the CR will reappear when the CS is presented. This is the phenomenon of _spontaneous_ _recovery_.

spontaneous recovery

13. Horizontal stripes on a card (CS) are paired with a puff of air to the eye (US), resulting in a conditioned eye blink response. Now, the first time the vertical stripes are presented, a conditioned eye blink is observed. This is an example of _stimulus_ _generalization_.

stimulus generalization

14. The greater the difference between a CS and another test stimulus, the weaker the CR to this test stimulus. This relationship is described as a _generalization_ _gradient_.

generalization gradient

15. Reinforcement (US presentation) after CS+, and nonreinforcement (no US) after CS− leads to _discrimination_.

discrimination

16. Animals show response suppression when a stimulus paired with shock is presented to them. This is called the _conditioned_ _emotional_ _response_.

conditioned
emotional response

17. According to a classical conditioning analysis, the object of a phobia or fetish can be considered a _conditioned_ _stimulus_.

conditioned stimulus

INSTRUMENTAL CONDITIONING

18. In classical conditioning, a relation between two stimuli is learned. In instrumental conditioning, however, the relation that is learned exists between a _response_ and a _reward_ .

response, reward

19. The experimental study of instrumental learning was begun by
Thorndike in the context of a debate over the mental continuity of
man and animals which was stimulated by the evolutionary
theories of _Darwin_.

(Edward L.) Thorndike

(Charles) Darwin

20. Thorndike's _law_ _of_ _effect_ states that the consequences of a response determine whether it becomes strengthened
or weakened.

law of effect

21. The most prominent figure in modern behavior theory was
Skinner.

(B. F.) Skinner

22. Skinner emphasized distinctions between classical conditioning
and instrumental learning. In the former, responses are
elicited , while in instrumental learning they are _emitted_ .

elicited, emitted

23. Skinner used the term "_operant_" to describe the "voluntary" or
"emitted" responses that are studied in instrumental learning.

He preferred to measure _response rate_ as a measure of
response strength.

operants

response rate

24. In instrumental conditioning, the delivery of an _appetitive_
stimulus (some preferred situation or substance, e.g., food)
following a particular response is called positive _reinforcement_.

appetitive

reinforcement

25. In instrumental conditioning, the situation in which an instrumental response eliminates or prevents an _aversive_ stimulus is
described as _negative reinforcement_.

aversive

negative reinforcement

26. Although operants are not elicited by external stimuli, the stimuli
can control behavior as _discriminative stimuli_

discriminative stimuli

27. Animals can be trained to perform difficult responses by the
method of _successive approximation_

successive
approximation (shaping)

28. After a neutral stimulus is paired with a reinforcer such as food,
the neutral stimulus acquires reinforcement properties. This is
called _conditioned reinforcement_

conditioned reinforcement

29. Conditioned reinforcement is established by a procedure that
seems to be the same as _classical_ conditioning.

classical

30. Reinforcements become less effective the longer the _delay_
between the response and the reinforcement.

delay (time)

31. The rule set up by the experimenter (or society) which determines the occasions on which a response is reinforced is called a
schedule of reinforcement

schedule of reinforcement

32. An animal that is reinforced for every five responses is on a
fixed ratio schedule.

fixed ratio

33. Responses acquired with intermittent reinforcement exhibit
greater resistance to extinction. This is termed the _partial
reinforcement effect_ .

partial

reinforcement effect

34. Loud noises, painful stimuli, bitter tastes, and social rejection are

    examples of _aversive_ stimuli.   aversive

35. In _punishment_ training, an aversive stimulus follows a particular   punishment
    response.

36. _Escape_ learning is a type of instrumental learning in which the   Escape
    organism is required to perform a response which terminates or
    reduces an aversive stimulus.

37. Avoidance learning presents problems for behavior theory

    because it is not easy to identify the _reinforcer_ for the avoidance   reinforcer
    response.

38. Avoidance responses are particularly resistant to _extinction_. This   extinction
    may account for the persistence in humans of certain intense

    fears, or _phobias_.   phobias

39. This graph illustrates the transition from _escape_ to _avoidance_   escape, avoidance
    learning.

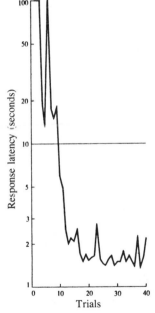

Response latency (seconds) vs. Trials

COGNITIVE LEARNING

40. Behavior theorists emphasize that learning modifies _responses_.   responses (action)
    In contrast, cognitive theorists argue that learning involves
                                                                             knowledge (cognitions)
    acquisition of _knowledge_.   (representations)

41. According to the most modern dominant view, in classical

    conditioning organisms acquire _representations_ of the relation between representations
    two stimulus events.

42. Learning of a conditioned response (CR) occurs most efficiently

    when the _conditioned stimulus_ precedes the _uncord. stimulus_ by a small time   CS, US

    interval. This is called _forward_ pairing.   forward

43. Pavlov and others claimed that togetherness in time, pairing, or

~~contiguity~~ forms the basis for classical conditioning.   contiguity

44. Later research suggests that what is critical for conditioning is

that the CS predicts the US, so that there is a ~~contingency~~ between   contingency
CS and US.

45. A stimulus (CS-1) is presented contingently with a US. Then a
second stimulus (CS-2) is also presented at the same time as
CS-1, and both are followed by the US. Often only CS-1 will show

classical conditioning. This phenomenon is called ~~blocking~~.   blocking

46. Two conditions that seem necessary for classical conditioning to

occur are that the CS must show a ~~contingent~~ relation to the US,   contingent

and the CS must provide ~~info.~~ that the organism did not   information
have before.

47. Evidence indicates that rather than strengthening specific

responses, instrumental reinforcement creates ~~act~~ - ~~outcome~~ act-outcome
associations.

48. Learning in the absence of reward indicates that responses need not

occur for learning to occur. This is called ~~latent~~ learning.   latent

49. Just as is the case with classical conditioning, what is learned in

instrumental learning is a ~~contingency~~   contingency

50. Dogs given inescapable shocks are then placed in an avoidance
situation shuttlebox where they could learn a jumping response to
escape and avoid shock. Instead, they lie quietly and take the
shocks. Their behavior has been interpreted as learning that the
presence or absence of shocks is not contingent on their behavior,

a state called ~~learned helplessness~~   learned helplessness

51. Helplessness training seems to increase susceptibility to cancer.

This may be because this training suppresses the ~~immune~~   immune
system.

52. Behavior theory assumes that the relation between stimuli in
classical conditioning, or between response and outcome in

instrumental learning, is ~~arbitrary~~. This assumption is known as   arbitrary
the ~~equipotentiality~~ principle.   equipotentiality

53. One criticism of behavior theory holds that there are certain

built-in limitations called ~~biological constraints~~ that determine   biological constraints
what a given animal can easily learn.

54. Belongingness in animal learning, as illustrated by taste aversion
learning, seems to fit well with the survival needs of animals.

Thus, rats, who rely heavily on ~~taste~~ in feeding, tend to   taste
associate that with the aftereffects of eating, while birds, which

rely on _vision_ in feeding, tend to associate this type of stimulus with the aftereffects of eating.

vision (sight)

55. The fact that rats learn to associate the taste, but not the sight, of food with illness is an instance of _prepared_ learning.

prepared

56. It can be argued that humans and some other animals seem relatively good at learning arbitrary relationships. In this sense, they can be seen as _generalists_, as opposed to _specialists_

generalists, specialists

COMPLEX COGNITION IN ANIMALS

57. Tolman's original work, later work on the radial-arm maze with rats, and food retrieval by chimpanzees suggest that animals have _cognitive map_ .

cognitive maps

58. Köhler claimed that animals can acquire _cognitions_, as well as responses.

cognitions

59. The photo below represents a situation studied by Köhler in which he demonstrated the phenomenon of _insight_.

insight

60. A chimpanzee solves the problem of knocking down a piece of fruit hung above the cage by throwing a ball at it. When the ball is taken away, it throws a piece of fruit. This demonstrates

transfer .

transfer

61. Behavior theory interprets transfer effects as instances of

stimulus generalization but transfer often seems to be based on

stimulus generalization

abstract _conceptual_ relationships.

conceptual

62. Successive improvement across a series of unrelated discrimination

problems demonstrates the acquisition of a _learning set_ .

learning set

63. An animal is shown one stimulus and, below it, two other stimuli. One of these two is identical to the upper stimulus. The correct response is to indicate this stimulus. This procedure is

called _matching to sample_ .

matching to sample

64. The idea of "sameness" developed by Sarah, the chimpanzee, is

an example of a _higher_ - _order_ relationship.

higher-order

65. A major criticism of behavior theory that emerges from recent work is that we must explore not only what animals (and

humans) _do_, but also what they _know_ .

know

Self-Test

1. Behavior theorists share with Descartes the conviction that:
   a. one must study the nervous system to understand behavior.
   b. learning is the most important aspect of animal behavior.
   c. complex behavior can be analyzed into simpler, more elementary processes.
   d. almost all behavior can be described as prewired.
   e. c and d

2. An animal startles when it is exposed to the sound of either a door slamming or a gong ringing. It is then exposed, about ten times, to the gong ringing followed by the door slamming. Now, when the gong rings, the animal does _not_ show startle. This is an example of
   a. habituation.
   b. classical conditioning.
   c. extinction.
   d. associations.
   e. a learning curve.

3. Classical conditioning and habituation have in common the fact that both:
   a. involve associations.
   b. require a conditioned stimulus.

   c. are built-in responses that animals show in laboratory situations.
   d. involve a change in response to a stimulus.
   e. occur primarily in dogs, though they may occur in some other species.

4. In a classical conditioning experiment in which a tone is paired with meat in the mouth, a dog comes to salivate to the sound of the tone. The tone is called the:
   a. conditioned stimulus.
   b. unconditioned stimulus.
   c. unconditioned response.
   d. stimulus generalization.
   e. reinforcer.

5. Ivan Pilaff developed a fear of German shepherds because, on a few occasions, he was bitten by them. Some weeks later, he became friendly with someone who had a German shepherd as a pet. After a few visits to this friend plus shepherd, he became fearful of the friend, even though this particular German shepherd never bit him. This is an example of:
   a. discrimination.
   b. extinction.
   c. reinforcement.
   d. learning with a long delay.
   e. higher-order conditioning.

6. A dog is first classically conditioned to seven stimuli (A–G) until he responds equally to all. He then gets some further training. At the end he produces the unusual generalization curve shown below. What was the further training the dog received?

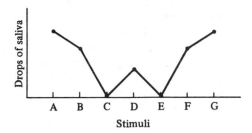

Stimuli

a. extinguish stimuli A, B, D, F, and G
b. extinguish B, D, and F; further condition A and G
c. extinguish C and E
d. extinguish C, D, and E
e. extinguish C and E; further condition D

7. This figure illustrated the phenomenon of:

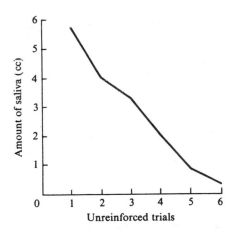

Unreinforced trials

a. conditioning.
b. generalization.
c. extinction.
d. reconditioning.
e. spontaneous recovery.

8. Classical conditioning has been:
a. shown to occur only with salivation.
b. used to explain responses to music, in conjunction with Romantic conditioning.
c. demonstrated only in vertebrates.
d. suggested as an explanation for phobias.
e. a and c

9. During World War II, air raid sirens preceded bombing raids. A person who, as a result of fear, stopped her ongoing activity (e.g., eating, working) when sirens sounded showed:
a. response suppression.
b. a siren phobia.
c. extinction.
d. spontaneous recovery.
e. a generalization gradient.

10. Instrumental learning differs from classical conditioning in that:
a. in instrumental learning, a response-reward association is learned, while in classical conditioning, a relation between stimuli is learned.
b. associations are formed only in classical conditioning.
c. responses are never involved in classical conditioning.
d. instrumental learning always occurs gradually, in trial-and-error fashion, whereas classical conditioning occurs very rapidly.
e. a and c

11. According to the law of effect, responses followed by reward:
a. increase latency.
b. are not always reinforced.
c. become trials or errors.
d. are strengthened.
e. all of the above

12. As described by Thorndike, instrumental learning:
a. is gradual.
b. involves no complex, uniquely human processes.
c. is accomplished on a trial-and-error basis.
d. is a means of strengthening particular responses.
e. all of the above

13. Skinner added to Thorndike's conception(s) the idea that the responses conditioned in instrumental learning were:
a. emitted or voluntary, as opposed to elicited as in classical conditioning.
b. increased in strength by the process of reinforcement.
c. selected from all responses emitted on the basis of the law of effect.
d. a and c
e. all of the above

14. The desire for good grades illustrates the phenomenon of:
a. stimulus generalization.

b. simultaneous discrimination.
c. conditioned reinforcement.
d. successive approximation.
e. a and d

15. In order to shape an animal to perform a difficult response, all but one of the following procedures should be followed. Which procedure is *not* appropriate?
    a. Provide a clear signal for the arrival of reinforcement.
    b. Present the reinforcement immediately after the response is performed.
    c. Initially reinforce approximations to the desired response.
    d. At first, reinforce those parts of the desired response sequence that come at the end of the sequence.
    e. Work with the most difficult component in the response sequence first.

16. A rat is placed in a chamber and is given a number of pellets of food, each preceded by a clicking sound. It is later trained to press a lever, with the reinforcement of the sounding of the click, but without food. Every other day the rat receives pairings of click and food, and on the alternate days, it presses only for the click. Eventually, it stops pressing the lever on the "click" days. This cessation could be explained as:
    a. generalization.
    b. loss of conditioned reinforcement properties by the click.
    c. discrimination between clicks in two different situations.
    d. an illustration of the importance of delay of reinforcement.
    e. spontaneous recovery.

17. Skinner and Thorndike share a belief in:
    a. the importance of schedules of reinforcement.
    b. the law of effect.
    c. the idea that instrumental behavior is emitted.
    d. the superiority of instrumental training with discrete trials.
    e. all of the above

18. A hippopotamus is placed in a puzzle box. On the first trial he performs a series of responses: R1 (ramming at the doors), R2 (bellowing), R3 (stamping on the floor), and finally, R4 (stepping on a pedal which opens a door and lets him out and gives him access to mountains of hippopotamus food). According to the law of effect, any response which is followed by reinforcement will be connected to the stimulus situation. This being

so, there should be a strengthening of R1, R2, and R3, but, in fact, we notice that these responses decline in probability. How would Thorndike explain this?
    a. by referring to the importance of conditioned reinforcement
    b. by invoking schedules of reinforcement
    c. by referring to the role of delay of reinforcement
    d. by referring to disinhibition
    e. by referring to generalization

19. Consider each swing by a baseball player as an operant response and every successful hit (single, double, etc.) as a reinforced swing. What schedule of reinforcement is a baseball batter on?
    a. continuous reinforcement (fixed ratio 1)
    b. fixed ratio
    c. variable ratio
    d. extinction
    e. variable interval

20. Paradoxically, when an operant is reinforced on a schedule (e.g., every third response is reinforced), the response shows a greater resistance to extinction than when it receives an equal number of reinforced responses on *every trial*. This effect (partial reinforcement effect) is paradoxical because:
    a. the nonreinforced trials in partial reinforcement training are extinction trials and should weaken the response.
    b. CS-US contingencies must be precisely controlled in order for good conditioning to occur.
    c. the animal on partial reinforcement performs more responses in training.
    d. the organism is learning a discrimination during training.
    e. all of the above

21. Avoidance learning presents a problem for behavior theory because:
    a. it is not clear what reinforces the avoidance response.
    b. it is particularly resistant to extinction.
    c. it occurs after the animal learns to escape.
    d. a and b
    e. none of the above

22. In a classic experiment (appropriately) on classical conditioning, it was shown that classical conditioning could occur when animals were temporarily paralyzed with a drug, so that they could not respond. (Of course, when testing for conditioning with a CS, the animals were no longer paralyzed.) Which position does this result support?

a. the cognitive learning view
b. the behavior theory view
c. Pavlov's position
d. Skinner's position
e. b and c

23. This figure demonstrates that it is very difficult to produce conditioning with:

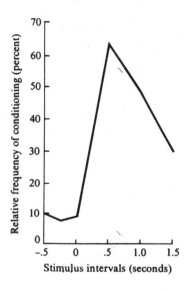

Stimulus intervals (seconds)

a. forward pairing.
b. higher-order conditioning.
c. extinction.
d. simultaneous pairing.
e. all of the above

24. Consider the following table of probabilities of CS and US. What predictions would the contiguity and contingency accounts make of whether conditioning would occur in this case?

	US	No US
CS	9	1
No CS	9	1

a. Both predict conditioning.
b. Both predict no conditioning.
c. Only contingency predicts conditioning.
d. Only contiguity predicts conditioning.
e. Neither predicts conditioning.

25. Consider the following table of occurrences of CS and US. What predictions would the contiguity and contingency accounts make of whether conditioning would occur in this case?

	US	No US
CS	7	3
No CS	3	7

a. Both predict conditioning.
b. Both predict no conditioning.
c. Only contingency predicts conditioning.
d. Only contiguity predicts conditioning.
e. Neither predicts conditioning.

26. In the case of unsignaled shock (a random relation between a signal and shock), the relation between a signal and the shock is one of:
a. anxiety.
b. absence of contingency.
c. contingency.
d. contiguity.
e. blocking.

27. Some properties of classical conditioning suggest that it functions to make predictions about events in the world, somewhat like a scientist makes. Which feature(s) of classical conditioning suggest(s) this property?
a. sensitivity to contingency
b. forward pairing
c. blocking
d. all of the above
e. b and c

28. Harriet gets very excited whenever she approaches the house of her boyfriend, Milton. She notices that her heart starts beating when she turns his corner and sees the name of his street on the corner sign. But she is surprised one day to note that the sign is down, and that she does not get excited on turning the corner, nor on passing Milton's street mailbox, just twenty feet from the corner. Why doesn't the mailbox cause her heart to increase beating?
a. blocking
b. backward pairing
c. Harriet is an amateur scientist.
d. The mailbox doesn't have a contingent relation with Milton.
e. Fear suppresses her response.

29. A rat learns to run down a runway when reinforced with a sugar solution in the end box. After learning this, it is then fed a bitter (negatively reinforcing) solution in this same end box. When put back in the start box of the runway, it runs to the end less quickly than before. This illustrates:
a. higher-order conditioning.
b. blocking.
c. learned helplessness.
d. the law of effect.
e. cognitive learning.

30. Animals exposed to lights randomly paired with shock (hence, unsignaled shock) sometimes develop pathologies related to stress. The relation of this finding to learned helplessness is the same as the relationship of:
   a. conditioning to extinction.
   b. the optimum CS-US interval to contingency.
   c. generalization in classical conditioning to generalization in instrumental conditioning.
   d. behavior therapy to the partial reinforcement effect.
   e. extinction of instrumental conditioning to establishment of classical conditioning.

31. Studies on learned helplessness in dogs and infants' responses to mobiles that they could or could not control are evidence for the importance of:
   a. the law of effect.
   b. contiguity.
   c. contingency.
   d. belongingness.
   e. none of the above

32. There is evidence that learned helplessness depresses the function of the immune system, resulting in greater susceptibility to cancer. What experience other than learned helplessness would also be likely to have these effects?
   a. avoidance learning
   b. unsignaled shock
   c. escape learning
   d. punishment training
   e. punishment

33. A simplified version of John Garcia's belongingness experiment would present sweetened water along with bright light and noise to rats, followed by X-ray produced illness. The rats would show an aversion only to the taste (one of the groups in the experiment described in the text). However, without the use of a second group in which shock is the US, this experiment could be criticized by a behavior theorist, because:
   a. bright-noisy type of stimuli don't associate well with US's like those induced by X-rays.
   b. the bright-noisy stimuli might have been generally less effective as CS's than the taste stimulus.
   c. this result would contradict the bird studies, showing selective association of visual stimuli and gastrointestinal effects.
   d. the selective association could have been previously learned by the rats.
   e. all of the above

34. Which of the following instances of human learning most clearly represents arbitrary, as opposed

to biologically specialized or prepared, learning?
   a. learning to avoid poisons
   b. learning to catch a ball
   c. learning the rules of chess
   d. learning to judge distance
   e. a and b

35. Which of the following phenomena presents a serious problem to behavior theory?
   a. learning without performing a response or without getting a reward
   b. taste aversion learning
   c. insight learning
   d. cognitive maps
   e. all of the above

36. Which of the following statements describes a fundamental difference between behavior and cognitive theorists?
   a. Behavior theorists think a response is necessary for learning, while cognitive theorists think responses may be merely an index of learning.
   b. Behavior theorists believe in reinforcement, and cognitive theorists deny its existence.
   c. Behavior theorists believe in belongingness, while cognitive theorists believe in preparedness.
   d. all of the above
   e. none of the above

37. In his attempts to demonstrate higher mental processes in animals, Köhler's experiments differed from those of Thorndike in that:
   a. Köhler used an animal which might have greater reasoning power.
   b. Köhler used situations in which it was possible to "reason" a solution.
   c. Köhler used problems which could be gradually understood.
   d. a and c
   e. a and b

38. Köhler suggested that a way to distinguish insightful from trial-and-error learning is that only insightful learning would:
   a. generalize.
   b. show transfer.
   c. be arbitrary.
   d. be accomplished by apes.
   e. show belongingness.

39. Primates seem superior to other nonhuman animals tested in learning situations in that they show:
   a. more rapid learning of initial discriminations.

b. more rapid instrumental conditioning.

c. more rapid classical conditioning.

d. clearer learning sets.

e. all of the above

40. Learning sets are a challenge to behavior theory because they imply that:

a. learning can be very rapid.

b. monkeys respond to perceptual relation-ships.

c. the particular form of the response is not important.

d. monkeys can employ "strategies" (e.g., win-stay, lose-shift).

e. belongingness occurs.

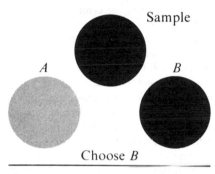

Choose *B*

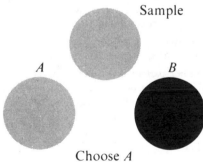

Choose *A*

41. The figure above sets out a problem used frequently in studies with primates. The problem is called:

a. discrimination.

b. symbol manipulation.

c. learning to learn.

d. matching to sample.

e. generalization.

42. Critical evidence for a concept of "sameness" in chimpanzees comes from the demonstration of:

a. discrimination.

b. generalization.

c. belongingness.

d. matching to sample.

e. transfer.

43. A relationship like "same," which holds regardless of the specific objects that are used to illustrate it, can be described as:

a. a good relationship.

b. a higher-order relationship.

c. an excellent relationship.

d. insightful.

e. matching to sample.

44. Which of the following pairs best expresses a distinction between behavior theory and cognitive theory?

a. discrimination versus generalization

b. same versus different

c. biological constraints versus higher-order relationships

d. insight versus out of sight

e. doing versus knowing

45. Cognitive theorists criticize behavior theorists on the grounds that behavior theorists:

a. assume animals are able to learn any arbitrary relationship.

b. underestimate the ability of some animals to show sophisticated learning in some specific situations.

c. rely too much on the response as a necessary part of learning.

d. a and c

e. all of the above

46–48. For the following three questions, the same set of answer alternatives are relevant.

Each question describes a major principle of behavior theory. For each one, choose the answer that describes a finding that casts doubt on this principle. The possible answers are listed below.

a. learning sets

b. random pairing of CS and US leads to no conditioning

c. insight learning

d. learned helplessness

e. taste-aversion learning

46. Contiguity in time of two stimuli is sufficient grounds for conditioning.

47. Any CS can be associated equally well with any US.

48. Learning occurs gradually.

Answer Key for Self-Test

1. c p. 70	26. b p. 90
2. a p. 71	27. d pp. 88–91
3. d pp. 71–73	28. a p. 90
4. a p. 73	29. d p. 91
5. e p. 74	30. c pp. 92–93
6. c p. 74	31. c pp. 93–94
7. c p. 74	32. b pp. 90, 94
8. d p. 76	33. b pp. 95–96
9. a p. 76	34. c p. 95
10. a p. 77	35. e pp. 87, 95–102
11. d p. 79	36. a pp. 87, 95
12. e pp. 77–78	37. e p. 99
13. a p. 79	38. b p. 100
14. c p. 82	39. d p. 101
15. e p. 81	40. d p. 101
16. c p. 81	41. d p. 101
17. b p. 79	42. e p. 101
18. c p. 83	43. b p. 102
19. c p. 84	44. e pp. 87, 91, 103
20. a p. 85	45. e pp. 87, 95,
21. d pp. 86–87	102–103
22. a p. 87	46. b p. 89
23. d p. 88	47. e pp. 95–96
24. d p. 89	48. c p. 100
25. a p. 89	

Investigating Psychological Phenomena

MAZE LEARNING

Equipment: Stopwatch or watch with second indicator
Number of subjects: One, yourself
Time per subject: Twenty to thirty-five minutes
Time for experimenter: Twenty to thirty-five minutes

This experiment illustrates a basic feature of learning: the acquisition curve, or the gradual acquisition of a skill or task. It employs a technique that was commonly used with animals in the earlier part of this century. The task is to find a way through a maze, presumably through learning a series of correct choices at the various choice-points. In the experiment you will proceed through the same maze four times: each time, a record will be kept of both your total time to completion and the number of errors (false entries). Learning would be demonstrated by a drop in either time to completion or the number of errors, as the number of trials increases.

Beginning on page 54, a maze is reprinted 4 times. In each case, using the second indicator on a wrist watch or a stopwatch, time yourself from the time you

begin with a pencil at the starting point to the time you leave the maze. You should never pick your pencil off the paper until the maze is completed. If you make an error, simply retrace your steps with the pencil. Upon completion of the maze, record the total time taken at the bottom of the page. Do not record the number of errors until you have finished all the mazes, since calculation of errors would be like another trial (you would have to work through the maze again).

Finish all four trials and then calculate errors for each trial. An error is defined as the crossing of the imaginary line at the mouth of an "alley" that leads to a dead end. One such entry can only count for one error, no matter how far you go up the blind alley before realizing that it is blind. In other words, once you have entered an alley which will ultimately be blind, you can only score one error, even if there is a further choice-point along this path (both of these choices would of course have to be blind alleys). The only way you can score two errors for the same blind alley is if you enter it twice.

Plot the time/trial and errors/trial on the two graphs provided below. Do you show evidence for gradual mastery of the maze? Compare your results with those from a group of undergraduate students that we have plotted on the same graph. We have plotted the mean (the average) scores. Individuals vary a lot; not all individuals show smooth curves like these averaged curves. In the graph, •——• represents the mean for eight subjects. H and L represent the range. H is the highest value of eight subjects; L is the lowest score of eight subjects.

In the earlier part of this century, psychologists speculated about what exactly is learned when a rat or human learns a maze. Some, like John B. Watson, took a "molecular" position and claimed that a sequence

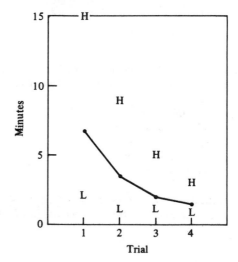

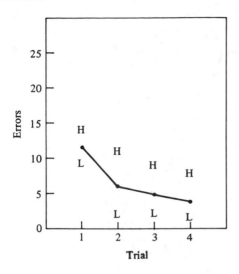

of responses is learned. The most critical responses would be those at the choice-points: From this point of view, the learning would be represented as a series of turning instructions (e.g., left, right, right), one for each successive choice-point. Others, such as Edward Chace Tolman, argued that the subject, rat or human, developed a spatial representation of the maze in his head, a "cognitive map," rather than a sequence of responses. What do you think you actually learned in this task?

You should realize that this type of maze differs markedly from the mazes used for rats or the life-size mazes for humans. In these cases, the subject does not get a direct picture of the whole layout; rather, the subject can only see the part of the maze in the immediate vicinity of the choice-point. This, of course, would make it much harder for the subject to build up a map of the maze. To get a feeling for the difference, cut out a hole about 1/2" square from the center of a full-sized piece of paper. Place it at the beginning of the fifth duplication of the maze, and attempt to move through the maze with the pencil again, moving the hole along as you move the pencil. If you had learned a series of turns or choices, this procedure should not seriously affect your performance. On the other hand, insofar as you used a "map," or some sort of larger view of the shape of the maze and your path through it, this procedure would seriously affect your performance.

(If your instructor collects the data, fill out the report sheet in Appendix B.)

FURTHER ACTIVITIES

We have included one extra copy of the maze. You can use this copy for further experiments: If you need more than one maze, you can make a copy of this unused maze.

You might wish to test the idea of a map of the maze versus a set of turning responses, by trying to run the maze backward (start at finish and end at start). What predictions would you make? A cognitive map view would hold that the backward run would be a lot easier than the first run in the "proper" direction, since the same maze map would work in both directions. But a response-learning view would not predict that having learned the maze in the original order would aid in the learning of the reversed maze. The sequence of turns (e.g., left, left, right, left, etc.) would be entirely different when running the maze backward.

Of course, there is a problem here. How do you know how long it would have taken to run the maze backward if you did that on your first trial? You don't. One possibility would be to run a few people on one trial forward and a few others on one trial backward. One could then see if one direction was harder than the other. Another possibility, not as satisfying, is just to assume that it should be about as easy forward as backward, since it wasn't designed to be more difficult one way than another.

Another activity would be to look at forgetting. Do the final maze in a few days or a week and compare your time and errors to your performance today. Would you expect your performance to be about the same as trial 4? Better than trial 1?

On the following three pages, cover the top (completed) maze while doing the bottom one.

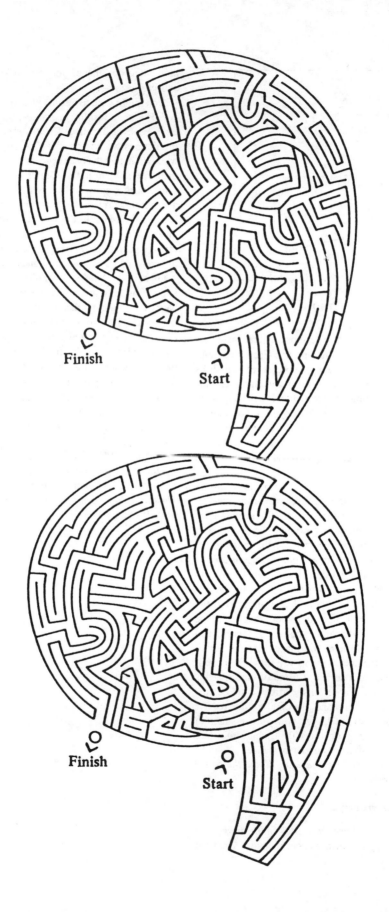

Finish

Start

Finish

Start

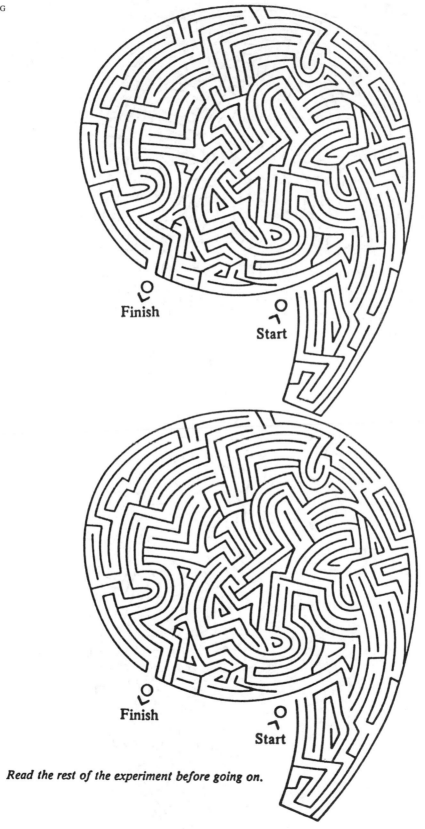

Finish

Start

Finish

Start

Read the rest of the experiment before going on.

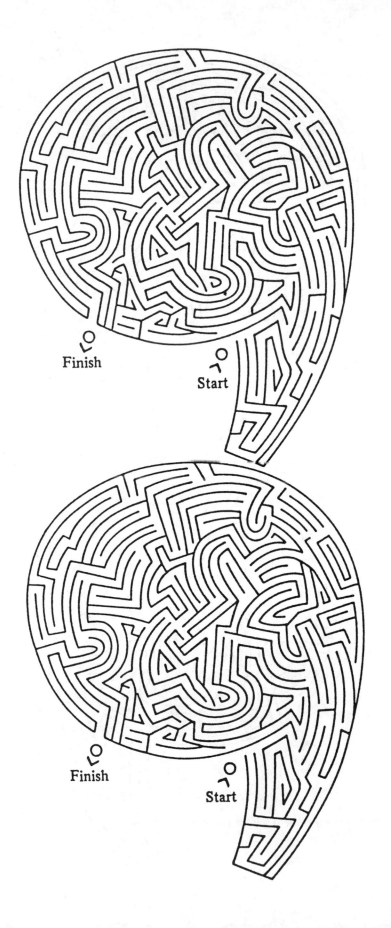

Finish

Start

Finish

Start

LEARNED TASTE AVERSIONS

Equipment: None
Number of subjects: Five to eight
Time per subject: Five minutes
Time for experimenter: Sixty minutes

One of the basic assumptions of behavior theory is that any conditioned stimulus (CS) could become associated with any unconditioned stimulus (US). That is, it is assumed that the relation of the CS to the US is arbitrary. This assumption has been seriously challenged by the discovery of the phenomenon of learned taste aversions in rats. As first documented by John Garcia and his colleagues, rats can learn in one trial to associate a taste (CS) with illness (US). They will subsequently avoid the taste. This learned taste aversion was of particular importance because Garcia and his colleagues showed that this rapid learning would only occur with tastes as the CS and certain types of illness as the US. This specificity of association between tastes and illness is an illustration of belongingness, the nonarbitrariness of associations.

Because learned taste aversions differ from most of the frequently studied types of learning, they were investigated in some detail. We now know that:

1. The specificity (belongingness) is between tastes and specific types of illness: symptoms from the upper gastrointestinal system, especially nausea, seem by far the most effective.

2. The learning typically occurs in one trial (thus allowing rats to avoid poisons without too many life-threatening trials).

3. The rat can accomplish this learning even if the illness follows the taste by more than one hour. This challenges the view that two stimuli must occur close together in time in order to be associated. CS-US intervals of more than an hour rarely, if ever, support conditioning in traditional classical conditioning, using salivation or startle responses, and tones, bells, and lights.

4. Novel tastes show much more conditioning than familiar ones. This makes sense: If eating of the familiar food has not been followed by illness, it is reasonable to associate the illness with the new food. This is true in other types of classical conditioning as well: There is generally more conditioning to novel stimuli.

It often happens that after a new phenomenon is described, it is found to be common, and one wonders how it could have escaped notice before. So it was with learned taste aversions. A phenomenon similar to that described by Garcia in the rat seems to occur in humans. Most commonly, someone eats a (usually new) food and gets ill within a few hours. Nausea and vomiting are particularly common symptoms. After this one experience, a person finds the food distasteful. Garb and Stunkard (1974) distributed a questionnaire about such experiences to about 700 people. They found that somewhat over one-third of people have had at least one such experience. The analysis of the results of their questionnaire confirmed the presence of the basic properties of learned taste aversions in humans:

1. Belongingness. Aversions were almost always limited to the food and its taste. Rarely were there reports of aversion to the restaurant, tablecloth, accompanying people, or other stimuli that were also associated, in time, with the illness. Furthermore, the illness in question almost always (87 percent of time) involved the gastrointestinal system.

2. One trial learning. The aversions usually occurred after one food-illness pairing.

3. Long CS-US intervals. There was often an interval measured in hours between food ingestion and illness.

4. Novelty. Novel foods (tastes) seem more effective. In spite of the fact that almost everything eaten on any given day would be familiar, 45 percent of the aversions involved foods that had been eaten no more than twice before the pairing with illness.

5. "Irrationality." In many cases, a subject knew that the food did not cause the illness (e.g., other people eating the same food did not get ill, and/or other friends not at the meal came down with the same viral illness at about the same time). Yet, this knowledge that the food did not cause the illness did not weaken the aversion.

We will attempt to confirm the phenomenon of learned taste aversion in humans and highlight its unusual properties. Since, according to Garb and Stunkard, about one-third of people show this phenomenon, we will ask you to interview five to eight people, in the hope that you will find one to four subjects with aversions. We will use an interview protocol that asks many of the same questions covered in Garb and Stunkard's questionnaire. Read the introduction, below, to each subject. If the subject has an aversion, ask each of the questions indicated and record the answers.

LEARNED TASTE AVERSIONS: INTERVIEW PROTOCOL

If a person becomes sick after eating a particular food, he may develop an intense dislike, called an aversion, for that food, whether or not it was responsible for the illness. For example, one person developed a high fever after eating pizza in a restaurant and found that he did not like pizza any more. Another person became very nauseous after eating a breakfast with hash-brown potatoes and found the potatoes distasteful after this experience. She also found she did not want to eat from the plate that the potatoes were on. Have you ever come to dislike a food because you became ill after eating it? If so, please answer the following questions:

1. Your current age.
   (Subject A) _18_ (B) _____
   (C) _____ (D) _____

2. Age when the aversion experience occurred.
   (A) _17_ (B) _____ (C) _____
   (D) _____

3. What is the food? (A) _yogurt_
   (B) _____ (C) _____
   (D) _____

4. Describe the experience in terms of what and where you were eating, and the symptoms of the illness. *(Use extra sheet of paper if necessary.)*
   (A) _I just had an operation on my mouth. I couldn't swallow the pills, so we crushed them up & put it in yogurt._
   (B) _____
   (C) _____
   (D) _____

5. Did this happen only once? If more than once, how many times? (A) _____ , _____
   (B) _____ , _____ (C) _____ ,
   _____ (D) _____ , _____

6. What was the most important symptom you had?
   (A) _the taste made me sick_ (B) _____
   (C) _____ (D) _____

7. Were you nauseous? Did you vomit (if not mentioned in answer above)? (A) _felt sick_ ,
   _____ (B) _____ , _____
   (C) _____ , _____ (D) _____ ,
   _____

8. About how long after you ate the food did the symptoms appear? (A) _____
   (B) _____ (C) _____ (D) _____

9. Do you believe that the food actually caused your illness? (A) _no_ (B) _____
   (C) _____ (D) _____

10. List all the foods that you can remember at the meal before you got sick. Indicate for each food whether it was relatively unfamiliar (you ate it no more than three times in your life). Indicate if you developed an aversion to any of these foods:

Food	Unfamiliar	Aversion
(A)		
___	___	___
___	___	___
___	___	___
___	___	___
(B)		
___	___	___
___	___	___
___	___	___
___	___	___
(C)		
___	___	___
___	___	___
___	___	___
(D)		
___	___	___
___	___	___
___	___	___
___	___	___

11. List all the other things or events that you can remember at this same meal and in the time after the meal and before the illness (e.g., the restaurant, table settings, people with you, books read, and

so on). Indicate if you acquired an aversion to any of these items.

(A) _____

_____

(B) _____

_____

(C) _____

_____

(D) _____

_____

12. Do you still have this aversion?

(A) _____   (B) _____   (C) _____

(D) _____

13. Was (Is) the aversion to the taste, smell, and/or sight of the food?

Taste	Smell	Sight
(A) _____	(A) _____	(A) _____
(B) _____	(B) _____	(B) _____
(C) _____	(C) _____	(C) _____
(D) _____	(D) _____	(D) _____

Summarize the results from all of your subjects below. You decide which questions are relevant to each feature of learned taste aversion, and summarize your results with respect to each of the features listed below.

BELONGINGNESS Relevant questions (Nos.)

_____

_____

_____

ONE TRIAL LEARNING Relevant questions (Nos.)

_____

_____

_____

LONG CS-US INTERVAL Relevant questions (Nos.)

_____

_____

_____

NOVELTY EFFECT Relevant questions (Nos.)

_____

_____

_____

"IRRATIONALITY" Relevant questions (Nos.)

_____

_____

_____

OTHER INTERESTING RESULTS:

_____

_____

_____

Do your data confirm the basic properties of learned taste aversion?

Comment: Interview protocols like this are quite common in psychological research. They are essentially questionnaires, but they are administered by a researcher or someone on his or her staff. In a way they are more subjective than questionnaires because the interviewer could influence the answers of the subject, especially if there is embarrassing material in the protocol. On the other hand, the interview allows for an interaction between the researcher and the subject. If a subject misunderstands a question, he or she can be corrected. If the subject says something that is ambiguous, it can be expanded upon. Similarly, if the subject says something of unusual interest, it can be followed up.

The introductory statement in the interview is critical. We tried to write it so as not to guarantee that subjects would only describe specific food aversions based on gastrointestinal illness. Note that we gave one example of another sort of illness and also suggested the possibility of an aversion to items other than tastes. This certainly does not guarantee an "unbiased" sample of aversions, but it allows for exceptions to the phenomena as described by Garcia and, later, by Garb and Stunkard. Garb and Stunkard's introductory paragraph was more suggestive of gastrointestinal illness than is the paragraph we use here. *(If your instructor collects the data, fill out the report sheet in Appendix B.)*

PROBLEMS AND FURTHER ACTIVITIES

Garb and Stunkard's questionnaire and our interview are not experiments. They can demonstrate that one-trial taste-illness aversions occur in humans. But by themselves they cannot demonstrate belongingness. Remember that Garcia's experiments with rats showed that although lights and tastes were equally paired with both illness and electric shock, the taste was much more strongly associated with illness and the lights with shock. Our introduction for the subjects (and more so Garb and Stunkard's) pointed the subject toward taste-illness associations. We did not ask the subjects if they ever got to dislike a restaurant or a person because they were "followed by" illness or whether they ever got to dislike a food because it was followed by pain or a variety of other unpleasant events. On the contrary, we could ask whether, as a consequence of a very unpleasant event such as a death in the family or painful injury, a subject developed an aversion to any object, event, or food. Such questions have not been asked systematically. Do you have any such aversion? Do any of your friends? If there are many aversions linking food with unpleasant events "outside of the body" or outside of the gastrointestinal system, or if there are aversions to visual or other objects paired with illness, then there is little evidence for the belongingness effects in humans. We don't think there *are* many such effects, but we are not sure at this time.

We have suggested that nausea and vomiting are especially important in generating taste aversion. See if you can get evidence for this. If you know anyone (including yourself) with a food allergy, interview him, using a protocol like the one we have used for aversions. (You will have to make a few modifications.) The critical question is whether people with food allergies develop aversions to these foods. In particular, if the allergy produces no symptoms in the gastrointestinal system, is there an aversion? There is some recent data (Pelchat and Rozin, 1982) that suggest that people with food allergies outside of the gastrointestinal system do not have aversions to these foods— that is, they don't dislike these allergenic foods.

References

Garb, F., and Stunkard, A. 1974. Taste aversions in man. *American Journal of Psychiatry* (131): 1204–7.

Logue, A. W., Ophir, I., and Strauss, K. E. 1981. The acquisition of taste aversion in humans. *Behavior Research and Therapy* (19): 319–33.

Pelchat, M. L., and Rozin, P. 1982. The special role of nausea in the acquisition of food dislikes by humans. *Appetite* (3): 341–51.

CHAPTER 4

Sensory Processes

Learning Objectives

THE ORIGINS OF KNOWLEDGE

The empiricist view
1. Be familiar with the viewpoint of the British empiricists. *knowledge* *senses*
2. Distinguish between proximal and distal stimuli.
3. Understand the difference between sensation and perception.
4. Understand the role of association in the empiricists' view of perception.
5. Explain the relevance of linear perspective in a discussion of association.

The nativist rejoinder
6. Describe how nativism differs from empiricism.

PSYCHOPHYSICS

7. Set forth the sequence of events leading from the stimulus to the reported sensation. Differentiate between the psychophysical and psychophysiological approaches.

Measuring sensory intensity
8. Explain why the just-noticeable difference (j.n.d.) is important in measuring sensory intensity. What is the implication for absolute threshold?
9. Define Weber's law and show how Weber's fraction is used to compare the sensitivities of different sensory modalities.
10. Understand the biological rationale for Fechner's law.

Detection and decision
11. List the various types of errors possible in a detection experiment. Show how payoff manipulations affect response bias.

AN OVERVIEW OF THE SENSES

Kinesthesis and the vestibular senses
12. Define kinesthesis.
13. Describe the function of the semicircular canals.

The skin senses
14. Be familiar with the four basic skin sensations and with what is known about the receptors that correspond to these sensations.
15. Explain the biological value of pain.

The sense of taste
16. List the four basic taste qualities.
17. Be aware of the different types of sensory interactions, both within and between sensory systems.

The sense of smell
18. List the primary smell sensations and be able to explain the underlying principle responsible for their elicitation.
19. Explain why olfaction is a minor distance sense in humans but why it is still important to humans.
20. Be familiar with the various functions of pheromones.

Hearing
21. Sound waves are auditory stimuli. Be aware of their physical and psychological dimensions.
22. Describe the mechanisms by which the ear conducts and amplifies sound waves en route to the auditory receptors.
23. Explain what the auditory receptors are and how they are stimulated.
24. Compare and contrast the place and firing-frequency theories of pitch perception.

The senses: some common principles
25. List four phenomena found throughout the sensory system and offer some examples of these phenomena.

VISION

The stimulus: light

26. Visual sensations register the emission and reflection of light. Know the characteristics of light and what their visual consequences are.

Gathering the stimulus: the eye

27. Explain how the eye is like a camera?
28. Describe the retinal image.

The visual receptors

29. Be familiar with the following terms: rods, cones, bipolar cells, ganglion cells, optic nerve, and blind spot.
30. Understand the nature of the two types of receptors, the evidence for these receptors, and why they are needed.
31. Know where visual acuity is greatest and why.
32. Explain the duplex theory of vision. Refer to dark adaptation in discussing the evidence.
33. Understand how visual pigments are similar to and different from the emulsions on film.

Interaction in time: adaptation

34. Explain what sensory adaptation is and what the organism gains by it.

Interaction in space: contrast

35. Recall that brightness contrast increases with progressive intensity difference between two regions.
36. Be familiar with the characteristics of receptive fields and the effects of lateral inhibition.

Color

37. Remember that color is a qualitative, rather than quantitative, psychological dimension.
38. List are the dimensions of color.
39. Describe the "unique" colors, and understand what it means to refer to a unique color as extraspectral.
40. Note whether differences in brightness are best observed in chromatic or in achromatic colors.
41. Be aware of the role of saturation in distinguishing between chromatic and achromatic colors.
42. Describe the color solid. Explain how different dimensions of color are represented in it. What is its relationship to the color circle?
43. Differentiate between additive and subtractive mixture of colors. Give examples illustrating each.
44. Explain what complementary colors are and how their complementary characters account for simultaneous color contrast and negative afterimages.

The physiological basis of color vision

45. Explain the difference among the three cone types in human color vision.
46. It is important to understand the opponent-process theory thoroughly. Be aware of the relevance of primary colors, color antagonists, and inhibition in the perception of hue and brightness.
47. Be able to give the physiological evidence for the opponent-process theory.
48. List some characteristics of color blindness and explain what might cause it.

Programmed Exercises

THE ORIGINS OF KNOWLEDGE

1. John Locke postulated that all knowledge comes by way of *senses* experience. This school of thought is known as _Empiricists_

   empiricism

2. Locke used the metaphor of a _blank_ _tablet_ in describing the human mind at birth.

   tabula rasa (blank slate)

3. An object in the real world is known as a _distal_ stimulus.

   distal

4. When the energy from an object impinges on a sensory surface, we say that this pattern of energy has become a _proximal_ stimulus.

   proximal

5. According to the empiricists, complex ideas are perceived by the linking together, or _Association_, of two or more sensations.

   association

6. Two identical objects have different retinal sizes. This clue that one object is closer than the other is known as _linear perspective_

   linear perspective

7. Kant believed that a number of aspects of perception are innate. This view has since been labeled _Nativism_

   nativism

PSYCHOPHYSICS

8. The study of the relationship between properties of the stimulus
   and sensory experience is known as _psychophysics_   psychophysics

9. The _absolute threshold_ is the minimal stimulus energy needed   absolute threshold
   to produce a sensation.

10. You find that you are unable to tell the difference between a
    25-lb. weight and a 28-lb. weight, but you can differentiate the
    25-lb. weight from any other weight over 28 lbs. Something
    slightly over 3 lbs. is your _different threshold_. It will produce   difference threshold
    a ___j__-_n___d___ in this weight range.   just-noticeable difference (j.n.d.)

11. A difference threshold is 2 lbs. when the standard is 40 lbs.
    Weber's law predicts that the difference threshold with a 20-lb.   Weber's
    standard would be __1__ lb(s).   1

12. The j.n.d. divided by the standard stimulus is known as
    Weber's fraction and, in general, seems to be constant.   Weber's fraction

13. Imagine that for a certain psychophysical task we found that
    sensation grew as a function of the logarithm of the physical
    stimulus intensity. This would be support for _Fechner's_ law.   Fechner's

14. Imagine that we toss a coin 100 times, each time asking a
    subject to predict the outcome (heads or tails). We find that 73
    times he predicts heads. We also find that he knows that on
    the average, 100 tosses will result in approximately 50 heads.
    We can then attribute his deviation from this figure to a
    Response bias .   response bias

15. One duty of an air traffic controller is to watch a radar screen
    and determine what planes are in the area. There are two kinds
    of errors he might make in this task. First, he may not see a
    small dot on the screen, thus committing a _miss_ , as it is   miss
    often called in signal-detection theory. On the other hand, he
    may report a plane when there is none there. This is called a
    false alarm . Considering the costs of these two errors,   false alarm
    the _false alarm_ error is probably more common than the   false alarm
    miss .   miss

16. Corresponding to the two types of errors, there are also two
    kinds of correct responses. When an event occurs in the world
    and we say that the event occurred, that is known as a _hit_ .   hit
    When an event hasn't occurred in the world and we say that it
    hasn't, we have given a _correct neg._ .   correct negative

17. We have looked at response bias that is caused by the costs of
    making various types of errors and response bias due to un-
    specified internal preferences. In a detection experiment, response
    bias can be altered by varying the _payoff matrix_ .   payoff matrix

18. Imagine the following payoff matrix.

Subject says:	yes	no
stimulus present	+$5.00	−$1.00
stimulus absent	−$10.00	+$5.00

Assuming that the subject would have no response bias if a payoff matrix was used which rewarded "yes" and "no" responses equally, it is most likely that the subject will produce more ___No___ responses with the above matrix.

no

AN OVERVIEW OF THE SENSES

19. The _semicircular canals_ indicate rotation of the head. They are located in the _inner ear_ .

semicircular canals

inner ear

20. The four basic skin sensations are: _pain_ , _cold_ , _pressure_, and _heat_ .

pressure, warmth

cold, pain

21. It is believed that pressure sensations are produced by specialized _receptors_ in the skin that sense movement and vibration of skin and hair.

receptors

22. Sensations of _temp._ and _pain_ are probably signaled by free nerve endings in the skin.

temperature, pain

23. The four basic taste qualities are: _sweet_ , _sour_ , _bitter_ , and _salt_ .

sour, sweet

salty, bitter

24. Sensory interaction in taste is manifested in ~~adaptation~~ to continually presented stimuli as well as in the influence of _smell_ ~~smell~~ on taste.

adaptation

smell

25. The technical term for smell is _olfaction_

olfaction

26. The olfactory receptors are located in a part of the nasal cavity called the _olfactory epithelium_. Here olfactory quality is not coded by particular receptors, but rather by a _pattern_ of excitation across different receptor groups.

olfactory epithelium

pattern

27. The sense of smell can be valuable in communication for organisms employing _pheromones_

pheromones

28. Light intensity is to vision as _pitch_ is to hearing.

amplitude

29. Hue is to vision as _amplitude_ is to audition.

pitch

30. The purpose of the middle ear, oval window, and inner ear is to _conduct_ and _amplify_ sound waves.

conduct, amplify

31. The structure that actually contains the auditory receptors is known as the _cochlea_.

cochlea

32. The actual auditory receptors are the _hair cells_ that are stimulated by deformation of the _basilar membrane_

hair cells

basilar membrane

33. Pitch perception seems to be based on two mechanisms. High

frequencies are coded using __place__ of excitation, while lower   place

frequencies are coded by __neural__ firing rate.   neural

34. For all modalities, stimulus energy must be converted into a
    form which can be used by the senses. The translation is termed
    __transduction__   transduction

35. Higher neural centers process all sensory input and __code__   code (translate)
    this input into various quantitative and qualitative dimensions.

36. Any part of a sensory system is in __interacting__ with the rest of that   interaction
    system.

VISION

37. Light energy can vary in __intensity__, thus giving rise to perceived   intensity

    brightness, and in __wavelength__ which determines perceived hue.   wavelength

38. The visible spectrum extends from roughly __400__ to roughly   400

    __750__ nanometers.   750

39. The first place at which light energy from the world interacts
    with the senses is at the __retina__.   retina

40. The focusing of the eye is effected by __accomodation__ of the lens.   accommodation

41. __Cones__ are most densely packed in the fovea, while __rods__   Cones, rods
    are most frequent in the periphery.
    Cones - chromatic - color   + Achromatic - grey, white, black

42. The first cells to be stimulated by light are the __receptor__, which   receptors

    activate the __bipolar__ cells, which in turn stimulate the __ganglion__ bipolar, ganglion
    cells.

43. The axons of the ganglion cells form a bundle which is known as

    the __optic nerve__.   optic nerve

44. One person is able to distinguish a one-inch "F" from a one-inch
    "E" at a distance of 300 feet. Another person is only able to
    make the same discrimination at 200 feet. These two people have

    different __visual acuity__   visual acuity

45. The fact that primarily nocturnal animals have no cones and
    many rods, while animals that operate in daylight have many

    cones and few rods, is evidence for a __duplex__ theory of vision.   duplex

46. The fact that sensitivity to dim light is greater in the periphery of
    the visual field (where rods are) than in the fovea (where cones

    are) supports the __duplex theory__ of vision.   duplex theory

47. The visual pigment that is in the rods is called __rhodopsin__   rhodopsin

48. __Lateral Inhibition__, the mechanism that causes brightness   Lateral inhibition
    contrast, is an example of spatial interaction.

49. The physical resolution of the eye is not very good. In terms of
    physics, we shouldn't be able to see as clearly as we do. How-

    ever, the exaggeration of contrast through __lateral inhibition__   lateral inhibition
    enhances the visual message.

50. The three attributes used to describe color are _hue_ , brightness, and _achromatic_

hue

brightness, saturation

51. _Achromatic_ colors cannot be distinguished on the basis of hue.

Achromatic

52. Unique red is that red which appears to have neither any

blue nor any _yellow_ in it.

blue, yellow

53. Only _chromatic_ colors can differ in saturation.

chromatic

54. The _color solid_ equates spatial relationships along three dimensions with the three dimensions of color.

color solid

55. Colored filters placed over two different lights which are focused

on the same spot produce an _additive_ color mixture.

additive

56. A _complementary_ hue is one which, when mixed with another hue in the correct proportion, will produce the color gray.

complementary

57. A gray color, when surrounded by green, appears reddish. This

is known as _sim. color contrast_ and is evidence for antagonistic pairing of colors.

simultaneous color contrast

58. _Neg. afterimages_ have the complementary hue and the opposite brightness of the original stimulus.

Negative afterimages

59. Human vision is termed _trichromatic_, since there are three cone types.

trichromatic

60. According to the opponent-process theory of color vision, it should never be possible to see a red hue with a trace of

green in it.

green

61. Color blindness is most common in _males_ and may entail the

absence of one of the opponent-process pairs.

males

absence

Self-Test

1. John Locke, the British empiricist, would most likely agree with which of the following statements?
   a. "All knowledge is determined by innate mechanisms."
   b. "We are born with a fair amount of innate knowledge, with experience playing a small role."
   c. "Knowledge arrives through the senses."
   d. John Locke was not an empiricist and would not have agreed with any of the above statements.

2. The metaphor which best describes the empiricists' view of the human mind at birth is:
   a. a camera.
   b. an encyclopedia.
   c. a pad and pencil.
   d. a blank slate.

3. An example of a distal stimulus would be:
   a. the patterns of light energy hitting the retina.
   b. a Chevrolet.
   c. the sensation (or perception) produced by a distant mountain.
   d. a hallucination.

4. An example of a proximal visual stimulus is:
   a. the activity of the retina hit by an array of photons.
   b. an object situated very close to the retina.
   c. a distant object which appears closer than it really is.
   d. all of the above

5. Linear perspective serves as a depth cue because:
   a. it produces a memory of the associated experience of depth.
   b. it mitigates the effect of convergence.

c. its use by painters has familiarized us with its symbolic representation of depth.

d. we are classically conditioned to accept it as such.

6. Immanuel Kant believed:
   a. in innately determined categories of perception.
   b. that all knowledge came through the senses.
   c. that associations of sensations determined perception.
   d. in none of the above

7. Which of the following is an example of transduction?
   a. sound waves in the air being translated into electrical energy by a microphone
   b. electrical waves being translated into sound waves by a loudspeaker
   c. light energy being converted into nerve energy by the retina
   d. all of the above

8. Psychophysics studies the relationship between:
   a. the distal and proximal stimulus.
   b. the distal stimulus and sensory experience.
   c. sensation and perception.
   d. the proximal stimulus and sensory experience.

9. The absolute threshold depends on:
   a. the magnitude of the difference threshold.
   b. the neurophysiological hierarchy of modalities.
   c. the critical stimulus energy level required by the sensory system.
   d. differences in quality of experience.

10. It can be argued that sensations cannot be measured directly. It should be possible, though, to compare sensations. For instance, we should be able to determine whether one sensation is the same as or different from another. This viewpoint would most likely be expressed by:
    a. Kant.
    b. Locke.
    c. Fechner.
    d. Berkeley.

11. You are shopping for a new car. You have test-driven a number of cars to determine which models have the best performance. You discover that you cannot tell the difference between models A and C. The difference (however measured) between cars A and C is below your:
    a. difference threshold.
    b. response bias.
    c. criterion.
    d. sensitivity.

12. Which of the following involves a search for an absolute threshold?
    a. trying to determine whether drink A or drink B has more sugar in it
    b. trying to determine which instrument in an orchestra is playing the loudest
    c. trying to determine whether you were cheated on your Irish coffee (i.e., whether there is really any whiskey in it or not)
    d. trying to determine if you detect any difference in your strength after three months of weight lifting

13. Which of the following agrees with Weber's law? (In each case, the first number represents the weight needed to produce a j.n.d., and the absolute stimulus energy is specified by the second number. Two pairs are provided for each possible answer.)
    a. 1,10/2,100
    b. 20,50/1,2.5
    c. 5,100/5,50
    d. all of the above are in agreement with Weber's law

14. As in 13 above, each of the pairs of numbers below represents a hypothetical Weber fraction with its associated stimulus energy value. Which of these fractions represents the greatest sensitivity?
    a. 1,100
    b. 1,10
    c. 100,1000
    d. 50,1000

15. Fechner's law states that the strength of the sensation increases _____ with stimulus intensity.
    a. inversely
    b. exponentially
    c. logarithmically
    d. linearly

16. A doctor is scanning a lung X-ray. He sees something which may be either the beginnings of a tumor or harmless scar tissue. It is likely that response bias will come into play when the doctor decides whether to operate or not. Which of the following factors might influence this response bias?
    a. probability that it is a tumor
    b. risks associated with surgery
    c. risks associated with an untreated tumor
    d. all of the above
    e. none of the above; response bias is constant and cannot be easily changed

17. In the above example, what type of error is worse to make?
    a. false alarm
    b. miss
    c. a and b are equally important
    d. cannot be determined without knowing associated costs and benefits

18. Still considering the example in question 16, imagine that there are five different types of tumors such that each is associated with a different death rate when left untreated. Type I has the highest death rate, and type V has the lowest rate (with the others falling between one and five, in order). Imagine further that these five tumors can be distinguished from each other with X-rays, but none of them can be distinguished from scar tissue (which is harmless). Assuming that everything else is constant from one tumor type to another, under which condition would the doctor be most likely to operate and risk putting the patient under the dangers of surgery?
    a. The patient has either scar tissue or type III tumor.
    b. The patient has either scar tissue or type V tumor.
    c. The patient has either scar tissue or type I tumor.
    d. If the doctor was good, the probability of his operating would be constant, despite the type of tumor.

19. Kinesthesis is:
    a. information from the muscles, tendons, and joints.
    b. a function of the ossicles in the inner ear.
    c. the movement of hair cells in the cochlea.
    d. the crystallization of the viscous liquid in the semicircular canals.

20. Head rotation is sensed via:
    a. the pressure of crystals on hair cells in the vestibular sacs.
    b. the deformation of hair cells in the semicircular canals.
    c. dynamic tension of the relevant musculature.
    d. the movement of the world relative to ourselves as we walk through it.

21. You are given an acidic solution of lemon and water to drink. After continuously drinking this solution, it appears to be almost tasteless. What phenomenon is being demonstrated?
    a. specificity
    b. adaptation
    c. difference threshold
    d. receptor interaction

22. Pressure:
    a. is assessed via the two-point threshold.
    b. is one of the four basic skin sensations.
    c. depends on the allocation of cortical space.
    d. is the sensation elicited by stimulation of capsule receptors.
    e. both b and d

23. A little sucrose is placed on the tongue prior to a little quinine. What will be the primary result?
    a. The bitter taste produced by the quinine will make the sucrose taste sweeter.
    b. Sensitivity to taste will decline rapidly as the taste buds adapt.
    c. The sweet taste produced by the sucrose will enhance the bitterness of the quinine.
    d. Since the sense of smell was not employed, both the quinine and the sucrose will be tasted equally.

24. The sense of smell, or olfaction, exhibits which of the following characteristics?
    a. It could classify odors as fragrant, spicy, and putrid.
    b. It could classify odors as aromatic, acrid, and rancid.
    c. It detects certain chemicals suspended in air.
    d. a and c

25. The physical stimulus for hearing is described in terms of amplitude and frequency. The corresponding psychological dimensions are:
    a. loudness and tone.
    b. amplitude and pitch.
    c. loudness and timbre.
    d. loudness and pitch.

26. The correct ordering of anatomical structures in the ear (from outside in) is:
    a. eardrum, middle ear, oval window, cochlea.
    b. oval window, middle ear, eardrum, cochlea.
    c. eardrum, oval window, middle ear, cochlea.
    d. none of the above

27. For low frequency tones (below 400 hz), pitch is detected by:
    a. a slow response.
    b. localization on the basilar membranes.
    c. firing frequency of the auditory nerve.
    d. none of the above

28. For frequencies between 400 and 1000 hz, pitch is detected by:
    a. a fast response.

b. localization on the basilar membranes.
c. firing frequency of the auditory nerve.
d. none of the above

29. Which of the following are characteristics common to most of the senses?
    a. the presence of anatomical structures
    b. the transduction of the physical stimulus to a neural impulse
    c. the coding of the neural impulse into a dimension of sensation
    d. the interaction of all parts of the sensory system
    e. all of the above

30. One light source appears bluish and another appears greenish. This difference in appearance is due to differences in:
    a. intensity.
    b. wavelength.
    c. opponent processes.
    d. none of the above

31. Intensity is to brightness as wavelength is to:
    a. sensitivity.
    b. darkness.
    c. wattage.
    d. hue.

32. Which of the following wavelengths is not considered to be part of the visible spectrum?
    a. 650
    b. 400
    c. 300
    d. 575

33. The structure that bends light rays so that they are projected onto a light-sensitive surface is the:
    a. retina.
    b. iris.
    c. lens.
    d. all of the above

34. During the process of accommodation, a close object will result in _____ of the lens.
    a. thickening
    b. flattening
    c. no change
    d. increased transparency

35. You arrive late to a movie theater and are forced to sit in the far right-hand seat of the first row. You must then look to your left to see the rectangular screen. What is the image of the screen that is projected onto your retina?

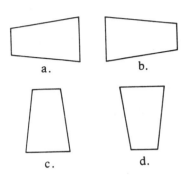

a.

b.

c.

d.

36. The two types of receptors in the human eye are known as _____ and _____ .
    a. bipolars, horizontals
    b. ganglions, bipolars
    c. rods, cones
    d. bipolars, cones

37. An area near the center of the retina has virtually no rods, consisting entirely of cones. It is approximately two degrees in diameter and is known as the:
    a. periphery.
    b. optic nerve.
    c. optic chiasm.
    d. fovea.

38. In order to maximize visual acuity you should:
    a. stare slightly away from the thing which you are trying to see.
    b. use only one eye at a time (to reduce interocular rivalry).
    c. reduce the luminance of the area, in order to engage the more sensitive rod system.
    d. look directly at the object.

39. Which of the following is not in agreement with the duplex theory of vision?
    a. The rods are the receptors for night vision, while cones serve day vision.
    b. Rods respond to low light levels, cones to high levels.
    c. Rod vision provides good acuity; cones provide poor acuity.
    d. Rods result in achromatic vision; cones provide color vision.

40. What happens when light hits a visual receptor?
    a. Silver bromide molecules combine with light to release silver.
    b. Light strikes the retina and generates rhodopsin.
    c. Energy is converted to nervous impulses via a photochemical process that bleaches rhodopsin.
    d. The reflected light from the receptor causes a photochemical alteration leading to neural excitation.

41. Which of the following is an example of sensory adaptation?
    a. the cold ocean feeling warmer after we've been in it for a while
    b. being able to see in a dark room after a period of adjustment
    c. increasing sensitivity to salt with continued exposure
    d. all of the above
    e. a and b

42. The first time you see a friend's new car, it is parked against a black wall. Later you see that same car parked against a white backdrop (at the same time of day) and comment that you remember the car as being much brighter. This is an example of:
    a. brightness contrast.
    b. adaptation.
    c. temporal interaction.
    d. none of the above

43. Which of the following is not used to classify colors?
    a. brightness
    b. hue
    c. wavelength
    d. saturation

44. White and black can be distinguished only on the basis of which dimension?
    a. brightness
    b. hue
    c. wavelength
    d. saturation

45. Red and green must differ on which dimension (at least)?
    a. brightness
    b. hue
    c. wavelength
    d. saturation

46. White and black cannot possibly differ on which dimension?
    a. hue

    b. saturation
    c. both of the above
    d. none of the above

47. The extent to which a color of some fixed hue is mixed with an achromatic color is represented by a value on the _____ dimension.
    a. brightness
    b. hue
    c. intensity
    d. saturation

48. Which of the following is true of the color solid?
    a. The central hoop consists of the colors red, green, yellow, blue, orange, purple, in that order.
    b. Horizontal distance from the central axis represents brightness.
    c. The tilt of the central hoop reflects saturation.
    d. none of the above

49. An example of a subtractive color mixture is:
    a. two spotlights, each with a different filter, trained on the same location.
    b. the use of two filters on one spotlight.
    c. the light as it enters the human eye.
    d. all of the above

50. All of the following are examples of additive color mixtures except:
    a. color printing.
    b. color TV.
    c. human color vision.
    d. mixing of paints.

51. In an additive color mixture, equal amounts of complementary hues mixed together will produce:
    a. a unique hue.
    b. a color with a hue intermediate to the two original hues.
    c. a hueless color.
    d. any of the above, depending on the choice of hues.

52. All of the following are used as evidence for color antagonism except:
    a. complementary colors.
    b. retinal bleaching.
    c. simultaneous color contrast.
    d. negative afterimages.

53. Most wavelengths of the visual spectrum will stimulate:
    a. all three receptor types, but unequally.
    b. all three receptor types, and equally.
    c. only one or two receptor types.
    d. from one to three receptors, depending on the intensity and wavelength.

54. In the opponent-process theory, the three pairs of

receptors are:
a. red-blue, green-yellow, black-white.
b. red-yellow, blue-green, black-white.
c. red-green, blue-yellow, black-white.
d. never specified.

55. An achromatic color results when which system(s) is(are) in balance?
a. red-green
b. blue-yellow
c. red-green and blue-yellow
d. black-white

56. Which of the following would be predicted by the opponent-process theory?
a. the dark gray appearance of black pepper placed against a gray background
b. chromatic contrast
c. negative afterimages
d. all of the above

57. A person who is color-blind will probably:
a. use color names appropriately.
b. be female.
c. be unable to distinguish any hues at all.
d. be unable to imagine how ultraviolet looks to a bee.

Answer Key for Self-Test

1. c p. 107	27. c p. 123
2. d p. 107	28. b p. 123
3. b p. 108	29. e p. 123
4. a p. 108	30. b p. 124
5. a p. 110	31. d p. 124
6. a p. 110	32. c p. 124
7. d p. 111	33. c pp. 124–25
8. b p. 111	34. a p. 125
9. c p. 111	35. a p. 125
10. c pp. 111–12	36. c p. 125
11. a p. 112	37. d p. 125
12. c p. 112	38. d p. 126
13. b p. 112	39. c p. 126
14. a p. 112	40. c p. 127
15. c p. 113	41. e pp. 126, 127
16. d p. 114	42. a pp. 127–128
17. d pp. 114–15	43. c p. 129
18. c pp. 114–15	44. a p. 130
19. a p. 115	45. b pp. 129–130
20. b p. 115	46. c p. 130
21. b p. 117	47. d p. 130
22. e p. 116	48. d p. 131
23. c p. 118	49. b pp. 131–32
24. d p. 118	50. d p. 131
25. d p. 120	51. c pp. 132–33
26. a p. 121	52. b pp. 133–34

53. a p. 135	56. d pp. 134–36
54. c p. 135	57. a p. 137
55. c p. 135	

Investigating Psychological Phenomena

MEASURING BRIGHTNESS CONTRAST

Equipment: Stimuli are included; one sheet of black construction paper needed
Number of subjects: One or more
Time per subject: Ten minutes
Time for experimenter: Twenty minutes

In the "Sensory Processes" chapter, Professor Gleitman describes a phenomenon that clearly illustrates the effect of context on perception. The phenomenon is brightness contrast. Examine Figure 4.15 in the text once again. Note how sharply different in brightness the four central gray squares appear to be; yet they are identical. (You can prove this to yourself by laying a sheet of paper over the figure with holes cut out where the squares are located.) The difference in brightness is apparently a result of interaction between each central square and its surrounding light or dark border. As the text explains, the surrounding border induces a contrast effect such that a patch will appear lighter when surrounded by a dark border and darker when surrounded by a light border. The greater the difference in lightness between the center and its surroundings, the greater the illusion.

Of course, as you have probably already suspected, brightness contrast has limits. That is, there is just so much illusion that can be produced by a surrounding context, no matter how great the difference between the center and its surroundings. The present experiment provides an opportunity to examine the extent to which the visual system can be fooled by context. More importantly, however, in this exercise you will have a chance to conduct an actual psychophysical experiment to measure quantitatively the relationship between physical stimuli and psychological experience.

The purpose of the experiment is to measure the magnitude of brightness contrast for a particular test patch of a given, fixed lightness. This test patch will be surrounded by several borders that differ in their lightness, one from another. With this arrangement, we should be able to produce different degrees of brightness contrast. But how do we measure the extent of the effect? One way would be to ask a subject to assign numbers to the test patch corresponding to how bright he thought it was. But we shall use a more accurate technique: Each time we present a border around the test patch, we shall ask the subject to match the apparent brightness of the test patch by choosing another patch that seems to match it. The matching patch that is chosen, having been carefully measured for its lightness, will then serve as an index of how light the subject perceived the test patch to be.

First, cut out the matching patches and the borders on the insert for Chapter 4. The matching patches are the ten squares on the left. Note that there is a number on the back of each that corresponds to its lightness. (The units for these numbers have to do with how various lightnesses are actually created by printers, and it is not necessary to know them for this exercise. It is sufficient that the patches are ordered correctly.) Now cut out the six borders on the right side of the insert, and cut out the central square area of each. Note that the borders are also marked with a lightness code on the back. Be very careful with both matching patches and borders to trim away any gray from the adjoining figures so that each cutout is an even gray. On the bottom of the insert is the test patch that has already been placed on a white surrounding region. The test patch has a lightness value of 6. Do not cut out the test figure! Leave it on its background and place this in turn on a sheet of black construction paper.

Now you are ready to run the experiment. The procedure is to select one background, place it over the test patch, and ask your subject to select a matching patch from among his ten choices that appears to match the test patch in brightness. (Be sure that he lays down the matching patch on the black area to the right of the background to be certain of his choice.) Be careful to tell the subject not to hesitate to select different matching patches with different backgrounds if he feels this is appropriate. Subjects may think that because the test patch remains the same, they should always select the same matching patch. Do not let the subject see the test patch without a border between trials, as this may also cause a bias toward a particular matching patch.

Place the matching patches at the top of the black construction paper haphazardly. Run the subject through eighteen trials of the experiment, three trials with each background. In order to have the backgrounds presented in a random order in each set of six, here are three random orders that you may use to determine the order in which the backgrounds are presented: 5, 10, 3, 1, 4, 7; 4, 3, 10, 7, 1, 5; 10, 4, 1, 5, 7, 3 (the numbers refer to the lightness codes on the back of each background).

After you have presented a background over the test patch and the subject has chosen his matching patch, place the value of the matching patch in the appropriate space in the table below. After the experiment is complete, add up the values in each column and divide by three to get an average matching patch value for each background.

Now you can plot these data in the graph provided. Along the x-axis are the six values of background that you used. Above each find the average value of matching patch that you calculated from the table, and place a dot at the value (as determined from the y-axis). Now connect the dots and note the shape of the function.

Recall that the test patch has a lightness value of 6. Given this, what shape should the function have? How much of a brightness contrast were you able to obtain? How could you improve the experiment to get an even larger effect?

Reference

Heinemann, E. G. 1955. Simultaneous brightness induction as a function of inducing- and test-field luminance. *Journal of Experimental Psychology* (50): 89–96.

Background values: 1   3   4   5   7   10

matching value 1:   _____   _____   _____   _____   _____   _____
matching value 2:   _____   _____   _____   _____   _____   _____
matching value 3:   _____   _____   _____   _____   _____   _____

Total matching value: _____   _____   _____   _____   _____   _____
Average matching value: _____   _____   _____   _____   _____   _____

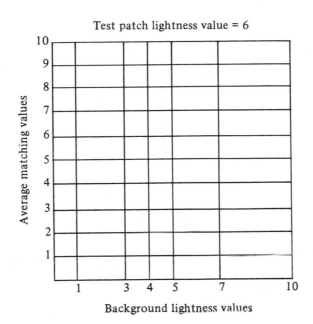

Test patch lightness value = 6

Background lightness values

CHAPTER 5

Perception

Learning Objectives

THE PROBLEM OF PERCEPTION

1. Know that the central issue of perception is not why a stimulus is recognized as a particular object, but why it is seen as an object at all.
2. Keep in mind the characteristics of the proximal stimulus in comparison with the distal stimulus.
3. Understand that to organize the sensory world, three questions must be asked of any given stimulus: Where is it? Where is it going? What is it?

THE PERCEPTION OF DEPTH: WHERE IS IT?

4. Be aware of the significance of binocular disparity in depth perception.
5. List the monocular cues to depth perception and relate the evidence that suggests that we must learn to attend to these cues. In what sense are they artificial?

The perception of depth through motion
6. Explain how motion parallax contributes to our perception of depth.

Innate factors in depth perception
7. Describe the evidence indicating that young infants have at least a rudimentary ability to perceive various aspects of form and space.

THE PERCEPTION OF MOVEMENT: WHAT IS IT DOING?

Illusions of movement
8. Be familiar with the explanations proposed to explain stroboscopic and induced movement, and the relevance of these phenomena to the study of real movement.
9. Describe how we are able to distinguish between a moving world with a stationary self (e.g., watching a car go by) and a stationary world with a moving self (e.g., looking out the window of a moving train).

FORM PERCEPTION: WHAT IS IT?

Recognizing the elements of form
10. Know how the early empiricists believed forms were perceived and how the nativists responded.
11. Give the evidence supporting the claim that some aspects of form perception are innate.
12. Explain what feature detector cells do, and offer two examples of features that these cells detect.

Perceptual segregation
13. Be able to explain the function that perceptual segregation serves. Name the phenomenon that illustrates this ability and describe the two types of processing involved.
14. State the laws of perceptual grouping, and tell how they relate to each other.

Pattern recognition
15. Be familiar with the arguments and demonstrations in support of a Gestalt viewpoint of form perception.
16. Provide evidence for the theories of bottom-up and top-down processing. Explain how bidirectional activation combines the two.

PERCEPTUAL PROBLEM SOLVING

Perceptual hypotheses
17. Be able to explain what purpose the perceptual hypothesis serves and how it involves bidirectional processing.

PERCEPTUAL SELECTION: ATTENTION

18. Know what attention is.

   Selection by physical orientation

19. Understand what the study of orienting movements can tell us about attention.

   Central selection

20. Be familiar with the concept of central selection and its manifestations in the auditory and visual modes. What is visual search?

21. Be able to give the evidence suggesting that attention is not an "all-or-none" phenomenon and the evidence for and against the filter theory of attention.

THE PERCEPTION OF REALITY

22. Understand that the goal of all perceptual processes is the perception of reality.

23. Know that the main problem encountered in the perception of reality is interpreting the number of different proximal stimuli produced by one distal stimulus. Be able to describe how this problem is addressed by perceptual constancies.

   Empiricism and nativism revisited

24. Know how the empiricists explain the discrepancy between the proximal stimulus and the perceived image.

25. Give the nativists' answer.

26. Regarding perceptual organization, understand the difference between the concept of unconscious inference (based on past experience) and the concept of direct response to the complex characteristics and invariant relationships of stimulus patterns.

   Lightness constancy

27. Understand lightness constancy and relevant terms such as reflectance, luminance, and illumination.

28. Explain how the nativists account for lightness constancy.

   Size and shape constancy

29. Be familiar with size and shape constancies. Know what types of cues are necessary for size constancy and how the empiricists and nativists explain these two phenomena.

   Inappropriate compensation and illusion

30. Be familiar with what an illusion is. Give the reasons for the moon illusion and the Ponzo and Müller-Lyer illusions. Of what benefit is the study of illusions?

Programmed Exercises

THE PROBLEM OF PERCEPTION

1. The properties of a three-dimensional distal stimulus are perceived as constant despite continuing variation of the _proximal_ stimulus.

   proximal

2. In order to perceive an object, the observer must _organize_ the sensory world into a coherent, meaningful scene.

   organize

THE PERCEPTION OF DEPTH: WHERE IS IT?

3. The two eyes look out on the world from slightly different positions and thus obtain a somewhat different view of any solid object on which they converge. This is called _binocular disparity_

   binocular disparity

4. Relative size is an example of a _monocular_ depth cue.

   monocular

5. Abrupt change in a _texture gradient_ can produce the impression of a sharp drop, a "visual cliff."

   texture gradient

6. Far-off objects are blocked from view by other opaque objects that obstruct their optical path to the eye. This is a depth cue called _interposition_

   interposition

7. As we move our head or body from right to left, the images projected by the objects outside will move across the retina. The direction and speed of this motion is an enormously effective monocular depth cue called _motion parallax_.

motion parallax

8. The reaction of infants to rapidly magnified forms in the visual field is called the _looming response_ and lends evidence to the theory of innate aspects of depth perception.

looming response

THE PERCEPTION OF MOVEMENT: WHAT IS IT DOING?

9. Suppose we briefly turn on a light in one location in the visual field, then turn it off, and after an appropriate period of time (somewhere between 30 and 200 milliseconds), turn on a second light in a different location. The resulting phenomenon is called _stroboscopic_ movement.

stroboscopic

10. If the ground is moving and a figure is stationary in the visual field, the figure is seen as moving. This phenomenon of illusory movement is called _induced_ movement.

induced

11. The perception of movement in one of two stimuli depends on which is seen as a stationary _frame_ of reference.

frame

FORM PERCEPTION: WHAT IS IT?

12. Infants appear to have an innate form preference for _human faces_.

human

faces

13. A nerve cell in a sensory system that is found to respond only to a narrow range of physical stimulation has been called a _feature detector_. A cell that reacts only to right angles is an example.

feature detector

14. The process known as _visual segregation_ enables us to separate figure from ground and is not a part of the stimulus but is performed by the perceptual system.

visual segregation

15. _Ambiguous_ figures are ones in which either of two figure-ground organizations is possible.

Reversible (ambiguous)

Royalist print from the French Revolution in which can be seen the profiles of Marie Antoinette and Louis XVI and their children.

16. Proximity, similarity, closure, and good continuation are examples of the laws of _perceptual grouping_   perceptual grouping

17. Contours that appear to continue smoothly along their original course follow the law of _good continuation_   good continuation

18. A melody can be recognized even when played in different keys. This indicates that we can recognize patterns even after _transposition_   transposition

19. A _Gestalt_ psychologist would argue that pattern recognition is due to the perception of certain relations between the component parts of a figure.   Gestalt

20. The _bottom-up_ processing approach to pattern recognition begins with component features and builds up to larger units.   bottom-up

21. The _top-down_ process of pattern recognition is often affected by higher-level knowledge and expectations.   top-down

22. _Context_ effects demonstrate that there is some top-down processing in the perceptual process.   Context

23. Perceptual processing is necessarily in both directions: from the _top down_ and also from the _bottom up_ .   top down, bottom up

PERCEPTUAL PROBLEM SOLVING

24. A _perceptual hypothesis_ is constantly compared to new stimuli in order to test its validity.   perceptual hypothesis

PERCEPTUAL SELECTION: ATTENTION

25. The ways by which we perceive selectively are grouped under the label _attention_.   attention

26. In the _visual search_ procedure, a subject must pick out a particular object from an array of stimuli.   visual search

27. During _internal selection_, the mind's eye moves although there is no physical movement of the eyes.   internal selection

28. Presenting stimuli over earphones so that each ear receives a different message is called a _dichotic_ presentation.   dichotic

29. When a subject is asked to _shadow_ a message, he is asked to repeat it aloud, word for word, as it comes over one of his earphones.   shadow

30. The attentional _filter_ attenuates irrelevant messages as a whole, but may pass items from them that are important or familiar.   filter

THE PERCEPTION OF REALITY

31. The perceptual system responds to real objects outside regardless of variations in their proximal images. This is best illustrated by the perceptual _constancies_ lightness, size, and shape.   constancies

32. According to the empiricists, prior learning of the rules relating retinal image and depth cues leads to the ___*unconscious*___ inference of true size.

unconscious

33. Nativists stress the importance of ___*invariant*___ relationships within a stimulus pattern in explaining perceptual organization.

invariant

34. The apparent lightness of an object remains fairly constant despite rather drastic changes in the amount of illumination that falls upon it. This is called ___*lightness constancy*___

lightness constancy

35. A Boeing 707 at a distance of 1,000 feet will look larger than a single-engine two-seater at a distance of 50 feet despite the fact that the retinal image of the latter will be greater than that of the former. This is called ___*size constancy*___. An analogous phenomenon occurs in the perception of ___*shape*___.

size constancy

shape

36. Since we compensate for distance when perceiving size, misjudgment of distance can lead to perceptual ___*illusions*___.

illusions

Self-Test

1. Which of the following is not true of the proximal stimulus?
   a. It is two-dimensional in vision.
   b. It can vary in size and shape.
   c. It alone enables us to perceive the constant properties of objects.
   d. It is the retinal image of the distal stimulus in vision.

2. Binocular disparity is caused by:
   a. a slight difference in the size of the two eyes.
   b. small imperfections in the lens and/or cornea.
   c. the slightly different position of each eye.
   d. the favoring of one eye over the other.

3. Binocular disparity:
   a. is an effective cue to depth for long distances.
   b. is due to the fact that our eyes receive virtually the same image.
   c. is not by itself a sufficient cue to depth.
   d. can be simulated by viewing specially designed 2-dimensional drawings.
   e. is only effective for familiar objects.

4. The figure at the right illustrates all of the following monocular cues to depth except:
   a. linear perspective.
   b. relative size.
   c. binocular disparity.
   d. texture gradients.
   e. interposition.

5. The impression of a "visual cliff" is accounted for by which depth cue?
   a. linear perspective
   b. relative size
   c. texture gradients
   d. interposition

6. Which of the following is not true of motion parallax?
   a. Nearby objects move in a direction opposite our own as we move through space.

b. Objects farther away move in a direction similar to our own as we move through space.

c. Objects farther away move at a lesser velocity.

d. Objects closer to us move at a greater velocity.

7. The depth cue known as motion parallax refers to:
   a. our ability to compare the size of two objects in motion.
   b. the opposing motion of two objects at variable distances as we move through space.
   c. the movement of objects away from us as we move through space.
   d. the apparent motion of objects toward us as we move through space.

8. One of the most effective monocular depth cues is _____ , which is absent in pictorial representations but present in real life.
   a. linear perspective
   b. relative size
   c. interposition
   d. motion parallax

9. The results of Gibson and Walk's visual cliff experiment (illustrated on this page) suggests that:
   a. infants cannot use motion parallax as a cue to depth.
   b. infants' eye fixations tend to be directed to edges and vertices.
   c. depth perception is largely innately given.
   d. texture gradients are not useful cues to distance.
   e. none of the above

10. Stroboscopic movement refers to:
    a. the perception of movement when two stimuli are presented in alternation at the proper temporal and spatial intervals.
    b. the perception of movement of a target when in fact it is stationary but the background is moving.
    c. the perception of self-movement when you are stationary but the scene that you are watching is moving.
    d. all of the above
    e. none of the above

11. Induced movement differs from stroboscopic movement in that:
    a. in the former case it is the figure that moves, while in the latter case it is the ground that moves.
    b. the former is a physical phenomenon, while the latter is a retinal phenomenon.
    c. induced movement is based on relative

displacement of the figure and background, while stroboscopic movement is based on absolute displacement of both.
    d. none of the above

12. Which two of the following are examples of induced movement?
    a. the moon moving through the clouds
    b. perceiving movement of a stationary spot of light in darkness
    c. perceiving movement of a stationary spot of light when the rectangular frame around it moves
    d. perceiving that the moon moves when you move with respect to it
    e. perceiving movement in the successive frames in a movie

13. Which of the following statements about perceptual parsing is *not* true?
    a. It is also called visual segregation.
    b. It is contributed by the individual and is not a part of the stimulus.
    c. It is the first stage of perceptual organization and separates the stimuli into various subcomponents.
    d. It occurs only in the realm of visual perception.

14. Segregating figure from ground (as in a reversible figure):
    a. is a high-level perceptual process that requires a good deal of preliminary analysis.
    b. can only be done with reversible figures.

c. is accomplished by perceiving the contour separating the two regions as belonging to the ground.

d. is too elementary a perceptual process to be used effectively by artists.

e. none of the above

15. For reversible figures such as the one in the next column, which of the following is false?

a. The figure is generally seen in front of the ground.

b. A reversible figure-ground display is characterized by two adjoining regions alternately acting as figures.

c. A contour can be seen as simultaneously belonging to figure and ground.

d. none of the above

Reversible figure that can be perceived either as two faces in profile or as a white vase.

16. All of the following are "laws of perceptual organization" *except*:

a. proximity.

b. similarity.

c. good continuation.

d. simplicity.

e. closure.

17. The law of proximity states that:

a. the closer an object is to an observer, the easier it is to identify it.

b. the closer two objects are to each other, the greater the chance that they will be grouped together perceptually.

c. given any two objects, one is always nearer (perceptually) to an arbitrary third object than the other.

d. none of the above

18. Closure may be a special case of:

a. proximity.

b. similarity.

c. good continuation.

d. perspective.

19. The phenomenon of transposition refers to:

a. figure-ground reversal.

b. the same percept resulting from different proximal stimuli.

c. the overlap of two figures, which causes the viewer to see them in depth.

d. the induced movement caused by the repositioning of a surrounding contour.

e. none of the above

20. According to the Gestalt point of view, we perceive _____ rather than individual retinal points per se.

a. features of forms

b. closure

c. relations among stimuli

d. all of the above

21. Pattern recognition is a:

a. top-down process.

b. horizontal process.

c. bottom-up process.

d. a and c

e. a and b

22. A professor is giving a lecture on the state of the U.S. economy. His lecture is suddenly broken up by several coughs that interrupt but do not stop his speech stream. Although there are physical gaps in the utterance, the students hear and understand the presentation. This is an example of:

a. feature analysis.

b. context effect.

c. bottom-up processing.

d. attention.

23. When a person makes sense of a previously unknown and meaningless stimulus:

a. she has trouble perceiving it in its original unorganized form.

b. she must constantly reinforce the new pattern in order to retain it in visual memory.

c. she has formed a cognitive construction.

d. a and c

24. A perceptual hypothesis:

a. once formed, provides fundamental and unchanging laws of perceptual organization.

b. represents the bottom-up aspect of perceptual processing.

c. is formed for every new stimulus encountered.

d. serves as the top-down aspect of visual processing that is compared to the stimulus.

25. Orienting movements like turning of the head and convergence and accommodation of the eyes are all external manifestations of:
   a. differentiation.
   b. attention.
   c. recalibration.
   d. proximity.

26. During a visual search procedure:
   a. a subject is asked to pick out the most relevant component of a stimulus pattern as quickly as possible.
   b. subjects may employ methods of physical orientation and central selection to locate the target.
   c. the orienting movements that a subject makes show little relation to the features of objects that are attended to during scanning.
   d. the internal selection process often hinders accurate scanning and location of the correct target.

27. Which of the following is untrue of dichotic presentations?
   a. The subject is asked to shadow the to-be-attended message.
   b. He is able to recall the message that came by way of the unattended ear.
   c. He does not notice if the speaker on the unattended ear shifts into another language.
   d. He wears two earphones and receives different messages through each of them.

28. Unconscious inference:
   a. is a nativist argument.
   b. operates independently of depth cues.
   c. operates independently of retinal image.
   d. depends on prior learning of a general rule.

29. The fact that a white object in the shade appears lighter than a gray object in the sunlight (even though the gray object has greater luminance) is called:
   a. relative luminance.
   b. perceived intensity.
   c. lightness constancy.
   d. none of the above

30. It is likely that six-month-old infants exhibit some measure of:
   a. angle constancy.
   b. depth constancy.
   c. lightness constancy.
   d. size constancy.

31. The moon looks larger at the horizon than it does when up in the sky because:
   a. the horizon looks farther away than the overhead sky.
   b. the sky looks farther away than the horizon.
   c. the retinal image of the moon is different in each case.
   d. none of the above

Answer Key for Self-Test

1. c p. 140	17. b p. 150
2. c p. 141	18. c p. 150
3. d pp. 141–42	19. b pp. 151–52
4. c pp. 141–43	20. c p. 152
5. c p. 143	21. d p. 154
6. b p. 144	22. b pp. 153–54
7. c p. 144	23. d p. 154
8. d pp. 142–44	24. d p. 154
9. c pp. 144–45	25. b p. 155
10. a p. 145	26. b p. 156
11. c pp. 145–46	27. b p. 157
12. a, c pp. 145–46	28. d p. 159
13. d p. 148	29. c p. 160
14. e p. 149	30. d p. 162
15. c p. 149	31. a p. 162
16. d p. 150	

Investigating Psychological Phenomena

THE EFFECT OF MENTAL SET

Equipment: Stimuli are included
Number of subjects: One
Time per subject: Twenty minutes
Time for experimenter: Twenty minutes

The issue of how past experience influences perception (an example of top-down processing) is an important one in psychology and has generated quite a bit of research. This is a difficult issue to resolve because there are many ways in which past experience might influence perceptual processes. In this problem you are asked to consider a series of hypothetical experiments (modeled after a study by Epstein and Rock, 1960) and to provide alternative interpretations of the hypothetical results. As you move through the experiments, try to develop one hypothesis which will account for all of the results that are described. The stimuli for all the experiments are the ambiguous and unambiguous versions of Leeper's old woman–young woman figure shown on the next page.

A   Y   O

Notice that the first picture (A) can be seen either as a young woman or as an old woman; that is, it is ambiguous. The second picture (Y) is quite similar to the first (A) except that some detail has been changed so that it has become a fairly unambiguous picture of a young woman. Likewise, the third picture (O) is a fairly unambiguous version of an old woman. The purpose of all the experiments is to determine how prior exposure to the unambiguous versions of the figure influences whether subjects call the ambiguous version an old woman or a young woman. Imagine that twenty subjects are run in each hypothetical experiment.

EXPERIMENT 1

Each subject is shown the following series of slides (at a rate of one slide every eight seconds) and asked to name each picture as "young" or "old" as it is presented: YYOOOOOOOOA (Y refers to a presentation of the unambiguous young woman, O refers to a presentation of the unambiguous old woman). All subjects name the Y and O versions of the figure correctly. On the critical trial, the ambiguous picture A, the results are as follows: Twenty subjects call it "old"; no subjects call it "young." One interpretation of this result is that the more frequently presented unambiguous version determined the perception of the ambiguous picture. This is listed as hypothesis 1 on the answer sheet. What alternative explanations can you propose to explain the responses of subjects in this hypothetical experiment? Write them on the answer sheet. There are at least three other plausible possibilities.

Before you go on to experiments 2 through 4, check to see whether the hypotheses you have developed coincide with those given in the answers to the prob-

lem. If not, use the given hypotheses as the basis for your answers to the questions posed in experiments 2 through 4.

EXPERIMENT 2

A new set of twenty subjects receives the series: YYYYYOOOOOA. Again the responses to all the Y and O stimuli are correct, and the responses to the A stimulus are as follows: Twenty subjects respond "old woman"; none respond "young woman." Consider each of the four hypotheses raised to account for the results of experiment 1 and evaluate how each fares with the results of the experiment.* Record your responses under experiment 2 on the answer sheet.

EXPERIMENT 3

Twenty subjects each receive the series: OOOOOOOYYYA. All respond correctly to the Y and O stimuli; the responses to A are: Twenty subjects call it "young woman"; none call it "old woman." Again evaluate the success of each of the four hypotheses at accounting for these results.

EXPERIMENT 4

Twenty new subjects are shown the series: YYOYYOYYOA. All O's and Y's are identified correctly; the data on the A presentations are: Eighteen subjects respond "old woman"; two subjects respond "young woman." (A reliable difference.) Which of the four hypotheses can explain these results? Is one of the four hypotheses confirmed by the results of all four experiments?

*We continue to consider hypothesis 1 even though experiment 2 cannot be explained by it; scientists do not typically discard an hypothesis because of a single contradictory finding.

ANSWER SHEET

Experiment 1

    Hypothesis 1   Frequency of presentation determines the response to the ambiguous figure.

    Hypothesis 2 _____

_____

    Hypothesis 3 _____

_____

    Hypothesis 4 _____

_____

Experiment 2

    Hypothesis 1 _____

_____

    Hypothesis 2 _____

_____

    Hypothesis 3 _____

_____

    Hypothesis 4 _____

_____

Experiment 3

    Hypothesis 1 _____

_____

    Hypothesis 2 _____

_____

    Hypothesis 3 _____

_____

    Hypothesis 4 _____

_____

Experiment 4

    Which of the four hypotheses can account for these results? _____

_____

_____

    Which hypothesis can account for the results of all four experiments? _____

_____

_____

Answers to Problems

EXPERIMENT 1

Hypothesis 2: It is possible that the interpretation of the ambiguous picture was entirely influenced by the perception of the immediately preceding picture of the old woman. If so, this would be called a "recency effect," because the most recently presented picture would have had the strongest influence on perception of the ambiguous picture.

Hypothesis 3: An alternative possibility has to do with what the subject might be expecting to be presented on the last trial. She has just seen eight consecutive pictures of the old woman and so she might reasonably expect that the next picture will also be that of an old woman. Thus, if this were the case, the subject's cognitive expectations would be guiding her perceptions.

Hypothesis 4: A final possibility is that subjects in general have a bias to respond with the name "old woman." One might suppose that such a bias exists (for some reason) even independently of what the subject actually sees. That is, subjects are biased to call the ambiguous version an "old woman" regardless of what precedes it.

EXPERIMENT 2

This experiment rules out hypothesis 1, the frequency hypothesis. Both unambiguous versions were presented equally frequently before the ambiguous version was presented. Thus, a subject's perception of the ambiguous version could not have been influenced by the more frequently presented unambiguous version. None of the alternative hypotheses is ruled out by these results: (a) The response to the ambiguous version was the same as that to the most recently presented unambiguous version. Thus, recency is a viable interpretation of these results. (b) Because the responses to the sixth through tenth stimuli were "old woman," the subjects may have built up an expectation that the eleventh stimulus would be an old woman as well. So cognitive expectations may well have guided their response to the ambiguous item. (c) The fact that most subjects identified the ambiguous picture as an old woman is consistent with the possibility that they have a bias to call it that regardless of their immediately prior perceptual experience.

EXPERIMENT 3

Once again this experiment disconfirms the frequency hypothesis. This time subjects responded to the test picture with the name of the *least* frequently presented unambiguous picture. Also, the experiment rules out hypothesis 4, which states that subjects have a predisposing bias to call the ambiguous version an old woman. But both the recency and the cognitive expectation hypotheses can account for the results.

EXPERIMENT 4

The cognitive expectation hypothesis probably is ruled out. In responding to the unambiguous versions, subjects were following a regular pattern of two "young woman" responses followed by one "old woman" response. The last unambiguous picture was that of the old woman; thus, subjects should have been expecting a young woman next. Instead most responded "old woman," a result that can only be explained by noting that the most recently presented unambiguous picture was that of the old woman. Thus, the recency explanation is compatible with these results. Once again the frequency hypothesis is disconfirmed because the most frequently presented unambiguous picture was the young woman. The response bias explanation might be brought up to explain the results of this experiment except that it was ruled out by experiment 3. Thus, the only explanation which satisfactorily can explain the results of all four experiments is hypothesis 2, which claims that the picture which a subject sees most recently will affect his current perception.

This exercise demonstrates how it is sometimes possible to start with several potential explanations of a phenomenon and successfully rule out the incorrect ones with further experimentation. Initially there were four plausible interpretations of the results of hypothetical experiment 1. The results of hypothetical experiments 2 through 4, however, rule out all but one of the alternatives.

Even though the experiments described above are only hypothetical, they illustrate this process of narrowing down alternative interpretations. You may want to try out any of these experiments to determine the actual results. On page 89 you will find sets of pictures of both the unambiguous versions and the ambiguous version of the figure. Cut them out and return to the previous pages of this section. Perform the experiments as described there and record the results. Do your results correspond to the hypothetical data? Do the same hypotheses apply?

Reference

Epstein, W., and Rock, I. 1960. Perceptual set as an artifact of recency. *American Journal of Psychology* (73): 214–28.

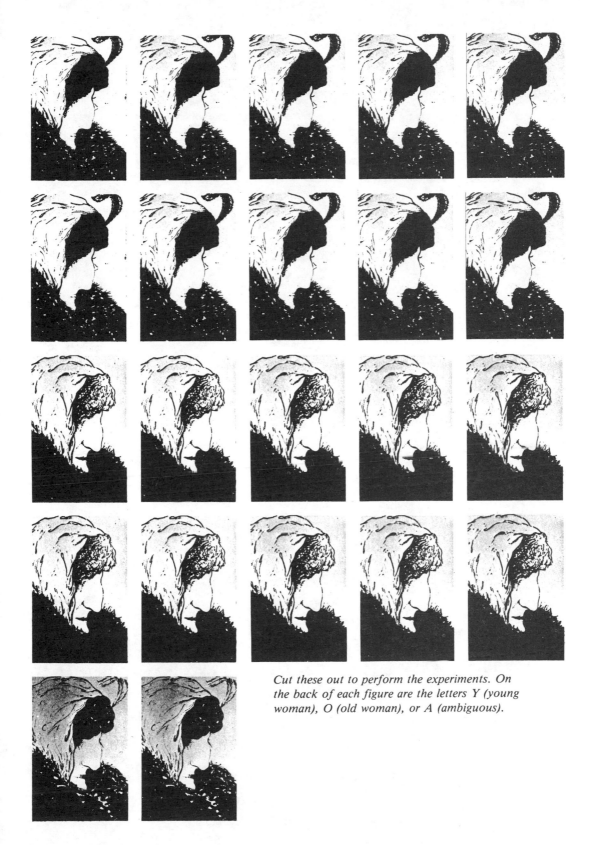

Cut these out to perform the experiments. On the back of each figure are the letters Y (young woman), O (old woman), or A (ambiguous).

Y   Y   Y   Y   Y

Y   Y   Y   Y   Y

O   O   O   O   O

O   O   O   O   O

A   A

CHAPTER 6

Memory

Learning Objectives

1. Understand what it means for perception to be concerned with organization in space and memory to be concerned with organization in time.

STUDYING MEMORY

2. Know that there are three major processes that must be understood in studying memory: acquisition, storage, and retrieval. Give examples of retrieval tasks.
3. List the characteristics of stage theory and the organizational view.

ENCODING

4. Explain what is meant by encoding.

   The stage theory of memory
5. Be familiar with the major assumptions of the stage theory of memory.
6. Know how the capacity of short-term memory is limited.
7. Rehearsal is a process important to short-term memory. Describe its function in relation to both short- and long-term memory.
8. One of the most robust phenomena in the study of memory is the appearance of primacy and recency effects in free recall. Describe these, and indicate what causes them. Be sure you can cite evidence that supports the presumed causes.
9. Be able to explain what a chunk is and how this concept applies to the capacity of short-term memory. How do chunks get created?

THE ORGANIZATIONAL APPROACH

10. Compare the concept of active memory with the concept of short-term memory.
11. Understand how chunking and reorganization affect the capacity of memory. Give examples.
12. Mnemonics are tools to increase the capacity of memory. Describe some mnemonics, and understand how they work to affect memory capacity.

RETRIEVAL

13. Understand the role of retrieval cues in increasing the accessibility of memory traces.

    The relation between original encoding and retrieval
14. Be able to explain the concept of encoding specificity and how it influences successful retrieval. Understand the range of contexts in which this principle operates.

    Memory search
15. Describe how memory is searched. What does the tip-of-the-tongue phenomenon tell us about memory search?

    Implicit memory
16. Be aware of the difference between implicit and explicit memory retrieval. What is the essence of an implicit measure, and what are some examples?

    Retrieval from active memory
17. Describe how reaction time methodology allows one to study retrieval from short-term memory. What are the predictions of serial versus parallel search theories about retrieval times? What does the evidence show?

CONCEPTUAL FRAMEWORKS AND REMEMBERING

    Memory distortions
18. Explain how memory for events is affected by prior knowledge. Give some examples

19. Memory is an important issue in the courtroom. Know what research tells us about the fallibility of eyewitness testimony.

The limits of distortion
20. Understand what limits our distortion of memory.

VARIETIES OF LONG-TERM MEMORY

Generic memory
21. Describe the differences between episodic and generic memory. What is semantic memory, and how is it related to episodic and generic memory?
22. Explain what is meant by the claim that semantic memory is organized hierarchically.
23. Describe how a spreading activation model of semantic memory differs from a hierarchical model. Offer some evidence that supports a spreading activation model.

Visual memory
24. Give the characteristics of eidetic imagery. How frequent and useful is it?
25. Discuss studies of scanning as evidence for visual memory.

FORGETTING

26. Know what a forgetting curve is.

Theories of forgetting
27. Recount the evidence both for and against a decay theory of forgetting.
28. Know the experimental techniques that are used to study proactive and retroactive inhibition.

29. Show how a theory based on changing retrieval cues might explain everyday forgetting. Explain how such a theory could be applied to the forgetting of childhood memories.

When forgetting seems not to occur
30. Some semantic memories seem to last quite a long time. Explain how we know this.
31. Some researchers claim that flashbulb memories are different from other memories. Explain how. Are these memories really treated differently by the memory system?

DISORDERED MEMORIES

Anterograde amnesia
32. Describe the symptoms of anterograde amnesia and give some of its causes. Describe the symptoms of patients such as H. M.
Retrograde amnesia
33. Explain how retrograde amnesia differs from anterograde amnesia, and discuss the mechanism proposed to account for retrograde amnesia.

Explicit and implicit memory revisited
34. Know what implicit memory measures tell us about the nature of anterograde amnesia. Show how the concepts of procedural and declarative knowledge are relevant here.

TAKING STOCK

35. Discuss the similarities among the topics of perception, memory, and thinking.

Programmed Exercises

STUDYING MEMORY

1. The first stage of memory is _acquisition_, in which information is brought into the system.

   acquisition

2. The records of experience made on the nervous system are called memory _traces_ .

   traces

3. The second stage of memory is _storage_, during which information is filed away. The final stage is _retrieval_, the point at which one tries to remember.

   storage

   retrieval

4. The term _encoding_ refers to the form in which a piece of information is stored.

   encoding

5. There are two general techniques for testing whether a person has remembered something. The first involves asking the person to produce or name the item and is known as _recall_ . The second requires that the person know the item when she sees or hears it and is called _recognition_

   recall

   recognition

ENCODING

6. The theory of memory that argues for separate memory systems working together is called the _stage_ theory.   stage

7. The approach to memory that emphasizes how memories are processed is called the _organizational_ view.   organizational

8. _Short-term_ memory holds information for a brief interval. _long-term_ memory stores information for longer periods of time.   Short-term

    Long-term

9. The storage _capacity_ of short-term memory is frequently claimed to be about 7 items.   capacity

10. The _memory span_ is the number of items an individual can recall after just one presentation. This quantity, 7 plus or minus 2, is sometimes called the _magic #_.   memory span

    magic number

11. _Rehearsal_ is one way of either keeping an item in short-term memory or allowing it to pass into long-term memory.   Rehearsal

12. The method of _free recall_ allows a subject who is presented with a list of unrelated items to report them in any order desired.   free recall

13. Of a long list of presented items, a subject is most apt to remember the first few (known as the _primacy_ effect) and the last few (known as the _recency_ effect).   primacy

    recency

14. The process that allows the contents of short-term memory to expand is called _chunking_. Recognition of this process foreshadows the current _organizational_ approach.   chunking

    organizational

15. When a subject repackages material into larger units, he is said to _recode_ that material into larger chunks.   recode

THE ORGANIZATIONAL APPROACH

16. The organizational approach focuses on how memories are _processed_, rather than where they are _stored_. So many psychologists prefer the term _active memory_ to the term short-term memory.   processed, stored

    active (working) memory

17. According to the stage theory, chunking affects _capacity_; according to the organizational approach, chunking affects _retrieval_   capacity

    retrieval

18. The various devices designed to improve memory are collectively called _mnemonics_   mnemonics

19. The method of _loci_ requires the learner to visualize each of the items he wants to remember in a different spatial location.   loci

20. The most effective kind of image for remembering is one in which the elements of the image are _interacting_.

interacting

RETRIEVAL

21. When you know a piece of information (i.e., you have stored it), but you cannot retrieve it at the moment, the trace is said to be _inaccessible_

inaccessible

22. A stimulus that provides a trigger to get an item out of memory is called a _retrieval_ _cue_ .

retrieval cue

23. The principle of _encoding_ _specificity_ states that retrieval success is most likely if the context at the time of retrieval approximates that during original encoding.

encoding specificity

24. Many investigators believe that retrieval is generally preceded by an internal process called _memory_ _search_ .

memory search

25. The _tip of tongue_ phenomenon is an example of unsuccessful retrieval in which the subject comes close to the searched-for item in his memory but cannot quite find the right memory location.

tip-of-the-tongue

26. Recall and recognition are both _explicit_ measures of memory, while word fragment completion is an _implicit_ measure.

explicit

implicit

27. A _parallel_ search process is one in which search proceeds simultaneously through all items in short-term memory, whereas a _serial_ search process is one in which search is sequential.

parallel

serial

CONCEPTUAL FRAMEWORKS AND REMEMBERING

28. As Bartlett demonstrated with subjects' recall of stories, retrieval is often a _reconstructive_ event, since partial knowledge of an event is pieced together in recall.

reconstructive

29. The conceptual framework that a person builds up on the basis of his knowledge of the world is called a _schema_. A subcase of this is a _script_ , which describes a scenario for a familiar event.

schema

script

30. Eyewitnesses to crimes seem to _reconstruct_ the past from their partial knowledge of it in the process of trying to remember it.

reconstruct

VARIETIES OF LONG-TERM MEMORY

31. _Episodic_ memory is the memory for particular events of one's own life. These memories are tagged by time and place.

Episodic

32. The term used to denote the sum total of a person's knowledge is _generic_ memory. One component of this is _semantic_ memory, the memory of words and concepts.

generic, semantic

33. A _network_ model of semantic memory asserts that words and concepts are stored in a complex, linked system of relationships.

network

34. In a semantic network, the words and concepts are represented by _nodes_ , while the associations between them are represented by lines or arrows.

nodes

35. A _spreading activation_ model of semantic memory has semantic relationships represented by links of varying lengths, showing their relative strengths.

spreading activation

36. The often-discussed phenomenon of "photographic memory" is also known as _eidetic imagery_.

eidetic imagery

37. Studies of _eidetic imagery_ and _image scanning_ reveal that in some ways mental images are like mental pictures.

eidetic imagery, image scanning

FORGETTING

38. The _retention interval_ is the time period between original learning and testing in a memory experiment.

retention interval

39. Ebbinghaus tested his subjects using lists of _nonsense syllables_ to avoid having items that have inherent meaning.

nonsense syllables

40. A _forgetting curve_ shows that most forgetting occurs early in the retention interval, followed by a gradual decline in the rate of forgetting.

forgetting curve

41. When relearning a list takes less time than original learning of that list, one is said to have achieved _saving_ .

saving

42. One example of an interference effect is _retroactive inhibition_, in which new learning hampers recall of old material. Another example is _proactive inhibition_, in which interference is from old material on the recall of newly learned items.

retroactive inhibition

proactive inhibition

43. One possible reason that we can't recall childhood memories is the drastic change in _retrieval cues_ between childhood and adulthood. This phenomenon is called childhood _amnesia_.

retrieval cues

amnesia

44. Some semantic information seems to be very long-lasting, suggesting that this information is moved into what is called a _permastore_

permastore

45. Brown and Kulik claim that certain salient and emotional events produce what are called _flashbulb_ memories, which are quite vivid.

flashbulb

DISORDERED MEMORIES

46. A patient suffers a hippocampal lesion. Subsequent recall of events that occurred before his accident is intact, but the patient is unable to remember new events (posttrauma) for very long. The patient suffers from _anterograde_ amnesia.

anterograde

47. An alcoholic with symptoms of anterograde amnesia likely suffers from _Korsakoff Syndrome_

Korsakoff syndrome

48. A patient has suffered an accident involving trauma to the head. Following this, his ability to learn things is unimpaired, but he seems to have forgotten some things that happened prior to the accident. This is an example of _retrograde amnesia_   retrograde amnesia

49. One theory to account for the loss of prior memories after a trauma to the brain is based on the notion of _trace_   trace
consolidation, according to which newly acquired memories undergo   consolidation
gradual change until they become more firmly established.

50. An amnesic's memory is relatively unaffected when the memory task involves _procedural_ knowledge, but his memory is drastically   procedural
impaired when it involves _declarative_ knowledge.   declarative

51. _Explicit_ tests of memory show great performance declines in   Explicit
amnesics, while _implicit_ tests show little difference from the   implicit
performance of normal subjects.

Self-Test

1. In order for us to remember something, we must first engage in the process of:
   a. storage.
   b. rehearsal.
   c. acquisition.
   d. recall.

2. An enduring physical record of a memory is called a:
   a. memory trace.
   b. chunk.
   c. memory span.
   d. none of the above

3. In principle, the stages of memory processes must be arranged in which of the following orders?
   a. memory trace – acquisition – storage – retrieval
   b. acquisition – memory trace – storage – retrieval
   c. acquisition – storage – memory trace – retrieval
   d. acquisition – memory trace – retrieval – storage

4. Suppose you are given a choice between a multiple-choice test and a short-answer test for the final exam in this course. You want to maximize the chance of doing well. Based on what you know about recall and recognition, all other things being equal, which test should you choose?
   a. short answer
   b. multiple choice

   c. Either; there is no difference.
   d. It depends on the difficulty of the material.

5. Complete the following analogy: Multiple-choice questions are to fill-in-the-blank questions as:
   a. recognition is to recall.
   b. recall is to retention.
   c. recognition is to retention.
   d. learning is to memory.

6. Which of the following are permissible forms of encoding?
   a. by sound pattern
   b. by visual pattern
   c. by meaning
   d. all of the above

7. The following are all characteristics of short-term memory except:
   a. limited capacity.
   b. contents disappear without rehearsal.
   c. primarily semantic representation.
   d. rapid access.

8. It has been found that people can hold about seven items in short-term memory. When more items are presented, complete recall is generally not possible. This demonstrates the _____ of short-term memory.
   a. retention interval
   b. memory trace
   c. displacement
   d. memory span

9. Suppose you are given driving directions by a gas station attendant and you repeat them over and over to yourself, "First left, second right, left at the first light, third right." Now suppose that your repetition of the directions is interrupted by an emergency driving maneuver. This would likely cause you to forget the directions, thereby demonstrating the importance of _____ in preserving short-term memory.
   a. storage capacity
   b. retrieval
   c. accessibility
   d. rehearsal

10. At a party you are taken around the room by the host and are introduced to the other guests. Some time after the introductions are finished, one of these people comes up to talk to you. All other things being equal, you have the best chance of remembering her name if she was one of the _____ people you met. This phenomenon is called _____ .
    a. first, primacy
    b. middle, inhibition
    c. last, recency
    d. first or last, partial report

11. Now imagine the same situation (as in No. 10) except that the person comes up to you immediately after you have been very quickly introduced to everyone. Again, other things being equal, you would have the worst chance of remembering her name if she was one of the _____ people you met and the best chance if she was one of the _____ .
    a. first, last
    b. middle, last
    c. middle, first, or last
    d. last, first, or middle

12. Suppose a subject is asked to memorize the following list of words: *apple, horse, desk, carpet, mug, milk, parrot, disk, street, tree.* Which of the following will occur?
    a. The word *street* will be rehearsed more than the word *horse*, causing *tree* to be stored in long-term memory.
    b. The word *parrot* will be rehearsed more than the word *mug*, causing *parrot* to be stored in short-term memory.
    c. The word *apple* will be rehearsed more than the word *carpet*, causing *apple* to be stored in long-term memory.
    d. The word *desk* will be rehearsed more than the word *parrot*, causing *desk* to be stored in short-term memory.

13. The figure above depicts recall curves for a list of 16 items. Two conditions were employed, I and II. What was the difference between the conditions?
    a. The interval between each item was longer for I than II.
    b. The interval between each item was longer for II than I.
    c. The interval between the last item and the recall test was longer for I than II.
    d. The interval between the last item and the recall test was longer for II than I.

14. Increasing the capacity of short-term memory is a misnomer because:
    a. all one does is to rehearse the material already there, keeping it fresh while new material is added.
    b. the number of items stored is the same, about 7, just the content of each item has changed.
    c. it is the number of chunks that has changed, not the capacity of short-term memory.
    d. it is not possible to increase the capacity of short-term memory.

15. Mnemonic devices (memorizing aids) use the principle of:
    a. consolidation of retrieval.
    b. recoding.
    c. retrieval of consolidation.
    d. all of the above

16. Short-term memory : long-term memory ::
    a. encoding : retrieval
    b. secondary memory : primary memory
    c. active : dormant
    d. retrieval : storage

17. Which of the following images would produce the greatest increase in recall performance for the pair of items horse-rock?
    a. a horse standing next to a rock
    b. a horse dragging a rock
    c. a horse and rock pictured separately
    d. All of the above would be equivalent.

18. You have been trying to remember the name of a street that a friend lives on. Despite all of your efforts you are unable to recall it. While in the kitchen looking for a snack (to console yourself) you reach for a can of nuts, and suddenly the street name comes to you—Walnut. This is an example of the role of:
    a. anterograde amnesia.
    b. retrograde amnesia.
    c. mnemonics.
    d. retrieval cues.

19. Retrieval cues are most effective if they:
    a. coincide with the way in which a trace was originally encoded.
    b. are presented at the time of recall not at encoding.
    c. are quite concrete.
    d. elicit visual images.

20. The tip-of-the-tongue phenomenon provides us with evidence concerning:
    a. the hierarchical organization of long-term memory.
    b. accessibility in short-term memory.
    c. the search process in long-term memory.
    d. the use of retrieval cues in short-term memory.

21. Having something "on the tip of the tongue" indicates a problem:
    a. in the way the item was chunked.
    b. with reconstruction.
    c. with proactive inhibition.
    d. with retrieval.

22. What is the relationship between implicit and explicit memory tests?
    a. They must be correlated because they both measure memory.
    b. They can be uncorrelated as shown by demonstrations of implicit memory without explicit memory.
    c. They must be uncorrelated because the tests measure different aspects of memory.
    d. Available evidence does not permit an answer.

23. A memory search experiment is conducted under two conditions, I and II. The results are shown above. Reaction time is plotted as a function of memory set size. What do you think might have been the difference between the two conditions?
    a. parallel search in I; serial search in II
    b. serial search in I; parallel search in II
    c. size of memory set smaller in I than II
    d. response key easier to press in I than II

24. It is believed that retrieval is generally preceded by:
    a. chunking.
    b. memory activation.
    c. memory search.
    d. recognition.

25. Bartlett's experiments and evidence about the fallibility of eyewitness testimony highlight the importance of which of the following factors about recall?
    a. reconstruction
    b. proactive inhibition
    c. retrieval cues
    d. retroactive inhibition

26. One could have a script for:
    a. mowing the lawn.
    b. visiting the eye doctor.
    c. going to a fast food restaurant.
    d. all of the above

27. Remembering what you did on your last birthday is an example of:
    a. semantic memory.
    b. generic memory.
    c. episodic memory.
    d. hierarchical memory.

28. Studies of image scanning draw on an analogy between image analysis and:
    a. feature analysis.
    b. concept analysis.
    c. picture analysis.
    d. semantic analysis.

29. If images were truly pictures, then a subject should be able to:
    a. scan the image.
    b. reinterpret the image of it as an ambiguous figure.
    c. all of the above
    d. none of the above

30. The typical effect of the forgetting curve is that:
    a. there is more saving with shorter retention intervals.
    b. there is more saving with longer retention intervals.
    c. relearning takes more trials than original learning.
    d. decline in saving is sharpest well after learning, not immediately after.

31. According to a decay theory of forgetting, if a subject learning a list of words was then subjected to one of the following procedures, he would forget the greatest number of words if:
    a. he slept for four versus two hours.

b. he learned other lists for four versus two hours.

c. he performed arithmetic problems for four versus two hours.

d. All of the above would be comparable.

32. Consider the following experimental design:

control group:
learn A → rest → test A
experimental group:
learn A → learn B → test A

This design would be used to test forgetting due to which factor?

a. proactive inhibition

b. retroactive inhibition

c. decay

d. generalization

33. A college sophomore participates in a nonsense syllable learning experiment. The first list takes him only four trials to learn. The second list takes five trials, and the third list takes eight trials. These results can be taken as a demonstration of:

a. memory activation.

b. retroactive inhibition.

c. proactive inhibition.

d. retrograde forgetting.

34. One hypothesis about forgetting is that it is due to a change in retrieval cues. Which of the following would be counterevidence for this hypothesis?

a. demonstration of proactive inhibition

b. demonstration of retroactive inhibition

c. demonstration that decay caused forgetting

d. none of the above

35. One of the potential causes of childhood amnesia is that the retrieval cues change massively between childhood and adulthood. Another plausible cause might be:

a. the poor quality of the initial encoding of memory traces.

b. retroactive inhibition.

c. decay.

d. all of the above

36. The concept of a permastore arises from the fact that:

a. some memories are not subject to any forgetting.

b. some memories, while they decline initially after learning, remain relatively intact thereafter.

c. some memories have a flashbulb character to them.

d. all of the above

37. The compelling nature of flashbulb memories has caused some to argue that they are caused by a special memory mechanism. Contrary to this hypothesis, though,

a. the accuracy of these memories may not be all that impressive.

b. some of the good memory may come from conversations about the event after it has occurred.

c. both of the above

d. none of the above

38. Retrograde amnesia may be caused by:

a. a disruption in the mechanism that causes new material to be placed into long-term memory, thus preventing any new learning.

b. a disruption of trace consolidation at the time of the trauma.

c. a difficulty in retrieving events that occurred just prior to the trauma.

d. more than one of the above

39. One experiment has shown that while amnesics get better at reading mirror-reversed text, they cannot recognize the words they have read later on, while normals can. This indicates that:

a. amnesics lose the ability to learn new information.

b. amnesics lose the ability to learn declarative information, but not procedural information.

c. amnesics can learn procedural skills, but only if the very same stimuli are repeated over and over.

d. anterograde amnesics are different from retrograde amnesics.

40. Three major symptoms characterize anterograde amnesia. They are:

a. accurate memory for pretrauma events, normal short-term memory, inaccurate memory for most posttrauma events.

b. inaccurate memory for pretrauma events, normal short-term memory, inaccurate memory for most posttrauma events.

c. accurate memory for pretrauma events, abnormal short-term memory, accurate memory for most posttrauma events.

d. inaccurate memory for pretrauma events, normal short-term memory, accurate memory for most posttrauma events.

41. H. M. (an anterograde amnesic) was tested for his memory span for unrelated nouns. What is your best guess about his span?

a. 0

b. 4

c. 7

d. 10

42. A theory of memory which says that memory needs time to be fixed into a permanent form is called:
    a. rehearsal.
    b. spreading activation.
    c. trace consolidation.
    d. memory priming.

43. You witness an automobile accident in which one of the drivers hits his head on the windshield. He appears uninjured, but when a policeman asks him what happened just prior to the accident, the man seems confused and is unable to answer. The policeman is about to haul the man off to jail (assuming that he must be drunk) when you step forward and (having studied your psychology text) say, "This man is suffering from _____ _____!"
    a. trace consolidation
    b. anterograde amnesia
    c. retrograde amnesia
    d. Korsakoff syndrome

Answer Key for Self-Test

1. c p. 171	23. d pp. 182–84
2. a p. 172	24. c p. 181
3. b pp. 171–72	25. a pp. 185–86
4. a pp. 172–73	26. d p. 185
5. a p. 173	27. c p. 187
6. d p. 172	28. c p. 189
7. c p. 173	29. c p. 189
8. d p. 174	30. a p. 190
9. d p. 175	31. d pp. 190–91
10. a p. 175	32. b p. 191
11. b p. 175	33. c p. 191
12. c p. 175	34. d p. 192
13. d p. 175	35. d p. 192
14. b p. 176	36. b p. 193
15. c pp. 178–79	37. c p. 194
16. c pp. 176–77	38. d pp. 195–96
17. b p. 179	39. b p. 196
18. d p. 180	40. a p. 194
19. a p. 180	41. c p. 194
20. c pp. 181–82	42. c p. 195
21. d pp. 181–82	43. c p. 195
22. b p. 182	

Investigating Psychological Phenomena

THE EFFECT OF IMAGERY INSTRUCTIONS ON MEMORY

Equipment: None
Subjects: One
Time per subject: Fifteen minutes
Time for experimenter: Twenty minutes

As Professor Gleitman discusses, there are several mnemonic techniques that will improve memory performance. One of these is the use of images. By now there is a good deal of research that demonstrates the memorial effectiveness of asking subjects to create images of the objects or events that they are trying to commit to memory. In the present experiment you will have an opportunity to demonstrate the effectiveness of imagery instructions for yourself in an experiment that involves learning paired-associate lists.

The procedure is quite simple. Below you will find two lists of twenty noun pairs each that you can use as a stimuli for the experiment. You will need just one subject to participate in the experiment. The procedure is as follows:

First, read the following instructions to the subject:

This is a memory experiment in which you will be required to memorize and recall two lists of words, each of which is composed of twenty pairs of fairly common nouns. First I will read aloud the twenty noun pairs from list 1 at the rate of one pair every seven seconds or so. While I am reading the pairs, just sit quietly and listen to them, trying as best you can to memorize the words in each pair. After I have presented all the pairs, I shall go through the list again, this time reading only the first noun in each pair. As I read each of these nouns, I would like you to recall the appropriate second noun that was paired with it when I originally presented the list. You will have seven seconds or so to recall the second noun for each pair and write it in the space provided on your answer sheet. Do you have any questions?

After you have read these instructions to the subject, give him or her the report sheet for this chapter in Appendix B. Then follow the testing procedure outlined in the instructions. After you have completed the procedure for list 1, read the following instructions to the subject:

Now I shall present you with another list of twenty noun pairs that I would like you to memorize. The procedure for this list will be identical to that for the first list except for one change: This time, when you are presented with each pair, try to form a mental image of the words in which there is some sort of interaction. For example, if you were presented with the pair "horse-rock," you might form an image of a horse that is harnessed to a large boulder and is dragging the boulder along the ground. Such images should help you memorize the words. Do you have any questions?

Now present list 2 exactly as list 1 was presented after you have given the subject another answer sheet for list 2.

To score the subject's performance, simply count up the number of items that were answered correctly on each list. If all went well, the subject should have scored better on list 2 (unless the subject was already forming mental images for the nouns in list 1).

Now at this point you may raise a question. Was the subject's performance on list 2 better because of the influence of the imagery instructions, or could it have been better for some other reason? For example, it may have already occurred to you that performance on list 2 may have been better than list 1 because list 2 was presented *after* list 1 and therefore the subject may simply have been better practiced at memorizing words. Before reading on, try to think of a way that you might have run this experiment that would have avoided this problem.

One way to have avoided a practice effect would have been to use two different subjects. The first subject would have received only list 1 with its instructions while the second would have received only list 2 with its imagery instructions. If performance on list 2 was still better than on list 1, you might feel more confident in attributing this difference to the effect of the instructions (assuming that your two subjects were fairly comparable in their overall memory ability). At least practice could not account for the difference.

But, you might object, there might *still* be an explanation for the difference between lists that has nothing to do with the effect of imagery instructions. Suppose, for instance, list 2 was composed of words that were more common or concrete than the words on list 1 (e.g., horse versus liberty). This alone might make list 2 more memorable. There are two ways that one might control for this possibility. The first is to choose words for the two lists that are equated for frequency of usage and concreteness (and, for that matter, whatever else you might think of that would affect the memorability of words). The second method is to balance experimentally which word lists are paired with which instructions. The following table shows

one arrangement that should work in which you would have to run at least 4 subjects:

	neutral instructions	imagery instructions
word list 1	subject 1	subject 2
word list 2	subject 3	subject 4

If you were to run this experiment, then you could tell whether the word lists differ from one another in memorability and/or whether there is an effect of instructions. If word list 2 is more memorable than word list 1, then subjects 3 and 4 should perform better than 1 and 2. If imagery instructions produce better performance than neutral instructions, then subjects 2 and 4 should perform better than 1 and 3. If list 2 is more memorable than list 1 *and* imagery instructions produce better performance than neutral instructions, then subject 4 should perform best of all.

If you want to check on the possible influence of practice in the experiment that you ran, and if you want to be sure that the word lists are comparable (they have actually been balanced for meaningfulness and commonness of the words), then you should try this last experiment. Whether you do try it or not, however, you should realize that one of the points of this exercise was to show that even a fairly simple experiment such as the one that you ran with the word lists is sometimes open to several interpretations. To find the right one requires careful experimentation.

Noun pairs for list 1	Noun pairs for list 2
1. building-letter	1. sail-bowl
2. grass-meat	2. coffee-lake
3. animal-village	3. girl-flood
4. house-lip	4. corn-river
5. sky-seat	5. stone-bottle
6. dress-apple	6. paper-shore
7. fur-mountain	7. dust-army
8. flag-coast	8. ocean-fire
9. sugar-ship	9. clothing-board
10. mother-city	10. door-king
11. market-church	11. butler-tree
12. plant-baby	12. gold-chair
13. sea-iron	13. flower-car
14. woods-engine	14. bird-skin
15. arm-boulder	15. hall-child
16. woman-forest	16. garden-book
17. table-wood	17. money-shoes
18. queen-college	18. cat-camp
19. bar-diamond	19. wife-storm
20. cotton-street	20. dollar-machine

CHAPTER 7

Thinking

Learning Objectives

THE COMPONENTS OF THOUGHT

Mental imagery

1. Understand the argument that thought is primarily guided by images. Be able to give the evidence against this position.

Abstract elements

2. Explain what it means for something to represent something else.
3. Be familiar with the terms "concept" and "proposition." You should be able to give examples of each.

PROBLEM SOLVING

4. Give the arguments that show that thinking is more organized than being simply the chaining of ideas.

Hierarchical organization and chunking

5. Explain how thinking is goal-directed. Explain how it is hierarchical. How do these features bear on Locke's position?
6. Describe the shape of the learning curve in the development of a skill, and understand what this shape tells us about the course of learning.
7. Be able to describe how chunking ability differentiates novices from experts. What is the role of automatization in skill development?
8. Describe the Stroop effect and discuss its relevance.
9. Be familiar with some of the classic puzzle problems that have been used to study thinking.
10. Show how research on problem solving demonstrates that subjects use hierarchical plans.
11. Know the major differences between masters and beginners in problem solving. What skills do masters have that novices don't?

Obstacles to problem solving

12. Be aware of the effects of set and motivation on problem solving. How does set influence solution strategies? Know what functional fixedness is and how it hinders problem solving.

Overcoming obstacles to solution

13. Understand how the strategy of working backwards is used.
14. Explain the role of analogy in problem solving. What factors govern whether people will retrieve analogies from memory and use them?
15. Understand what it means to change the way a problem is represented in order to facilitate solving that problem. How do changes in representation help in problem solution?

Restructuring

16. Know what restructuring is and how it is related to creative thinking.
17. Understand how incubation is related to the effects of set, as well as how it is related to creative thinking.

ARTIFICIAL INTELLIGENCE: PROBLEM SOLVING BY COMPUTER

18. Be able to explain why computers are valuable analogs to humans as problem solvers, as well as how the analogy is weak.
19. Understand the goal of the field of artificial intelligence.

Algorithms and heuristics

20. Define the terms "algorithm" and "heuristic." Describe some useful heuristics in problem solving. Why are algorithms often inefficient but exact?

How do expert chess programs use algorithms and heuristics in their operation?

21. Describe what MYCIN is and what it can do, as well as what its limitations are.

SOME LIMITATIONS OF ARTIFICIAL INTELLIGENCE

22. Explain why different strategies are required for well-defined versus ill-defined problems. Know what the difference between these two kinds of problems is and how this difference is relevant to the comparison of humans and computers.

23. Understand how the concept of "common sense" is important in understanding the limitations in the ability of computers to solve problems.

SPATIAL THINKING

Spatial problem solving and imagery

24. Explain how mental pictures help solve spatial problems.

25. Explain the difference between mental maps that are picture-like and those that are conceptual.

26. Know what makes our spatial knowledge not entirely picture-like. Be able to give an example to substantiate this statement.

REASONING AND DECISION MAKING

27. Understand whether the laws of logic are the laws of thought.

Deductive reasoning

28. Define a syllogism. What reasons cause many

subjects to do poorly in solving syllogisms?

Inductive reasoning

29. Be able to explain the difference between deductive and inductive reasoning and give examples of each.

30. Define the confirmation bias. Why are disconfirmations more helpful in testing hypotheses than confirmations? Give an example of the confirmation bias.

Decision making

31. People are poor at estimating probabilities, but they can use shortcuts to get at these estimates. List some of these shortcuts.

32. Be able to explain what the representativeness heuristic is. How does it affect people's use of base-rate information?

33. Know why the availability heuristic can sometimes lead to grave errors in estimating likelihoods. Be able to state two examples in which the availability heuristic may affect estimations.

34. Give examples of errors in reasoning that are due to the way a problem is framed. How do people feel about gains and losses in their willingness to take on risk?

A BACKWARD LOOK AT PERCEPTION, MEMORY, AND THINKING

35. Understand how the broad domains of cognition (perception, memory, and thinking) overlap. Explain the importance of this overlap.

Programmed Exercises

THE COMPONENTS OF THOUGHT

1. According to Berkeley and other British empiricists, all thought is ultimately comprised of _____ _____ , which enter and exit from consciousness.   mental images

2. Unlike pictures, _____ are abstract and symbolic.   words

3. The term "_____" is generally used to describe a class that subsumes a number of individual instances.   concept

4. A _____ concept doesn't apply to any one item in isolation; it can only be defined with respect to two or more objects.   relational

5. A _____ makes some assertion that relates a subject and a predicate in a way that can be true or false.   proposition

PROBLEM SOLVING

6. Hobbes, Locke, and their many descendants believed that the stream of activity that characterizes thinking is produced by a chain of _____ ideas, each triggered by the one before.

associated

7. The use of master plans to organize subsidiary actions suggests that thought is organized into _____ .

hierarchies

8. The ability to organize many details into larger _____ is one of the crucial features of directed activity, including thinking.

chunks

9. Much of the difference between a master and an apprentice is in the degree to which subcomponents of an activity have been chunked hierarchically; to the master, the substeps have become _____ .

automatic

10. The _____ and subsequent rise found in many learning curves for motor skills suggest that the learner gradually transforms this task.

plateau

11. The _____ effect is an example of how reading letter strings has become an automatized activity for adults. Reading incompatible color names interferes with naming colors in which the color words are printed.

Stroop

12. Associationists' explanation for chunking involves _____ : a first movement provides a kinesthetic stimulus for a second movement, which in turn is a stimulus for a third, etc.

chaining

13. Karl Duncker demonstrated that _____ organization is a common feature of problem solving; his subjects first formulated a plan of attack and then generated specific solutions.

hierarchical

14. As Adrian de Groot demonstrated with chess, master problem solvers use _____ that contain more information than do those of beginners.

chunks

15. When a person becomes _____ on one approach to a task, it is hard for him to approach it any other way.

fixated

16. A person who attempts to solve a problem by thinking along a line of thought created by previous thinking is operating under a _____ _____ .

mental set

17. The water jug problem, an example of mental set, is one of the classic demonstrations of _____ in problem solving.

mechanization

18. In general, the greater the _____ for reaching a solution, the stronger the _____ with which the problem is approached.

motivation

set

19. Thinking of objects in terms of their normal function is termed _____ _____ and can hinder problem solving.

functional fixedness

20. When two problems have a similar structure, using one as a(n) _____ to the other can be an effective problem-solving strategy.

analogy

21. Sometimes it is necessary to change the way a problem is

_____ to achieve a solution.   represented

22. Solutions of difficult problems often involve a perceptual

_____ of the problem in order to break a false perceptual set.   restructuring

23. The phenomenon whereby one arrives at an insightful solution to a problem after intense preparation followed by rest is called

_____ .   incubation

ARTIFICIAL INTELLIGENCE: PROBLEM SOLVING BY COMPUTER

24. One way in which humans and computers are similar is that both

are _____-_____ systems.   information-processing

25. The field of _____ _____ is concerned with programming   artificial intelligence
computers to solve various intellectual problems.

26. A procedure in which all of the operations required to achieve

the solution are specified step by step is called an _____ .   algorithm

27. A _____ differs from an algorithm in that it is a rule of   heuristic
thumb rather than a fixed sequence of steps.

28. One chess program includes a heuristic in which the computer

strives toward _____ such as occupation of the center squares. subgoals

29. _____ _____ are problem-solving programs that deal   Expert systems
with problems in a limited domain of knowledge.

30. _____ is an example of a problem-solving program that helps MYCIN
doctors in the treatment of infectious diseases.

31. A newspaper proofreader is asked to check a piece of text for

spelling errors. This is an example of a(n) _____-_____   well-defined
problem.

32. A student is asked to write a "good" paper. This is an example

of a(n) _____-_____ problem.   ill-defined

33. Some computer scientists feel that the crucial difference between human and artificial intelligence is that computer programs lack

_____ _____ .   common sense

SPATIAL THINKING

34. When we try to determine a shortcut between two locations, we

are using _____ reasoning.   spatial

35. A _____ _____ is a picturelike image of a geographical   mental map
area that is formed in the mind.

36. In addition to mental maps that are picturelike, there are those

that are abstract and _____ .   conceptual

REASONING AND DECISION MAKING

37. A _____ contains two premises and a conclusion.   syllogism

38. The statement "All A are B and therefore all B are A" is a(n)

    _____ inference.   invalid

39. In _____ reasoning we apply a general rule to a particular case.   deductive

40. In _____ reasoning we consider different cases and try to find the rule that covers them all.   inductive

41. The fact that people primarily seek evidence that will confirm their

    hypotheses suggests that there is a strong _____ _____ .   confirmation bias

42. One _____ shows that a hypothesis is false, but countless   disconfirmation

    _____ cannot prove that it is true.   confirmations

43. The _____ heuristic involves judging the probability that an object belongs to a category by judging the similarity of that object to the category.   representativeness

44. One of the factors that might lead to people's paying too much attention to a description as opposed to a base rate is that the

    description bears a close resemblance to a _____ they accept.   stereotype

45. When we estimate the frequency of certain events by considering how many such events readily come to mind, we are using the

    _____ _____ .   availability heuristic

46. The way a problem is _____ can influence the way people will solve it.   framed

A BACKWARD LOOK AT PERCEPTION, MEMORY, AND THINKING

47. There are no clear boundaries between the domains of

    _____ , _____ , and _____ .   perception, memory, thinking

Self-Test

1. Imageless thought:
   a. does not exist.
   b. is not found even in persons who are capable of vivid images.
   c. has been described as wordless and image-less but having a sense of relationships.
   d. none of the above

2. A concept:
   a. must have a finite number of instances.
   b. must not refer to a relationship.
   c. may designate qualities or dimensions.
   d. all of the above

3. A proposition:
   a. can be simply a mental image.
   b. has a truth value.

   c. can be simply a sentence.
   d. none of the above

4. All of the following are examples of directed thinking *except*:
   a. discovery of a geometric proof.
   b. deciding on the next move in a chess game.
   c. daydreaming about last night's meal.
   d. trying to figure out why a car will not start.

5. Learning curves involving such tasks as receiving Morse code have a characteristic plateau preceded and followed by rises. This is because:
   a. people tend to get bored with tasks like this, and so their performance falls off.
   b. people begin to use mental imagery after a little practice.

c. with practice people can make more efficient use of chunks.

d. none of the above

6. Which of the following is not a characteristic of learning for a new motor skill?
   a. periods in which there is no apparent change in the learning curve
   b. periods of relatively sharp increases in skill
   c. a steady increase in skill from the beginning of learning to the end
   d. a scalloped shape to the learning curve

7. The Stroop effect clearly shows that:
   a. certain mental activities become automatized.
   b. colors are named faster than words.
   c. words are named faster than colors.
   d. Lashley was wrong in his description of behavior sequences.

8. To explain chunking, many associationists claim that skilled acts are highly practiced stimulus-response strings. For such strings the first movement serves as a stimulus for the second, which does the same thing for the third, etc. This is known as:
   a. a heuristic.
   b. an algorithm.
   c. mental set.
   d. none of the above

9. Typical solutions to Karl Duncker's X-ray problem:
   a. involved hierarchical thought patterns.
   b. involved reformulating the problem to produce a plan of attack.
   c. show that subjects entertain classes of solutions before converging on one.
   d. all of the above

10. Research has shown that master chess players are better than novices in:
    a. solving algorithms.
    b. chunking chess moves.
    c. looking farther ahead to plan chess moves.
    d. memorizing random patterns of chess pieces.

11. A person is asked to solve a series of math problems. The first five problems can only be solved one way, each the same. The sixth problem can also be solved using this method, but there is also a much simpler solution. The subject solves this problem in the way he solved the first five. This person's problem-solving ability has been hampered by:
    a. functional fixedness.
    b. a lack of motivation.
    c. mental set.
    d. an improper heuristic.

12. Several subjects are told that they will receive ten dollars if they are able to solve a problem in fifteen minutes. A second group is given no such promise. These groups demonstrate the inverse relationship between _____ and _____ .
    a. motivation, set
    b. effort, success
    c. attitude, money
    d. none of the above

13. An inability to think of objects except in terms of their normal function can be a hindrance in problem solving and is known as:
    a. perceptual set.
    b. restructuring.
    c. functional fixedness.
    d. none of the above

14. The use of analogy in problem solving:
    a. seems to be a habitual characteristic of the human problem solver.
    b. seems to work only when the analogy is somehow pointed out to the problem solver by someone else.
    c. requires that there be several potential analogs in memory for a single problem.
    d. depends on the problem solver noticing a structural similarity between two problems.

15. Some problems require a change in representation in order for the problem solver to work toward a solution. This phenomenon is quite different from:
    a. restructuring.
    b. incubation.
    c. functional fixedness.
    d. analogy.

16. All of the following problems discussed in the text require perceptual restructuring for a solution *except*:
    a. the nine-dot problem.
    b. the match puzzle.
    c. the horse-and-rider problem.
    d. unscrambling words (anagrams).

17. All of the following often contribute to insights *except*:
    a. a period of intense preparation.
    b. a period of retreat.
    c. a different environment.
    d. functional fixedness.

18. One likely reason that incubation helps in reaching a solution is that:
    a. it allows for perceptual restructuring.
    b. it helps break mental set.
    c. it gives time to set up subgoals.
    d. none of the above

19. The concept of an incubation period (in the explanation of insight) is unsatisfactory because:
    a. it tells us nothing of the underlying processes.
    b. the term "unconscious thought" is too vague.
    c. it has been demonstrated to be false.
    d. a and b but not c

20. Incubation works best when
    a. mental set is broken.
    b. people work on problems continuously.
    c. the time between problem presentation and solution is short.
    d. all of the above

21. The use of the computer as an analog to the human problem solver depends on:
    a. the sequential nature of computer programs.
    b. the fact that computers use algorithms to solve their problems.
    c. the fact that computers are limited to solving well-defined problems.
    d. the irrelevance of the underlying hardware in humans and computers.

22. Humans and computers are similar in that:
    a. both are information-processing systems.
    b. both can use heuristics.
    c. both can use algorithms.
    d. all of the above

23. A food recipe specifies what ingredients are to be added together, in what amounts, and in what order. Such a recipe would be:
    a. a heuristic.
    b. an algorithm.
    c. a subgoal.
    d. a scheme.

24. Which of the following would make most efficient use of heuristics?
    i. an initial diagnosis made by a physician
    ii. an architect designing a hotel
    iii. a search for a particular word in a dictionary
    iv. deciding where to hang a new picture
    a. i, ii, iii
    b. ii, iii, iv
    c. iii, iv
    d. i, ii, iv

25. Examples of the appropriate use of subgoals and heuristics might be:
    a. trying for a position in the center of a board in a game of chess.
    b. going for a checkmate.
    c. finding the general area of an automotive

problem (i.e., electrical vs. mechanical).
    d. all of the above

26. Recently developed chess programs differ from novice chess players in that they rely on
    a. better memory for chess positions.
    b. brute force techniques for calculating moves.
    c. better evaluation of chess board configurations.
    d. all of the above

27. In general, expert problem solvers seem to excel at using:
    a. hierarchical strategies.
    b. subgoals.
    c. heuristics.
    d. all of the above

28. Ill-defined problems differ from well-defined problems in that:
    a. ill-defined problems have more difficult and complex solutions.
    b. well-defined problems always have solutions, while ill-defined problems are unsolvable.
    c. it is hard to define what changes are needed to reach the goal stated in ill-defined problems.
    d. all of the above

29. The analogy between computers and the human mind is weak because:
    a. computers are made of transistors.
    b. the mind uses nerve signals, not electrical impulses.
    c. humans can solve well-defined problems.
    d. none of the above

30. Expert systems are limited in their similarity to human problem solving in that:
    a. they are too rigid in their approaches to problems.
    b. they are restricted to a narrow area of competence.
    c. they are confined to working on well-defined problems.
    d. all of the above

31. One of the limitations of artificial intelligence is its lack of common sense. This could be addressed by:
    a. giving the computer a better set of algorithms to map out all possibilities that might occur in any given situation.
    b. providing the computer with better background knowledge so that it can anticipate what might occur.
    c. making ill-defined problems well-defined.

d. having the computer stick strictly to relevant information, ignoring any information about a problem that is not directly relevant to its algorithm for the solution.

32. One would most likely construct a mental map for all of the following activities except:
    a. getting from one end of the college campus to the other.
    b. rearranging furniture in a living room.
    c. taking a walk around the block.
    d. finding a shortcut to work.

33. Suppose subjects are required to provide estimates of certain distances. The estimation time of which distance would be the longest?
    a. 1/2 mile
    b. 1 mile
    c. 2 miles
    d. 3 miles

34. Spatial knowledge is sometimes affected by:
    a. rotation.
    b. conceptual knowledge.
    c. perceptual knowledge.
    d. none of the above

35. All A are B
    Some B are C
    Therefore some A are C. This is a(n):
    a. invalid syllogism.
    b. valid syllogism.
    c. invalid algorithm.
    d. valid algorithm.

36. Which of the following statements is true?
    a. People often set out to see whether their hypotheses are false.
    b. People rarely set out to see whether their hypotheses are false.
    c. People do not seek evidence that will confirm their hypotheses.
    d. none of the above

37. In making predictions about the outcome of situations, people seem to make too little use of:
    a. salient information that is presented in the form of a memorable scenario.
    b. base-rate information that tells one the past history of a situation.
    c. rules of discourse that dictate what one should say on particular occasions.
    d. none of the above; people appropriately balance these sources of information.

38. When a decision is affected by events that come readily to mind, this is a manifestation of:
    a. an algorithm.
    b. deductive reasoning.

c. conjunction.
d. the availability heuristic.

Answer Key for Self-Test

1. c pp. 200–1	20. a p. 211
2. c p. 201	21. d p. 211
3. b p. 201	22. d pp. 211–13
4. c p. 201	23. b p. 212
5. c p. 202	24. d pp. 212–13
6. c p. 202	25. d p. 213
7. a p. 203	26. d p. 213
8. d p. 203	27. d pp. 202–13
9. d p. 204	28. c p. 214
10. b, c pp. 204–5	29. d pp. 211–14
11. c p. 206	30. d pp. 213–14
12. a p. 207	31. b pp. 214–15
13. c pp. 207–8	32. c pp. 215–16
14. d p. 209	33. d p. 216
15. c pp. 207–10	34. b p. 216
16. d pp. 209–10	35. a p. 217
17. d pp. 210–11	36. b p. 218
18. b p. 211	37. b p. 221
19. d p. 211	38. d p. 221

Investigating Psychological Phenomena

THE STROOP EFFECT

Equipment: Included (see insert)
Number of subjects: One
Time per subject: Thirty minutes
Time for experimenter: Forty minutes

It is frequently observed that as people are given more experience at the task of reading, the skill becomes more and more automatic in character. One symptom of this increasing automatization is that it is difficult to prevent a skilled reader from reading material that he is exposed to. This appears to be a general characteristic of skills that become automated. Given the proper conditions for the occurrence of such a skill, it is difficult to inhibit it.

Since automatization is a prominent characteristic of skilled activities ranging from reading to motor behavior to problem-solving routines, it is useful to investigate it to determine its characteristics. One task that has been studied extensively in this regard is the Stroop task (turn to p. 203 in the text for a full description of the task). The following three experiments are designed to demonstrate the basic Stroop effect and to extend it somewhat so that you can develop some intuitions about why it occurs.

EXPERIMENT 1

First, before performing Stroop's actual demonstration you should conduct a simple version of it that will provide some baseline data on the effectiveness of our ability to ignore irrelevant information (see Chapter 5, "Perception," for a full discussion of this ability). In this experiment subjects are required to name colors. (Use the insert for the stimulus in each of the following experiments.) In the control condition of the experiment the colors are simply displayed in patches. In the experimental condition the colors are presented by having randomly ordered letter strings, each string of a different color. The question is whether having the letters present interferes with a subject's ability to name the colors. In principle, if the subject is capable of selectively attending to color, having the letters present should not interfere with his color-naming performance. Thus, naming the colors of the letter strings should be as easy as naming the colors of the color patches. On the other hand, the extent to which the subject cannot ignore the letter information is the extent to which his performance in color naming will decline.

Your measure of ease of color naming will be the amount of time it takes a subject to name a string of fifteen colors. To obtain reliable data you should have the subject name the colors in five lists of color patches and in five lists of letter strings, alternating between the two kinds of lists (see the number below each list).* The procedure is as follows: Cut out the ten lists of stimuli for experiment 1. On each trial have the appropriate list in front of the subject turned over so that he cannot see the stimuli (see book insert for these lists). Then read the following instructions:

> When I say "go," turn over the list in front of you and name the colors in the list from top to bottom. There will be fifteen colors total. Name these colors as fast but as accurately as possible. After you have named the last color, say "stop!" We will do this with ten different lists. Five have the colors printed in patches of ink, the other five have the colors printed in strings of randomly arranged letters. You should *ignore* how the colors are presented and simply name them. Any questions?

You should keep time from when you say "go" until when the subject says "stop." Make sure to present

the ten lists in the order indicated by the number under the list. Record the time elapsed for each list and the number of errors for each list in the spaces provided on the report sheet.

Average the times for each type of list and total the errors. Does it appear that there is a difference between the average naming time or the total number of errors comparing the two types of lists? How would you interpret the data?

EXPERIMENT 2

In this experiment you are going to duplicate Stroop's demonstration. In the previous experiment you probably found either no effect or a very small effect of list type. The question we now ask is: Are there any conditions under which the subject cannot selectively attend well? In this experiment we have constructed such a condition by having the letters in the experimental condition spell color words themselves. Subjects are still required to name the color of the word, not what it spells, but now the name of what it spells is itself going to be a color name. If selective attention is not very effective, these names should interfere with the subject's response and slow him down relative to a control condition that has neutral (noncolor) words printed in color.

Follow the same procedure as before, but read the following set of instructions:

> In this experiment you are going to perform the same task as in the previous experiment. This time, however, the ink colors will be printed in the form of words. For half the lists, the words will be randomly chosen. For the other half, they will be color words. In both lists, however, you are to ignore the meaning of the words themselves and simply name the colors in which they are printed from the top to the bottom of each list. Remember that you should be as fast and as accurate as possible. Don't turn over each list until I say "go," and when you have finished be sure to say "stop!"

When you record the data, keep track of both the time to read the list and the number of errors made. Average the time and errors for each type of list. Is the difference in average time and total errors between list types greater than the difference found in experiment 1? How would you interpret this?

EXPERIMENT 3

Now we will try a somewhat more subtle version of the Stroop experiment to get a better idea of the extent to which the subject can selectively attend. In the experimental condition, the words printed in color

---

*Notice that the two types of lists are matched for the length of the stimulus. That is, the color patches of lists 1, 3, 5, 7, and 9 are matched in length to the letter strings of length 2, 4, 6, 8, and 10. Why is this an important control? How have the lists of experiments 2 and 3 been matched? Why?

represent nouns whose referents themselves have a characteristic color (this color is never the same as the color in which the word is written). If the word suggests the characteristic color of its referent to the subject, this color might interfere with naming the color in which the word is printed (Majeres, 1974).

Follow the same procedure as in experiments 1 and 2, but read the following instructions to the subject:

In this experiment you are going to perform the same task as in the previous experiments; that is, you will be naming colors. This time the ink colors will be printed in the form of words that themselves are not colors. For example, one of the lists might contain the word "stove" printed in green ink. Disregard the word that is present and simply name the ink color of each word in the list. Remember that you should not turn over the list until I say "go," you should name the colors as quickly as possible, and you should say "stop" when you are done.

Conduct this experiment as you did the others. Is there a difference in performance between the lists? Is it larger or smaller than in experiment 2? What does this suggest about selective attention? What does it suggest about the automaticity of the reading process? *(If your instructor collects the data, fill out the report sheet in Appendix B.)*

References

Stroop, J. R. 1935. Studies of interference in serial verbal reactions. *Journal of Experimental Psychology* (18): 643–62.

Majeres, R. L. 1974. The combined effects of stimulus and response conditions on the delay in identifying the print color of words. *Journal of Experimental Psychology* (102): 868–74.

Language

Learning Objectives

MAJOR PROPERTIES OF HUMAN LANGUAGE

Language is creative
1. Describe some everyday phenomena that undermine the view that language is a habit.

Language is structured
2. Explain the difference between descriptive rules and prescriptive rules of language.

Language is meaningful
3. Know whether a grammatical pattern is always related to the meaning of words. Why or why not?

Language is referential
4. Understand why reference is a critical feature of language.

Language is interpersonal
5. Give examples of how an unspoken principle of conversation can make communication successful in two separate social situations.

THE STRUCTURE OF LANGUAGE

Phonemes
6. List the major hierarchical levels of linguistic structures.
7. Define phoneme. Give examples.
8. Know whether phonemes are combined haphazardly. Give examples to support your answer.

Morphemes and words
9. Define morpheme. Give examples.
10. Be able to explain how morphemes are combined.

Phrases and sentences
11. Define syntax.

THE LINGUISTIC HIERARCHY AND MEANING

12. Explain the human ability to deal with the infinite number of items in any language.

The meaning of words
13. Define semantics.
14. Be prepared to argue why meaning is not the same as reference.
15. Know how word meanings are stored in memory, according to the definitional theory.
16. Offer convincing evidence for the prototype theory, and explain how this theory differs from the definitional theory.
17. Know what a family resemblance structure is.

Organizing words into meaningful sentences
18. Explain how phrase structure is related to meaning.
19. Name the two main types of phrases.
20. Describe how linguists represent phrase structure.

THE GROWTH OF LANGUAGE IN THE CHILD

The problem of language learning
21. Name some of the problems of the language learner and some of the factors that play an important part in language learning.

Is language learning the acquisition of a skill?
22. Explain why imitation is insufficient to account for either sentence or word acquisition.
23. Characterize the kinds of speech corrections that children often receive. What false hypothesis about language learning can be derived from observing speech corrections?

LANGUAGE DEVELOPMENT

The social origins of language

24. Characterize the verbal behavior of the pre-linguistic child.

Infants' discovery of the phonemes

25. Initially, infants are capable of responding to all sound distinctions made in any language. Know what change occurs in the later stages of language learning. Describe how the habituation paradigm is used to reveal this developmental change.

The one-word speaker

26. List the kinds of words that children learn first, and the kinds of words children rarely learn first. Why?

27. Relate theories of children's word meaning to comparable theories of adults' word meaning.

28. Cite two common problems for the language learner who is trying to comprehend the meaning of a word.

29. Describe the selective looking experiment and its use in answering this question: Can propositions be conveyed by the child's single words?

The two-word (telegraphic) speaker

30. Describe the changes in language that take place around two years of age.

31. Know how words are ordered in two-word speech. What is the underlying propositional structure of this speech?

Later stages of language learning: syntax

32. Know what typical language errors are made by a two-and-a-half year old and what these errors indicate about the structure of language.

Further stages of language learning: word meaning

33. Given what you've learned about syntax, suggest some explanations for children's remarkably rapid learning of language.

34. Explain the categorization bias held by most language learners. What evidence helps psychologists to observe this bias?

35. Describe how children use their growing knowledge of word classes and semantics to interpret a word meaning.

LANGUAGE LEARNING IN CHANGED ENVIRONMENTS

36. Cite the characteristic about the course of language acquisition which suggests that it is a biological process.

Wild children

37. Offer arguments for the nature-nurture controversy from data about wild children.

Isolated children

38. Offer arguments for the nature-nurture controversy from data about isolated children.

Language without sound

39. Describe the characteristics of American Sign Language (ASL). Why is this an important example of language from a theoretical point of view?

Language without a model

40. Describe the language-learner studies with deaf children of hearing parents. What do the results imply?

Children deprived of access to some of the meanings

41. Theoretically, blind children should learn sentence meanings more slowly than sighted children because blind children are cut off from opportunities to observe word referents. Nevertheless, evidence shows that the rate of language acquisition is not significantly different. Explain this finding, and relate it to what you have learned about categorization.

The case of Helen Keller

42. If isolated from language forms, a human infant begins to invent her own language. Describe how Helen Keller and Anne Sullivan invented language. Which characteristics of communication were carefully developed by Sullivan?

LANGUAGE LEARNING WITH CHANGED ENDOWMENTS

The critical period hypothesis

43. Summarize the evidence that points out the importance of critical periods in language learning.

44. Describe the initial difference between young learners of a second language and old learners. How does this difference change over time?

45. Explain how age relates to achieving native-level fluency.

46. Know whether there is general evidence to support the idea that "You can't teach an old dog new tricks."

Language in nonhumans

47. Compare vocabulary learning in chimpanzees and humans. Which method works best to teach chimpanzees vocabulary?

48. Describe the evidence that suggests the use of primitive propositions by chimpanzees.

49. Cite evidence that has suggested early syntax acquisition in chimpanzees. Be able to evaluate the quality of this evidence.

50. If we say that trained chimpanzees use language, know what we must exclude from our definition of language.

LANGUAGE AND ITS LEARNING

51. Evidence suggests that language acquisition is a complex interaction of the child's innate capabilities, the social, cognitive, and specifically linguistic supports in the child's environment. Give examples of how each factor plays a role in learning language.

Programmed Exercises

MAJOR PROPERTIES OF HUMAN LANGUAGE

1. There are about _____ human languages now in use on earth.

   4,000

2. Although animal and human languages are similar in that both have sounds and words (or something like words), animal

   languages do not have _____ .

   sentences

3. We are able to make up novel sentences at will. This tells us

   that language is _____ .

   creative

4. An estimate of the number of English sentences that are twenty

   words or fewer is _____ .

   10^{30}

5. A rule such as "it is not correct to say ain't" is a _____ rule.

   prescriptive

6. Each _____ in a language expresses a meaningful idea or concept.

   word

7. We are able to understand which words refer to which things, scenes, and events in the world. This tells us that language is

   _____ .

   referential

8. A communicating pair takes the utterance and its context as the basis for making a series of complicated inferences about the meaning

   of a conversation. This tells us that language is _____ .

   interpersonal

THE STRUCTURE OF LANGUAGE

9. We can think of language as existing at a number of levels, from

   sounds to ideas. The structure of language, then, is _____ .

   hierarchical

10. The spoken words *bed* and *dead* differ only in the "b" and "d"

    sounds at the beginning. This is a difference in one _____ .

    phoneme

11. English uses about _____ speech sounds.

    forty

12. Some of the facts about how phonemes combine in words are

    accidental choices. Others are _____ choices.

    systematic

13. Morphemes are the smallest language units that carry _____ .

    meaning

14. "Strange," "er," and "s" are all _____ .

    morphemes

15. The system by which we combine words into meaningful

    sentences is known as _____ .

    syntax

16. An organized grouping of words is known as a _____ , the   phrase
    unit from which sentences are composed.

THE LINGUISTIC HIERARCHY AND MEANING

17. The fact that _____ of units exists at each level of the   organization
    hierarchy enables us to generalize what we know about con-
    structing sentences.

18. An old (and insufficient) view of word and phrase meaning is
    that meaning is whatever a word or phrase points to in the real

    world. This view equates meaning and _____ .   reference

19. Another theory says that the meaning of a word is synonymous

    with a list of characteristics, or _____ . This theory of   features

    meaning is called the _____ theory.   definitional

20. The _____ theory of meaning is similar to the feature theory,   prototype
    except that no one feature is necessary or sufficient. Instead, a
    whole group of features may be present. This theory accounts
    nicely for the fact that certain words are better examples of their
    respective categories than other words.

21. Words are related through groups of features shared unequally among

    word meanings. This concept is termed the _____ _____   family resemblance
    structure.

22. When we say, "The girl climbed the tree," "climbed the tree" is

    the _____ of the sentence, and "the girl" is the _____ .   predicatc, subject

23. A tree structure of phrases and words is referred to as a

    _____ _____ _____ of a sentence.   phrase structure description

24. In the sentence, "The boy saw the ice cream truck," the phrase

    "the boy" is called the _____ phrase.   noun

25. A _____ _____ is a useful way of partitioning a sentence   tree diagram
    to show its hierarchical structure.

THE GROWTH OF LANGUAGE IN THE CHILD

26. Language learning by _____ is not a sufficient explanation,   imitation
    since children often speak novel sentences.

27. _____ cannot account for language learning, since it is   Reinforcement
    impossible for the child to know what parts of a sentence are
    being praised.

28. _____ cannot account for language learning, since grammati-   Correction
    cal errors are seldom successfully changed by parents.

LANGUAGE DEVELOPMENT

29. Childish sounds that make no real sense, but often sound like

    real words, are called _____ .   babbles

30. Speech production is preceded by __ ____ interactions such as   social (interpersonal)
    looks, gestures, and caresses.

31. Although infants can respond to all sound distinctions made in

    any language, they learn to _____ the distinctions that don't   ignore
    matter in their language.

32. Two-word speech is known as _____ speech.   telegraphic

33. Even though children utter only two-word sequences at one stage
    in their acquisition of language, there is reason to believe that

    they have _____ parts to their propositional ideas.   three

34. After a child learns that the past tense of verbs *play* and *walk*
    are *played* and *walked*, *runned* may be given as the past tense of
    run although *ran* was previously used. This phenomenon is

    known as _____ .   overgeneralization

35. By two years old, the child seeks _____ rules that operate   general
    over the whole vocabulary or set of sentence structures.

LANGUAGE LEARNING IN CHANGED ENVIRONMENTS

36. Cases of wild children raised by animals were initially regarded

    as crucial cases for the _____ _____ controversy about   nature/nurture
    language development.

37. Evidence that language can develop without sound comes from

    studies of _____ children.   deaf

38. A widely used manual communication system among deaf people

    is _____ _____ _____ .   American Sign Language (ASL)

39. A biological _____ enables children to learn language basics,   predisposition
    whether they invent the basics themselves (if there is no language
    model) or follow the model that they are exposed to.

LANGUAGE LEARNING WITH CHANGED ENDOWMENTS

40. When language capacities are lost or diminished because of
    damage to a cerebral hemisphere (usually the left), this state is

    termed _____ .   aphasia

41. One hypothesis of language learning postulates an ideal time to
    learn languages, after which the learning process is significantly

    more difficult. This time is known as the _____ _____ .   critical period

42. In comparing adults with children, it is clear that _____ pick   children
    up a second language more quickly in the long run than

    _____ do.   adults

43. After having been taught ASL for four years, Washoe had learned

    _____ signs. Some of these were acquired by _____ ,   130, imitation
    others by having her hands physically molded into a desired
    position.

44. Premack's studies of the concept of _____ in chimpanzees   causation
    showed that they were quite successful in performing a task in
    which they were required to identify an object that could produce
    a change of state in another object.

45. Even if chimpanzees were shown to have some sense of _____ ,   sequence
    this would not be sufficient to claim that they have knowledge of
    syntax.

46. Studies with chimpanzees show that a precursor to language may

    be primitive _____ thought.   propositional

LANGUAGE AND ITS LEARNING

47. Language acquisition is a task combining the child's innate

    capacities as well as the _____ , _____ , and _____   social, cognitive, linguistic
    environment of the child.

Self-Test

1. A new group of people is discovered possessing a language that has never been studied before. After a good deal of work, linguists are able to translate anything said in this language into English. This is further evidence that all language:
   a. is unrelated.
   b. is similar in the ideas that can be expressed.
   c. uses the same sounds.
   d. uses the same words.

2. All of the following describe language use except:
   a. it is creative.
   b. it has a rule-governed structure.
   c. it is imitative.
   d. it is interpersonal.

3. The fact that there is an infinite number of sentences that can be uttered upon seeing a rabbit is an argument against the behaviorist position and demonstrates the _____ of language.
   a. uncertainty
   b. variability
   c. creativity
   d. rigidity

4. The fact that the words *boys*, and *kiss*, and *girls*, can be arranged in different orders to give different meanings (i.e., "Boys kiss girls," "Girls kiss boys") demonstrates another universal characteristic of language. Language is:
   a. rule-governed.
   b. unpredictable.
   c. implicit.
   d. prototypical.

5. The rules of grammar that structure a language are called:
   a. features.
   b. morphemes.
   c. semantics.
   d. descriptive rules.

6. The actual speech acts that pass between people are merely hints about the thoughts being conveyed. Hidden from the observer are the unspoken, yet guiding:
   a. descriptions of conversation.
   b. principles of conversation.
   c. dialects.
   d. utterances.

7. When we say that language is hierarchical, we mean that:
   a. different language uses demonstrate social class differences.
   b. language structure exists at many levels.
   c. language has developed from other cognitive functions.
   d. modern languages are descended from other languages.

8. Which of the following represents the actual hierarchy of language structures?
   a. phrase, word, phoneme, morpheme
   b. word, morpheme, phrase, phoneme
   c. phoneme, morpheme, word, phrase
   d. morpheme, phoneme, word, phrase

9. The perceptual units of speech are:
   a. phonemes.
   b. morphemes.
   c. syllables.
   d. words.

10. One reason foreign languages sound strange is that:
    a. the same phonemes are pronounced differently.
    b. other languages are spoken more rapidly than English.
    c. there are fewer "gaps" in foreign languages than in English.
    d. some of the phonemes are different from those of English.

11. New words are being coined every day. Some sound combinations are not used, though. This is due to _____ rules.
    a. syntactic
    b. semantic
    c. pragmatic
    d. none of the above

12. A morpheme is a:
    a. word.
    b. single sound.
    c. perceptual unit.
    d. unit of meaning.

13. A phrase is:
    a. several sentences put together.
    b. unrelated to the meaning of the sentence.
    c. an organized group of words.
    d. always delineated by grammatical markings.

14. What makes possible the understanding of infinite items in a language?
    a. human memory alone
    b. the organization of units and patterns
    c. Psychologists and neurolinguists cannot agree on what makes it possible.
    d. It is not possible for humans.

15. The area of knowledge dealing solely with meaning is called:
    a. linguistics.
    b. semantics.
    c. phonetics.
    d. none of the above

16. A view of meaning as simply referring to objects in the world is not sufficient, since:
    a. the same object can be referred to in more than one way.
    b. it's difficult to describe the reference of words like *truth*.
    c. both of the above
    d. none of the above

17. The definitional theory attempts to define the _____ attributes that define a given concept.
    a. necessary
    b. sufficient
    c. both of the above
    d. none of the above

18. One problem with the definitional theory is that:
    a. some attributes are used to describe more than one concept.
    b. some concepts involve more than one attribute.
    c. some concepts have no attributes.
    d. some members of a category seem to be better examples of that category than other members.

19. The major characteristic of a prototype theory of meaning is that:
    a. no feature is individually necessary.
    b. no feature is individually sufficient.
    c. a whole set of features describes word meaning.
    d. all of the above

20. A robin will be judged to be an exemplary member of the bird family because:
    a. it has wings.
    b. it has feathers.
    c. the robin is close to the presumed prototype of a bird.
    d. a robin is more like a bird than an ostrich.

21. A family resemblance structure is an analogy to support which theory?
    a. prototype
    b. definitional
    c. interpersonal
    d. language attribution

22. Sentence meanings are often called:
    a. propositions.
    b. predicates.
    c. syntax.
    d. phonemes.

23. A two-branch tree diagram of a sentence structure would include these parts:
    a. principle rules and prescriptive rules.
    b. verb phrase and noun phrase.
    c. morphemes and phonemes.
    d. syntax and verb phrases.

24. Which of the following can be used to explain first-language learning?
    a. imitation
    b. reinforcement
    c. correction
    d. none of the above

25. All of the following are forms of preverbal communication *except*:
    a. crawling.
    b. babbling.
    c. gesturing.
    d. touching.

26. Which of the following statements is true about sound discrimination in early language learning?
    a. Initially infants respond only to the sounds of their own language.
    b. Initially infants respond to all sounds in all languages.
    c. Initially infants cannot respond to sound

distinctions at all.

d. Initially infants respond only to the most common sound distinctions of their own language.

27. Two-word speech is known as _____ speech.
   a. functor
   b. telegraphic
   c. syntactic
   d. propositional

28. By two-and-a-half years of age knowledge of _____ begins to develop.
   a. language
   b. propositions
   c. syntax
   d. synapses

29. The use of a word form like "sitted" by a child is known as:
   a. telegraphic.
   b. undergeneralization.
   c. overgeneralization.
   d. syntactics.

30. Children are disposed to organize the world into broad:
   a. categories.
   b. syntax.
   c. phrases.
   d. ideas.

31. Which statement(s) describe(s) how children learn language?
   a. They use the forms of new words as clues to their meanings.
   b. They use their knowledge of words to predict their forms.
   c. They use their knowledge of sentence structure to plug in new words.
   d. all of the above

32. Evidence from wild children reveals that:
   a. some can be rehabilitated so as to use language without problems.
   b. some can learn to speak a few words.
   c. all can learn to speak a few words.
   d. none of the above

33. Language development does not depend on hearing language, as evidenced by:
   a. wild children.
   b. deaf signers of American Sign Language (ASL).
   c. isolated children.
   d. retarded children.

34. Deaf children whose parents did not teach them sign language demonstrated language development similar to that of normal language in that:

a. the children went through one-word speech, two-word speech, etc.
b. they began by pointing to "action objects," and only later "talking" about things like "walls".
c. they eventually put signs together to form sentences.
d. all of the above

35. The following individuals were deprived of exposure to language since birth. Which one has the best chance of learning to speak?
   a. an eight-year-old girl
   b. a fourteen-year-old boy
   c. a twenty-year-old man
   d. a thirty-year-old woman

36. Helen Keller's experience is an example of how when human infants are isolated from language forms, they will:
   a. become incommunicative until adolescence.
   b. need to be taught how to think.
   c. begin to invent their own language.
   d. become permanently uncommunicative.

37. The loss of language function is known as:
   a. aphasia.
   b. anorexia.
   c. asphyxia.
   d. aphaeresis.

38. The speech disorder characterized by loss of content words is often due to damage in:
   a. Broca's area.
   b. Washoe's area.
   c. Wernicke's area.
   d. none of the above

39. First-language learning, second-language learning, and recovery from aphasia may depend on:
   a. intelligence.
   b. the particular language involved.
   c. generalization.
   d. the critical period.

40. When Washoe teaches some of her human signs to an adopted chimpanzee baby, it is an example of:
   a. cultural transmission.
   b. language acquisition among chimpanzees.
   c. syntax.
   d. both a and b

41. Language in chimpanzees:
   a. seems to involve propositions.
   b. uses a hierarchical structure.
   c. approaches the complexity of human language.
   d. progresses at about the same rate as for children.

42. Some linguists argue that chimpanzees are held back by their lack of understanding of basic:
    a. syntax.
    b. vocabulary.
    c. intonation.
    d. words.

43. The nature of human language can be described by which following statement(s)?
    a. Fundamentally, languages are the same all over the world.
    b. All languages consist of a hierarchy of sentences.
    c. Language can flourish in virtually any exposure condition.
    d. all of the above

Answer Key for Self-Test

1. b p. 225	23. b pp. 235–36
2. c p. 226	24. d p. 238
3. c p. 227	25. a p. 239
4. a p. 227	26. b p. 239
5. d p. 227	27. b p. 242
6. b p. 228	28. c p. 243
7. b p. 229	29. c p. 244
8. c pp. 229–31	30. a p. 244
9. a p. 229	31. d pp. 244–45
10. d pp. 229–30	32. b p. 246
11. d p. 230	33. b p. 247
12. d p. 230	34. d p. 248
13. c p. 231	35. a p. 246
14. b p. 232	36. c p. 251
15. b p. 232	37. a p. 251
16. c p. 232	38. c p. 251
17. c p. 233	39. d pp. 251–53
18. d p. 233	40. a p. 254
19. d p. 234	41. a p. 254
20. c p. 234	42. a p. 255
21. a p. 234	43. d pp. 255–56
22. a p. 235	

Investigating Psychological Phenomena

IMPLICIT LEARNING

Equipment: A stopwatch or a watch that indicates seconds, index cards
Number of subjects: One
Time per subject: Thirty minutes
Time for experimenter: Forty minutes

One of the most impressive aspects of language is its acquisition: Children learn an enormous amount about their language without ever being explicitly taught. Consider syntax, for instance. Not until children have already learned a substantial number of syntactic rules do parents correct syntactic constructions that their children use. Somehow the growing child manages to induce the syntactic rules of language from the variety of utterances that he or she happens to encounter. This ability to induce complex rules from examples is an ability that we use all the time, but its use without intention, or even awareness, and with complex linguistic construction is what makes it impressive as a characteristic of language acquisition. Having just learned about language acquisition, you can now begin to appreciate how complex the language-learning process must be, especially since it is largely mediated by implicit induction.

You can demonstrate this implicit induction process using the following experiment modeled after one by Arthur Reber (1967). There are two phases to the experiment. In the first place, your subject will memorize a series of strings of letters after being told only that he is a subject in a memory experiment. In the second phase, the subject will be told that the letter strings from the first phase were constructed using a rule. Then the subject will be shown twenty-four new strings that he has never seen before and asked to judge which twelve of these were constructed from the same rule used in phase 1. If the subject correctly categorized more of these twenty-four strings than we would expect by chance alone (twelve by chance, since there are only two responses the subject can make), then we can conclude that the subject has learned something about the rule even though he wasn't trying to in phase 1.

PHASE 1

Instruct your subject as follows:

"This experiment concerns memory for unmeaningful material. You will be presented with twenty strings of letters that you must memorize and recall. These strings of letters will be presented in groups of four which you can study for fifteen seconds. Then the groups will be taken away and you will be required to recall all four strings (in any order). Following this you will be presented with the same strings again for another fifteen-second study period. This will be followed by another recall attempt. In all, each of the five groups of strings will be presented five times each for study and recall."

The stimulus materials for this first phase are at the end of this section. Write each of the five lists of strings on index cards and present them to the subject individually. Provide the subject with twenty slips of paper on each of which he can write the recall for one quadruplet of strings. Be sure to remove each recall attempt before showing the next repetition of a set of strings or before going on to a new set of strings.

PHASE 2

Instructions:

"The strings of letters were constructed according to a rule. The rule dictated the orders in which letters were allowed to follow one another. In the second phase you will be shown twenty-four new strings of letters, and you must decide for each one whether it was or was not constructed according to the same rule for the letter strings in phase 1. When you decide, you should place your answer in the appropriate place on the answer sheet."

Score the subject's answers after he has completed phase 2, using the answer key provided. Did he do better than chance? Ask him whether he has any guesses about what the rule is. You will probably be surprised to discover how little the subject appears to be aware of the rule even though he can use it (in some sense) to make judgments about individual instances.

A diagrammatic representation of the rule is shown below. It works as follows: If you begin at "start" and trace through the diagram along any path in the direction of the arrows, you can get to "end." By noting the order of the letters that you pass along the way, you can construct a string. Notice that because of loops, some strings may be quite long but still permissible according to the rule.

Think about some of the following issues: In what way does this experiment mimic language learning? In what way is language learning different? As a model of language learning, why was it important not to tell subjects about the rule until the end of phase 1? What do the results suggest about language learning?

Reference

Reber, A. S. 1967. Implicit learning of artificial grammars, *Journal of Verbal Learning and Verbal Behavior* (6): 855–63.

PHASE 1: STIMULUS LISTS

(Write these on index cards or pieces of paper for presentation to the subject.)

List 1	List 2	List 3	List 4	List 5
VVTRXRR	VVRXRR	VTRRR	VVTRXR	XMVTRX
XMVTTRX	XXRR	XMVRXRR	VTRR	XMTRRRR
XMVRXR	VVRMVRX	VVTTRMT	VVRMTRR	XMVRX
VVTRX	XMVRMT	VVRMTR	XMVTRMT	XXRRR

PHASE 2: LIST OF ALTERNATIVES FOR RECOGNITION TEST

(Write these on index cards as well.)

1. RXTTVMXR		13. VVTTRX
2. XMTR		14. VVRX
3. MXXR		15. VVRRTX
4. XMVRXRRR		16. MT
5. VVRXR		17. VVTRMVRX
6. VTTX		18. VM
7. MVTTTXVR		19. XXR
8. XX		20. XMT
9. VRT		21. RXTMV
10. VVTTTRX		22. XXM
11. TTV		23. TTRXXM
12. VT		24. VTR

RECOGNITION TEST REPORT SHEET

(You can find this report sheet in Appendix B; cut it out and give it to the subject.)

ANSWERS

1. no	9. no	17. yes
2. yes	10. yes	18. no
3. no	11. no	19. yes
4. yes	12. yes	20. yes
5. yes	13. yes	21. no
6. no	14. yes	22. no
7. no	15. no	23. no
8. yes	16. no	24. yes

RULE FOR LETTER-STRING CONSTRUCTION

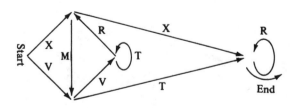

CHAPTER 9

The Biological Basis of Social Behavior

Learning Objectives

THE SOCIAL NATURE OF HUMANS AND ANIMALS

1. Explain Hobbes's conception of human nature.

   Natural selection and survival
2. Outline the basic principles of Darwin's theory of evolution.
3. Distinguish personal from genetic survival, and indicate the role of sexual competition in the latter.
4. Know whether natural selection operates on behavior as well as on physical traits.
5. Know whether humans are an inherently social species and whether Darwin's theory of evolution explains this.

   Built-in social behaviors
6. Describe the basic principles of ethology, including the concepts of display, fixed-action patterns, and releasers.
7. Define sociobiology.

BIOLOGICAL SOURCES OF AGGRESSION

   Conflict between species: Predation and defense
8. Explain whether aggression is a component of predatory attack.
9. Discuss whether it is fair to describe much of aggressive behavior between different species as defensive.

   Conflicts between like and like
10. Discuss the relation between testosterone and aggression.
11. Discuss the nature and function of territory.
12. Explain mechanisms for limiting aggression in humans and in animals.
13. Define dominance hierarchies and explain their functions.
14. Be able to discuss whether humans are territorial.

THE BIOLOGICAL BASIS OF LOVE: THE MALE-FEMALE BOND

15. Define bonding, and explain the role of grooming in primates in cementing relationships.

   Sexual behavior
16. Understand what the selective advantage of sexual reproduction is.

   Sexual choice
17. Describe the nature and function of courtship rituals.
18. Discuss the evolutionary origin of displays, and indicate how the comparative method helps to discover this.
19. Explain why the female is generally choosier in mate selection than the male.
20. Discuss the adaptive value and means of synchronizing male and female reproductive behavior. Explain why it is said that the human female is emancipated from hormonal control.

   Evolution and mating systems
21. Define polygyny, polyandry, and monogamy. Explain why most bird species are monogamous, while most mammal species are polygamous.
22. Understand the relation between polygyny and sexual dimorphism.

23. Give the sociobiological explanation of the pre-dominance of polygyny in human cultures and the widespread tendency of men to be more interested in multiple sexual partners than women. Give the culturally oriented rejoinder to the sociobiological explanation.

THE BIOLOGICAL BASIS OF LOVE: THE PARENT-CHILD BOND

The infant's attachment to the mother

24. Know to what extent the child's love for the mother is explained by the fact that the mother fulfills the child's basic biological needs.

The mother's attachment to the infant

25. Describe the function of maternal attachment.
26. List the characteristics of the infant that are important in establishing maternal attachment.

COMMUNICATING MOTIVES

Expressive movements: animal display

27. Describe the role of displays in communication.

Why are displays sometimes called expressive movements?

The expression of emotions in humans

28. Review the evidence for human facial expressions as products of both biology and culture.

SELF-SACRIFICE AND ALTRUISM

Altruism in animals

29. Explain how self-sacrifice (altruism) is consistent with evolutionary theory.
30. Distinguish among enlightened self-interest, kin selection, and reciprocal altruism as accounts for altruistic behavior.

Altruism in humans

31. Discuss sociobiological accounts of altruism in humans and the criticism of this approach.

ETHOLOGY AND HUMAN NATURE

32. Indicate the extent to which human social behavior can be explained in biological terms.

Programmed Exercises

THE SOCIAL NATURE OF HUMANS AND ANIMALS

1. The view that man is an inherently solitary creature, who invents society as a means of taming his brutish nature, is associated

   with the British philosopher _Hobbes_ .   (Thomas) Hobbes

2. According to Darwin, evolution proceeds because variants of a species with superior characteristics are more likely to survive.

   This process is called _natural selection_   natural selection

3. Essentially, natural selection is not about literal survival, or

   personal survival, but about reproductive success, which   personal

   amounts to _genetic_ survival. The latter leads to selection of   genetic

   traits that produce an advantage in _sexual_ competition.   sexual

4. Those characteristics that confer survival and reproductive

   advantage are considered to have high _adaptive value_ .   adaptive value

5. The branch of biology that studies animal behavior, particularly under natural conditions and within an evolutionary framework,

   is called _ethology_ . It focuses on _species_-specific behavior.   ethology, species

6. Stereotyped, species-specific movements are called

   fixed - action patterns   fixed-action patterns

7. When a female stickleback enters a nest, the male prods her rhythmically at the base of her tail. This action causes the female to deposit her eggs, a species-specific response. We can term

such prodding a _releasing stimulus_   releasing stimulus

8. Since this prodding stimulus is a product of the male's behavior,

   it can also be called a _display_ .   display

9. _Sociobi_ is a branch of biology that emphasizes the evolutionary   Sociobiology
   basis of social behavior.

THE BIOLOGICAL SOURCES OF AGGRESSION

10. An attack by a lion on a zebra seems qualitatively different from
    a fight or threat sequence between two members of the same

    species. We call the former _predator_ and the latter _aggressiveness_   predation, aggression

11. The generally higher level of aggression seen in males of most
    species has been attributed to higher levels of the male hormone

    testosterone (male hormone)   testosterone

12. Animals often defend a particular area against other members of
    their species. This area probably serves to guarantee them

    essential _resources_ and is called a _territoriality (territory)_   resources, territory

13. Animals limit aggression by making ritualized communications,

    called _threat displays_   threat displays

14. One mechanism for limiting aggression involves a display that
    essentially indicates "surrender." Such a display is called an

    appeasement signal.   appeasement signal

15. In a _dominance hierarchy_, a group of animals of the same   dominance hierarchy
    species develops a stable social order based on the establishment
    of ranks as a result of mutual aggressive encounters.

16. A person walks up to a stranger, approaching her until their
    bodies are just inches apart. This can be considered a violation

    of _personal space_ .   personal space

THE BIOLOGICAL BASIS OF LOVE: THE MALE-FEMALE BOND

17. The tendency to affiliate with others of one's own kind is called

    bonding .   bonding

18. This is accomplished in some animals, such as monkeys, by
    activities including caring for the fur of another member of the

    species. This activity is called _grooming_   grooming

19. In sexual reproduction, the _ovum_ and _sperm_ unite to   sperm, ovum

    produce the fertilized egg, or _zygote_.   zygote

20. The rooster's comb, the stag's antlers, and possibly the enlarged breast

    of the human female are all instances of structural _displays_   displays

21. The relatively complex behavior patterns that constitute sexual

    displays in many animals are called _courtship rituals_   courtship rituals

22. Courtship rituals indicate both the animal's _intention_ and _species_.   intentions, species

23. In most species the _female_ (male or female) has the major
role in "deciding" whether or not to mate.

female

24. Except for primates, mammals mate only when the female is in
"heat" or _estrus_.

estrus

25. Implantations of male hormones, that is, _androgens_, into the part
of the brain called the _hypothalamus_ can cause a castrated male
animal to show male sexual behavior.

androgens

hypothalamus

26. While the biological aspects of the human female reproductive
cycle are controlled by hormones, in the human female,
sexual activity is relatively independent of hormones.

sexual activity (sexual behavior)

27. In general, in terms of mating systems, bird species are
monogamous, whereas mammal species are _polygynous_.

monogamous, polygynous

28. There is usually more _sexual dimorphism_, that is, structural
differences between the sexes, in species that are _polygynous_

sexual dimorphism

polygynous

29. The sociobiological view predicts that, because of the lower
investment that male mammals have in any reproductive act, the
mating system of _polygyny_ will be more common than its
opposite, _polyandry_ and that males will seek more _variety_ in
sexual partners than will females.

polygyny

polyandry, variety

THE BIOLOGICAL BASIS OF LOVE: THE PARENT-CHILD BOND

30. The human infant's cry or the chirp of a newly hatched bird are
examples of _distress_ calls.

distress

31. The _smile_ is the human infant's built-in means of communicating with adults and maintaining their attention while indicating
a generally positive state.

smile

COMMUNICATING MOTIVES

32. The message of a display can be inferred by noting the _relation_
between the occurrence of the display and the animal's behavior
just before and after the occurrence.

correlation (relation)

33. Some prefer to describe displays as indications of an animal's
emotional state. In this respect, displays are referred to as
expressive movements

expressive movements

34. Human _facial expressions_ are displays that probably indicate
emotional states.

facial expressions

35. Although there are some variations across cultures, there seem to
be a number of _universal_ human facial expressions.

universal

SELF-SACRIFICE AND ALTRUISM

36. "Self-sacrifice" by a parent animal can be understood within an
evolutionary framework, since it may ultimately serve to increase

the number of the parent's _genes_ in the population. genes

37. When this (question 36) is accomplished by sparing the lives of

relatives, it is called _kin selection_ kin selection

38. "Unselfish" acts may also be adaptive because the recipients of these acts may later return the favor. This is called

reciprocal altruism reciprocal altruism

39. Edmund Wilson's view, that altruism in humans is based in our

genes, is part of the general position of _sociobiology_ sociobiology

40. The sociobiological view emphasizes genetic relatedness, or

kinship , in explaining altruism. kinship

ETHOLOGY AND HUMAN NATURE

41. Contrary to the position taken by Hobbes, it now seems clear

that the human organism is, in its biological nature, a _social_ social
creature.

Self-Test

1. Hobbes and Darwin agree that:
   a. natural selection is the key to understanding human nature.
   b. humans are basically solitary creatures.
   c. humans are basically destructive.
   d. humans enter a "social contract" to protect themselves from their brutish nature.
   e. none of the above

2. Animal A lives 10 years and has 6 offspring. Animal B lives 8 years and has 10 offspring. Therefore:
   a. A has greater personal, B has greater genetic survival.
   b. B has greater personal, A has greater genetic survival.
   c. B is more successful in sexual competition.
   d. A is more successful in sexual competition.
   e. a and c

3. The Darwinian principle of natural selection implies that:
   a. social behavior cannot be subject to evolution because it is not inherited.
   b. in the struggle to survive and reproduce, human beings are self-centered and solitary creatures restrained only by the constraints imposed by society.
   c. social or altruistic behavior may evolve only if it serves to increase the frequencies of the genes of the animal showing this behavior.
   d. coupled with the principles of ethology and

genetics, social and altruistic behavior will evolve as long as there is appropriate display or communication.
   e. a and b

4. Ethologists are particularly concerned with the study of:
   a. species-specific behavior.
   b. behavior in natural settings.
   c. social behavior.
   d. all of the above
   e. none of the above

5. Releasing stimulus : fixed-action pattern ::
   a. species-specific : general
   b. cause : effect
   c. learned : innate
   d. predation : aggression
   e. house : door

6. Sociobiology:
   a. is concerned with evolutionary explanations of behavior.
   b. claims a biological, evolutionary origin for some human social behavior.
   c. holds, along with ethology, that many behaviors have a genetic basis.
   d. all of the above
   e. none of the above

7. An observer notes that animal A, a male of a particular species, is, at a particular time, more aggressive than animal B. In an effort to increase the aggressiveness of animal B, the observer could:

a. introduce a dominant animal of the same species into B's environment.

b. inject B with any sex hormone in an appropriate dose.

c. place B in its own territory and arrange for another male to approach the territory border.

d. place B in the territory of another male.

e. limit B's resources and deprive B of the releasers it would normally encounter.

8. Aggressive encounters between members of the same species are often concerned with the establishment of:

a. mobbing.

b. predation.

c. appropriate defense mechanisms.

d. territories.

e. displays.

9. The adaptive value of territories is that they:

a. increase the aggressiveness of the territory holder.

b. preserve resources for the territory holder.

c. prevent threat displays.

d. decrease personal space and allow for greater reproduction.

e. c and d

10. The damage caused by aggressive encounters within a species is controlled by all but one of the following. Which of the alternatives is not a means of controlling aggression?

a. appeasement signals

b. displays

c. establishment of territories

d. imprinting

e. All of the above limit aggression.

11. Dominance hierarchies:

a. exist only in males.

b. are the basis of personal space.

c. confer reproductive advantages on those at the top.

d. guarantee equal distribution of resources.

e. increase aggressive encounters.

12. This picture illustrates one stage of:

a. predation.

b. defense.

c. feeding.

d. courtship.

e. contact comfort.

13. Courtship rituals serve all but one of the following purposes. Which of the items below is *not* a function of courtship rituals?

a. to synchronize the sexual activities of male and female

b. to attract members of the opposite sex

c. to increase the size of a territory

d. to identify the sex and sexual readiness of the partners

e. all of the above are functions of courtship rituals

14. To the extent that the male of a species spends time and energy in the care of the young, we would expect that:

a. he would be more selective about mating partners.

b. he would have higher levels of testosterone than expected.

c. he would show more structural sexual displays.

d. he would be less likely to have a territory.

e. he would show more appeasement signals.

15. During estrus, the female (nonprimate) mammal is:

a. secreting estrogen.

b. most receptive to sexual approach of males.

c. fertile.

d. all of the above

e. none of the above

16. In some species where the female has a clearly defined estrus cycle, the male is always ready for sexual activity. This would make sense if it were the case that in these species:

a. all females come into estrus at the same time.

b. estrus is dependent on the season.

c. estrus occurs throughout the year and females are not synchronized in their cycles.

d. a and b

e. hormonal factors are especially important in determining the receptivity of the female.

17. Which of the following features of human sexual behavior is shared most completely with other mammals?

a. the hormone independence of female receptivity

b. the existence of sexual displays

c. the importance of learning in the sexual

response
d. the persistence of sexual behavior following castration
e. b and d

18. Sociobiologists' predictions about male-female differences in mammalian mating systems and variety seeking in sexual partners are based on the fact that female mammals have a greater investment in reproduction because they:
a. carry the offspring during pregnancy.
b. take the greater responsibility for the early care of infants.
c. account for a greater part of the genetic material of their offspring.
d. all of the above
e. a and b

19. If you knew that in a particular species, the males sought more variety in sexual partners than did the females, you would guess that this species had a _____ mating system.
a. monogamous
b. polyandrous
c. polygynous
d. dimorphic
e. b or c

20. Features of the human infant, such as the upturned nose and chubby cheeks, are:
a. the stimuli through which we learn to recognize specific children.
b. the vehicles for the establishment of basic trust.
c. releasers of parental behavior.
d. instances of distress displays.
e. more common in monogamous cultures.

21. Expressive movements by animal A may inform other members of its species about:
a. its current motivation.
b. a motivational conflict that it is in.
c. how likely it is that it will behave in one way or another.
d. a and b
e. all of the above

22. Some claim that at least some human facial displays are innately linked to certain emotional states. Which of the following invalidate such a view?
a. Across many cultures, people seem to associate the same facial expressions with the same situations (emotions).
b. Blind children show some of the basic facial expressions in appropriate situations.
c. Deaf children show some of the appropriate facial expressions in some situations.

d. On some occasions, some people can mask the facial expression they would normally make under the circumstances.
e. none of the above

23. Consider a case in which an animal risks death from a predator by distracting it from the children of the animal's sister. Which of the possibilities listed below is a likely account of this "altruistic" behavior?
a. kin selection
b. reciprocal altruism
c. emancipation from hormonal control
d. all of the above
e. none of the above

24. Consider a different case, one in which animal A risks death from a predator by distracting the predator from another adult, B, of its species. And suppose that B is not related to A and, furthermore, that B is not a member of A's group and is only transiently in A's presence. This apparently altruistic act would be easily accounted for as:
a. kin selection.
b. reciprocal altruism.
c. emancipation from hormonal control.
d. a and b
e. none of the above

25. On a sociobiological (evolutionary and genetic) account, which of the following "altruistic" human acts would be most difficult to explain?
a. a man sacrificing his life to save four of his sister's children
b. a woman sacrificing her life to save four of her sister's children
c. a grandmother sacrificing her life to save one grandchild
d. a grandchild sacrificing his life to save one grandparent
e. a or c

26. Hobbes and the sociobiologists would agree that:
a. there is something that might be called basic (biological) human nature.
b. humans are inherently social.
c. any apparently unselfish act of humans is a result of culture and works against basic human nature.
d. humans are basically aggressive.
e. none of the above

Answer Key for Self-Test

Investigating Psychological Phenomena

PERSONAL SPACE: BEHAVIOR IN ELEVATORS

Equipment: A bank of at least two public elevators
Number of subjects: None
Time per subject: None
Time for experimenter: Thirty minutes to one hour

Whatever one's view of the precise way in which the basic phenomena of territoriality in animals are experienced in humans, it is clear that humans prefer to avoid close contact with strangers. Strangers interact at respectable distances, and one typically feels uncomfortable when a stranger approaches to within much less than a meter. Observations of this sort lead to the notion of personal space, a "territory" around the body. The distant spacing of students seated at libraries or riders on public transportation speaks to the same issue.

In this study we will attempt to gather direct evidence for the idea of personal space. To do so, we must find a common situation in which strangers find themselves in close confinement. Elevators seem particularly suited for this study.

Our study will be based on observations of where people stand in elevators. Given that an elevator already requires that all riders stand in close proximity, a personal space approach would certainly predict that *strangers* would maximize the distance between themselves. In order to test this idea, we will have to make some decisions about where, when, and how to make observations. (Although it would seem easy just to go and observe people in elevators, to do so without some thought, planning, and preliminary casual observation, would almost surely result in unreliable and not very meaningful data.)

What are the predictions? We must realize that elevators are typically asymmetrical: there is a door on one wall, and there is usually a button panel on one or both sides of the door. When people enter, they normally go to the panel to see if their floor has been pressed. Since it is likely that each person who gets on will go to the panel, it would be natural to maximize the distance from the panel in anticipation of the arrival of the next person. A personal space approach would also predict that strangers would not look at each other, but rather would tend to look straight ahead (toward the door) or up or down. On the basis of personal space, we would make the following predictions with respect to the positions in the schematic elevator diagrammed below.

1. In elevators with only one rider, the rider would usually stand along the back wall. In anticipation of a second rider, the first rider would be expected to stand in one back corner, thus leaving the other back corner for the second rider (and keeping both away from the button panels, which an additional rider would approach on entering). In terms of the schematic elevator layout on the next page, a single person should be located either in square 7 or square 9.

2. The second rider would be inclined to maximize distance from both the first rider and a potential third rider, who would be expected to approach the button panel(s) on entering the elevator. Therefore, in the schematic elevator layout below, two people should occupy squares 7 and 9. (Note: squares 7 and 6, 4 and 9, and 4 and 6 would also constitute reasonable distributions, but would not be as optimal as 7 and 9.)

1	2	3
4	5	6
7	8	9

Schematic elevator, divided into a 3 × 3 unit array. The door is at 2.

Conditions of observation: The observer cannot be on the elevator, as he would then be influencing the results. Therefore, observations must be made when an elevator arrives or departs and the door is open. Since people are likely to be leaving or entering, quick observation will be necessary at a stable moment: just as the doors open or just as they close. (If you are lucky enough to be near an office or other building with video security monitors for the elevators in the lobby, you can use the monitors to record the positions of people between floors.)

Personal space rules would not necessarily hold among friends and certainly not between lovers. Therefore, a fair test of personal space should eliminate any data including people who know each other well. To do this as best as possible, we will adopt two policies:

1. We will eliminate any observation (that is, the data collected from any particular elevator at a particular time) if any two people in the elevator are talking to one another or showing personal involvement in any way (e.g., holding hands).

2. We will try to make observations at places and at times when the number of people knowing each other well would be minimal. Ideal locations would be elevators in department stores or office buildings. Time would also be an important factor. We should avoid taking observations around the noon hour. (Why? Because it is very common to go out to lunch with friends, so the level of friend pairs or groups in elevators might be particularly high. This holds as well for people returning from lunch.)

Finally, precise conditions of measurement must be determined. Only record stable patterns: No one should be moving. Your critical time for observation is the moment before the doors close (it is harder to use the moment they open, because it is likely that a passenger intending to exit has moved toward the door as the elevator comes to his or her floor). If, at the time of departure, the elevator contains one or two people who have settled into position and if they do not appear to be friends (by the criteria above) then record their location on the data sheet. Assign each person to whichever of the nine squares best locates him or her.

To minimize data collection time, try to find a bank of elevators (at least two), and try to go at a time of moderate use, so you won't have to deal with infrequent or empty elevators. But don't use the lunch period, as discussed above. Normally the first floor is the natural place to make observations. But if you have a great deal of trouble with subjects moving in the elevator, you could go to another floor and push the call button, so that the elevator will stop on your floor. (The second floor would be best for these purposes. Why?)

Make sufficient observations so that you can get fifteen cases of elevators with one rider and fifteen of elevators with two riders. Indicate on the two data sheets the plan of the elevator, its location, and the time of day. Record one-person elevators on one data sheet and two-person elevators on the other.

When you have fifteen observations of each type, enter your data in the boxes in the table below. Do your data support the personal space theory? In order to help you make this evaluation, we have given you an indication of what would be statistically significant findings.

For the one-person elevator, there are nine possible positions. The theory predicts that one of two (positions 7 or 9) will be occupied. If people positioned themselves randomly in the elevator, we would expect them to be at 7 or 9 2/9 of the time, or for fifteen cases, $2/9 \times 15 = 3.3$ times (see table). By statistical calculations, we have determined that if there was actually an equal chance of someone's standing in any square, the chances of finding nine or more subjects out of fifteen in squares 7 or 9 is less than one in 100. This seems highly unlikely, so we would reject the idea that people stand randomly in the elevator and claim that the results supported the personal space hypothesis. These calculations are worked out in the table.

For the case of two people in the elevator, we have made similar calculations. It turns out that there are thirty-six different pairs of spaces that could be occupied in our 9-square elevator. The 7-9 combination is just one of them, and hence, if people were standing in random positions, there would only be one case in thirty-six where the 7-9 position was occupied. Therefore, the expected number of 7-9 locations in fifteen trials would be $15 \times 1/36 = 0.4$. A value of three or more people in this pair of locations would come about by chance less than one time in 100.

We can use one other measure with the two-person elevators. Personal space theory predicts, in general, that these people will stand far apart. We can translate this into the prediction that two people will not stand in boxes that are touching (even on the diagonal). Pairs 7-9, 4-6, 1-9 and others would meet this criterion. Altogether, of the thirty-six pairs of locations, twenty are touching (contiguous). Thus, we would expect that (since there are sixteen nontouching pairs), in $16/36 \times 15$ cases, we would expect people in nontouching pairs, assuming that people distributed themselves randomly. A score of twelve or more pairs in nontouching squares would come about less than one time in 100 by chance and would be evidence for the personal space hypothesis. (See calculations in table below.)

For comparison purposes, we have made measurements like those we asked you to make in this study. We took advantage of a special situation that allows unusually easy data collection. The data we present comes from elevators in an office building in New York City. In this building, there is a video security camera in the ceiling of each elevator. Therefore, we could watch the bank of video monitors and record the location of people. Furthermore, we could make the measurements between floors, so that there was no movement to or from the door. *(If your instructor collects the data, fill out the report sheet in Appendix B.)*

Analysis of Results

Elevator type	Location prediction	# in predicted place/Total	Expected random #	# significant*
1 person	7 or 9	□/15	3.3	9
2 person	7 and 9	□/15	0.4	3
New York data				
1 person	7 or 9	28/57	12.7	20
2 person	7 and 9	15/32	0.9	5
		# in noncontiguous squares/Total	Expected random #	# significant*
2 person	16 noncontiguous pairs out of 36 total pairs	□/15	6.7	12
New York data				
2 person	16 noncontiguous pairs out of 36 total pairs	31/32	14.2	21

*# significant means that one would expect this or a larger number of cases by chance no more than one time in one hundred.

Indicate panel location and other unusual features on diagram below.

Name _____ Location _____

1 Person in Elevator   Time _____

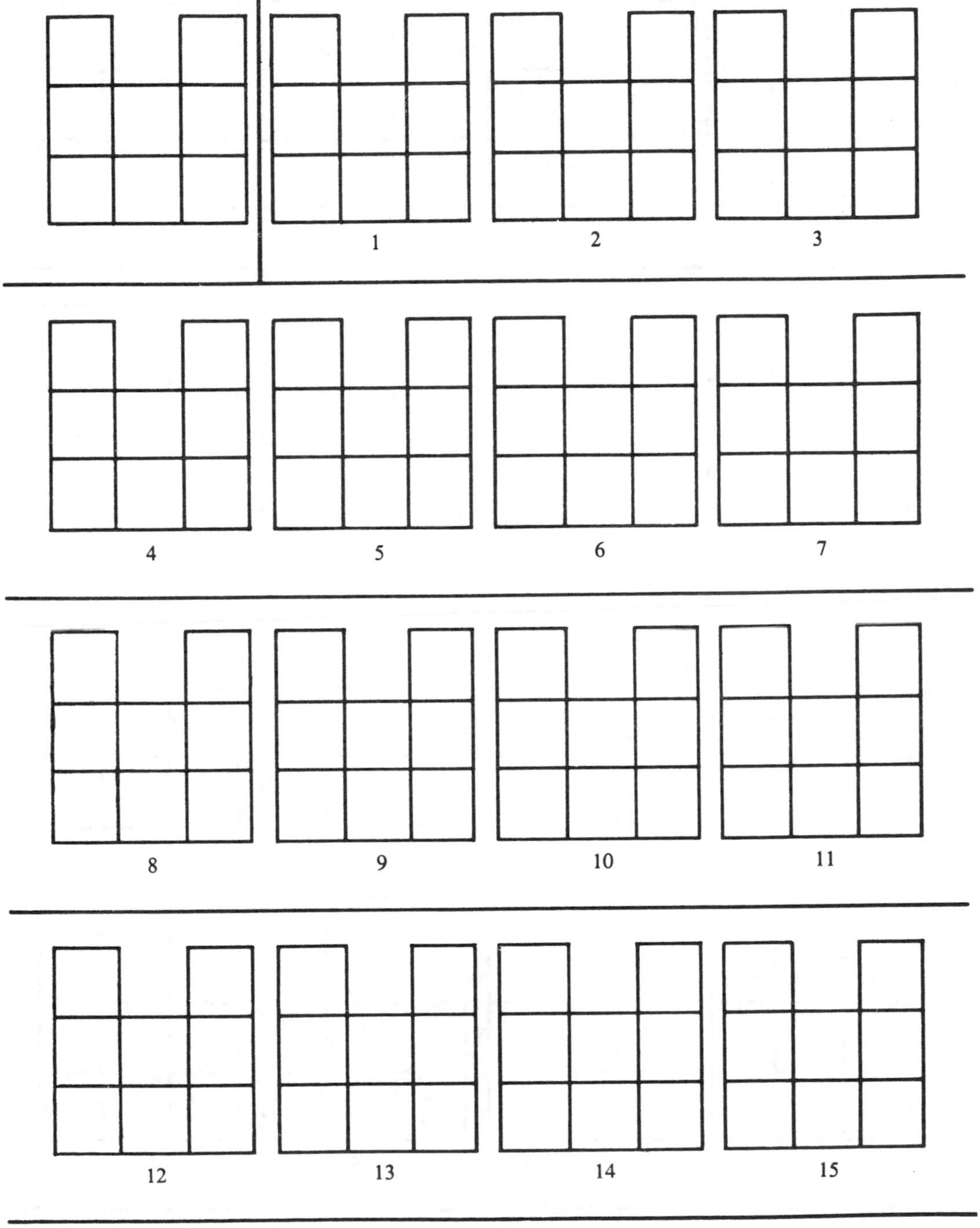

1   2   3

4   5   6   7

8   9   10   11

12   13   14   15

Indicate panel location and other unusual features on diagram below.

Name _____   Location _____

2 Persons in Elevator   Time _____

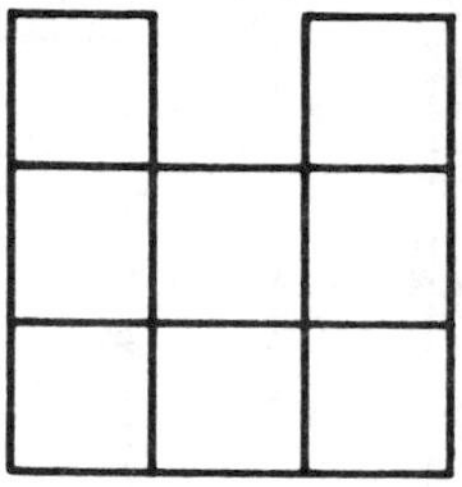

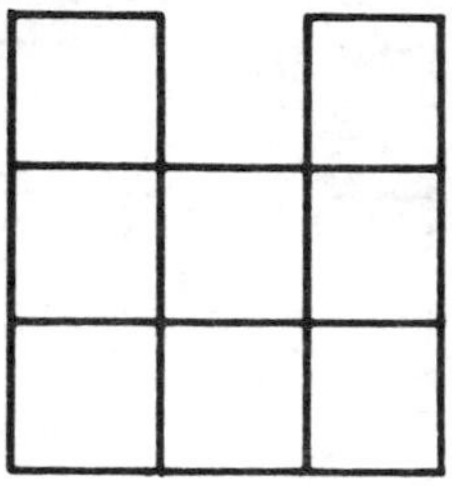

1

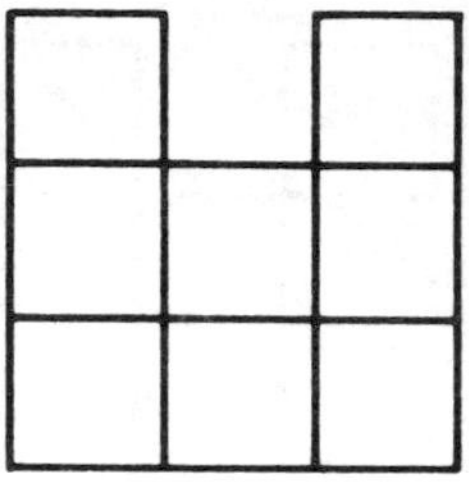

2

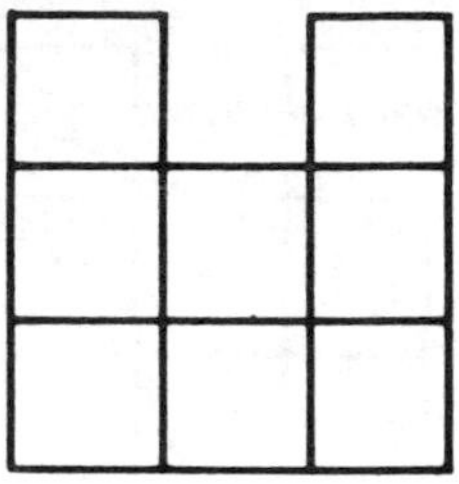

3

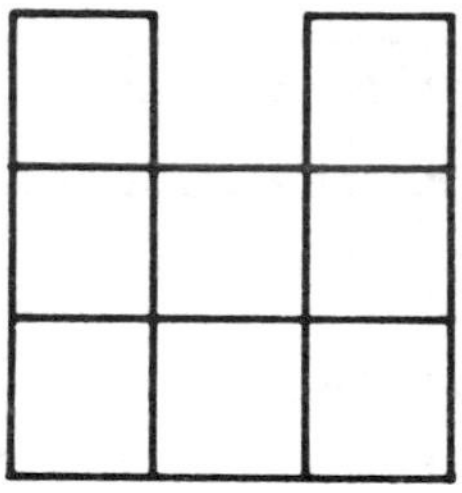

4

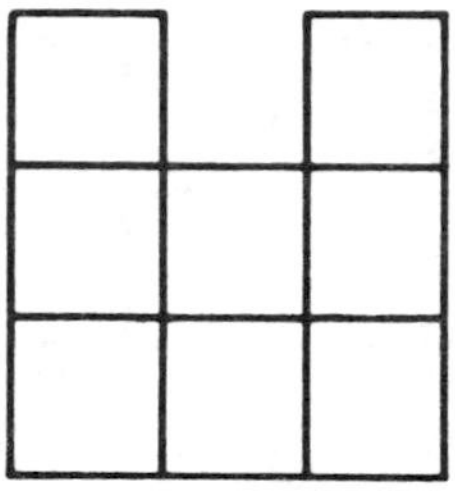

5

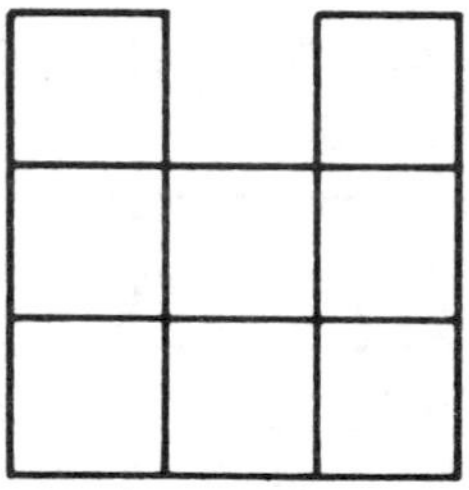

6

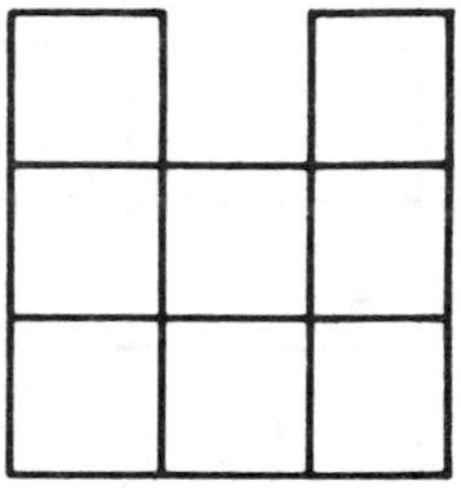

7

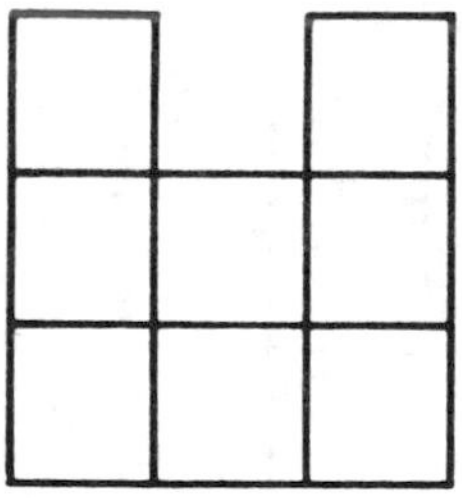

8

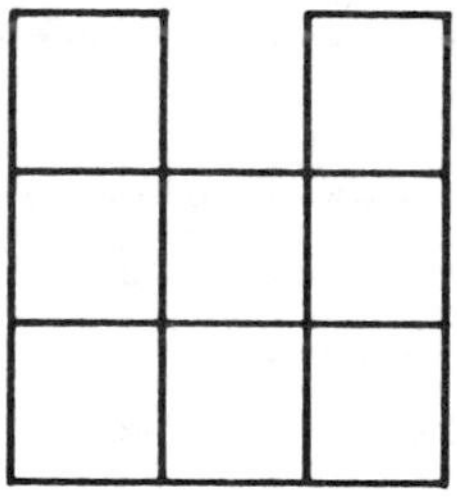

9

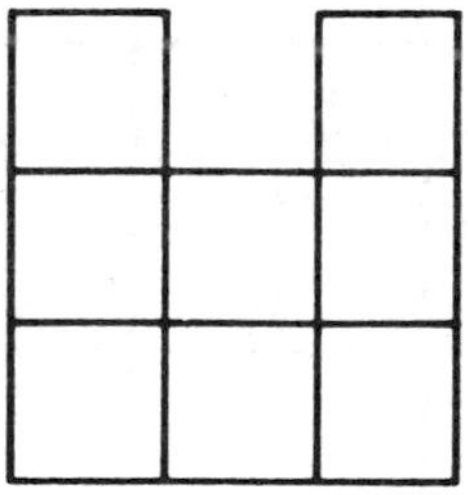

10

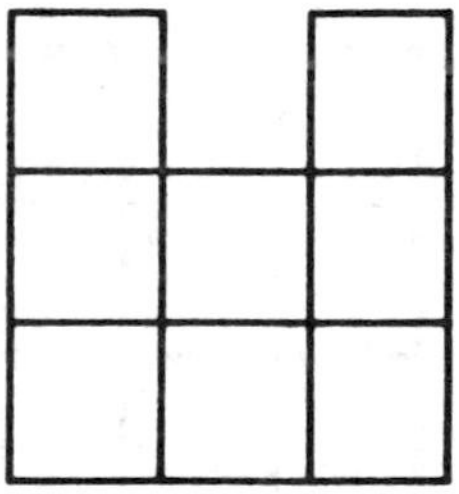

11

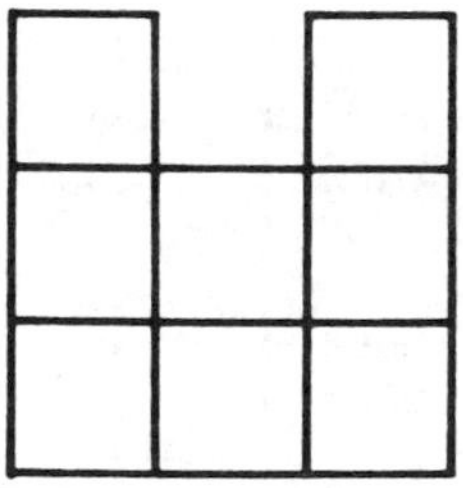

12

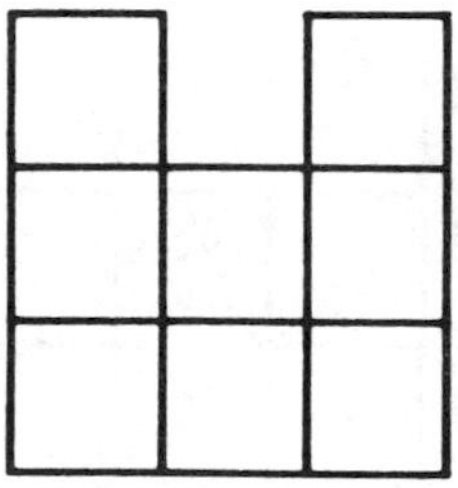

13

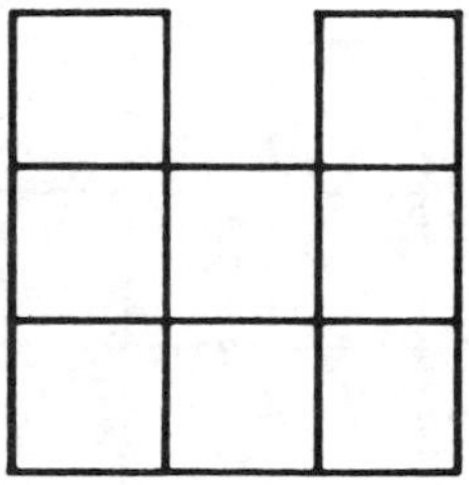

14

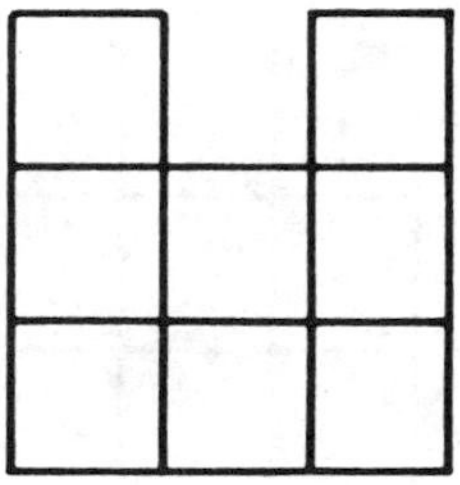

15

FURTHER STUDIES

1. You can extend these observations. In elevators with a button panel on one side of the door, you can make the further predictions that: 1. the first person will stand in the back corner opposite to the panel; 2. in three-person elevators, the third person should stand in the front corner that does not have the button panel.

2. You can extend this study to elevators with three persons. In elevators with two button panels, it is hard to make precise predictions about where people will stand (see item 1 above, for predictions in single-panel elevators). However, personal space theory would predict that people would stand as far apart as possible, so that they should not stand in contiguous squares. There are eighty-four possible arrangements of three people, assigned to three of the nine squares. Only nine of these eighty-four arrangements involve no person in a square contiguous to another (e.g., 1, 3, 9; 6, 1, 7; 1, 3, 8). Run another fifteen elevators, this time with three persons. How many have no one in a square contiguous with any other? We would predict, based on random location of people, $9/84 \times 15 = 1.6$ cases of people in noncontiguous squares. A significant result (less than one time in 100, by chance) would be six or more cases out of fifteen with no one in contiguous squares.

3. You can make observations like the elevator observations in any place where strangers are in an enclosed area. Library tables or seats on vehicles of public transportation are natural places to see if distances between strangers are maximized.

4. What do you think would happen if the rules of personal space were purposely violated? How would the desire for privacy and isolation from strangers affect the behavior of the person violated? Also, would you think that the sex of the subjects, in cases when there are two or more persons per elevator, would be influential in any way?

The Individual and Society:
The Contributions of Sigmund Freud

Learning Objectives

THE ORIGINS OF PSYCHOANALYTIC THOUGHT

1. Understand how Freud viewed the process of taming the savage, selfish human nature and how this process is related to unconscious conflicts.

Hysteria and hypnosis

2. Describe the symptoms of hysteria. Why is this illness termed a psychogenic disorder?
3. Understand the relationship between hysteria and hypnosis and the central role of suggestibility.
4. Explain how Freud proposed to treat hysteria.

Resistance and repression

5. Describe the method of free association and the significance of resistance.
6. Understand the central role played by repression in Freud's theory. Know what happens to repressed material and how it is expressed by the conscious self.

UNCONSCIOUS CONFLICT

The antagonists of inner conflict

7. Understand the nature of unconscious conflict and its effect on behavior.
8. List the three divisions of personality according to Freud. Be able to explain how these develop and how they interact to give rise to conflict and resolution.

The nature of unconscious conflict

9. Be cognizant of the major role of anxiety as a motivating force in keeping unacceptable urges repressed.

10. Explain how repression affects the realm of thought in addition to that of behavior.
11. Define displacement.
12. Describe additional defense mechanisms invoked to keep conflicts hidden.

Origins of unconscious conflict

13. List Freud's stages of psychosexual development and the conflicts that arise during each.
14. In Freud's view, the Oedipus complex is the most important aspect of psychosexual development. Discuss this theory.
15. Understand what the delayed effect of the resolution of the Oedipus conflict is as expressed in adolescence.

Windows into the unconscious

16. Describe the psychopathology of everyday life, and understand how it reflects underlying motives and conflicts.
17. Freud's theory of dreams focused on the content of dreams. Understand the motive of wish fulfillment and its symbolic expression, and the difference between the latent and the manifest dream.

A REEXAMINATION OF FREUDIAN THEORY

18. Recount some of the empirical difficulties with Freud's theories.

Testing Freud's theories of repression and defense

19. Summarize the issues and arguments against and in favor of Freud's reliance on repression and defense mechanisms in dealing with unconscious conflicts.

Problems of Freud's dream theory

20. Be able to give evidence for Freud's theory that

dreams reflect the conscious and unconscious pre-occupations of the dreamer in condensed and symbolic form.

21. Offer evidence that militates against Freud's emphasis on wish fulfillment in the interpretation of dreams.

22. Freud believed that the manifest dream was a disguised and censored version of the latent dream that deals with unacceptable urges. Give an alternative view.

Biology or culture?

23. Freud's theories are often attacked under the rubric of the nativist/empiricist debate. Explain Freud's view and the argument of the neo-Freudians.

24. Discuss the contribution of cultural anthropology in evaluating Freud's theories.

Critiques of Freud's theories of development

25. Know how universal the Oedipus complex is.

FREUD'S CONTRIBUTIONS IN RETROSPECT

26. Review Freud's major contributions to our understanding of human nature and to the field of psychology.

Programmed Exercises

THE ORIGINS OF PSYCHOANALYTIC THOUGHT

1. To understand human social nature, we must ask how people transmit their _culture_ from one generation to the next.

   culture

2. Freud has been compared to Hobbes, since both men believed that man is basically _savage_. But Freud differs from Hobbes in that he believed that the taming force of society is _internalized_ in each of us.

   savage (or selfish)

   internalized

3. According to Freud's view, forbidden impulses are never completely controlled, despite repressive measures by the individual. This division of the individual (one part fighting another) gives rise to _unconscious_ conflicts.

   unconscious

4. In the early 1900s a patient exhibiting partial blindness, glove anesthesia, and memory gaps would likely have been diagnosed as suffering from _hysteria_.

   hysteria

5. If organic damage is ruled out in glove anesthesia, then the origin of the symptoms must be _psychogenic_

   psychogenic

6. Due to the similarities of the characteristics of hysteria and _hypnosis_, it was believed at one time that the two might be related.

   hypnosis

7. Because of the similarities between hysteria and hypnosis, it was hypothesized that hysterical symptoms could be eliminated by _suggestion_

   suggestion

8. A subject asked to forget everything that happened while under hypnosis will generally demonstrate _posthypnotic amnesia_ upon awakening, but will nonetheless respond to _posthypnotic_ suggestions.

   posthypnotic amnesia

   posthypnotic

9. Freud and Breuer came to the conclusion that the symptoms of hysteria could not be just suggested away; the underlying _memories_ that such symptoms block must be recovered. The resulting _catharsis_ will then have therapeutic effects.

   memories

   catharsis

10. Although Freud began by using hypnosis, he later abandoned this approach, since not all of his patients were hypnotizable and since the same crucial memories could be obtained in the waking

state through the method of _free_ _association_   free association

11. A patient is told to say anything that enters his mind, yet struggles at times to change the subject or forgets what he was

going to say. This subject is demonstrating _resistance_ to the   resistance

recovery of _repressed_ memories.   repressed

12. According to Freud, repression is a _defense_ against the   defense
intolerable pain that would be caused by unacceptable thoughts and wishes.

13. Freud investigated unconscious conflicts: their origin, effects, and removal. He termed his exploration and interpretation of

these phenomena _psychoanalysis_   psychoanalysis

UNCONSCIOUS CONFLICT

14. The two major aspects of Freud's theory concern the _mechanisms_   mechanisms

of unconscious conflicts and the _origins_ of these conflicts.   origins

15. The three distinct systems of the human personality, according to

Freud, are the _id_ , the _ego_ , and the _superego_   id, ego, superego

16. The most primitive portion of personality is the _id_ .   id

It operates according to the _pleasure_ principle, with the single   pleasure
goal being immediate satisfaction.

17. As the id-dominated infant encounters the frustration of the real

world, he develops a(n) _ego_ , which attempts to satisfy the   ego

urges of the id according to a _reality_ principle.   reality

18. The young child refrains from doing wrong only through fear of being caught. As the rules and admonitions of the parents are

internalized however, the _superego_ develops and suppresses for-   internalized, superego
bidden behavior even in the absence of negative consequences.

19. _Anxiety_ is the crucial factor in the mechanism underlying   Anxiety
repression. Internal thoughts and feelings that evoke this state must be escaped and are thus suppressed.

20. When fear of retaliation blocks the expression of anger, a person may vent his feelings on another recipient, resulting in

displaced aggression   displaced aggression

21. When a repressed thought or wish manifests itself as a diametrically opposite wish or thought, it is a result of

reaction formation   reaction formation

22. _Rationalization_ is another defense mechanism in which a repressed   Rationalization
thought is reinterpreted in more acceptable terms.

23. Cognitive reorganization also plays a role in _projection_ in which   projection
forbidden urges are attributed to others rather than to the self.

24. _Isolation_ is another defense mechanism in which memories are   Isolation
in consciousness, but the emotions that accompany them are not.

25. Freud's theory of _psychosexual_ development postulates biologically   psychosexual
determined stages of emotional and sexual development.

26. Freud maintained that the young child seeks pleasure. This
pleasure is often obtained by touching body parts which are
particularly sensitive, such as the mouth, anus, and genitals.

These areas are known as _erogenous zones_ .   erogenous zones

27. Seeking pleasure through the mouth is characteristic of the

oral stage, which yields to the _anal_ stage as toilet   oral, anal

training begins. The _phallic_ stage focuses on the stimulation   phallic
of the genitals, while interest in the satisfaction of others as well

as one's own satisfaction characterizes the _genital_ stage.   genital

28. The family drama from which grows the child's internalized
morality and identification with the same-sex parent is called the

Oedipus complex .   Oedipus complex

29. The _phallic_ urges of the boy at ages three and four are   phallic

directed toward the _mother_ as the source of previous gratifica-   mother
tion during the oral stage.

30. The young boy's _jealousy_ of the father leads to _hostility_ and a   jealousy, hostility

fear of retaliation which is termed _castration anxiety_   castration anxiety

31. As the young boy's anxiety about retaliation increases, the boy

identifies with the father in the hope that this will eventually   identifies
secure him an erotic partnership like the father's.

32. The renunciation of genital pleasures endures from about five to

twelve years of age and is termed the _latency period_ .   latency period

33. Through his study of dreams, Freud came to the conclusion that

dreams are an attempt at _wish fulfillment_. Desires suppressed   wish fulfillment
by considerations of reality and by the superego emerge and are
gratified in dreams.

34. The _manifest_ dream is the disguised expression of the _latent_   manifest, latent
dream, which represents hidden and forbidden wishes.

35. The manifest dream employs _symbolism_ in representing the   symbolism
hidden wishes and concerns of the dreamer.

A REEXAMINATION OF FREUDIAN THEORY

36. The fact that clinical psychologists cannot be totally objective
about a patient's behavior patterns and problems is one of the

difficulties of _psychoanalytic_ theory.   psychoanalytic

37. Repression, or _motivated forgetting_, has been studied through   motivated forgetting

analysis of _memory_ lapses.   memory

38. A word association test described in the text employing emotionally charged words measured anxiety according to the patterns of

    heart rate and of _galvic skin response_   heart rate, galvanic skin response

39. Freud's belief that dreams reflect current emotional preoccupations

    is supported by the dreams of _preoperati_ patients.   preoperative

40. The same urge may sometimes be disguised and sometimes be expressed openly in a dream. Freud's assertion that the manifest

    dream represents a _defensive_ disguise cannot handle this facet,   defensive

    but C. S. Hall's proposal that the dream functions to _express_   express
    an underlying idea can.

41. Freud believed that the progression of emotional development is

    rooted in _biology_ and is thus universal.   biology

42. Some psychoanalytic practitioners acknowledge the importance of social factors in development. These psychologists are termed

    neo-Freudians   neo-Freudians

43. Freud maintained that neurotic conflict centers on the repression

    of _erotic_ impulses. Others, such as Erich Fromm, emphasize   erotic

    the area of _interpersonal_ relationships.   interpersonal

44. Evidence from _cultural_ anthropology supports an antibiological   cultural
    bias in the analysis of personality development.

45. Studies of other cultures have indicated that the hostility of the young boy toward the father in our culture is a product, not of

    sexual _jealousy_ , but rather of the father's role as a _disciplinarian_ jealousy, disciplinarian

46. The method of _cross_ - _cultural comparison_ looks for correla-   cross-cultural comparison
    tions between various cultural and/or psychological factors over a
    large number of different societies.

FREUD'S CONTRIBUTIONS IN RETROSPECT

47. Despite the criticisms of Freud's theoretical proposals, his

    conception of _internal_ conflict and the sheer scope of his ideas   internal (or unconscious)
    rank him as one of the giants of psychology.

Self-Test

1. Which of the following adjectives would not be used by Freud to describe basic human nature?
   a. sexually motivated
   b. selfish
   c. pleasure-seeking
   d. conflict-free

2. At first the child's behavior is based on a fear of direct social consequences. Later he will avoid certain behaviors even when there is no chance of punishment. Freud would say that the control put on the child by society is then:
   a. eliminated.
   b. internalized.
   c. externalized.
   d. repressed.

3. Freud made a major contribution to the understanding of human nature when he suggested that the apparent irrationality of much human behavior was a symptom of:
   a. basic insanity.
   b. severe hysteria.
   c. unconscious conflicts.
   d. wish fulfillment.

4. Which of the following are symptoms of hysteria?

   i. partial or total blindness
   ii. paralysis
   iii. feelings of helplessness
   iv. uncontrollable tremblings
   v. uncontrollable urges

   a. i, iii, v
   b. i, ii, iv, v
   c. ii, iii, iv
   d. i, ii, iv

5. Jean Charcot discovered that hysteria is:
   a. inherited.
   b. psychogenic.
   c. the result of physical trauma (injury to the brain).
   d. incurable.

6. It was suggested at one time that hysteria and _____ were related, due to the similarity of effects produced in the two conditions.
   a. drug addiction
   b. true (physiological) paralysis
   c. hypnosis
   d. none of the above

7. Due to the similarities mentioned in question 6, it was hypothesized that the two conditions were related through:
   a. suggestion.
   b. neurosis.
   c. organic damage.
   d. amnesia.

8. The explosive release of emotions that accompanies the remembrance of certain long-forgotten memories is called:
   a. resistance.
   b. memory release.
   c. transference.
   d. catharsis.

9. A patient is asked merely to say whatever comes to mind during a therapy session. The term applied to this psychoanalytic technique is:
   a. transference.
   b. free association.
   c. resistance formation.
   d. wish fulfillment.

10. All of the following statements (made by a patient during free association) are examples of resistance *except*:
   a. "I really can't think of anything right now."
   b. "I just forgot what I was about to say."
   c. "I'm thinking of something which has nothing to do with my problem."
   d. "I just remembered a terrible experience from my childhood."
   e. "What I'm thinking about now is too unimportant to tell you."

11. Freud was interested in unconscious conflicts. This interest included which of the following?
   a. the origin of these conflicts
   b. their present effects
   c. treatment
   d. all of the above
   e. a and c

12. Which of Freud's subsystems would be responsible for a desire to eat or drink?
   a. ego
   b. superego
   c. id
   d. a combination of ego and superego

13. If a child wants a drink, we often find that he asks for something rather than just taking it. Which subsystem is responsible for this?
   a. ego
   b. superego
   c. id
   d. a combination of ego and superego

14. The reality principle controls:
   a. the ego.
   b. the superego.
   c. the id.
   d. all of the subsystems to one degree or another.

15. When a child begins to think of himself as if he were the parent, the _____ has begun to develop.
   a. ego
   b. superego
   c. id
   d. impossible to tell from this description

16. Conflicts develop because the _____ and _____ often issue conflicting commands to the _____ .
   a. id, ego, superego
   b. id, superego, ego
   c. ego, superego, id
   d. all three systems issue commands to every other system

17. On what is the mechanism underlying repression based?
   a. irrationality
   b. biological urges
   c. anxiety
   d. fear

18. Why are thoughts and memories repressed as well as actions?

a. Thinking about an act is similar to performing it.
b. Young children cannot properly distinguish between thought and action, nor do they realize that thoughts are private.
c. Both of the above are possible explanations.
d. Neither of the above is a possible explanation.

19. A child is punished for something he did. He then hits his brother. This is an example of:
a. repression.
b. transference.
c. hysteria.
d. displaced aggression.

20. Three defense mechanisms that come into play once a forbidden impulse cannot be kept down any longer are:
a. transference, projection, reaction formation.
b. repression, transference, reaction formation.
c. reaction formation, projection, rationalization.
d. displaced aggression, repression, rationalization.

21. A child has deeply hidden feelings of hostility toward a younger sibling. However, the child treats his sibling with apparent love. This is an example of the defense mechanism known as:
a. projection.
b. reaction formation.
c. rationalization.
d. transference.

22. A child who displays a behavior diametrically opposed to his frustrated true desires is demonstrating:
a. reaction formation.
b. displacement.
c. projection.
d. none of the above

23. After failing to be offered a good job, an applicant decides that he wouldn't have liked the job anyway. This person is displaying a defense mechanism called:
a. rationalization.
b. projection.
c. reaction formation.
d. paranoia.

24. When a person attributes his own thoughts and feelings to someone else, we call this:
a. rationalization.
b. projection.
c. reaction formation.
d. repression.

25. Parts of the body which are particularly sensitive to touch are called:

a. arousal zones.
b. pleasure zones.
c. sensitivity zones.
d. erogenous zones.

26. Which of the following presents the correct stages of psychosexual development in the right order?
a. oral, anal, erogenous, phallic, genital
b. oral, anal, phallic, genital
c. anal, oral, erogenous, phallic
d. oral, anal, phallic, erogenous

27. All of the following are components of Freud's family triangle except:
a. love.
b. inadequacy.
c. fear.
d. jealousy.

28. The drama of the Oedipus complex unfolds according to the following progression of events:
a. identification, love, fear, hate, renunciation.
b. love, fear, hate, renunciation, identification.
c. hate, fear, renunciation, identification, love.
d. love, hate, fear, renunciation, identification.

29. The motivation for the young boy's identification with his father is:
a. perception of sexual similarities.
b. castration anxiety.
c. the father's acts of retaliation.
d. vicarious enjoyment of the mother through the father.

30. The stage following resolution of the Oedipus complex comprises:
a. the latency period.
b. increased masturbation.
c. puberty.
d. all of the above

31. Freud believed that the basis of every dream was:
a. projection.
b. schizophrenia.
c. wish fulfillment.
d. day residues.

32. Freud distinguished between two parts of the dream, which he termed:
a. conscious and unconscious.
b. latent and manifest.
c. normal and deviant.
d. wish fulfillment and disguise.

33. Dreams, metaphor, and poetry all involve:
a. displaced activity.
b. repression.
c. suppression.
d. symbolism.

34. In a recent study, a test was made of Freud's view

of the dream as an attempt at gratification. Most very thirsty subjects reported:

a. dreams in which they drank.
b. dreams in which they did not drink.
c. no dreams whatsoever.
d. dreams in which the act of drinking was represented symbolically.

35. Which of the following statements is *not* in accordance with C. S. Hall's view about dreams?
a. The dream symbol expresses, rather than disguises, an underlying idea.
b. The dream is a concrete form of mental shorthand that embodies a feeling or emotion.
c. The dream is an abstract form of mental longhand that elaborates on a feeling or emotion.
d. The function of the dream is analogous to that of a cartoonist's picture.

36. Neo-Freudians believe that Freud erred in:
a. emphasizing sexual motivations.
b. his view of dreams as wish fulfillment.
c. his perception of oral and anal characteristics.
d. his assertion that the key to emotional development is in biology.

37. There is little evidence for all of the following assertions of psychoanalytic theory except:
a. the existence of unconscious conflict.
b. the general theory of psychosexual development.
c. the importance of biology in emotional development.
d. personality is essentially fixed by the age of five or six.

Answer Key for Self-Test

1. d pp. 286–87
2. b p. 287
3. c p. 287
4. d p. 287
5. b p. 287
6. c p. 287
7. a p. 288
8. d p. 288
9. b p. 289
10. d p. 289
11. d p. 289
12. c p. 290
13. d pp. 290–91
14. a p. 291
15. b p. 291
16. b p. 291

17. c p. 293
18. c p. 292
19. d p. 292
20. c pp. 292–93
21. b pp. 292–93
22. a pp. 292–93
23. a p. 293
24. b p. 293
25. d p. 294
26. b p. 294
27. b pp. 294–95
28. d pp. 294–95
29. b p. 295
30. a p. 295
31. c p. 296
32. b p. 297

33. d p. 297
34. b p. 300
35. c p. 300

36. d p. 300
37. a pp. 302–3

Investigating Psychological Phenomena

ANALYSIS OF DREAM CONTENT

Equipment: None
Number of subjects: One or more
Time per subject: Thirty minutes
Time for experimenter: Thirty minutes

The study and analysis of dream content has been of considerable concern to psychologists at least since the publication of Freud's classic work on dreams in 1900. A variety of hypotheses have been proposed to account for the content of dreams and for the way in which our past experiences and expectations about the future are frequently incorporated into our dreamwork.

Given the sparse evidence concerning dream content, there is still a good deal of controversy concerning the facts. One phenomenon of particular interest that is still controversial is whether present motivational states or expectations about the future (e.g., wish fulfillment) influence our dream content.

The present experiment further tests the hypothesis that dream content is influenced by present motivational state. The test is similar to the experiment of William Dement and Edward Wolpert cited in the Gleitman text in which these investigators induced thirst in their subjects, then analyzed the subjects' dreams to determine whether there was evidence in the dream content for increased thirst.

You will be the subject in the present experiment. Starting on the next page, you will find eight pairs of dream reports. These are the reports of actual dreams from eight students enrolled in an introductory psychology course. One of the reports in each pair is the report of a dream from early in the term in which these students were enrolled in introductory psychology. The other report in each pair represents a dream that occurred on the night preceding a major midterm examination in the psychology course. The question we ask in this experiment is whether the specific issues involved in this examination or general anxiety about the examination was reflected in the dreams of these eight subjects.

In order to address the question, you should read each dream and try to decide which dream in each pair was the one that occurred prior to the examination.

Be careful to consider the possibility, as Freud theorized, that conflicts or concerns may be either manifest or latent in dream content. That is, there may be direct or transformed reference to the event in question. For each dream pair, mark your answer sheet A or B according to which member of the pair you think was the dream that preceded the examination. In each case, think about the reasons for your choice and assess your confidence in your decision. After listing your choices, check them with the answers given.

DREAM PAIRS

1A Someone was singing a rousing song about a coat. An audience of women, mostly of the type interviewed in commercials, was sitting on the floor of a large room. They were asked to describe how they had put together their outfits. Most were wearing the sweater-and-skirt sort of thing, but one woman in a peculiar-looking caftan told how she had bought the trim first and had then searched for something to use it on. The trim didn't look very good on the caftan.

1B A record store: The stuff that had been pasted up all over the walls (posters, clippings, etc.) had yellowed, creating an antique atmosphere. Some balloons: The store was giving away something for free — furniture I think. There was some argument, something about a snake who liked a trollop. A young and quarrelsome married couple from a film I'd seen more or less reenacted their roles. I was in a strange room in a hotel or dormitory. There was, to my surprise, a small wrought-iron balcony. Night: From the balcony I could see the lights and reflections of the city gleaming white and yellow all around me. The lights began to go out, all at once — the restaurants and bars were closing. I was seeing into a little restaurant or ice cream parlor, very white and empty. Three people wearily got up and left as the place closed up for the night.

2A I was knocking at the door of my best friend's house. (Earlier in the dream I had seen her working on campus and spoken to her. [She lives in San Antonio, Texas.]) I covered the peephole to the front door, as is my custom, when she became very excited and yelled for her parents. She seemed to be very frightened. This is when the dream ended and I woke up.

2B Someone I didn't recognize was walking down Locust Walk wearing shoes exactly like some of mine, except for the color. Mine are red and blue. Hers were green and blue.

3A I dreamed I was sitting at a table with several people eating brownies with whipped cream and soap suds, fighting with one of my friends.

3B I dreamed that my kitten looked like a guinea pig. (I went home for the weekend and she had changed.) She wasn't tiger striped, she was only solid black and rust colored. Her ears were not pointed; they were small and flat. She had no tail and her legs were short.

4A I was going to go swimming. I sat on a bench on the side of the street waiting for a taxi or bus. With me were a girl and a German teacher. The man had a beach umbrella. He grew tired of waiting and left. I went to a different beach to look for the father from a foreign family I spent a year with.

4B I was with a boyfriend while he was making sandwiches for a party. Beaded strings were in the crevice between the wall and the ceiling. Another girl was there making coffee with a weird machine. Outside I played catch with a friend. First we used a ball, then an orange, and lastly a key. We almost lost the key in the snow. I was skiing with another girl and she kept complimenting Yamaha skis. I tried to park the car in front of my house but there were no spaces. Two guys who I didn't particularly like from high school were in one of the cars drinking. They were not my type. When they asked me to go drinking I declined. Finally I went to a party. A minister I know said grace. A guest commented that a girl's jewelry didn't match her clothes, yet it really did. A lot of people were talking and eating.

5A The dream opened with me having just had a baby, but for some reason the kid (a boy) was about the size of a year-old baby — maybe a couple of months younger. I didn't recall getting pregnant or delivering the kid. Somehow I knew that the kid (baby) had my boyfriend's nickname. I got extreme pleasure from hugging the baby and knowing he was mine, although I didn't know who the father was. Suddenly I realized that I was in high school and my mother would never let me keep the baby. So I had to give him up for adoption. I was very sad at handing him over to a stranger and the thought that I would never see him grow up was upsetting. This was a pleasurable dream until the last scene.

5B I went back to visit my prep school and I bumped into my favorite teacher there. She was terribly aged and frail, having had some sort of drastic operation. I kissed her hello on the cheek and she was very cold, as though I had misbehaved recently at school or something. I don't remember the rest of the dream clearly except that the teacher kept turning into my mother and back into the teacher, and evidently I had done something awful but no one would tell me what. It was a very anxiety provoking and unpleasant dream.

6A I was riding on a trolley coming home from high school. The driver asked me for my fare and I found out I didn't have any money. I ran to the back to try to get out. Then I woke up.

6B I dreamt I had a sexual affair with my psychology professor. He told me I was one of his best friends.

7A I dreamt about color vision. I repeatedly remembered seeing one page in the reading.

7B I dreamt that I woke up late for chemistry lab and that experiment failed.

8A I rode on a short train ride and on the return trip I met a very good friend who is coming to visit me for the weekend. However, the train departure is delayed so I sit down to lunch with my family and another three friends (I don't know where they came from). My family wants me to tell them about school, but I am more interested in seeing one of my friends—procuring tea bags and knives for my apartment (which I need). Another incident—I pass a stand with two older ladies selling homemade doughnuts (and cake) but I don't buy any, even though I see a girl sinking her teeth into one. Also, while I am walking toward the train station, the sidewalk is being paved (by males and females).

8B I have been waiting three weeks to see my boyfriend. Finally the weekend arrives and he comes to visit me. But, of course, we can't be alone since my best friend also drops in on me. Then I find out my grandmother has passed away (however, she is still among us when we all sit down to a mourning feast). When we finally get a chance to be alone again, my boyfriend and I are walking down a street. A car honks its horn and it turns out to be his old girlfriend asking for a ride home. During this same dream I remember buying a new bicycle and a pair of army boots.

Answer Sheet

Dream pair	Dream preceding examination (A or B)	Reason for choice
1.	_____	_____
2.	_____	_____
3.	_____	_____
4.	_____	_____
5.	_____	_____
6.	_____	_____
7.	_____	_____
8.	_____	_____

ANSWERS

1. B 2. A 3. A 4. B 5. B 6. B 7. A 8. B

QUESTIONS TO THINK ABOUT

1. Were you accurate? What does this suggest about the content of dreams and about how well they blend with life events?

2. Were there certain pairs where the choice seemed more obvious than for other pairs? Were you more accurate on these?

3. How might you improve on the experiment?

CHAPTER 11

Social Cognition and Emotion

Learning Objectives

1. Distinguish the approach of modern social psychology from those of Freud and sociobiology.

SOCIAL COGNITION AND SOCIAL REALITY

The interpersonal nature of belief

2. Know what social cognition is.
3. Describe Asch's experiment on the social basis of physical "reality," and indicate why subjects become upset in this study.

Social comparison

4. Define social comparison, and explain how it functions in ambiguous situations.

Cognitive processes and belief

5. Understand what is meant by cognitive consistency.
6. Explain cognitive dissonance and give an example.

ATTITUDES

7. Distinguish between attitudes and beliefs.

Attitudes and behavior

8. Explain how close the relation between attitudes and behavior is. Indicate some factors that could explain discrepancies between attitudes and behavior.

Attitude change

9. List two of the factors that account for the effectiveness of persuasive communications. Review the role of the message source and the message.

10. Describe the two routes to persuasion incorporated in the elaboration-likelihood model.
11. Explain how aspects of cognitive dissonance, particularly bringing one's own behavior into line with one's attitudes, causes attitude change. Include justification of effort and forced compliance in the discussion.
12. Describe how protecting the self-picture can account for many instances of attitude change, and distinguish this motivation from cognitive consistency.

Attitude stability

13. List the factors that account for the stability of most attitudes.

PERCEIVING OTHERS

Forming impressions

14. Show how visual perception is analogous to social perception.

Impressions of others as patterns

15. Describe Asch's experiments on impression formation.
16. Be able to explain what a central trait is and in what sense people are perceived as more than the sum of their attributes.

Impressions of others as cognitive constructions

17. Draw parallels between cognitive constructions of the physical and social worlds.
18. Indicate the roles of schemas and implicit theories of personality in social cognition and impression formation.
19. Define stereotypes, and explain the role of illusory correlation in maintaining inaccurate stereo types.

ATTRIBUTION

Attribution as a rational process
20. Indicate the parallels between scientific thinking and the attribution process.
21. Define situational factors and dispositional factors in the attribution process.

Errors in the attribution process
22. Evaluate the roles of situational and dispositional factors in judgments about other people. What is the fundamental attribution error?
23. Describe the actor-observer difference.
24. Explain why people are more inclined to make situational attributions about their own behavior, as opposed to the behavior of others (the actor-observer difference). Indicate the role of different perspectives.
25. Define the self-serving attributional bias.

PERCEIVING ONESELF

The self-concept and others
26. Describe the factors that contribute to the developing perception of the self.

Self-perception and attribution
27. Understand what self-perception theory is. Be able to offer the evidence for the influence of one's own behavior on one's attitudes.

EMOTION: PERCEIVING ONE'S OWN INNER STATES

The James-Lange theory
28. Describe the James-Lange theory of emotion and the major objections to it.

The cognitive arousal theory of emotion
29. Describe the cognitive arousal theory of emotion put forth by Schachter and Singer. Contrast this theory with the James-Lange theory. What is the role of physiological state in each of these theories?
30. Discuss the misattribution of emotion in light of the cognitive arousal theory. How do results from false feedback and excitation transfer effects support this theory?

Beyond cognitive arousal theory
31. Describe the relation between facial expressions and emotion. Be able to offer the evidence for a group of fundamental emotions.

TAKING STOCK

32. Evaluate the contribution of motivational and cognitive factors in social cognition and emotion.

Programmed Exercises

1. Modern social psychologists emphasize the _present_ situation in their accounts of behavior.

present

SOCIAL COGNITION AND SOCIAL REALITY

2. The way we try to interpret and understand social events, that is,

social cognition is like the way we comprehend nonsocial events.

social cognition

3. In Asch's experiment on judging line length, subjects become disturbed because the behavior of the confederates challenges

their shared sense of _phys. reality_.

physical reality

4. When people have to make difficult judgments, they often seek the opinion of others, demonstrating the need for

social comparison

social comparison

5. The perception by a person of inconsistency in beliefs, feelings, or behavior sets up an unpleasant internal state called

cognitive dissonance

cognitive dissonance

6. Cognitive consistency refers to the fact that people try to
   resolve contradictions between their attitudes and beliefs.   resolve

ATTITUDES

7. An _attitude_ is a rather stable, evaluative mental position held   attitude
   toward some idea or object or person.

8. Unlike beliefs, attitudes are _evaluated_   evaluative (or emotionally tinged)

9. _Specific_ as opposed to _general_ attitudes are better predictors   Specific, general
   of behavior.

10. Messages that openly try to convince us of something, called
    persuasive communications, are more effective if they come from   persuasive
    a _credible_ and _trustworthy_ source.   credible, trustworthy

11. According to the _elaboration-likelihood_ model, there are two   elaboration-likelihood

    routes to persuasion. One, the _central_ route to persuasion,   central

    involves careful consideration of arguments. The other, the

    peripheral route to persuasion, demands less attention and makes   peripheral

    use of shortcuts, or _heuristics_   heuristics

12. According to dissonance theory, a goal will be valued all the

    higher, the _harder_ it was to reach.   harder

13. Attitudes toward a goal often become more positive after a
    person makes sacrifices to attain the goal. This is called retro-

    spective _justification_ of _effort_ .   justification, effort

14. If people behave inconsistently with their beliefs under

    forced _compliance_ they are unlikely to change their beliefs or   forced compliance
    attitudes.

15. An alternative to cognitive consistency as an explanation of
    attitude change involves more emotional or evaluative factors and

    is described as protecting the _favorable self - picture_   favorable self-picture

16. Although attitudes can change, cognitive consistency and the
    constancy of one's personal environment tend to produce attitude

    stability .   stability

PERCEIVING OTHERS

17. In both object and person perception, the observer extracts

    certain _consistencies_ from the flow of events.   consistencies (invariances)

18. According to Asch, both form perception and person perception

    result from combinations of attributes into _organized_ wholes.   organized

19. Asch's experiments on impressions of others showed that certain
    attributes had an organizing effect on the integration of other
    attributes. Such "organizing" attributes were called

    central traits .   central traits

20. Impressions of others can be seen as patterns, based on the relations among elements. One basis for this process is a set of organized expectations about the way in which different behaviors of people hang together, called a _schema_ or an _implicit theory_ of personality.

schema, implicit theory

21. Simplified schemas applied to whole groups are called _stereotypes_ Some inaccurate stereotypes are maintained by a tendency for people to see expected relations, even if these relations do not actually exist. This process is called _illusory correlation_.

stereotypes

illusory correlation

ATTRIBUTION

22. _Attribution_ is a process through which people infer the causes of other people's behavior.

Attribution

23. Studies of attribution show that in judging others people tend to rely too much on internal causation, or _dispositional_ factors, as opposed to _situational_ factors in explaining behavior. This is called the _fundamental attribution error_.

dispositional

situational

fundamental attribution error

24. People are more likely to attribute their own (as opposed to others') behavior to situational factors. This is called the _actor - observer difference_

actor-observer difference

25. The tendency to make dispositional attributions for one's own successes, and situational attributions for one's own failures, is called the _self - serving_ bias.

self-serving

PERCEIVING ONESELF

26. Bem and some other cognitive social psychologists believe that conceptions of the self are built up from attribution processes of the same type used in forming conceptions of other people. This position is called _self -perception theory_.

self-perception theory

27. According to this theory, _behavior_ determines attitudes, rather than the other way around.

behavior

28. The "foot-in-the-door" technique is an example of how _behavior_ can lead to attitude change.

behavior

EMOTION: PERCEIVING ONE'S OWN INNER STATE

29. According to the _James - Lange_ theory, the subjective experience of emotion results from our awareness of bodily changes in the presence of certain stimuli.

James-Lange

30. According to Schachter and Singer's cognitive arousal theory of emotion, emotion depends on the interpretation of _autonomic arousal_ by a subject, in light of the total situation.

autonomic arousal

31. Studies of facial response patterns in different emotional situations suggest that there arc about six to ten _fundamental_ emotions.

fundamental

Self-Test

1. In explanations of current behavior, in contrast to the approaches of Freud and the sociobiologists, modern social psychologists emphasize:
   a. effects of early childhood.
   b. evolutionary factors.
   c. genetic causes.
   d. unconscious determinants.
   e. situational factors.

2. In Asch's experiment on the effect of social pressure on judgments of noticeably different line lengths, he found that:
   a. many subjects yielded to social pressure, but their perceptions of line length did not necessarily change.
   b. the actual perceptions of line length were changed in the subject.
   c. the perceptions of line length were changed in the confederates.
   d. the shared sense of physical reality can affect perception.
   e. a and b

3. Indicate which of the following statements about social comparison is *false*:
   a. Social comparison is more likely to occur when someone is faced with a difficult decision.
   b. Social comparison is more likely to occur in a situation in which there is some ambiguity.
   c. Social comparison is more likely to occur when people feel they need more information.
   d. Social comparison is more likely to occur when the decision involves social issues.
   e. none of the above are false

4. Fred supports the cause of the A's, in their war against the B's. He then sees on television that the A's are killing innocent children. He decides that the A's must be being forced to do this by the B's, and that the A's have no choice. This type of thinking in Fred is an example of:
   a. social comparison.
   b. stimulus-response association.
   c. resolution of cognitive dissonance.
   d. reference to comparison groups to change attitudes.
   e. all of the above

5. Sandy holds that French food is good and Canadian food is bad. These views represent:
   a. attitudes.
   b. beliefs.

   c. cognitive consistency.
   d. cognitive dissonance.
   e. actions.

6. Attitudes are usually measured by:
   a. questionnaire.
   b. observation of behavior.
   c. experimental studies.
   d. physiological measures.
   e. a and c

7. Attitudes do not always predict behavior. This could be because:
   a. attitudes, as measured, are often very general, and behavior deals with specific situations.
   b. attitudes are evaluative and behavior is not.
   c. behavior is not affected by cognitive consistency or cognitive dissonance.
   d. a and c
   e. all of the above

8. Someone using the peripheral route to persuasion is likely to:
   a. have cognitive dissonance.
   b. use heuristics.
   c. show more cognitive consistency.
   d. have moderate elaboration-likelihood.
   e. pay special attention to events in the periphery.

9. According to cognitive dissonance theory, which of the following would be the best way to cause people to change attitudes?
   a. Pay them a lot to make them believe they hold the new attitude.
   b. Force them to behave as if they support the new attitude for at least a few weeks.
   c. Tell them that they will be prejudiced if they continue with their current attitude.
   d. Show them that their current attitude is inconsistent with their actual behavior.
   e. Urge them to consult with an appropriate social comparison group.

10. This graph illustrates the relation between:

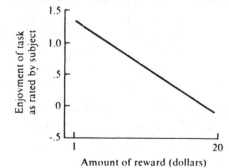

a. attitudes and beliefs.
b. cognitive dissonance and forced compliance.
c. cognitive dissonance and cognitive consistency.
d. social comparison and ambiguity.
e. cognitive dissonance and beliefs.

11. After working as a volunteer for a political candidate for a month, Jonathan finds that his support for the candidate has increased, even though he has never met her. This is an instance of:
a. forced compliance.
b. justification of effort.
c. persuasive communications.
d. a and b
e. all of the above

12. Which of the following techniques is *not* considered an effective way to produce a positive change in attitude toward a message?
a. use of a credible and trustworthy source
b. use of a message that is regarded favorably by a social comparison group
c. openly forcing a person to behave in a way that supports the message
d. linking the message to past behavior by the person that supports the message
e. c and d

13. An alternative to the view that attitude change results from attempts to create logical consistency invokes emotional factors that motivate creation of:
a. cognitive consistency.
b. a favorable self-picture.
c. retrospective reevaluation.
d. justification of effort.
e. post-decision dissonance.

14. Which of the following is involved both in maintaining stable attitudes and in attitude change?
a. attitude questionnaires
b. forced compliance
c. cognitive consistency
d. striking and unexpected events
e. changing reference groups

15. Perception of objects and people have in common the fact that:
a. both rely almost exclusively on vision.
b. both involve the construction of stable or invariant characteristics.
c. both are fixed in their nature by first impressions.
d. both involve the resolution of cognitive dissonance between the object (or person) and its perception.
e. none of the above

16. After a few encounters, Susan decided that Gary was stupid. She maintained this impression even after she discovered that he got the highest grade on a physical chemistry examination and assumed that he cheated. Susan's behavior is an example of:
a. resolution of cognitive dissonance.
b. forced compliance.
c. persuasive communication..
d. a and c
e. all of the above

17. There are many parallels between nonsocial and social cognitions. Which of the following processes does *not* appear in both types of situations?
a. illusory correlation
b. use of heuristics
c. use of schemas
d. attempts to simplify complex situations
e. All of the above appear in both situations.

18. The decision by a person that another person's behavior was internally caused, e.g., as a result of his aggressive nature, is an example of:
a. a central trait.
b. illusory correlation.
c. stereotypes.
d. attribution.
e. situational factors.

19. People have a tendency to believe that actors in the theater are really like the roles that they play. This is an example of:
a. the resolution of cognitive dissonance.
b. the dominance of dispositional over situational factors in attribution.
c. the primacy effect in impressions.
d. the distinction between the bodily self and the social self.
e. the interaction of social and biological factors in the determination of behavior.

20. The actor-observer difference describes the fact that people are *less* likely to make _____ attributions about themselves than others.
a. dispositional
b. correct
c. cognitively consistent
d. situational
e. c and d

21. Explanations of the actor-observer difference include the fact that:
a. people are more situational.
b. people cannot literally see themselves in social situations.
c. attribution theory only applies to judging other people.

d. a and b
e. all of the above

22. The self-serving bias is designed to explain:
    a. the fundamental attribution error.
    b. the actor-observer difference.
    c. the greater inclination to make dispositional attributions about the self in cases of success.
    d. a and b
    e. all of the above

23. According to self-perception theory:
    a. one's own behavior can influence one's attitudes.
    b. cognitive dissonance is a self-fulfilling prophecy.
    c. social roles determine behavior.
    d. social factors are not involved in the concept of the self.
    e. attitudes are formed more or less independent of behavior.

24. Which of the following illustrates how one's feelings or beliefs may be the result of one's actions?
    a. the "foot-in-the-door" technique
    b. forced compliance
    c. stereotypes
    d. the need for comparison groups
    e. none of the above

25. Both self-perception theory and the James-Lange theory of emotion make the similar claim that:
    a. the bodily self must interact with the social self to produce emotion.
    b. behavioral or bodily events cause mental changes.
    c. subjective phenomena cannot be studied.
    d. attribution plays no role in emotion.
    e. impression formation is of central importance.

26. After running for a quarter mile, a person shows increased heart rate and various other signs of arousal but may not feel any strong emotion. This fact is particularly damaging to which of the following theories?
    a. the cognitive arousal theory of emotion
    b. the James-Lange theory
    c. Cannon's idea that subjective emotion leads to physiological responses
    d. a and b
    e. all of the above

27. An experiment has shown that subjects alter their ratings of the attractiveness of nude photos in response to feedback about the increase or decrease of their heart rate. This result can be taken to support:

a. the cognitive arousal theory (Schachter-Singer) of emotion.
b. the James-Lange theory.
c. Cannon's theory (subjective emotion leads to the physiological responses, but the latter do not cause the former).
d. a and b
e. all of the above

28. Suppose a person was completely paralyzed. If this person experienced the normal intensity and range of emotions, this would be evidence against:
    a. the James-Lange theory.
    b. the fundamental attribution error.
    c. a role for cognition in emotion.
    d. the foot-in-the-door technique.
    e. the existence of fundamental emotions.

29. Forced compliance, interpretation of emotions, and the self-serving bias all share:
    a. cognitive interpretations.
    b. motivational interpretations.
    c. an involvement with attitude change.
    d. a and b
    e. a and c

Answer Key for Self-Test

1. e p. 305	16. a pp. 315–16
2. a p. 307	17. e pp. 315–17
3. e p. 308	18. d p. 317
4. c p. 308	19. b pp. 318–19
5. a p. 309	20. a p. 319
6. a p. 310	21. b p. 319
7. a pp. 310–11	22. c p. 320
8. b p. 312	23. a pp. 321–22
9. d p. 312	24. a pp. 321–22
10. b p. 313	25. b pp. 321–23
11. b p. 312	26. b p. 323
12. c p. 313	27. d pp. 322–24
13. b p. 313	28. a p. 323
14. c p. 314	29. d p. 327
15. b p. 315	

Investigating Psychological Phenomena

PERSON PERCEPTION: THE EFFECT OF CONTEXT OR SET ON FIRST IMPRESSIONS

Equipment: A stopwatch or a watch that indicates seconds
Number of subjects: At least eight
Time per subject: Five minutes
Time for experimenter: Forty minutes

Social perception bears many analogies to more traditional areas of perception (see p. 315 in the text). In both cases, information is taken in selectively and put together into some organized percept. This aspect of person perception was illustrated in the text with special reference to the classic studies of Solomon Asch. Asch's work argued for an organizational basis for impression formation. This approach is in keeping with the position of Gestalt psychology. In Asch's view, impressions were not formed by "summing" different items of information about a particular person. One particular aspect of the active process of impression formation is the effect of set. One is constantly forming impressions of people. New information on any person is integrated with an already existing impression: the new information will be interpreted to be as consistent as possible with the existing impression. Under the circumstances, one would expect that the first information one gets about a person would be especially important, since it might color what comes in later. Therefore, an organizational view would predict that the *order* of items of information about a person would affect the resulting impression, whereas a simple *summation* hypothesis would predict that order would not matter.

Asch tested his hypothesis in a very simple manner: He gave college students a list of six adjectives that ostensibly described someone and recorded the impressions that they subsequently formed of this imaginary person. By manipulating the types of adjectives used and the order of their presentation, Asch attempted to produce systematic changes in the elicited impression formations. We will repeat his experiment on word order in precisely the same way that it was performed by Asch.

Try to get at least eight (student) subjects. It might be useful for you to team up with a few friends from the course and run up to twenty subjects, so that your results might be more meaningful. Subjects must be divided into two groups. You can run as many subjects as you want at the same time, so long as they are all from the same group. Since this experiment will compare the results of subjects from one group with the results from another group, it is important that the two groups be similar in general characteristics. For example, keep the percentage of females the same in both groups and try not to run a group of friends together, since they may share many similar characteristics. If you run one subject at a time, simply assign the first subject to group A, the second to group B, and so on. This should give you a random and "unbiased" sample.

The list for group A	The list for group B
intelligent	envious
industrious	stubborn
impulsive	critical
critical	impulsive
stubborn	industrious
envious	intelligent

Note that the adjectives in group B are in the reverse order of group A. This arrangement is designed to enhance any effect of order, by putting adjectives that would lead to quite different impressions on opposite ends of the adjective list.

Subjects should be seated comfortably, and should have in front of them a blank piece of paper and a pencil. Make sure to put the group letter (A or B) on the paper and on the checklist. The experimenter reads the following instructions:

I shall read you a number of characteristics that belong to a particular person. Please listen to them carefully and try to form an impression of the kind of person described. You will later be asked to give a brief characterization of the person in just a few sentences. I will read the list slowly and will repeat it once.

Read the list of six adjectives out loud in a steady voice, with an interval of five seconds between terms. Then say:

I will now read the list again.

(Repeat the reading of the list)

Now please write a brief characterization of this person.

(Subject writes)

Finally, tell the subjects while handing them the checklist (see pages 146 and 147):

Here is a list of pairs of adjectives. For each pair, please circle the adjective that better characterizes the person we have been describing.

After the subject has completed this task, he or she is finished.

NOTES ON PROCEDURE

In setting up any experiment, many decisions must be made. Here, these include selecting the adjectives for the list and for the checklist, deciding on the number of adjectives in the list, and so on. In most cases there are specific reasons for making these decisions. In this experiment, for example, ask yourself:

1. Why does the experimenter read the list instead of allowing the subject to read the list?

2. Why is the subject asked to write an impression before seeing the checklist rather than after filling out the checklist?

RESULTS

You should end up with eight or more written sketches and eight or more marked checklists. About half should be in each group. There is no simple way to score the written impressions. Read them over and try to summarize the impressions written by the two groups (the procedure used by Asch). You could also give the written impressions to another person and ask that person to sort them into piles, about equal in size. One pile would be for the more desirable impressions (persons) and the other for the less desirable ones. See if the impressions based on the adjective list with more desirable traits first are usually classified as more desirable. (It would be a good idea to fold back the part of the impressions paper with the group letter on it before reading and analyzing the character summaries.)

It is easier to analyze the data from the checklists. Simply record the percent of subjects who selected the more favorable adjective of each pair for each group. This is the procedure used by Asch. His results, based on twenty-four student subjects in group A and thirty-four in group B, are presented in the table on the next page. Record your data in the columns next to his data. Compare your results with his. If we take a difference of 20 percentage points as worthy of note, he reported big differences, in favor of group A, on happy, humorous, sociable, popular, good-looking, and restrained.

(You can increase the significance of your data by combining it with data from a few friends in the class, so that you would have 20 or more subjects in each group.)

Based on your results, what is the conclusion about the validity of the organization (set, Gestalt) versus simple summation explanations of impression formation?

Try to explain why some particular adjectives show clear effects and others do not. Obviously, in real life people form impressions from interactions with other people or by hearing about them from other people. To what extent do you think that Asch's procedure gives an indication of how people actually form impressions? The hallmark of a good experiment is that it simplifies a situation but still preserves its essential features. Is that true of this experiment?

FURTHER STUDY

You can use Asch's technique to address other questions. You can change specific adjectives on the list. You can use brief statements about a person's *behavior* (e.g., John consistently drives over the speed limit; John is always on time, etc.), rather than general characteristics. You can see which types of adjectives cause a subject to guess that a person is male or female. There are many possibilities, should this problem interest you. Some of the possibilities that you will come up with may never have been investigated.

Reference

Asch, S. E. 1946. Forming impressions of personality. *Journal of Abnormal and Social Psychology* (41): 258–90.

	Percent of subjects checking favorable adjective at left			
	Asch's Data		Your Data	
Adjective Pair	group A (24 students)	group B (34 students)	group A (__ students)	group B (__ students)
generous	24	10		
wise	18	17		
happy	32	5		
good-natured	18	0		
humorous	52	21		
sociable	56	27		
popular	35	14		
reliable	84	91		
good-looking	74	35		
serious	97	100		
restrained	64	9		
honest	80	79		

CHECKLISTS

There are eight checklists on the next two pages. Cut one out for each subject. (Asch used eighteen adjective pairs. We use twelve of these pairs.)

Circle the most relevant adjective:

generous–ungenerous

shrewd–wise

unhappy–happy

irritable–good-natured

humorous–humorless

sociable–unsociable

popular–unpopular

unreliable–reliable

good-looking–unattractive

frivolous–serious

restrained–talkative

dishonest–honest

Group _____

Circle the most relevant adjective:

generous–ungenerous

shrewd–wise

unhappy–happy

irritable–good-natured

humorous–humorless

sociable–unsociable

popular–unpopular

unreliable–reliable

good-looking–unattractive

frivolous–serious

restrained–talkative

dishonest–honest

Group _____

Cut here

Circle the most relevant adjective:

generous–ungenerous

shrewd–wise

unhappy–happy

irritable–good-natured

humorous–humorless

sociable–unsociable

popular–unpopular

unreliable–reliable

good-looking–unattractive

frivolous–serious

restrained–talkative

dishonest–honest

Group _____

Circle the most relevant adjective:

generous–ungenerous

shrewd–wise

unhappy–happy

irritable–good-natured

humorous–humorless

sociable–unsociable

popular–unpopular

unreliable–reliable

good-looking–unattractive

frivolous–serious

restrained–talkative

dishonest–honest

Group _____

Circle the most relevant adjective:

generous–ungenerous

shrewd–wise

unhappy–happy

irritable–good-natured

humorous–humorless

sociable–unsociable

popular–unpopular

unreliable–reliable

good-looking–unattractive

frivolous–serious

restrained–talkative

dishonest–honest

Group _____

Circle the most relevant adjective:

generous–ungenerous

shrewd–wise

unhappy–happy

irritable–good-natured

humorous–humorless

sociable–unsociable

popular–unpopular

unreliable–reliable

good-looking–unattractive

frivolous–serious

restrained–talkative

dishonest–honest

Group _____

Cut here

Circle the most relevant adjective:

generous–ungenerous

shrewd–wise

unhappy–happy

irritable–good-natured

humorous–humorless

sociable–unsociable

popular–unpopular

unreliable–reliable

good-looking–unattractive

frivolous–serious

restrained–talkative

dishonest–honest

Group _____

Circle the most relevant adjective:

generous–ungenerous

shrewd–wise

unhappy–happy

irritable–good-natured

humorous–humorless

sociable–unsociable

popular–unpopular

unreliable–reliable

good-looking–unattractive

frivolous–serious

restrained–talkative

dishonest–honest

Group _____

CHAPTER 12

Social Interaction

Learning Objectives

RELATING TO OTHERS:
ONE-ON-ONE INTERACTIONS

Social exchange
1. Be able to explain what social exchange is.

Reciprocity
2. Explain the reciprocity principle.
3. Understand how the reciprocity principle is used in bargaining and persuasion. What is the door-in-the-face technique?

Altruism
4. Know under what circumstances people fail to help others in distress. Consider the role of ambiguity, pluralistic ignorance, and diffusion of responsibility.
5. Describe the bystander effect.
6. Indicate the possible costs that someone who offers aid might incur.
7. Consider whether there is any genuine altruism. Explain how vicarious distress accounts for altruistic behavior. Is empathic concern a truly altruistic feeling?

Attraction
8. Discuss proximity as a major determinant of attraction.
9. Review the evidence for similarity and physical attractiveness in attraction.
10. Offer the evidence for the importance of physical attractiveness in attraction.
11. Describe the matching hypothesis.
12. Evaluate the roles of biological and cultural factors as determinants of sexual attractiveness.

Love
13. Distinguish romantic from companionate love.

14. Describe the phenomenon of romantic love.
15. Define the Romeo-and-Juliet effect.

SOCIAL INFLUENCE:
MANY-ON-ONE INTERACTIONS

16. Explain social influence.

Social facilitation:
Social influence by mere presence
17. Define social facilitation. Indicate the conditions under which it occurs, and in particular, the role of arousal and facilitation of dominant responses.

Conformity
18. Define conformity. Be able to explain the role of cognitive and motivational factors in causing conformity.
19. Know under what conditions minorities successfully oppose the conformity influence of the majority.

Blind obedience
20. List the characteristics of the authoritarian personality and understand its relevance to blind obedience.
21. Describe Milgram's basic study on obedience.
22. Discuss the importance of seeing oneself as another's agent.
23. Discuss how dehumanization, psychological distance, and gradual escalation influence blind obedience. Illustrate these influences with the example of the Milgram experiment.
24. Contrast personality factors with situational factors as causes of blind obedience.

CROWD BEHAVIOR:
MANY-ON-MANY INTERACTIONS

Deindividuation and crowd behavior
25. Define deindividuation. Give the evidence linking

it to crowd behavior and to antisocial acts.

Cognitive factors and the panicky crowd

26. Evaluate the statement that "people become 'primitive' or irrational in crowds."
27. Describe the circumstances under which panic is likely to spread in a crowd.
28. Understand what the prisoner's dilemma is. Provide examples of payoff matrices as illustrations, and show how the prisoner's dilemma analysis can account for panic in crowds.

Cognitive factors and the hostile crowd

29. Discuss the motivation for hostile behavior in crowds, using lynching as an example.
30. Explain the role of anonymity, diffusion of responsibility, and pluralistic ignorance in hostile crowd behavior.
31. Indicate how pluralistic ignorance and diffusion of responsibility can explain apathetic behavior in crowds in the face of some apparent offense.
32. Compare and contrast the causes of panic, hostility, and apathy in crowds.

THE GENERALITY OF SOCIAL PSYCHOLOGY

33. Evaluate the extent to which principles of social psychology discussed in this and the preceding chapter are general features of human nature, as opposed to principles specific to United States culture in the late twentieth century.

Programmed Exercises

RELATING TO OTHERS: ONE-ON-ONE INTERACTIONS

1. According to the principle of _social__ _exchange_ each partner in a relationship gives something to the other and expects to receive something in return.

social exchange

2. The notion that favors and gifts must be repaid is embodied in the _Reciprocity_ principle.

reciprocity

3. An application of this principle is the _Door_-_in_-_the_-_face_ technique, in which, after a major request is refused, a smaller request from the same source is more likely to be granted.

door-in-the-face

4. Three factors that account for people's failure to help someone in distress are _ambiguity, plur with ignoran_ and _diffusion of responsibility_

ambiguity, pluralistic ignorance
diffusion of responsibility

5. The larger the size of the group a person is in the less likely he is to come to a victim's assistance. This is called the _Bystander Effect_.

bystander effect

6. The costs of helping include loss of _time_ and possible _physical danger_.

time
physical danger

7. Two people who have spent a fair amount of time in physical _proximity_ to one another are more likely than not to become friends.

proximity

8. In addition to proximity, two major factors that cause one to like another are _similarity_ and _phys. attractiveness_

similarity, physical attractiveness

9. The strong tendency for people to marry other people very similar to themselves is called _homogamy_

homogamy

10. The personal characteristic that most influences initial liking for a person in American culture is _phys. attraction_

physical attractiveness

11. The tendency for people to select mates who are similar to them on many characteristics (such as physical attractiveness) is called

    the _matching hypothesis_   matching hypothesis

12. Although there may be some universal characteristics that lead to sexual attraction, to a large extent the criteria of sexual attrac-

    tiveness vary in different _cultures_.   cultures

13. Two contrasting types of love are a passionate type, or _romantic_   romantic
    love, and another type that emphasizes mutual trust, care, and

    sharing, called _companionate_ love.   companionate

14. Parental opposition tends to intensify romantic love. This is

    called the _Romeo_ - _&_ -_Juliet_ effect.   Romeo-and-Juliet

SOCIAL INFLUENCE: MANY-ON-ONE INTERACTIONS

15. The study of the way an individual is affected by different social

    forces, acting simultaneously, is the study of _social influence_   social influence

16. The improvement in performance in the presence of other

    members of one's species is called _social facilitation_   social facilitation

17. According to Zajonc, social facilitation operates by producing

    arousal , which strengthens the tendency to perform the   arousal

    dominant response.   dominant

18. Going along with what other people think or do is called

    conformity   conformity

19. Conformity is more likely if the other persons involved are

    un _animous_ in the position they take.   unanimous

20. People who emphasize the importance of power, dominance, and

    obedience have been described as having an _authoritarian_ personality.   authoritarian

21. In Milgram's first experiments on obedience, approximately

    _65%_ percent of subjects shocked the learner up to the   65 (50-75 percent would be
    maximum amount.   acceptable)

22. Milgram's experiments suggest that it is not necessary to have an

    authoritarian personality to exhibit blind obedience.   authoritarian

23. An important factor that causes people to perform acts that they might otherwise consider abhorrent is the feeling that they are

    another person's _agent_ .   agent

24. Blind obedience is more likely when _psychological distance_   psychological distance
    between the "subject" and the "victim" is increased.

25. The obedient person who causes pain to another person may treat

    that person as an object. This is called _dehumanization_   dehumanization

26. The cognitive reorientation required in producing obedience is best

    accomplished by a _gradual increase_ in obedience requirements.   gradual increase

CROWD BEHAVIOR: MANY-ON-MANY INTERACTIONS

27. *Deindividuation*, a weakened sense of personal identity, disinhibits impulsive actions that are normally under restraint. It occurs

    more often in *crowds*.

    Deindividuation

    crowds

28. The prisoner's dilemma presents an individual with a choice in a situation with mixed risks and benefits, described in a

    payoff matrix.

    payoff matrix

29. The prisoner's dilemma analysis is an attempt to explain the apparently *irrational* behavior of a crowd in terms of the *rational* behavior of individuals.

    irrational, rational

30. The large size and apparent unanimity of the mob causes some of its members to perform acts that they would not normally

    perform, because of a *diffusion* of responsibility.

    diffusion

31. Although the mob may be far from homogeneous, the apparent

    unanimity leads to *pluralistic ignorance* of the crowd members.

    pluralistic ignorance

32. Feelings of anonymity in the violent crowd may precipitate

    antisocial acts of *commission*. However, in a crowd of onlookers observing a violent encounter, the resultant behaviors are more

    likely to be antisocial acts of *omission*.

    commission

    omission

THE GENERALITY OF SOCIAL PSYCHOLOGY

33. Some principles of social psychology described in this and the

    preceding chapter may be universal aspects of *human nature*,

    or they may be much more specific to this *culture* and this

    time.

    human nature

    culture

    time

Self-Test

1. The idea of social exchange is:
   a. tit-for-tat (exchange of favors).
   b. the money economy.
   c. the slavery system.
   d. forced compliance.
   e. altruism.

2. The bystander effect is accounted for by:
   a. ambiguity.
   b. diffusion of responsibility.
   c. pluralistic ignorance.
   d. a and c
   e. all of the above

3. Diffusion of responsibility is:
   a. dependent on the structure of the social environment.
   b. an example of a cost of intervention.
   c. lessened as group size decreases.
   d. b and c
   e. a and c

4. Proximity is an important factor in attraction. There is evidence that this relation results from the fact that:
   a. one must ordinarily meet someone in order to be attracted to him/her.
   b. familiarity promotes attraction, and familiarity is increased by proximity.
   c. proximity explains the matching hypothesis.
   d. a and b
   e. all of the above

5. Mildred and Herb have been dating for years. Both are physically unattractive, and one acquaintance wonders what they see in each other. Which of the following factors could contribute to their mutual attractiveness?
   a. proximity
   b. similarity
   c. matching
   d. a and c
   e. all of the above

6. In a particular culture, relatively thin males tend to marry relatively plump females. According to the matching hypothesis, this implies that:
   a. relative thinness in males is as desired (attractive) as relative plumpness in females.
   b. physical attractiveness is not important in this culture.
   c. body shape is not important in this culture.
   d. the plumpness and thinness of relatives is important in this culture.
   e. c and d

7. Romantic love:
   a. tends to be more short-lived than companionate love.
   b. is intensified by parental approval.
   c. can be almost completely explained in terms of the matching hypothesis.
   d. differs from companionate love in that romantic love depends heavily on similarity.
   e. c and d

8. Baseball player A is a better hitter in batting practice than in actual games, while player B shows the opposite pattern. We can say that:
   a. A shows social facilitation and B does not.
   b. B shows social facilitation and A does not.
   c. hitting optimally is more likely to be a dominant response for player A.
   d. hitting optimally is more likely to be a dominant response for player B.
   e. b and d

9. The situations that lead to conformity are similar to those that lead to failure to help a person in distress. Both conformity and failure to help others in distress are increased by all *except* which of the following?
   a. ambiguity in the situation
   b. a need for additional information
   c. presence of a large number of other people
   d. a desire to be liked by others
   e. c and d

10. A single dissenter in a conformity experiment is most likely to have an effect on an otherwise lone nonconforming subject if:
    a. she is in agreement with the nonconforming subject.
    b. her dissent is clear, whether or not it is in agreement with the nonconforming subject.
    c. the problem in question is a matter of fact, rather than an opinion.
    d. a and c
    e. all of the above

11. An explanation of blind obedience that emphasizes the authoritarian personality of the person in question relies on:
    a. factors within the situation.
    b. factors within the person.
    c. reciprocity.
    d. homogamy.
    e. attribution of emotional experience.

12. Which of the following would tend to *prevent* obedience in a situation of the type that Milgram studied?
    a. making a person feel like the agent of another
    b. dehumanizing the person being punished
    c. describing the experiment as a scientific enterprise
    d. decreasing the psychological distance between the subject and the person being punished
    e. none of the above

13. It is probably easier for a bombardier to drop bombs on an inhabited building than for the same person to kill a person standing in front of him. This presumed fact can be accounted for in terms of:
    a. anonymity.
    b. psychological distance.
    c. deindividuation.
    d. all of the above
    e. none of the above

14. Brown suggests that panic is more likely in situations where:
    a. a serious danger is perceived.
    b. the escape routes appear to be inadequate.
    c. the people involved have well-defined roles.
    d. a and b
    e. all of the above

15. The prisoner's dilemma analysis explains:
    a. the use of payoff matrices.
    b. how obedience is based on a past history of stern parental treatment.
    c. how maladaptive crowd behavior can result from rational behavior of individuals.
    d. the importance of roles in controlling the crowd panic reaction.
    e. b and c

16. Hostile behavior of mobs is encouraged by:
    a. diffusion of responsibility.
    b. bystander apathy.
    c. the prisoner's dilemma.
    d. cognitive reinterpretations.
    e. c and d

17. The behavior of hostile crowds is motivated. In the case of lynching, an important motive was:
    a. forestalling a socioeconomic threat.

b. diffusion of responsibility.
c. extermination of the lower class.
d. countering bystander apathy.
e. all of the above

18. Bystander apathy and mob violence are both more likely to occur in situations where there is:
a. high motivation and aggressiveness.
b. diffusion of responsibility.
c. a blurring of roles.
d. cognitive dissonance.
e. b and c

Answer Key for Self-Test

1. a pp. 329–30	10. a p. 341
2. e p. 332	11. b p. 342
3. e p. 332	12. d p. 344
4. d p. 334	13. d pp. 344–45
5. e pp. 334–36	14. d p. 347
6. a p. 336	15. c p. 348
7. a p. 338	16. a p. 350
8. e p. 339	17. a p. 350
9. d pp. 332, 340	18. b p. 350

Investigating Psychological Phenomena

MATCHING FOR INTELLIGENCE AND ATTRACTION

Equipment: None
Number of subjects: One, yourself
Time per subject: Twenty minutes
Time for experimenter: Twenty minutes

As described in the text, one of the major features of romantic couples is that they are similar along a wide variety of dimensions. Much of this similarity seems to be a reason for the formation of the relationship, rather than a consequence of it. Although certain characteristics may become more similar the longer a couple is together, this cannot be so for the many characteristics unlikely to change in adulthood, such as height. Furthermore, individuals are likely to seek a partner with a high rating on characteristics for which there can be a clear positive or negative evaluation (such as intelligence or attractiveness), with competitive selection and fear of rejection tending to sort people out with others at their own level of achievement, ability, beauty, and so forth. Thus, one would expect similar ratings on almost all traits.

This study will demonstrate the principles of homogamy and matching by examining the similarity of couples on two characteristics: physical attractiveness and intelligence. You will be the one subject in this study. First, select ten heterosexual (or ten homosexual) couples that you know fairly well. The couples should be selected according to the following criteria:

1. All should be romantically involved: married or together for at least one year.

2. The couples should be about the same age in two senses: The members of the couple should be no more than ten years apart in age and the oldest person should be no more than twenty years older than the youngest person of the same sex on the list. (If you cannot generate the ten couples that this study calls for, you can ask a friend to generate the data for you.)

DO NOT INCLUDE YOURSELF IN ANY OF THESE COUPLES.

List the couples (by the first name of each partner) in the tables on the next page. Now rank the ten women and the ten men separately for both physical attractiveness and intelligence. Thus, for physical attractiveness, rank the most attractive man number one, the next most attractive number two, and so on until all ten numbers have been assigned. Rank the women in the same fashion.

Now calculate a rank-order correlation, a statistic that represents the correlation between the ranking for men and women in each couple. (See the Statistical Appendix, pages A15–A19 of the text, but use the formula on page 157 to calculate the correlation.) If the members of a couple match perfectly on a characteristic (that is, if the man ranked number one for attractiveness is involved with the woman ranked number one on this same trait, and so on), the correlation coefficient would equal 1.00 – the highest possible value for correlation. If the members of a couple are inversely matched (that is, if the man ranked number one for attractiveness is involved with the woman ranked number ten on that trait), then the correlation coefficient would equal −1.00 (the lowest possible value). If there is no relation between the ranking of the man and woman in a couple on the trait in question, then the correlation coefficient would be 0. (For a sample calculation and table, see page 158.)

Attractiveness

Couple (man's/woman's name)	Man's Rank	Woman's Rank	Difference	Difference^2
1 _____	_____	_____	_____	_____
2 _____	_____	_____	_____	_____
3 _____	_____	_____	_____	_____
4 _____	_____	_____	_____	_____
5 _____	_____	_____	_____	_____
6 _____	_____	_____	_____	_____
7 _____	_____	_____	_____	_____
8 _____	_____	_____	_____	_____
9 _____	_____	_____	_____	_____
10 _____	_____	_____	_____	_____

Correlation for attractiveness = _____

Intelligence

Couple (man's/woman's name)	Man's Rank	Woman's Rank	Difference	Difference^2
1 _____	_____	_____	_____	_____
2 _____	_____	_____	_____	_____
3 _____	_____	_____	_____	_____
4 _____	_____	_____	_____	_____
5 _____	_____	_____	_____	_____
6 _____	_____	_____	_____	_____
7 _____	_____	_____	_____	_____
8 _____	_____	_____	_____	_____
9 _____	_____	_____	_____	_____
10 _____	_____	_____	_____	_____

Correlation for intelligence = _____

Use the formula below to calculate the correlation, r.

$$r = 1 - \frac{6(\text{Sum of the difference in ranking between couple members}^2)}{\text{number of couples (number of couples}^2 - 1)}$$

For the sample table below, the equation would read:

$$r = 1 - \frac{6(68)}{10(100 - 1)} = -.59$$

Couple (man's/woman's name)	Man's Rank	Attractiveness Woman's Rank	Difference	Difference^2
1 A/B	1	2	−1	1
2 C/D	5	3	2	1
3 E/F	3	1	2	4
4 G/H	9	6	3	9
5 I/J	2	7	−5	25
6 K/L	7	5	2	4
7 M/N	4	4	0	0
8 O/P	8	9	−1	1
9 Q/R	10	8	2	4
10 S/T	6	10	−4	16

Sum of Difference^2 = 68

Correlation for attractiveness = .59

Compare your results to those in the list below generated by other students in introductory psychology. These correlation coefficients were calculated by eleven students for intelligence and thirteen students for attractiveness and have been arranged in order of increasing correlation. How do your values compare to theirs?

Finally, try to think of the characteristic that would be most likely to show similarity in mates, as well as the characteristic that might, perhaps because of its lack of importance, not show matching in mates. Calculate the correlation coefficient for each of these characteristics, using the same ten couples you have already used. You might also consider doing a similarity/matching score for ten same-sex non-romantic friends. Would you expect them to show similarity/matching effects as well? Would you expect this on the same characteristics as with romantic partners?

Correlations

Attractiveness	Intelligence
−.16	−.01
−.01	.18
.02	.26
.07	.35
.36	.39
.45	.42
.46	.56
.50	.63
.55	.68
.60	.75
.60	.76
.76	
.76	
Mean .38	.45

CHAPTER 13

Physical and Cognitive Development

Learning Objectives

WHAT IS DEVELOPMENT?

Development as differentiation

1. Define differentiation, and explain how it accounts for similarities in the embryos of different species.

Development as growth

2. Review the major events in physical growth of humans from conception to adulthood.
3. Compare humans' physical growth (especially of the nervous system) with that of other animals.
4. Review the basic sensory and response capacities of the human infant.

Development as orderly progression

5. Describe the sequence of early development of locomotion in humans, and indicate how the order of many accomplishments is fixed.

PIAGET'S THEORY OF COGNITIVE DEVELOPMENT

6. Discuss the major philosophical positions on development. Explain how Piaget's theory relates to these positions. What is the major characteristic of Piaget's theory?

Sensory-motor intelligence

7. Describe the hallmarks of this stage. Explain how the child sees himself and objects around him. What distinctions develop during this period?
8. Know why object permanence is seen as an end to this stage of development.
9. Define assimilation and accommodation as Piaget would use these terms.
10. Define representation as Piaget would use this term, and offer some examples of representations.

The preoperational period

11. Explain how the name of this period is derived.
12. Be familiar with various tests of conservation. Understand how the child's conservation ability develops during this period. Know why children fail to conserve at the beginning of this period. What operations are crucial for conservation?
13. Describe a test that demonstrates egocentrism.

Concrete and formal operations

14. Be able to explain the difference between the stages of concrete and formal operations. Know how Piaget studies formal operations. Give examples of thinking patterns that would qualify for this stage.

PERCEPTION AND MOTOR ACTION IN INFANCY

The perception of objects

15. Know what occlusion is and how it affects adult object perception.
16. Explain the habituation procedure and how it is used to study perception.
17. Offer the evidence which suggests that infants have some notions of the principles that govern objects in space.
18. Cite the evidence that indicates that infants do have a notion of object permanence.

THE PRESCHOOLER AND THE STAGE CONCEPT

The meaning of mental stage

19. List the characteristics of a developmental "stage" as Piaget uses the term.

The question of discreteness

20. Explain how a recent finding has suggested that Piaget overestimated the extent of egocentrism during the preoperational period.

21. Describe recent research on conservation of number. What does this reveal about Piaget's theory? What does it suggest about children's conceptions of number?
22. Preschool children are apparently capable of conservation in simple, constrained situations. Explain what this implies about their general intellectual maturity. Have they necessarily mastered the skills of the preoperational period?

Sequences or stages?
23. Cite the evidence for a sequence in development.

THE CAUSES OF COGNITIVE GROWTH

The nativist approach: maturation
24. Be aware of the role of cross-cultural data in evaluating the maturational hypothesis.

The empiricist approach: specific learning
25. Be able to discuss the basic issue distinguishing the position of specific learning and maturation. What is Piaget's position? What is the relevant evidence?

26. Discuss how a specific learning position explains the fairly fixed orders of development that characterize various stages.

Piaget's approach: assimilation and accommodation
27. Describe how Piaget sees assimilation and accommodation as explanations of cognitive growth.

The information-processing approach: chunking and strategies
28. Know what adults are better at remembering than young children. How do the neo-Piagetians explain this difference?
29. Describe some strategies for remembering that adults use. How do young children approach a memory task, and how does their approach change as they mature?
30. Define metacognition. How is metacognition manifested in memory, perception, language, thinking, and problem solving? At what approximate age does metacognition manifest itself?

Programmed Exercises

WHAT IS DEVELOPMENT?

1. The process of differentiation involves a progressive change from the more general to the more particular, from the simpler to the more complex. — differentiation

2. Differentiation predicts and accounts for the fact that development occurs in an _orderly_ progression. — orderly

3. Physical growth continues until approximately the end of the _second_ decade of life. — second

4. The part of the human body that grows at a disproportionately high rate before birth is the _head_. — head (brain)

5. Because of extensive growth of the brain after birth, humans have a longer period of _dependency_ than most other species. — dependency

6. The _rooting_ reflex is elicited in an infant by a touch to the cheek, which makes the infant turn his head toward the stimulating object. — rooting

7. In general, the infant's sensory capacities are _more_ advanced at birth than her _response_ capacities. — more / response (motor)

8. The human baby begins to walk alone at an age of about _15_ months. — 15 (12 to 18)

9. The first words typically occur at about _10_ months. — 10 (8 to 12)

10. Although some children develop faster than others, the major motor and language accomplishments occur in a _fixed_ sequence. — fixed (orderly)

PIAGET'S THEORY OF COGNITIVE DEVELOPMENT

11. Jean Piaget and other developmental psychologists usually look

    for _qualitative_ differences between children and adults; they do   qualitative
    not see children as adults in miniature.

12. Piaget regards cognitive development as a dynamic process in

    which the child progresses through several _stages_ .   stages

13. A child has begun to learn that he lives in a stable world which
    can be distinguished from his sensory impressions. This child is

    most likely in the _sensory - motor_ stage.   sensory-motor

14. Children develop the notion of _object permanence_ near the end   object permanence
    of the sensory-motor stage as they become aware that objects
    exist independently of their sensory experience and motor
    manipulations.

15. Perhaps the most significant accomplishment of children in the

    last phase of the sensory-motor stage is their ability to _represent_   represent
    objects or events in their absence, rather than merely reacting to
    their presence.

16. Recurrent action patterns (such as sucking, swallowing, and head

    and eye movement) are the first mental elements, or _schemas_ .   schemas
    It is in terms of these that the infant organizes the world.

17. Representations may be internalized actions, images, or words;

    in all cases they function as _symbols_ , which stand for what-   symbols
    ever they may signify.

18. _Deferred_ imitation is a case in which a child imitates an action   Deferred
    that occurred in the past, such as a playmate's temper tantrum
    observed a day before.

19. According to Piaget, a conceptual system of thought can only be

    constructed by means of higher-order schemas. These _operations_   operations
    allow the internal manipulation of ideas according to a stable set
    of rules and emerge at age seven or so; the period from two to

    seven is therefore termed _preoperational_   preoperational

20. Piaget states that the ability to form _representations_ precedes linguistic representations
    expression and is a prerequisite for it.

21. A characteristic of children in the preoperational stage is their

    inability to _conserve_ quantity, as shown by their lack of   conserve
    knowledge about relative quantities of liquids in two glasses.

22. One of the crucial concepts that children must grasp if they are

    to conserve is that manipulations upon objects are _reversible._   reversible

23. A preoperational child is incapable of attending to all of the

    relevant _dimensions_ of an object simultaneously.   dimensions

24. Piaget believes that a child can learn to chunk dimensions

    together when he learns to focus upon the _transformations_ from one   transformations
    experience to another rather than upon the individual experiences
    themselves.

25. A preoperational child believes his point of view is the only one.

    Such a belief is known as **egocentric**   egocentrism

26. A child can determine whether a given number is odd or even
    and can also add one to any number. The child finds that 3 + 1
    is even, and 5 + 1 is even, but doesn't understand that any odd
    number added to one results in an even number. This child

    would be categorized as being in the **concrete operations** stage.   concrete operations

27. A child in the concrete operations stage has operations that are

    applicable to **concrete** events but that do not work very well   concrete

    when applied to **abstract** concepts.   abstract

28. The ability to entertain hypothetical possibilities and deal with
    potential relationships is characteristic only of the stage of

    Formal   operations   formal operations

PERCEPTION AND MOTOR ACTION IN INFANCY

29. The fact that an infant can perceive an object that is partially
    blocked by another object gives evidence that infants are capable

    of reacting appropriately to the perceptual effect of **occlusion**.   occlusion

30. The procedure in which a perceptual display is kept in view until

    an infant becomes bored is called **habituation**   habituation

31. It appears that young infants have some knowledge of the fact

    that two objects cannot occupy the same **space** at the same   space (place)
    time.

THE PRESCHOOLER AND THE STAGE CONCEPT

32. Piaget asserts that cognitive development goes through several

    distinct **stages** , each one having its own consistent and   stages
    discrete characteristics.

33. Recent results with a task in which young children were required
    to show their mothers a picture demonstrate that these children

    are not as **Egocentric** as Piaget has claimed.   egocentric

34. Recent, more sensitive tests of **#** conservation, using a   number
    "surprise" technique, demonstrate that spatial rearrangement of

    objects is not a cause for surprise, but a change in **#**   number
    (same word as above) is.

35. Examination of early concepts of number suggest that children

    do have a consistent way of **counting** even though their number   counting
    tags may not match those of adults.

36. Most developmental psychologists would say that Piaget's cogni-
    tive milestones are not a succession of mental stages, similar to

    those found in embryological development, but rather a **sequence**   sequence
    of mental steps.

THE CAUSES OF COGNITIVE GROWTH

37. Nativists would state that mental development depends on
    Maturation, a pre-programmed growth process based on changes   maturation
    in underlying neural structures.

38. While children of different cultures may reach each Piagetian
    stage at different *times (ages)*, they pass through these stages in   ages
    the same *order* .   order

39. The alternative to the maturation-centered approach is one that
    emphasizes the acquisition of specific *patterns* through exposure   patterns
    to the environment.

40. Piaget believes that at the same time that the environment is
    assimilated to the child's schemas, the schemas are *accommodated* to   assimilated, accommodated
    the environment.

41. A more current approach to cognitive development asserts that it
    results from a change in *information processing*   information processing

42. According to this approach, mental growth is partly based on the
    acquisition of better and larger *chunks* of information and of   chunks
    various *strategies* for thinking and remembering.   strategies

43. As children get older, rote repetition is substituted by various
    forms of active *rehearsal* in which the items to be remembered   rehearsal
    are grouped and organized.

44. The fact that adults can reflect on the cognitive operations
    whereby they gain knowledge shows that they are capable of
    not Metacognition   metacognition

Self-Test

1. The fact that at early stages embryos of many very
   different species look very much alike and have
   a much simpler structure than adults can be taken
   as evidence for:
   a. physical development.
   b. differentiation.
   c. the inheritance of behavior.
   d. all of the above
   e. b and c

2. The photo shows a human being of about what
   age (beginning with conception as zero)?
   a. one month
   b. four months
   c. eight months
   d. birth (nine months)
   e. one year (postconception)

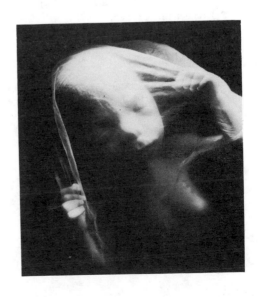

3. All but one of the following are distinctive features of human development, in comparison with most other mammals. Which is not a distinctively human feature?
   a. long period of dependency on the parent
   b. being born at a very immature stage
   c. presence of reflexes at birth
   d. continuation of growth until about twenty years of age
   e. b and c

4. Major features of motor, language, and other types of development often occur in a fixed order in children who develop at different rates. A major reason for this is that:
   a. development must occur in stages.
   b. some capacities depend on the existence of other capacities.
   c. sense organs mature before response capacities.
   d. language depends on locomotion ability.
   e. the infant begins with reflexes like rooting before it can learn.

5. A nativist:
   a. thinks of the child's mind as similar to an adult's, only with fewer associations.
   b. thinks of a child's mind as qualitatively different from an adult's.
   c. conceptualizes the growth of a child's mind as progression through a series of natural stages.
   d. views basic cognitive categories as given a priori at birth.

6. A child has learned that whether a toy box is open or closed, there are toys inside. It could be said that the child has attained the concept of:
   a. object permanence.
   b. representations.
   c. directed action.
   d. solipsism.

7. When a child becomes aware that objects exist independent of his own sensory experience, he would most likely have just completed which Piagetian stage?
   a. sensory-motor
   b. preoperational
   c. concrete operations
   d. formal operations

8. Recurring action patterns such as sucking and swallowing are:
   a. simple reflexes which have little developmental interest.
   b. the first mental elements with which the infant organizes the world.
   c. examples of intentional acts.
   d. none of the above

9. The two processes that Piaget sees as being responsible for cognitive development are:
   a. deferred imitation and assimilation.
   b. schemas and representations.
   c. assimilation and accommodation.
   d. none of the above

10. A toy is hidden under a box in the presence of a child. The child is prevented from reaching the box for a few seconds. When she is released she immediately lifts the box off the toy. The earliest stage that this child could be in is:
    a. sensory-motor.
    b. preoperational.
    c. concrete operations.
    d. formal operations.

11. Demonstrations of the child's understanding that symbols (i.e., internalized actions, images, or words) may stand for objects but are not equivalent to them include all of the following except:
    a. object permanence.
    b. deferred imitation.
    c. make-believe play.
    d. metacognitions.

12. The concept unknown to a child who doesn't conserve quantity is:
    a. reversibility.
    b. accuracy.
    c. size.
    d. weight.

13. Children who don't conserve are:
    a. unable to attend to all of the relevant dimensions of a stimulus.
    b. usually in the concrete operations stage.
    c. usually in the formal operations stage.
    d. none of the above

14. The social counterpart of an inability to attend to more than one dimension in a conservation task is:
    a. aggressive behavior.
    b. having only one friend during a particular time interval.
    c. egocentrism.
    d. none of the above

15. The major difference between a child in the concrete operations stage and one in the formal operations stage is:
    a. The former is incapable of following the rules.
    b. The former cannot deal with numbers.
    c. The former cannot deal with abstract

concepts.

d. all of the above

16. Piaget's assertion is that perception:
   a. is achieved because of the innate capacity of the organism.
   b. is not present in an organism until the age of two.
   c. is built out of piecemeal impressions provided by the different senses.
   d. has little to do with experience and learning.

17. Some developmental psychologists have challenged Piaget's views on what is given to the infant at the start of life. Which of the following would these critics agree with?
   a. Infants have some sense of object permanence.
   b. Four-month-old infants can perceive partially hidden objects similar to the way adults do.
   c. Infants have some notion that two objects cannot occupy the same place at the same time.
   d. all of the above

18. What are two characteristics of a developmental stage as Piaget uses the term?
   a. consistent, continuous
   b. operational, discrete
   c. consistent, concrete
   d. consistent, discrete

19. The fact that cognitive achievements like conservation have precursors that appear possibly years before the concrete operational stage leads investigators to question the _____ of Piaget's developmental stages.
   a. concreteness
   b. discreteness
   c. consistency
   d. validity

20. According to the theory of maturation:
   a. behavior change is associated with neurological changes.
   b. environmental changes have great impact on the development of the child.
   c. learning takes place independently of age.
   d. all of the above

21. According to the theory of specific learning:
   a. learning is the acquisition of specific patterns.
   b. most things could be learned at any time.
   c. the speed with which a child learns depends on his age.
   d. a and b but not c

22. Which of the following statements about Piaget is true?
   a. He asserts that development involves a constant interchange between the child and the environment.
   b. He asserts that specific learning causes the progression from one stage to another.
   c. He asserts that the age at which each stage begins is consistent across cultures.
   d. He says that the child's schemas assimilate to the environment, as well as the environment being accommodated to the schema.

23. An approach to cognitive development asserts that mental growth is based partly on the acquisition of better and larger chunks of information. This approach explains cognitive development as a change in:
   a. maturation.
   b. information processing.
   c. specific learning.
   d. assimilation.

24. Which of the following is *not* an example of metacognition?
   a. being realistic about how many numbers you can recall at one time
   b. recognizing the difference between reality and illusion
   c. using strategies for reaching solutions
   d. reading and following directions for a recipe

Answer Key for Self-Test

1. b p. 356	13. a p. 365
2. b p. 357	14. c p. 366
3. c pp. 358–59	15. c p. 366
4. b pp. 359–60	16. c p. 366
5. d p. 361	17. d pp. 367–69
6. a pp. 361–62	18. d pp. 369–70
7. a p. 363	19. b p. 370
8. b p. 362	20. a p. 372
9. c p. 362	21. d p. 373
10. a p. 363	22. a p. 374
11. d p. 363	23. b p. 375
12. a p. 364	24. d p. 376

Investigating Psychological Phenomena

CONSERVATION OF NUMBER

Equipment: Thirty-three red poker chips and thirty-four blue ones
Number of subjects: One, age four or five (preoperational stage, according to Piaget)
Time per subject: Fifteen minutes
Time for experimenter: Thirty minutes

In Chapter 13, Professor Gleitman discusses the development of conservation ability as children move into what Piaget calls the stage of concrete operations. The characteristic of this ability is that children come to use a set of mental rules, or operations, to govern their thought about objects in the world. For example, they learn that a certain volume of water is unchanged by the characteristics of the container that happens to contain it. Thus, pouring a certain amount of water from a low and wide container into one that is tall and thin does not change its volume even though the water achieves a greater height in the tall container.

There is also research suggesting that Piaget may have underestimated the ability of children to conserve. Apparently, when faced with somewhat less demanding tasks, which nevertheless are formal tests of conservation ability, young children who should be in a preoperational stage show some signs of conservation. This has been shown most impressively with the conservation of number. The problem that preoperational children face in conserving number is that they confuse numerosity with the physical length of the series which contains the items whose number must be judged. For example, they frequently judge that a row of items contains more items if it is simply longer than another row of items.

The present exercise allows you to take an empirical look at this issue. One of the variables that may influence whether children show evidence of conservation or not is the number of items that are included in a test. Common sense suggests that the more objects in a set whose number must be judged, the more difficult will be the judgment. We shall test this hypothesis in the context of a number conservation test in which the number of objects whose number must be judged will vary. In both conditions of the experiment, your subject will be asked to judge which of two rows contains more objects. In one condition, the number of objects in each row will be less than in the other condition.

In order to conduct this experiment most efficiently, and with the greatest chance of keeping the attention of your subject, prearrange the stimulus arrays before you begin. The figure on page 167 shows you the five

stimulus arrangements for each of the two numerosity conditions. Each letter in the figure represents a chip of the appropriate color (B = blue, R = red). On the left are the arrangements for the lower numerosity condition. The first arrangement is the control condition in which each row contains the same number of chips and in which the two rows are of equal length. In the second figure, the two rows contain the same number, but the lengths of the rows differ. In the third figure, the lengths are equal, but one row contains more chips than the other. The fourth arrangement pits the two variables against one another: the row that is longest also contains fewer chips than the shorter row. On the right are comparable arrangements for the condition in which more chips are used. The four arrangements are in the same order as the ones on the left of the figure.

Make each of the eight arrangements on a separate piece of cardboard, and place them out of sight. Then seat your subject comfortably and explain that you are going to play a game in which the child has to say which row has more chips. Take out arrangement 1 first and ask the child, "Which row has more, the one with red or the one with blue, or are they the same?" If the child answers that they are not the same, then lengthen or shorten one of the rows so that the child agrees that they are equal. Be sure that the red and blue chips line up above one another, so there is a one-to-one correspondence.

Now move on to arrangement 2. Continue with the same line of questioning, asking which row contains more, the red one or the blue one. After getting an answer, which you should record on the protocol form that is given on page 167, ask your subject to explain his/her response. That is, ask why he/she judged one of the rows as having more (or less, or equal, depending upon his/her answer) chips, and record the substance of this answer on the protocol form. Continue with arrangements three and four after which you should move on to arrangements five through eight. In each case, record the data in the spaces provided on the answer sheet. For each arrangement decide whether your subject was paying attention to the number or the length of the series in making his/her judgment. Which condition shows better number conservation overall?

The critical comparison that is of interest in this experiment is whether your subject shows evidence of competence in number conservation with fewer chips, but falters with a greater number of chips. If this is so, how does it fit in with the discussion in the text about the development of conservation? What does it imply about a stage theory of development?

Some other questions that might be raised by this exercise are the following: Would your results have been any different if the two conditions had been run in the opposite order, from the more to the less difficult? Is there something inherent in the questioning of the subject that may bias him/her to attend to length rather than number? Why might number conservation be better with fewer chips in the stimuli? What kinds of operations did your subject seem to be using as the basis for his/her judgments? What kinds of tests could be constructed to discover whether other conservation skills might also develop earlier than previously thought?

STIMULI FOR NUMBER CONSERVATION EXPERIMENT

Small Numbers

1. B   B   B
   R   R   R

2.   B   B   B
    R   R   R

3. B   B
   R   R   R

4. B   B
    R   R   R

Large Numbers

5. B B B B B B
   R R R R R R

6.   B B B B B B
    R R R R R R

7. B   B   B   B   B
    R R   R   R R R

8. B   B   B   B   B
     R R   R R   R R

ANSWER SHEET FOR NUMBER CONSERVATION EXPERIMENT

1. More blue _____
   More red _____
   Both equal _____

   Explanation:

2. More blue _____
   More red _____
   Both equal _____

   Explanation:

3. More blue _____
   More red _____
   Both equal _____

   Explanation:

4. More blue _____
   More red _____
   Both equal _____

   Explanation:

5. More blue _____
   More red _____
   Both equal _____

   Explanation:

6. More blue _____
   More red _____
   Both equal _____

   Explanation:

7. More blue _____
   More red _____
   Both equal _____

   Explanation:

8. More blue _____
   More red _____
   Both equal _____

   Explanation:

CHAPTER 14

Social Development

Learning Objectives

1. Discuss the major ways in which the individual's social world expands as the individual develops.

ATTACHMENT

The roots of attachment

2. Describe the view (the "cupboard" theory) that attributes the infant's love for the mother to the fact that she fulfills basic biological needs.
3. Understand how Harlow's experiments on monkeys cast doubt on the "cupboard" view.
4. Explain Bowlby's theory of attachment, including both positive and negative aspects of attachment seeking. Contrast Bowlby's theory with Freud's "cupboard" theory.
5. Describe the process of imprinting in animals.

Separation and loss

6. Describe the origin of fear of strangers and the effect of long separation from the mother.
7. Describe Ainsworth's procedure for measuring attachment. What characterizes the securely attached child?
8. Cite the evidence that the early parent-child relationship, as assessed in the Strange Situation, is a major determinant of later social and emotional adjustment.
9. Give evidence for the child's attachment to the father. What is the difference between paternal and maternal attachment?
10. Summarize the effects of maternal deprivation on young monkeys and humans. To what extent are the effects similar in monkeys and humans?
11. Describe the circumstances under which it is possible to reverse effects of early maternal deprivation in monkeys and humans.

12. Discuss the effects of maternal separation and the effects of career mothers and day care on later social adjustment.
13. Evaluate the Freudian claims that early experience is a critical factor in social development and that its effects are irreversible. Describe the general process of social development.

CHILDHOOD SOCIALIZATION

Mechanisms of socialization

14. Describe observational learning and modeling. Indicate the way in which this process differs from Pavlovian or instrumental learning.
15. Discuss the relation between imitation and performance, and the importance in imitation of the characteristics of the model.
16. Outline cognitive developmental theory. Indicate how it views imitation and the role it ascribes to a desire for competence.
17. Summarize the basic differences among the Freudian-reinforcement, social learning, and cognitive developmental approaches to socialization.

Patterns of child rearing

18. Describe the autocratic, permissive, and authoritative-reciprocal patterns of child rearing. What are the characteristic behaviors of children raised under each of these approaches?

The child's effect on the parents

19. Explain the interaction between the child's temperament and the parent's pattern of child rearing, and indicate how this interaction complicates the task of relating patterns of child rearing to the child's personality.

THE DEVELOPMENT OF MORALITY

Not doing wrong

20. Know what it means to internalize moral values. Discuss the role of punishment in internalization and the principle of minimal sufficiency.

Doing good

21. Understand how empathy functions in supporting altruistic behavior.

Moral reasoning

22. Describe Kohlberg's stages of moral reasoning.
23. Describe the fundamental sex difference in moral attitudes or reasoning according to Gilligan.
24. Discuss the relation between moral reasoning and moral behavior.

THE DEVELOPMENT OF SEX AND GENDER

25. Distinguish among gender roles, sexual orientation, and gender identity.

Gender roles

26. Describe what gender typing and gender role stereotypes are.

Constitutional factors and sex differences

27. Evaluate the role of nature (biological-genetic factors) in establishing gender roles, with respect to gender differences in aggression and patterns of intellectual abilities.

Social factors and sex differences

28. Discuss how small constitutional differences can be amplified by social forces.

29. Discuss sex reassignment and the possibility of a critical period for gender identity determination.

Theories of gender typing

30. Compare and contrast three theories of gender typing: psychoanalytic, social learning, and cognitive developmental. Be able to explain the critical mechanism of gender typing for each theory.

Sexual orientation

31. Discuss the incidence and cross-cultural aspects of homosexuality. What is the relation between sexual orientation and gender identity?
32. Discuss some possible cases of homosexuality or, more generally, sexual orientation. Include consideration of genetic effects, prenatal effects, early and current hormonal environment, and events in early childhood.

DEVELOPMENT AFTER CHILDHOOD

33. Describe Erik Erikson's conception of human growth. Cite his "eight ages of man." To what extent do they hold across cultures?

Adolescence

34. Discuss the particular problems of adolescence as a transition to adulthood in the United States and in other cultures. Is adolescence always turbulent?

Adulthood

35. Describe the mid-life transition. Indicate how changes in American society have markedly changed the experience of old age.

Programmed Exercises

ATTACHMENT

1. According to Freud, love for the mother derives from the fact that she is associated with the _____ of hunger, thirst, and pain.

alleviation (reduction, decrease)

2. Harlow's experiments with terry-cloth mothers suggest that, in monkeys, the nutrient provided by the mother is less important for attachment than the _____ _____ that she provides.

contact comfort

3. According to Bowlby's theory of attachment, fear of the _____ forms one basis of attachment. Another basis is a tendency to engage in _____ _____ .

unknown (unfamiliar)

social interaction

4. The built-in fear referred to above is initially unspecific, and corresponds to what psychiatrists call _____-_____ anxiety.

free-floating

5. The formation of strong attachments by the young of a species to objects (typically the parent) encountered early in life is called _____ .

imprinting

6. This type of attachment (imprinting) tends to occur during a special time, early in life, called the _____ _____ .

sensitive period

7. According to Bowlby, proximity to an attachment figure provides _____ and _____ , and separation from it leads to _____ .

comfort, security

distress

8. Fear of strangers and specific recognition of the mother occur at about the same time, cross-culturally. This time is from _____ to _____ months of age.

six, eight

9. In Ainsworth's "Strange Situation" measurements, a child who explores freely when the mother is present, shows some distress at her leaving, and greets her return with enthusiasm is called _____ _____ .

securely attached

10. In Ainsworth's "Strange Situation" measurements, a child who doesn't explore even in the mother's presence, becomes intensely upset when she leaves, and shows ambivalence during reunion is called _____ .

resistant

11. In Ainsworth's "Strange Situation" measurements, a child who is distant and aloof toward the mother, shows little distress when she leaves, and ignores her when she returns is called _____ .

avoidant

12. In the "Strange Situation," disappearance of the father produces some _____ , but _____ than that shown when the mother disappears.

distress, less

13. While mothers are preferred sources of care and comfort for most children, fathers are often the preferred _____ .

playmate

14. Motherless monkeys and humans reared in some _____ show marked deficits in social performance.

institutions

15. Maternal deprivation has severe effects in both monkeys and humans, but not if it occurs for no more than a few _____ .

months

16. Freud claimed that early experience (in the first six years or so of life) was _____ for appropriate adult social adjustments, and that the effects of abnormal early experience were _____ .

critical

irreversible

17. Studies using younger monkey therapists with motherless monkeys and studies on children put in nurturant environments after being in institutions indicates that many of the effects of maternal deprivation are _____ .

reversible

18. Evidence indicates that the effects of maternal separation in humans are _____ , and that maternal _____ , with consequent day care, may not compromise social adjustment.

reversible, employment (careers)

CHILDHOOD SOCIALIZATION

19. _____ is the process by which the child acquires the patterns of thought and behavior that are characteristic of the society in which she is born.

Socialization

20. Both Freudian and reinforcement theories explain socialization in terms of the opposite influences of _____ and _____ .

pain (punishment), pleasure (reward)

21. Researchers who believe that the basic Pavlovian and instrumental learning processes must be supplemented to explain socialization are called _____ _____ theorists.

social learning

22. Social learning theorists add to the basic learning processes the mechanism of _____ _____ .

observational learning (modeling)

23. Performance of an observed act depends, in part, upon the characteristics of the _____ .

model

24. The _____ approach to socialization emphasizes the role of understanding or competence in the socialization process.

cognitive (cognitive developmental)

25. According to cognitive theories, imitation is motivated by a desire for _____ .

competence

26. The child-rearing style in which the parent controls the child strictly and does not explain the justification for the governing rules to the child is called the _____ pattern. The opposite

autocratic

extreme is called the _____ pattern. An intermediate approach, in which the parents exercise power, but also recog-

permissive

nize the child's point of view, is called the _____-_____ pattern.

authoritative-reciprocal

27. Of the autocratic, permissive, and authoritative-reciprocal patterns, the one that leads to the best-adjusted children is the

_____-_____ pattern.

authoritative-reciprocal

28. Some differences in the pattern of child rearing may result from differences in _____ in children, some of which are present at birth.

temperament

THE DEVELOPMENT OF MORALITY

29. We say a moral value is _____ when an individual avoids transgressions because he feels that they are wrong and not because he is afraid of being punished.

internalized

30. According to the principle of _____ _____ , internalization occurs best under mild social pressure.

minimal sufficiency

31. A direct emotional response to another person's emotions is called _____ .

empathy

32. Kohlberg has interviewed both adults and children in an attempt to describe the development of _____ _____ .

moral reasoning

33. Kohlberg describes this development, in accordance with the theories of Piaget, in a series of successive _____ .

stages

34. According to Kohlberg, moral reasoning develops along a course in which right and wrong are defined by, first:

_____ _____ _____ ; second: _____ ; and third:

_____ _____ _____ .

1. fear of punishment and/or desire for gain; 2. convention; 3. internalized (or abstract) moral principles

35. According to Gilligan, in making moral decisions, men tend to

emphasize _____ , while women tend to be more influenced   justice

by _____ .   compassion

36. A criticism of Kohlberg's cognitive approach to moral behavior

is that although it may be able to _____ moral rules, these   describe

rules may not actually guide _____ .   behavior

THE DEVELOPMENT OF SEX AND GENDER

37. A definition of maleness or femaleness would have to consider
three different "domains" or aspects. One is our inner sense of

being male or female, called _____ _____ .   gender identity

38. A second aspect (see above) is a group of behavior patterns
that our culture deems appropriate for each sex, called

_____ _____ .   gender roles

39. A third aspect (see above) is our choice of sexual partner, called

_____ _____ .   sexual orientation

40. The expectation that someone "labeled" as a male will be more
aggressive and more interested in things than people is an

example of _____ _____ .   gender typing

41.

This figure illustrates the phenomenon of gender role _____ .   stereotypes

42. Characteristics of the female gender role stereotype in American   submissiveness, interest in peo-
                                                                      ple, emotionality, fear of suc-
society include (list 3) _____ , _____ , and _____ .   cess, talkativeness, gentleness

43. There seems to be a constitutional basis for some sex differences: for example, in the area of motivation, males tend to be more

    _____ than females.   aggressive

44. There may also be a constitutional basis for male superiority in

    _____ ability.   spatial

45. In many cases, culture or social factors act to _____ existing small constitutional sex differences.   exaggerate (or amplify or increase)

46. A child that has reproductive organs that are difficult to classify

    as male or female is called a _____ .   hermaphrodite

47. People who are genetically male but raised as female from

    infancy usually show normal female gender _____ .   identity

48. A female who sees herself as female and is sexually attracted to males but is aggressive and athletic could be said to have some

    characteristics of the male _____ _____ .   gender role

49. Most sex reassignment studies indicate that if the reassignment is

    made within the first _____ years of life, the child will grow   three (or four)

    up with a normal gender _____ , appropriate to his or her   identity
    sex of rearing. However, studies from the Dominican Republic

    suggest that successful sex reassignment can occur at _____ .   puberty

50. According to Freud, the basic mechanism of gender typing is

    _____ .   identification

51. According to the social learning view, little girls show typical

    female interests because they are _____ for doing so.   rewarded (reinforced)

52. Cognitive developmental theories point out that a three-year-old who believes that a girl can become a boy if given a haircut fails

    to show _____ _____ .   gender constancy

53. According to cognitive developmental theory, and in contrast to social learning theory, identification with a same-sex model

    (precedes or follows) _____ the acquisition of gender identity.   follows

54. According to social learning theories, the first aspect of sex

    differences that is established is _____ _____ .   gender role

55. The majority of men and women are _____ in that they seek sexual partners of the opposite sex.   heterosexual

56. The incidence of male homosexuality in the United States is

    about _____ percent of all adult males (as of 1948).   4

57. At this time, there is not clear evidence for a biological basis for homosexuality, in terms of either different levels of

    _____ _____ or _____ predisposition.   sex hormones (androgens), genetic

DEVELOPMENT AFTER CHILDHOOD

58. Erikson's "Eight Ages of Man" span the entire life cycle, each
stage accompanied by a critical _____ .   conflict (or crisis)

59. The stage of transition from childhood to adulthood is called
_____ . At this stage, the major conflict is described as an   adolescence
_____ _____ .   identity crisis

60. In some cultures, the transition to adulthood is marked clearly,
with a ceremony or more extended set of activities called
_____ _____ .   initiation rites

61. In the _____-_____ _____ , people of middle age   mid-life transition
reappraise what they have done with their lives and may
reevaluate their marriage and career.

62. In Erikson's scheme, although there are some important biological
markers in growth past childhood, such as _____ , the   puberty (or menopause)
quality and duration of each stage is substantially influenced by
_____ .   culture

Self-Test

1. Harlow's results, showing a preference for a "terry-cloth mother" over a wire mother that provides food by infant monkeys, argue:
   a. in favor of Freud's view of attachment.
   b. in favor of Bowlby's view of attachment.
   c. that nutrition has no effect in producing attachment between infant and mother.
   d. a and b
   e. all of the above

2. Bowlby's theory of attachment:
   a. may include imprinting to a familiar object.
   b. assumes that infants fear unfamiliar objects.
   c. assumes infants have a tendency to interact socially.
   d. all of the above
   e. none of the above

3. Which of the following statements about imprinting is false?
   a. Imprinting depends on the fact that the parents will be the most salient objects around the offspring in the first part of life.
   b. Imprinting is based on experience.
   c. Animals may lose the capacity to imprint after a certain age.
   d. One would not expect to find imprinting in a "parasitic" species that is typically raised by adults of another species.
   e. none of the above

4. Proximity : comfort :: separation :
   a. imprinting
   b. sensitive periods
   c. providing nutrients
   d. distress
   e. satisfaction

5. The effects of maternal deprivation for more than a few months on subsequent behavior of monkeys and humans are:
   a. severe, and almost the same.
   b. severe for humans, mild for monkeys.
   c. severe for monkeys, mild for humans.
   d. minimal.
   e. irreversible.

6. A conclusion that can be drawn from monkey and human maternal deprivation studies is that:
   a. adequate nutrition is not sufficient to produce normal social behavior.
   b. behavior to peers is unaffected by maternal deprivation.
   c. imprinting does not have anything to do with later sexual or maternal behavior.
   d. the effects of maternal deprivation are very different in humans and monkeys.
   e. maternal deprivation effects are especially severe if the deprivation occurs in the first few months of life.

7. Monkeys deprived of mothers in about the first six months of life:

a. show a temporary depression in social behavior.

b. are abnormal in social behavior, but will usually be successful parents.

c. are permanently deficient in all domains of social behavior.

d. show severe deficits in social behavior that are completely irreversible.

e. show severe deficits in social behavior that can be at least partly cured by carefully designed "therapy."

8. Institutionalized human children and motherless monkeys show social abnormalities characterized by:
a. a "critical period" beginning at the time of birth and ending at about three months.
b. social withdrawal.
c. long-term effects that are irreversible.
d. a and b
e. all of the above

9. Freud claimed that early experience had (1) a critical and (2) an irreversible effect on social development. Results from research up to this time suggest that:
a. these two principles are basically correct.
b. early experiences have important effects, but many are reversible.
c. these two principles arc totally incorrect.
d. early experiences have some significant effects, and these effects are irreversible.
e. none of the above

10. Both the Freudian approach and social learning or reinforcement theory agree that _____ is a major factor in socialization.
a. imitation
b. modeling
c. the child's understanding of the importance of older people
d. gender identity
e. none of the above

11. According to social learning theory, a critical aspect of socialization is:
a. observational learning from models.
b. making models.
c. Pavlovian conditioning.
d. imprinting.
e. none of the above

12. Little Bertram watches a seedy character steal a tip from a restaurant table and get away with it. Is Bertram likely to imitate this behavior? According to social learning theorists the answer is:
a. yes, because the stealing was reinforced.
b. no, because the seedy character is a poor

model.
c. yes and no; the act is reinforced, but the actor is a poor model.
d. yes and no; the act is not violent, but the consequences are not performed or modeled.
e. none of the above

13. Wendy sees her big sister smoking a cigarette. A few hours later she sneaks over to a pack of cigarettes, takes one out, holds it with two fingers, and puts it into her mouth, looking as debonair as possible. Then she lights it up, inhales her first breath, and proceeds to cough and gag. But she continues to smoke the whole cigarette. This performance presents problems for a simple reinforcement view of socialization because:
a. there is observational learning without immediate performance.
b. there seems to be negative reinforcement (gagging) for smoking.
c. there seems to be no basic biological reinforcement for her smoking.
d. it is not clear why she would want to imitate her sister.
e. all of the above

14. According to cognitive developmental theory, the motivation for imitation is _____ , while according to social learning theory, the motivation for imitation is _____ .
a. to increase competence, to gain reinforcements
b. to understand the model, to model
c. to gain reinforcements, to gain social reinforcements
d. to increase competence, to decrease competence
e. to model competence, to model reinforcement

15. Ironically, children raised in the opposing autocratic and permissive styles share some common behavioral characteristics. Both types of children tend to:
a. be socially responsible.
b. be more attached to their father.
c. lack independence.
d. be high in originality.
e. a and c

16. Imagine that a study reports that most cranky five-year-olds had parents who closed the door to their infants' bedrooms at night, so the baby wouldn't wake them. What might be possible explanations of this result?
a. Isolating infants causes them to be cranky later in life.

b. Cranky infants are more likely to be isolated by their parents.

c. Parents who isolate their children in this way also do other things in child rearing that cause crankiness.

d. Crankiness is inherited; cranky parents are more likely to be irritated by a crying child, and so are more likely to isolate it.

e. all of the above

17. Authoritative-reciprocal rearing style : optimal adjustment :: mild social pressure :
   a. doing good
   b. not doing wrong
   c. maximum internalization
   d. permissive rearing style
   e. autocratic rearing style

18. Forced compliance is an ineffective way of producing attitude change. This finding is in accord with:
   a. the permissive rearing style.
   b. the principle of minimal sufficiency.
   c. the principle of imitation.
   d. attachment theory.
   e. none of the above

19. In order to show altruistic or unselfish helping behavior, a child (or adult) must:
   a. experience empathic distress.
   b. be at a high stage of moral reasoning.
   c. know how to be helpful in the particular situation.
   d. a and b
   e. a and c

20. Consider the following three objections to making three reservations on different airlines at the same time for one person: A. It is against the unwritten rules of the airlines. B. It interferes with the access of others with no tangible gain to the party in question. C. It can be detected, and penalties can be assessed. According to Kohlberg, how would these three reasons be arranged in terms of the development of moral reasoning; indicate the earliest stage first.
   a. A, B, C
   b. B, C, A
   c. C, B, A
   d. B, A, C
   e. C, A, B

21. A person says that one shouldn't double park because it is against the law. This explanation is an example of:
   a. preconventional morality.
   b. conventional morality.

c. postconventional morality.
   d. empathy.
   e. none of the above

22. According to Gilligan, moral reasoning in men is relatively more influenced by justice, while in women it is relatively more influenced by compassion. But men and women don't differ on scores on Kohlberg's tests of moral reasoning. Why?
   a. Kohlberg's tests value compassion as much as abstract principles.
   b. Compassion is more abstract than justice.
   c. The male-female difference has more to do with emphases than abilities.
   d. a and b
   e. a and c

23. Seymour speaks eloquently on the issue of equal rights for all races and religions but is actually quite racially prejudiced when he hires workers at his business. This illustrates:
   a. the effects of reinforcement.
   b. the influence of the Freudian unconscious.
   c. the distinction between moral reasoning and moral conduct.
   d. the conflict between the social learning view and more traditional reinforcement explanations of moral behavior.
   e. egocentrism.

24. Which of the following is illustrative of gender role?
   a. thinking of oneself as a female
   b. attraction to the opposite sex
   c. submissiveness and emotionality in a female
   d. homosexual tendencies
   e. none of the above

25. The finding that, in American culture, females express emotion more readily than do males, should be interpreted to mean:
   a. that females are constitutionally more inclined to express emotions.
   b. that our society teaches females to be more expressive.
   c. that the average female is more emotionally expressive than the average male, but that there is a great deal of overlap.
   d. gender typing is not a sufficient explanation of sex difference, and one must also consider gender identity.
   e. a and d

26. The idea that there is a constitutional factor contributing to sex differences in aggression or spatial orientation is (or would be) supported by all but which of the following?

a. In early humans, the stronger male was responsible for almost all hunting and fighting.

b. These differences are seen in many cultures.

c. Some of these differences are also seen in animals.

d. Male hormone increases aggression.

e. all of the above

27. According to the psychoanalytic view, the basic mechanism of gender typing is:

a. imitation.

b. conditioning.

c. repression.

d. identification.

e. imprinting.

28. Kohlberg's cognitive developmental view criticizes both the Freudian concept of identification and the social learning notion of imitation in the first few years of life on all but which of the following grounds?

a. Little children don't show gender constancy.

b. Little children don't have a basis for recognizing which of their parents is of their sex.

c. Gender role precedes gender identity.

d. Young children may not understand that males have a penis and females don't.

e. b and c

29. The psychoanalytic notion that the young boy identifies with his father in order to avoid punishment for his erotic feelings toward his mother assumes:

a. a necessary linkage among gender role, gender identity, and sexual orientation.

b. that the boy understands his fundamental sexual similarity to his father.

c. that erotic factors form the basis for gender typing.

d. all of the above

e. none of the above

30. According to Kohlberg's cognitive view of gender typing, gender identity depends critically on:

a. identification.

b. constitutional factors.

c. achievement of gender constancy.

d. hormones.

e. imprinting.

31. For which theory (or theories) of sex typing is the fact that the little boy has a penis of special importance?

a. psychoanalytic

b. social learning

c. cognitive developmental

d. a and b

e. all of the above

32. The psychoanalytic view suggests that male homosexuality may result when the child resolves fears aroused during the Oedipal conflict by identifying with the mother instead of the father. This theory would have difficulty explaining:

a. the fact that many homosexuals do not consult psychiatrists.

b. the absence of sex hormone differences between male homosexuals and heterosexuals.

c. the reported high frequency of hostile and detached fathers of homosexual males who seek psychiatric help.

d. the fact that, typically, male homosexuals have traditional male gender identity and roles.

e. all of the above

33. The data from sex reassignment and the fact that, in most cases, homosexuals report homosexual tendencies early in life both argue for:

a. the psychoanalytic approach.

b. attachment to the mother at the time of the Oedipal crisis.

c. a genetic basis for important aspects of sexual orientation or gender identity.

d. all of the above

e. none of the above

34. A clear and substantial difference has been documented between male homosexuals and heterosexuals with respect to:

a. gender role.

b. gender identity.

c. testosterone (androgen) levels.

d. passivity.

e. none of the above

35. The transition from adolescence to adulthood:

a. occurs at about the same age in all cultures.

b. is always a turbulent period.

c. usually occurs at the onset of sexual maturity.

d. all of the above

e. none of the above

36. Initiation rites, retirement parties, and marriages have in common that they:

a. explicitly mark important life transitions.

b. occur in virtually all cultures.

c. are explicitly predicted by Erikson's scheme.

d. match Freud's views of major life events.

e. make for gradual transitions from one stage to another.

37. In some societies, children gradually assume adult responsibilities, and in some societies, old family members live in the home, taking care of grandchildren (or great-grandchildren) and giving advice. These traditions:
    a. emphasize transitions from one stage of life to another.
    b. ease transition from one stage of life to another.
    c. emphasize the importance of biological factors in life history.
    d. prove the correctness of Erikson's stages.
    e. none of the above

Answer Key for Self-Test

1. b pp. 380–81
2. d p. 381
3. e p. 382
4. d p. 383
5. a pp. 384–86
6. a pp. 384–86
7. e p. 386
8. b pp. 385–86
9. b pp. 386–87
10. c pp. 389–90
11. a p. 389
12. c p. 390
13. e pp. 389–90
14. a pp. 390–91
15. c p. 392
16. e p. 393
17. c pp. 392, 394
18. b p. 394
19. e pp. 395–96

20. e p. 396
21. b p. 397
22. c p. 397
23. c p. 398
24. c p. 398
25. c p. 400
26. e pp. 399–401
27. d p. 403
28. c pp. 403–4
29. d p. 403
30. c p. 404
31. a p. 403
32. d p. 406
33. e pp. 406–7
34. e pp. 406–7
35. c pp. 408–11
36. a p. 410
37. b pp. 411, 413

Investigating Psychological Phenomena

SEX DIFFERENCES

Equipment: None
Number of subjects: Twelve
Time per subject: Five minutes
Time for experimenter: Sixty minutes

Sex differences can be analyzed into three different categories:
1. Gender identity—thinking of oneself as male or female.
2. Sexual orientation—sex of desired sexual partners, leading to the heterosexual-homosexual distinction.
3. Gender role—behavior patterns or attitudes associated with one or the other sex.

The relative role of experience (nurture) and genes (nature) has been debated for each of these aspects of sex. But before such studies can be done definitively, we must be clear on the nature of the differences to be explained. This is more or less clear for gender identity and sexual orientation. But the major behavioral and attitudinal differences between the sexes are not that obvious and surely differ across cultures.

This study is an attempt to define some reliable sex differences among American college students. We have developed seventeen questions that promise to reveal sex differences (we will use as a criterion of a question that discriminates between the sexes a response pattern in which there is at least a 25 percent difference between males and females).

First: Answer the questionnaire. *Do not read on until you finish it.*

QUESTIONNAIRE ON SEX DIFFERENCES

| Sex: Male   Female |
| (Circle one) |

1. Would you be willing to kill a cockroach by slapping it with your hands?
    a) yes　　　　　　　　b) no
2. What is Queen Anne's lace?
    a) flower　　　　　　　d) doily
    b) embroidery　　　　　e) spice
    c) perfume
3. How many times in the last twenty-four hours have you used the word "shit"?
    a) less than 5 times　　b) 5 or more times
4. Can you sew well enough to make clothes?
    a) yes　　　　　　　　b) no
5. Do you believe in sexual intercourse only after a spiritual love exists between you and your partner?
    a) yes　　　　　　　　b) no
6. Do you walk around freely in the nude in a locker room?
    a) yes　　　　　　　　b) no
7. How often do you cry?
    a) very often　　　　　d) very infrequently
    b) often　　　　　　　e) never
    c) only with good
       reason
8. At times I feel like smashing things.
    a) true　　　　　　　　b) false
9. Do you know your chest measurement?
    a) yes　　　　　　　　b) no
10. Can you change a tire easily?
    a) yes　　　　　　　　b) no
11. I spend no more than one hour during an average school day playing the radio or listening to records.
    a) true　　　　　　　　b) false

12. Would you prefer to be the dominant one in a relationship?
   a) yes   b) no
13. Do you think that you are overweight?
   a) yes   b) no
14. When you get depressed, does washing your hair make you feel better?
   a) yes   b) no
15. Do you sleep in the nude?
   a) yes   b) no
16. Which parent are you closest to?
   a) mother   b) father
17. I try to keep my room as neat as possible.
   a) true   b) false

These questions have been made up by faculty and students in introductory psychology courses. Each question has been "tested" with at least 100 undergraduate students in psychology courses. Therefore, we know how well these questions discriminate between college age males and females (at least in 1971–1973, when the questions were tested). Of the seventeen questions, we know from past testing that five do *not* discriminate males from females. Try and guess, in advance, which questions would not discriminate. Then, check your guesses against the data presented on the final page of this study. *Guess before you read on.*

List questions that would not discriminate.

Note the type of successful questions in this questionnaire. Some relate to traditional male-female differences. Thus, males are more aggressive (item 12 on dominance, but note no difference on item 8 — smashing things. Similarly males are less squeamish (item 1, cockroach) and more restrained emotionally (item 7, crying).

Other questions refer to knowledge or abilities that tend to go with gender in our society. This would include information about flowers (item 2, Queen Anne's lace), sewing ability (item 4), ability to change a tire (item 10), and knowledge of body measurements (item 9).

There are in addition some "miscellaneous" questions that tap into reliable differences (item 5, attitudes toward intercourse; item 6, attitude toward walking around nude in a locker room; item 13, perception of fatness in self; item 14, washing of hair as a response to depression; and item 17, neatness).

Second, collaborate with at least one or two other students in the class, so that you can collect enough data. Give the twelve copies of this questionnaire, located on pages 183–93 to twelve undergraduates, six males and six females. (Try to get them to fill out the questionnaire when you give it to them; otherwise, you will find that you don't get a very high return rate.) Aim for a minimum of five completed questionnaires for each sex. Combine your results with the results of as many classmates as you can: It would be desirable to end up with at least fifteen students of each sex.

Third, tabulate your results (see page 180 in the following way. For the "yes" or "no" questions (e.g., item 1), add up the number of subjects who answered "yes." Then calculate what percentage answered "yes." For the "true" or "false" questions (e.g., item 8), record those who answer "true." For other items (e.g., item 2), add up the number of subjects whose answers are the same as those indicated in parentheses under "Item" (e.g., item 1 – flower).

Fourth, we have devised a "femaleness" score, by indicating the more common female response to each of the questions that discriminates sex. Compute such a score for each of your subjects by counting one point for each of the following answers:

1. no	9. yes
2. flower	10. no
4. yes	12. no
5. yes	13. yes
6. no	14. yes
7. very often, often, or with good reason	17. yes

Indicate here the total number of subjects of each sex from whom you have collected data:

Male _____   Female _____

	Your data (combined with classmates' data)				U. of Pa. Students**	
	Male		Female		Male	Female
Item	#	%	#	%	%	%
1. Killing cockroach	_____	_____	_____	_____	37	* 7
2. Queen Anne's lace (correct answer: flower)	_____	_____	_____	_____	50	*82
3. Using word "shit" (less than 5 times)	_____	_____	_____	_____	49	50
4. Sew clothes	_____	_____	_____	_____	4	*59
5. Intercourse only after spiritual love	_____	_____	_____	_____	30	*75
6. Nude in locker room	_____	_____	_____	_____	72	*31
7. Crying frequently (very often, often, or only with good reason)	_____	_____	_____	_____	22	*78
8. Feel like smashing things	_____	_____	_____	_____	75	70
9. Chest measurement	_____	_____	_____	_____	28	*78
10. Change tire	_____	_____	_____	_____	76	*13
11. Playing radio	_____	_____	_____	_____	41	42
12. Prefer dominance in relationship	_____	_____	_____	_____	72	*10
13. Overweight	_____	_____	_____	_____	17	*60
14. Washing hair when depressed	_____	_____	_____	_____	19	*53
15. Sleep in nude	_____	_____	_____	_____	39	44
16. Closest parent (mother)	_____	_____	_____	_____	61	72
17. Keep room neat	_____	_____	_____	_____	51	*77

*A male-female difference of at least 25 percent.
**Responses to items in the sex difference questionnaire by undergraduate introductory psychology students at the University of Pennsylvania (1971–1973). Responses are based on from 70 to 270 males and from 88 to 292 females, depending on the item.

SCORES OF MALES AND FEMALES ON "FEMALENESS" SCORE

Plot the number of males and females with each score. Use solid lines for the males and broken lines for the females. The graph at the left contains data gathered from fifteen undergraduate males and seventeen undergraduate females in 1980. Plot your data on the blank graph on the right. How well does this score separate biological females from biological males? What percent of females score less than the highest male? How would you go about making a better behavioral discriminator of the sexes? (Note: We have avoided asking questions that might trivially distinguish males from females, such as: Do you wash the hair on your chest? or Do you ever wear dresses?)

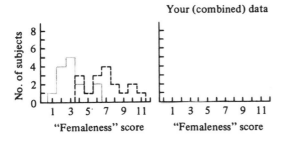

You may note some major differences between your data and the data we reported in 1971–1973. In fact, we tried the questionnaire on fifteen male and seventeen female undergraduate students in 1980 (the subjects used in the femaleness ratings), and found some differences from our 1971–1973 study. The biggest effects were that male-female differences disappeared for Queen Anne's lace (question 2), overweight (question 13: Over half of the men as well as women thought they were overweight), and washing hair when depressed (question 14: Practically no one in our recent sample answered yes to that).

There are basically three ways to explain discrepancies (our recent data or your data) from the original large sample of 1971–1973:

1. A general change in society over the last decade. It would seem fair to say that female gender roles have become more like male gender roles in this period. Does your data show this trend for any items? (Note that this would mean that female scores could move closer to male scores, and *not* that male scores would move closer to female scores. Of course, it is also possible to argue that the roles are becoming less distinct, but not necessarily moving toward the traditional male role.)

2. A difference in the populations sampled. Students from different parts of the country or from institutions with different styles or emphases might differ markedly in gender roles. Do you think your student sample would be likely to be very different from University of Pennsylvania students? In what ways? Is this reflected in differences on any scores? (Note, the differences might not just appear as male-female differences, but as generally higher or lower levels of response. For example, one might expect a generally higher positive response on sewing or changing a tire in people from rural backgrounds.)

3. Sampling error. Some observed differences may simply result from the fact that all samples from the same population don't have precisely the same scores (see Statistical Appendix to the textbook). With a small sample such as you have collected (as opposed to the large sample that we originally used), a wider variation from sample to sample would be expected. We would ordinarily use statistical methods to indicate how confident we would be that a difference between samples was not due to chance.

FURTHER ACTIVITIES

You might wish to try out some other questions that would relate gender identity to gender role. You could get a suggestion as to whether your questions were good discriminators with samples as low as twenty.

You can also try to use behavior rather than verbal responses to questionnaires. Can you think of obvious differences in such activities as: manner of walking or eating, facial expressions, behavior in front of mirrors, motorcycle riding, etc. Test your hypotheses by direct observation.

(If your instructor collects the data, fill out the report sheet in Appendix B.)

QUESTIONNAIRE ON SEX DIFFERENCES

> Sex: Male   Female
> (Circle one)

1. Would you be willing to kill a cockroach by slapping it with your hands?
   a) yes   b) no
2. What is Queen Anne's lace?
   a) flower   d) doily
   b) embroidery   e) spice
   c) perfume
3. How many times in the last twenty-four hours have you used the word "shit"?
   a) less than 5 times   b) 5 or more times
4. Can you sew well enough to make clothes?
   a) yes   b) no
5. Do you believe in sexual intercourse only after a spiritual love exists between you and your partner?
   a) yes   b) no
6. Do you walk around freely in the nude in a locker room?
   a) yes   b) no
7. How often do you cry?
   a) very often   d) very infrequently
   b) often   e) never
   c) only with good
      reason
8. At times I feel like smashing things.
   a) true   b) false
9. Do you know your chest measurement?
   a) yes   b) no
10. Can you change a tire easily?
    a) yes   b) no
11. I spend no more than one hour during an average school day playing the radio or listening to records.
    a) true   b) false
12. Would you prefer to be the dominant one in a relationship?
    a) yes   b) no
13. Do you think that you are overweight?
    a) yes   b) no
14. When you get depressed, does washing your hair make you feel better?
    a) yes   b) no
15. Do you sleep in the nude?
    a) yes   b) no
16. Which parent are you closest to?
    a) mother   b) father
17. I try to keep my room as neat as possible.
    a) true   b) false

QUESTIONNAIRE ON SEX DIFFERENCES

> Sex: Male   Female
> (Circle one)

1. Would you be willing to kill a cockroach by slapping it with your hands?
   a) yes   b) no
2. What is Queen Anne's lace?
   a) flower   d) doily
   b) embroidery   e) spice
   c) perfume
3. How many times in the last twenty-four hours have you used the word "shit"?
   a) less than 5 times   b) 5 or more times
4. Can you sew well enough to make clothes?
   a) yes   b) no
5. Do you believe in sexual intercourse only after a spiritual love exists between you and your partner?
   a) yes   b) no
6. Do you walk around freely in the nude in a locker room?
   a) yes   b) no
7. How often do you cry?
   a) very often   d) very infrequently
   b) often   e) never
   c) only with good
      reason
8. At times I feel like smashing things.
   a) true   b) false
9. Do you know your chest measurement?
   a) yes   b) no
10. Can you change a tire easily?
    a) yes   b) no
11. I spend no more than one hour during an average school day playing the radio or listening to records.
    a) true   b) false
12. Would you prefer to be the dominant one in a relationship?
    a) yes   b) no
13. Do you think that you are overweight?
    a) yes   b) no
14. When you get depressed, does washing your hair make you feel better?
    a) yes   b) no
15. Do you sleep in the nude?
    a) yes   b) no
16. Which parent are you closest to?
    a) mother   b) father
17. I try to keep my room as neat as possible.
    a) true   b) false

QUESTIONNAIRE ON SEX DIFFERENCES

Sex: Male   Female
(Circle one)

1. Would you be willing to kill a cockroach by slapping it with your hands?
   a) yes   b) no
2. What is Queen Anne's lace?
   a) flower   d) doily
   b) embroidery   e) spice
   c) perfume
3. How many times in the last twenty-four hours have you used the word "shit"?
   a) less than 5 times   b) 5 or more times
4. Can you sew well enough to make clothes?
   a) yes   b) no
5. Do you believe in sexual intercourse only after a spiritual love exists between you and your partner?
   a) yes   b) no
6. Do you walk around freely in the nude in a locker room?
   a) yes   b) no
7. How often do you cry?
   a) very often   d) very infrequently
   b) often   e) never
   c) only with good
      reason
8. At times I feel like smashing things.
   a) true   b) false
9. Do you know your chest measurement?
   a) yes   b) no
10. Can you change a tire easily?
    a) yes   b) no
11. I spend no more than one hour during an average school day playing the radio or listening to records.
    a) true   b) false
12. Would you prefer to be the dominant one in a relationship?
    a) yes   b) no
13. Do you think that you are overweight?
    a) yes   b) no
14. When you get depressed, does washing your hair make you feel better?
    a) yes   b) no
15. Do you sleep in the nude?
    a) yes   b) no
16. Which parent are you closest to?
    a) mother   b) father
17. I try to keep my room as neat as possible.
    a) true   b) false

QUESTIONNAIRE ON SEX DIFFERENCES

Sex: Male   Female
(Circle one)

1. Would you be willing to kill a cockroach by slapping it with your hands?
   a) yes   b) no
2. What is Queen Anne's lace?
   a) flower   d) doily
   b) embroidery   e) spice
   c) perfume
3. How many times in the last twenty-four hours have you used the word "shit"?
   a) less than 5 times   b) 5 or more times
4. Can you sew well enough to make clothes?
   a) yes   b) no
5. Do you believe in sexual intercourse only after a spiritual love exists between you and your partner?
   a) yes   b) no
6. Do you walk around freely in the nude in a locker room?
   a) yes   b) no
7. How often do you cry?
   a) very often   d) very infrequently
   b) often   c) never
   c) only with good
      reason
8. At times I feel like smashing things.
   a) true   b) false
9. Do you know your chest measurement?
   a) yes   b) no
10. Can you change a tire easily?
    a) yes   b) no
11. I spend no more than one hour during an average school day playing the radio or listening to records.
    a) true   b) false
12. Would you prefer to be the dominant one in a relationship?
    a) yes   b) no
13. Do you think that you are overweight?
    a) yes   b) no
14. When you get depressed, does washing your hair make you feel better?
    a) yes   b) no
15. Do you sleep in the nude?
    a) yes   b) no
16. Which parent are you closest to?
    a) mother   b) father
17. I try to keep my room as neat as possible.
    a) true   b) false

QUESTIONNAIRE ON SEX DIFFERENCES

> Sex: Male   Female
> (Circle one)

1. Would you be willing to kill a cockroach by slapping it with your hands?
   a) yes   b) no
2. What is Queen Anne's lace?
   a) flower   d) doily
   b) embroidery   e) spice
   c) perfume
3. How many times in the last twenty-four hours have you used the word "shit"?
   a) less than 5 times   b) 5 or more times
4. Can you sew well enough to make clothes?
   a) yes   b) no
5. Do you believe in sexual intercourse only after a spiritual love exists between you and your partner?
   a) yes   b) no
6. Do you walk around freely in the nude in a locker room?
   a) yes   b) no
7. How often do you cry?
   a) very often   d) very infrequently
   b) often   e) never
   c) only with good
      reason
8. At times I feel like smashing things.
   a) true   b) false
9. Do you know your chest measurement?
   a) yes   b) no
10. Can you change a tire easily?
    a) yes   b) no
11. I spend no more than one hour during an average school day playing the radio or listening to records.
    a) true   b) false
12. Would you prefer to be the dominant one in a relationship?
    a) yes   b) no
13. Do you think that you are overweight?
    a) yes   b) no
14. When you get depressed, does washing your hair make you feel better?
    a) yes   b) no
15. Do you sleep in the nude?
    a) yes   b) no
16. Which parent are you closest to?
    a) mother   b) father
17. I try to keep my room as neat as possible.
    a) true   b) false

QUESTIONNAIRE ON SEX DIFFERENCES

> Sex: Male   Female
> (Circle one)

1. Would you be willing to kill a cockroach by slapping it with your hands?
   a) yes   b) no
2. What is Queen Anne's lace?
   a) flower   d) doily
   b) embroidery   e) spice
   c) perfume
3. How many times in the last twenty-four hours have you used the word "shit"?
   a) less than 5 times   b) 5 or more times
4. Can you sew well enough to make clothes?
   a) yes   b) no
5. Do you believe in sexual intercourse only after a spiritual love exists between you and your partner?
   a) yes   b) no
6. Do you walk around freely in the nude in a locker room?
   a) yes   b) no
7. How often do you cry?
   a) very often   d) very infrequently
   b) often   e) never
   c) only with good
      reason
8. At times I feel like smashing things.
   a) true   b) false
9. Do you know your chest measurement?
   a) yes   b) no
10. Can you change a tire easily?
    a) yes   b) no
11. I spend no more than one hour during an average school day playing the radio or listening to records.
    a) true   b) false
12. Would you prefer to be the dominant one in a relationship?
    a) yes   b) no
13. Do you think that you are overweight?
    a) yes   b) no
14. When you get depressed, does washing your hair make you feel better?
    a) yes   b) no
15. Do you sleep in the nude?
    a) yes   b) no
16. Which parent are you closest to?
    a) mother   b) father
17. I try to keep my room as neat as possible.
    a) true   b) false

QUESTIONNAIRE ON SEX DIFFERENCES

> Sex: Male   Female
> (Circle one)

1. Would you be willing to kill a cockroach by slapping it with your hands?
   a) yes   b) no
2. What is Queen Anne's lace?
   a) flower   d) doily
   b) embroidery   e) spice
   c) perfume
3. How many times in the last twenty-four hours have you used the word "shit"?
   a) less than 5 times   b) 5 or more times
4. Can you sew well enough to make clothes?
   a) yes   b) no
5. Do you believe in sexual intercourse only after a spiritual love exists between you and your partner?
   a) yes   b) no
6. Do you walk around freely in the nude in a locker room?
   a) yes   b) no
7. How often do you cry?
   a) very often   d) very infrequently
   b) often   e) never
   c) only with good
      reason
8. At times I feel like smashing things.
   a) true   b) false
9. Do you know your chest measurement?
   a) yes   b) no
10. Can you change a tire easily?
    a) yes   b) no
11. I spend no more than one hour during an average school day playing the radio or listening to records.
    a) true   b) false
12. Would you prefer to be the dominant one in a relationship?
    a) yes   b) no
13. Do you think that you are overweight?
    a) yes   b) no
14. When you get depressed, does washing your hair make you feel better?
    a) yes   b) no
15. Do you sleep in the nude?
    a) yes   b) no
16. Which parent are you closest to?
    a) mother   b) father
17. I try to keep my room as neat as possible.
    a) true   b) false

QUESTIONNAIRE ON SEX DIFFERENCES

> Sex: Male   Female
> (Circle one)

1. Would you be willing to kill a cockroach by slapping it with your hands?
   a) yes   b) no
2. What is Queen Anne's lace?
   a) flower   d) doily
   b) embroidery   e) spice
   c) perfume
3. How many times in the last twenty-four hours have you used the word "shit"?
   a) less than 5 times   b) 5 or more times
4. Can you sew well enough to make clothes?
   a) yes   b) no
5. Do you believe in sexual intercourse only after a spiritual love exists between you and your partner?
   a) yes   b) no
6. Do you walk around freely in the nude in a locker room?
   a) yes   b) no
7. How often do you cry?
   a) very often   d) very infrequently
   b) often   e) never
   c) only with good
      reason
8. At times I feel like smashing things.
   a) true   b) false
9. Do you know your chest measurement?
   a) yes   b) no
10. Can you change a tire easily?
    a) yes   b) no
11. I spend no more than one hour during an average school day playing the radio or listening to records.
    a) true   b) false
12. Would you prefer to be the dominant one in a relationship?
    a) yes   b) no
13. Do you think that you are overweight?
    a) yes   b) no
14. When you get depressed, does washing your hair make you feel better?
    a) yes   b) no
15. Do you sleep in the nude?
    a) yes   b) no
16. Which parent are you closest to?
    a) mother   b) father
17. I try to keep my room as neat as possible.
    a) true   b) false

QUESTIONNAIRE ON SEX DIFFERENCES

> Sex: Male   Female
> (Circle one)

1. Would you be willing to kill a cockroach by slapping it with your hands?
   a) yes   b) no
2. What is Queen Anne's lace?
   a) flower   d) doily
   b) embroidery   e) spice
   c) perfume
3. How many times in the last twenty-four hours have you used the word "shit"?
   a) less than 5 times   b) 5 or more times
4. Can you sew well enough to make clothes?
   a) yes   b) no
5. Do you believe in sexual intercourse only after a spiritual love exists between you and your partner?
   a) yes   b) no
6. Do you walk around freely in the nude in a locker room?
   a) yes   b) no
7. How often do you cry?
   a) very often   d) very infrequently
   b) often   e) never
   c) only with good
      reason
8. At times I feel like smashing things.
   a) true   b) false
9. Do you know your chest measurement?
   a) yes   b) no
10. Can you change a tire easily?
    a) yes   b) no
11. I spend no more than one hour during an average school day playing the radio or listening to records.
    a) true   b) false
12. Would you prefer to be the dominant one in a relationship?
    a) yes   b) no
13. Do you think that you are overweight?
    a) yes   b) no
14. When you get depressed, does washing your hair make you feel better?
    a) yes   b) no
15. Do you sleep in the nude?
    a) yes   b) no
16. Which parent are you closest to?
    a) mother   b) father
17. I try to keep my room as neat as possible.
    a) true   b) false

QUESTIONNAIRE ON SEX DIFFERENCES

> Sex: Male   Female
> (Circle one)

1. Would you be willing to kill a cockroach by slapping it with your hands?
   a) yes   b) no
2. What is Queen Anne's lace?
   a) flower   d) doily
   b) embroidery   e) spice
   c) perfume
3. How many times in the last twenty-four hours have you used the word "shit"?
   a) less than 5 times   b) 5 or more times
4. Can you sew well enough to make clothes?
   a) yes   b) no
5. Do you believe in sexual intercourse only after a spiritual love exists between you and your partner?
   a) yes   b) no
6. Do you walk around freely in the nude in a locker room?
   a) yes   b) no
7. How often do you cry?
   a) very often   d) very infrequently
   b) often   e) never
   c) only with good
      reason
8. At times I feel like smashing things.
   a) true   b) false
9. Do you know your chest measurement?
   a) yes   b) no
10. Can you change a tire easily?
    a) yes   b) no
11. I spend no more than one hour during an average school day playing the radio or listening to records.
    a) true   b) false
12. Would you prefer to be the dominant one in a relationship?
    a) yes   b) no
13. Do you think that you are overweight?
    a) yes   b) no
14. When you get depressed, does washing your hair make you feel better?
    a) yes   b) no
15. Do you sleep in the nude?
    a) yes   b) no
16. Which parent are you closest to?
    a) mother   b) father
17. I try to keep my room as neat as possible.
    a) true   b) false

QUESTIONNAIRE ON SEX DIFFERENCES

Sex: Male   Female
(Circle one)

1. Would you be willing to kill a cockroach by slapping it with your hands?
   a) yes   b) no
2. What is Queen Anne's lace?
   a) flower   d) doily
   b) embroidery   e) spice
   c) perfume
3. How many times in the last twenty-four hours have you used the word "shit"?
   a) less than 5 times   b) 5 or more times
4. Can you sew well enough to make clothes?
   a) yes   b) no
5. Do you believe in sexual intercourse only after a spiritual love exists between you and your partner?
   a) yes   b) no
6. Do you walk around freely in the nude in a locker room?
   a) yes   b) no
7. How often do you cry?
   a) very often   d) very infrequently
   b) often   e) never
   c) only with good
      reason
8. At times I feel like smashing things.
   a) true   b) false
9. Do you know your chest measurement?
   a) yes   b) no
10. Can you change a tire easily?
    a) yes   b) no
11. I spend no more than one hour during an average school day playing the radio or listening to records.
    a) true   b) false
12. Would you prefer to be the dominant one in a relationship?
    a) yes   b) no
13. Do you think that you are overweight?
    a) yes   b) no
14. When you get depressed, does washing your hair make you feel better?
    a) yes   b) no
15. Do you sleep in the nude?
    a) yes   b) no
16. Which parent are you closest to?
    a) mother   b) father
17. I try to keep my room as neat as possible.
    a) true   b) false

QUESTIONNAIRE ON SEX DIFFERENCES

Sex: Male   Female
(Circle one)

1. Would you be willing to kill a cockroach by slapping it with your hands?
   a) yes   b) no
2. What is Queen Anne's lace?
   a) flower   d) doily
   b) embroidery   e) spice
   c) perfume
3. How many times in the last twenty-four hours have you used the word "shit"?
   a) less than 5 times   b) 5 or more times
4. Can you sew well enough to make clothes?
   a) yes   b) no
5. Do you believe in sexual intercourse only after a spiritual love exists between you and your partner?
   a) yes   b) no
6. Do you walk around freely in the nude in a locker room?
   a) yes   b) no
7. How often do you cry?
   a) very often   d) very infrequently
   b) often   e) never
   c) only with good
      reason
8. At times I feel like smashing things.
   a) true   b) false
9. Do you know your chest measurement?
   a) yes   b) no
10. Can you change a tire easily?
    a) yes   b) no
11. I spend no more than one hour during an average school day playing the radio or listening to records.
    a) true   b) false
12. Would you prefer to be the dominant one in a relationship?
    a) yes   b) no
13. Do you think that you are overweight?
    a) yes   b) no
14. When you get depressed, does washing your hair make you feel better?
    a) yes   b) no
15. Do you sleep in the nude?
    a) yes   b) no
16. Which parent are you closest to?
    a) mother   b) father
17. I try to keep my room as neat as possible.
    a) true   b) false

CHAPTER 15

Intelligence: Its Nature and Measurement

Learning Objectives

1. Explain the relation between the rise of mental testing and the structure of society.

MENTAL TESTS

2. Distinguish between achievement and aptitude tests.

The study of variation

3. Define mean, variance, standard deviation, and normal curve.

4. Explain the meaning of correlation.

Evaluating mental tests

5. Explain the concept of reliability and different measures of reliability.

6. Explain predictive and construct validity and the procedure of standardization.

Using tests for selection

7. Indicate the meaning and use of a cutoff score.

INTELLIGENCE TESTING

8. Indicate the difficulties in defining intelligence.

Measuring intelligence

9. Outline the major events in the history of intelligence testing.

10. Define and explain the rationale behind intelligence quotients (as calculated by Binet) and deviation IQs.

11. Describe the different types of intelligence tests. Contrast the Wechsler, Binet, and the Kaufman Assessment Battery for Children.

An area of application: mental retardation

12. Discuss the definition of mental retardation and the relation between retardation and productive functioning in society.

13. What are some causes of mental retardation?

THE PSYCHOMETRIC APPROACH TO INTELLIGENCE

The structure of mental abilities

14. Describe the evidence for "g," and differentiate general factor and group factor theories.

15. What are Gardner's multiple intelligences, and what is the evidence for them?

Intelligence and age

16. Outline the major changes in intellectual ability in adulthood, including mention of fluid and crystallized intelligence.

THE INFORMATION-PROCESSING APPROACH TO INTELLIGENCE

Simple cognitive correlates

17. Indicate the logic and evidence behind the suggestion that simple cognitive processes may be components of intelligence.

Complex cognitive components

18. What are the limitations on explanations of intelligence in terms of simple cognitive processes, and how does involvement of complex cognitive processes solve some of these problems?

19. Explain how analogical reasoning has been ana-

lyzed into components, and the possible relation of analogical reasoning to intelligence.

NATURE, NURTURE, AND IQ

Some political issues

20. Review the history of positions on genetic factors in intelligence differences related to racial groups or social class.

21. Note some of the results on the effect of preschool enrichment programs on intelligence and school performance. How are these interpreted by those inclined to genetic or environmental explanations?

Genetic factors

22. Review basic terms in genetics (phenotype, genotype, dominant, recessive) and the relation between genotype and phenotype.

23. Describe the cause and genetic basis of phenylketonuria, and know how it illustrates the fact that inborn characteristics may be changeable.

24. Explain polygenic inheritance.

25. Explain why studies of the similarity in intelligence of members of the same family cannot be used to distinguish between genetic and environmental factors.

26. Explain how twin and adoption studies can be used to make this same distinction. Summarize the results of these studies and indicate problems in interpreting them.

Environmental factors

27. Summarize the evidence for and against genetic and environmental explanations of differences in intelligence (IQ) in American whites, from twin and adoption studies and from situations where major environmental differences were studied.

Group differences in IQ

28. Evaluate each of the following explanations of the reported difference between average IQ scores of American whites and blacks:
   1. the difference doesn't exist
   2. unfairness of the tests and test situations for blacks
   3. differences in environments between the groups
   4. genetic differences between the groups

29. What would be the consequences of a clear finding that some of the black-white IQ difference was attributable to genetic factors?

Programmed Exercises

MENTAL TESTS

1. Tests of **achievement** measure what an individual can do now, his present knowledge and competence in a particular area.

   achievement

2. Tests of **aptitude** predict what an individual will be able to do later.

   aptitude

3. The frequency with which individual cases are distributed over different intervals of some measure is called a(n)
   Frequency Distribution

   frequency distribution

4. The most common measure of central tendency is the **mean**.

   mean

5. The most common measure of variability is the
   standard deviation

   standard deviation

6. Many physical and mental attributes show symmetrical bell-shaped frequency distributions, which are described as
   normal curves.

   normal curves

7. Each point in the figure here represents the weight and IQ of one
person. This display is called a *scatter diagram*.

scatter diagram

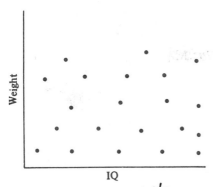

8. The *correlation coefficient* is a statistic that describes the relations
between two sets of measures.

correlation coefficient

9. If a test shows consistency in repeated measurements in similar
circumstances, it is said to be *reliable*.

reliable

10. This is measured as the *correlation* of the scores on two versions
of the same basic test.

correlation

11. The higher the positive correlation between the score on a
driving test and the number of years driving without an accident,
the greater the *predictive validity* of this test.

predictive validity

12. A test based on a theoretical scheme that accounts for the
attribute being measured is said to have *construct validity*.

construct validity

13. In order to obtain norms against which to evaluate a test score,
the test is administered to a large number of people, called the
standardization sample.

standardization sample

14. The *cut-off* score in a test for selection is the minimal score
for acceptance.

cut-off

INTELLIGENCE TESTING

15. According to Binet's system, a six-year-old who passed all the
items at the nine-year-old level and none at the ten-year level
would have a *mental age* of nine years.

mental age

16. A person who gets the mean score for people of his age would
have a deviation IQ of *100*.

100

17. A person with an IQ of 100 would have a *percentile rank*
of 50.

percentile rank

18. The Wechsler Adult Intelligence Scale was in part a response
to the emphasis on language in the Binet-Simon IQ tests. The
Wechsler test has two parts, labeled *verbal* and *performance*

performance, verbal

19. The Kaufman Assessment Battery for Children focuses on intelligence as a form of *information* processing. It has nonverbal scales

information

which make it particularly appropriate for testing of _handicapped_ or   handicapped
minority children.   minority (non-English-speaking)

20. The majority of people classified as mentally retarded can

    function _adequately_ in relatively simple life situations.   adequately

21. Retardation can be caused by _genetic_ factors or by an _impoverished_   genetic, impoverished
    environment.

THE PSYCHOMETRIC APPROACH TO INTELLIGENCE

22. In the _psychometric_ approach, the results of intelligence tests are   psychometric
    studied and analyzed in an attempt to discover the structure of
    intelligence.

23. The fact that scores from a variety of different intelligence tests,

    specific and general, are positively _correlated_, led Spearman to   correlated

    introduce the factor of _general intelligence_.   general intelligence (g)

24. The technique used to try to extract the structure of intelligence

    from correlation matrices is called _factor analysis_.   factor analysis

25. The fact that some specific parts of intelligence tests correlate
    very highly with only some other parts, and that there are
    clusters of tests which highly correlate with one another, is

    evidence for the _group factor_ theories.   group factor

26. Spearman also recognized that certain very specific abilities were
    involved in the performance of any particular test, and named

    these abilities _s_ .   s

27. Gardner's theory of _multiple intelligences_ holds that there are six   multiple intelligences

    different, _independent_ mental capacities.   independent

28. Evidence for these independent capacities is the presence of
    retarded people who show outstanding performance on a task
    related to one of these activities. Such people are called

    Idiot Savants .   idiot savants

29. It seems to be the case that as one goes to older age, ability to

    deal with new problems or to respond rapidly, called _fluid_   fluid
    intelligence, tends to deteriorate, while the repertoire of basic

    cognitive skills, knowledge, and strategy, called _crystallized_ intelli-   crystallized
    gence, remains intact.

30. Measurements of changes in intelligence in later life are ideally
    done by testing the same person at different ages in what is

    called a _longitudinal_ study.   longitudinal

THE INFORMATION-PROCESSING APPROACH TO INTELLIGENCE

31. A problem such as "car is to garage as person is to house" is an

    example of _analogical reasoning_ Some believe that such tasks   analogical reasoning
    can be analyzed into _cognitive components_   cognitive components

NATURE, NURTURE, AND IQ

32. The observed characteristics of an organism are called its

    phenotype But the underlying genetic blueprint is called the
    genotype.

    phenotype

    genotype

33. Assume that color of rat skin is determined by the genes at one locus. If a brown and a white rat mate and all the offspring are brown, we can guess that the gene for brown is _dominant_ and and that these brown offspring have a different _genotype_ from their brown parent.

    dominant

    genotype

34. A form of mental retardation that is caused by a single recessive gene is _PKU_.

    phenylketonuria (PKU)

35. Traits that are controlled by genes but show many different values are determined by _polygenic_ inheritance.

    polygenic

36. The fact that members of the same family have positively correlated intelligence and often share special abilities can be used as evidence for both _hereditary_ and _environmental_ factors.

    hereditary (genetic), environmental

37. The pattern of a higher correlation of IQ scores in _identical_ twin pairs than in _fraternal_ twin pairs, argues for a role for heredity in intelligence.

    identical

    fraternal

38. Two basic methods for estimating the role of inherited factors in intelligence or other traits are _twin_ and _adoption_ studies.

    twin, adoption

39. The negative effects of poor environments on IQ are illustrated by data showing that the longer a child is in a deprived environment, the lower his IQ. This appears as a _negative_ correlation between IQ and age.

    negative

40. Some have argued that at least part of the American black-white difference in average IQ scores can be attributed to the fact that the test was designed for the white middle class, that is to say, that the tests are not _culture_ fair.

    culture

41. A number of studies indicate that when differences in the environments of blacks and whites during childhood are markedly reduced or equated, the black-white IQ difference is markedly _reduced_.

    reduced (diminished)

Self-Test

1. Mental testing is primarily an American product, dating from the beginning of this century. America was a natural place for mental testing because:
   a. Americans embraced Freudian theory.
   b. the American idea that all men are created equal required mental tests to show up their subtle differences.
   c. of the high social and occupational mobility in America.
   d. reinforcement was a popular concept in America.
   e. Binet and Simon were Americans.

2. One group of five people gets the following scores on a mathematics test: 85, 85, 90, 95, 95. Another group gets these five scores: 80, 80, 90, 100, 100. Which of the following statements about these groups is true?

a. Both have the same means and different standard deviations.

b. Both have the same means and the same standard deviation.

c. Both have different means and the same standard deviation.

d. Both have different means and standard deviations.

e. It is impossible to say which group has a greater standard of deviation.

3. The diagram below represents the hypothetical scores of individual subjects on an IQ test and on a history achievement test. The correlation displayed would be closest to:

a. +1.00.

b. + .50.

c. 0.00.

d. − .50.

e. −1.00.

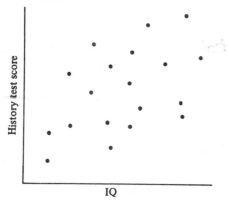

4. For which of the following pairs of variables would one expect to see a negative correlation?

a. age and vocabulary

b. height and visual acuity

c. brain size and intelligence

d. long-distance running ability and weight (among adults)

e. social security number and intelligence (among adults)

5. A hypothetical air force needs a test to help select people for training as pilots. There is no adequate theory of the acquisition of flying skills, but air force investigators discover that the speed with which one can tap with the third finger correlates + .80 with survival in flying school. On the basis of this observation, one could say that the test had:

a. high reliability.

b. high predictive validity.

c. high construct validity.

d. good standardization.

e. b and c

6. A student takes the same test of reaction time at 10:00 A.M. on two consecutive days. She gets very different scores on these two days. If this was true of many other test takers, it would suggest that this test is not:

a. valid.

b. standardized.

c. reliable.

d. none of the above

e. all of the above

7. An appropriate standardization sample for a test of artistic talent in elementary school children would be:

a. elementary school children.

b. elementary school children fifty years ago.

c. older children who have selected art as a career.

d. elementary school children with artistic talent.

e. representative adults from the same country.

8. Intelligence testers have faced special problems because:

a. intelligence changes with age.

b. intelligence tests are not reliable.

c. all questions require prior knowledge, so that past experience determines the test score.

d. there is no clear basis for determining construct or predictive validity.

e. it is difficult to calculate percentile ranks for intelligence.

9. The deviation IQ is a better measure than the older intelligence quotient (mental age/chronological age), because:

a. it is newer.

b. the deviation IQ is more reliable and is based on better tests.

c. a person's deviation IQ will stay about the same, from age fifteen to fifty, for example.

d. the deviation IQ increases with age, as does intelligence.

e. it is based on the idea of 100 being average.

10. Harry is eighteen and has a deviation IQ of 110. Carol is ten and has the same deviation IQ. In comparing them, we can say that:

a. both have the same percentile rank in their age group.

b. both have the same mental age.

c. both get the same number of questions correct.

d. a and b

e. none of the above

11. The SATs are a type of intelligence test. The scores are calculated as deviation IQs, with 500

as the mean score of those who have taken the test over the past few years. The mean deviation IQ of people with SAT scores of 500 is well over 100. This can be explained as a result of:

a. different types of questions on the two tests.
b. high reliance on verbal ability in most IQ tests.
c. superior intelligence in the standardization population for the SATs.
d. a higher cutoff score for the SATs.
e. a higher intake of cheese and other high protein foods in high school seniors.

12. A test administered like the SAT but measuring subjects' abilities to do jigsaw puzzles would be _____ test.

a. group performance
b. group verbal
c. unreliable performance
d. standardized performance
e. verbal performance

13. A psychometrician examines a verbal and a spatial intelligence test and finds that the scores on these two tests correlate +.38. From this he might conclude that:

a. performance on both tests is partly determined by g but mostly by specific factors.
b. these tests measure very different things, and there is no g component here.
c. both of these tests are excellent measures of g.
d. these results constitute proof of the group factor theories.
e. none of the above

14. g : group factor :: group factor :

a. correlation matrix
b. IQ
c. Spearman
d. s
e. factor analysis

15. One occasionally finds people who are highly intelligent, but terrible at spatial relations. This fact supports:

a. Gardner's theory of multiple intelligences.
b. group-factor theory.
c. the idea of s.
d. a and c
e. all of the above

16. Gordon is really pretty ignorant, but he has a way of seeing relationships among ideas and figures and quickly comes up with new ways of doing things. He could be described as:

a. high in g.
b. high in fluid, low in crystallized intelligence.

c. evidence for one-factor theories of intelligence.
d. someone who would do well on vocabulary tests.
e. someone who would do poorly on Raven's progressive matrices.

17. Studies indicate that certain types of "intelligence" decline with age in adulthood and others do not. A type that improves or at least holds its own through most of adulthood is:

a. g.
b. fluid intelligence.
c. crystallized intelligence.
d. group factors.
e. none of the above

18. The observation that people on the political left tend to think of intelligence as more under environmental control, while those on the right tend to think of it as more under genetic control, suggests that:

a. one must distinguish between within- and between-group differences.
b. the study of genetic and environmental influences on intelligence is inherently political.
c. sociopolitical factors influence judgments about the role of heredity in intelligence.
d. there is no way to study scientifically the issue of the role of heredity and environment in intelligence.
e. c and d

19. The fact that in the period between the two World Wars IQ scores of Eastern European immigrant groups improved, the longer they were in the United States:

a. justified a policy of excluding Eastern Europeans from immigrating to the United States.
b. raises questions about U.S. immigration policy in the period between the wars.
c. demonstrates that intelligence is primarily under genetic control.
d. demonstrates that intelligence is primarily under environmental control.
e. none of the above

20. Jane and Phyllis have brown eyes. All of Jane's relatives have brown eyes. Phyllis's father has brown eyes, but her mother has blue eyes (brown eye color is dominant). From this information, we can guess that Jane and Phyllis have:

a. the same genotype and phenotype.
b. the same genotype and different phenotypes.
c. different genotypes and the same phenotype.
d. different genotypes and phenotypes.
e. c or d

21. A genetic female who is exposed to androgens as a fetus and develops male genitals, and a person with phenylketonuria who is treated at birth and develops no symptoms, both illustrate that:
    a. inborn, genetically determined traits can be changed by environmental factors.
    b. recessive traits can occur in both sex and intelligence.
    c. behavior is inherited.
    d. environmental factors, under some circumstances, have no influence on behavior.
    e. behavior is related to sex chromosomes.

22. Suppose the unlikely occurrence that a severely mentally retarded person married someone of normal intelligence, and that they had many children together. Suppose, further, that half of these children were severely retarded. This would suggest that this retardation was probably due to:
    a. a single recessive gene effect.
    b. recessive genes.
    c. a single dominant gene.
    d. polygenic inheritance.
    e. a or b

23. The clustering of specific talents (e.g., music in the Bach family) or high intelligence in particular families, *across generations*, argues for:
    a. a significant role for genetics in these abilities.
    b. a significant role for environment in these abilities.
    c. polygenic inheritance.
    d. a and b
    e. a and/or b

24. If, counter to the results actually found, it was reported that fraternal and identical twins had the same high correlation in intelligence and that this was *higher* than the correlation between other siblings (e.g., brothers and sisters of different ages), one would be most justified in concluding that:
    a. the higher correlation in twins was due to environmental factors.
    b. the higher correlation in twins was due to genetic factors.
    c. fraternal twins are more closely related, genetically, than are other siblings.
    d. a and c
    e. none of the above

25. Environmentalists explain the significant correlation between the IQ of adopted children and their biological parents in terms of *selective placement* of these children in adopted homes. (Children with higher IQ biological parents are placed with higher IQ adoptive parents.) This argument, however, is strongly weakened by:

    a. the studies on identical twins.
    b. the fact that the IQ of adopted children correlates more highly with biological than adoptive parents.
    c. the fact that there is a positive correlation between the IQ of adopted children and their adoptive parents.
    d. b and c
    e. none of the above

26. All but one of these findings supports or is consistent with the idea of a hereditary component in intelligence differences. Which finding does not support such a view?
    a. higher IQ correlation in identical than fraternal twins
    b. higher IQ correlation between adoptive children and their biological parents than between these same children and their adoptive parents
    c. higher IQ correlation between siblings than between half siblings (sharing only one parent)
    d. higher correlations in IQ between fraternal twins than between other siblings
    e. the stability of IQ over decades

27. On the whole, the IQs of biological parents giving children up for adoption are below those of adopting parents (since the latter are screened by agencies). The observation that, whatever the correlation between IQ of adopted child and biological parent, the actual IQ of such adopted children tends to be considerably higher than that of the biological parents, is evidence for:
    a. hereditary effects.
    b. environmental effects.
    c. a and b
    d. a heritability value.
    e. polygenic inheritance.

28. Many have argued that IQ tests and the circumstances under which they are given favor whites over blacks. All but one of the following reported findings argue against this view: that is, all but one indicate that the tests are reasonably fair culturally. Select the one reported finding that does not argue in favor of the cultural fairness of tests or test situations.
    a. The black-white IQ difference remains about the same when the black version of the test is translated into black English.
    b. The black-white difference is about the same for verbal tests and for the abstract Raven's progressive matrices.
    c. The black-white difference remains about the same whether the tester is black or white.

d. The black-white difference remains about the same for tests of verbal and tests of spatial intelligence.

e. The black-white difference decreases in the children in families that have children of both races through adoption.

29. A fair summary of studies on environmental matching or change, as applied to the black-white IQ difference, would be:

a. There is generally a decreased black-white IQ difference when attempts are made to equalize environments in the comparison groups and an improvement in black IQs when the environment is improved.

b. Appropriate manipulation of environments, to provide blacks with the full advantages of the white environment, leads to elimination of the black-white IQ difference.

c. There is very little effect of environmental change or equalization on black IQ or black-white differences.

d. a and b

e. none of the above

30. What would be educationally and scientifically *appropriate* sociopolitical responses to a *hypothetical* proof that a fair proportion of the difference in IQ scores between American blacks and whites could be assigned to hereditary factors?

a. curtailment of early enrichment programs

b. establishment of racial quotas

c. inclusion of race as an important factor in determining the ability of applicants for jobs involving intelligence

d. cessation of affirmative action programs

e. none of the above

Answer Key for Self-Test

1. c p. 419	14. d pp. 433–34
2. a pp. 420–21	15. e pp. 433–34
3. b p. 423	16. b p. 436
4. d pp. 422–23	17. c p. 436
5. b pp. 423–25	18. c pp. 436–37
6. c p. 424	19. b p. 437
7. a p. 425	20. c p. 438
8. d p. 426	21. a p. 439
9. c p. 428	22. c p. 438
10. a p. 428	23. e pp. 440–43
11. c pp. 425, 429	24. a p. 440
12. a p. 429	25. b p. 442
13. a p. 433	26. d pp. 440–43

27. b p. 442	29. a pp. 446–47
28. e pp. 444, 446	30. e pp. 446–47

Investigating Psychological Phenomena

"INTELLIGENCE TESTS"

Equipment: None
Number of subjects: One, yourself
Time per subject: Thirty minutes
Time for experimenter: Thirty minutes

This is an experiment that will help you to understand the construction of intelligence tests. The procedure that you will go through will be like the procedure that might be used in the development of an intelligence test. The main concern is that you understand how a distribution of test scores is generated and how an individual score is interpreted with respect to that distribution.

For this purpose, rather than making up a so-called intelligence test, we have chosen to try out a measure of a characteristic that is rarely tested: One's knowledge of foods and cooking. In this case, one begins with some idea of the ability or knowledge base that one is trying to assess. Questions or tasks are constructed that seem to measure these. Then, pilot tests, like those we will give you, are distributed to a representative sample of the population for which the tests are intended. In your case, your class might serve as a sample of college undergraduate. Of course, students differ in different schools and in different regions, so this would not be anything like the random sample we would actually need were this a real test.

The results of the test are examined. Typically, most of the questions which all subjects get right or all get wrong are discarded, because such questions do not help to measure *differences* among people in the abilities under study. Then, some sort of retest studies are done, to make sure the test is reliable, and a validity study is done, to assure that the test measures what it is supposed to measure.

We will only deal with one phase of test construction here. We have made up a test that has never been used by psychologists before. (It is certainly not clear why a food knowledge test would be of interest to anyone in the real world.) We ask each of you to take the test. It is brief. The food knowledge test is in the format of a written test, with unlimited time. It is, of course, "closed book." Fill it out in a quiet place. Then score your answers, using the list of correct answers at the end of this section.

FOOD KNOWLEDGE TEST

Sex _____

Listed below are five countries:
Italy (southern Italy)
China
India
Mexico
Germany

Each of the following food items (1–14) is particularly characteristic of the cuisines of one of the five countries listed above. Write the name of the appropriate cuisine (country) beside the food item.

1. potatoes _____

2. corn _____

3. sesame oil _____

4. olive oil _____

5. soy sauce _____

6. cumin (two possible answers) _____

7. oregano _____

8. curry _____

9. chili pepper (two possible answers) _____

10. liverwurst _____

11. turmeric _____

12. yogurt _____

13. bean curd _____

14. ghee _____

Write in the name of the country associated with each of the following items:

15. sushi _____

16. lasagna _____

17. taco _____

18. paella _____

19. moussaka _____

20. goulash _____

21. sukiyaki _____

22. mousse _____

23. sate (pron: sā′·tāy) _____

24. biryani _____

25. mole (pron: mǒ′·lāy) _____

26. trifle _____

27. kim chee _____

28. champagne _____

29. What is the primary ingredient used in raising (leavening) bread? _____

30. What is yogurt made from? _____

31. What are raisins made from? _____

32. What is meringue made of? _____

33. What animal does bacon come from? _____

34. What are prunes made from? _____

35. What type of fish is lox made from? _____

36. What vegetable are pickles usually made from? _____

37. What fruit is wine usually made from? _____

38. What is sauerkraut made from? _____

39. What are chitterlings made from? _____

40. What does caviar come from? _____

41. What is marzipan made from? _____

42. What is the primary ingredient in guacamole? _____

Indicated below are five common cooking methods:
   baking
   sautéing or pan frying
   braising
   boiling
   broiling

For each dish or food below, indicate by writing in the correct term from those listed above the primary cooking method used.

43. chicken soup _____

44. bread _____

45. scrambled eggs _____

46. pot roast _____

47. shish-kebab _____

48. spaghetti _____

49. soufflé _____

50. hash-brown potatoes _____

51. collard greens _____

TEST RESULTS AND "IQ" CALCULATIONS

The food knowledge test was taken by 153 University of Pennsylvania undergraduates in the introductory psychology course and twenty-one students in a University of Michigan class in learning and memory. The results were:
   Mean score: 35.9 for 174 subjects
   Standard deviation: 5.03
   Range of scores: 22 (lowest) to 47 (highest)
Females do slightly better than males on this test (mean female score: 36.8; mean male score: 35.1).

CALCULATION OF A "CULINARY IQ"

As we will discuss below, much more work would have to be done with this test before it could actually be used in a meaningful way. For the sake of illustrating the scaling of psychological tests, we will use the data generated by undergraduates taking this test to develop a "deviation" scale like that used in IQ tests. You can then calculate your "culinary IQ."

The basic principle behind scaling of tests is the deviation score. Like a percentile score, it expresses where a particular score stands with respect to all of the other scores. The distribution of scores for tests usually falls into what is called a normal distribution. An ideal normal distribution is drawn in the next column. Normal distributions are typically described by their mean value and their standard deviation, a measure of the spread or variability of the curve (see the statistical appendix to the text). In a normal distribution, 68 percent of all observations fall within one standard deviation of the mean, and 96 percent of all observations fall within two standard deviations of the mean (see figure in the next column). Test scores are measured in units of deviation from the mean. For all IQ type tests, 100 is set as the mean value and 15 points

as the standard deviation. Thus, an IQ of 115 corresponds to the score one standard deviation above the mean (85 to one standard deviation below); 130 corresponds to a score of two standard deviations above the mean (70 to two below), and so on. (An IQ of 105 would then be one third of a standard deviation above the mean.) In percentile terms, an IQ of 130 would be at the 98th percentile, and an IQ of 85 would be at the 16th percentile (see figure).

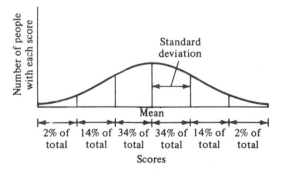

Normal distribution

| 2% of total | 14% of total | 34% of total | 34% of total | 14% of total | 2% of total |

Scores

Applying these ideas to our test, the mean score (35.9) on the food test would be assigned a scaled score of 100. Subtracting one standard deviation (5.03) from this score, we get approximately 31, a score that would be assigned a scaled score of 85 (one standard deviation below the mean corresponds to 15 scaled points). We have performed the appropriate arithmetic for the food test, and provided the raw score (your actual score) and scaled score (converted to deviation units) equivalents in the table on the next page. Because the standard deviation for the food knowledge scores is almost exactly 5, each additional point on the test is worth one-fifth of a standard deviation, or 3 "IQ" points.

FOOD TEST

Raw score (your actual score)	Scaled score ("IQ")
18	46
19	49
20	52
21	55
22	58
23	61
24	64
25	67
26	70
27	73
28	76
29	79
30	82
31	85
32	88
33	91
34	94
35	97
36	100
37	103
38	106
39	109
40	112
41	115
42	118
43	121
44	124
45	127
46	130
47	133
48	136
49	139
50	142
51	145

The next step in developing a test would be to improve the first version. For example, in the food knowledge test, there are a number of useless items: These are items that do not contribute to the measurement of differences in people. For three items (number 16 — lasagna, 37 — wine, and 44 — bread), all 174 subjects got the right answer. Because of this, these items would normally be discarded. Three additional items were missed by less than 2% of the subjects and might also be discarded. There were no questions that were missed by all subjects. The "hardest" question was about the country of origin of sate (number 23 — Indonesia), and 8.6% of subjects were correct on this item.

We would also eliminate any questions that turned out to be ambiguous. In this test, for example, some of the "What is X made from?" questions need clarification. Thus, for number 39 — chitterlings (chitlings), some people answered "pig," and others said "intestine." We scored both as correct, but should have been more specific in the question. Similarly, for number 30 — what is yogurt made from? — we intended that milk be the correct answer. But bacteria cultures are also components of yogurt. We should have asked, "What is the primary ingredient in yogurt?" See if you can find some other ambiguous questions. Finally, we would examine the correlation of correctness on each question with the total score on the test. Are there any items which don't seem to be measuring the same sort of thing as the rest of the test? (See the experiment on personality testing in the next chapter.) Such items might or might not be included but would at least be reexamined. Along these same lines, one might look at any questions which the top performers on the test all missed. Often such items are badly worded, or perhaps even in error. For the food test, there was no single item missed by all of the six top scorers.

Having streamlined the test, we would then use some type of test-retest procedure to determine reliability. (Will the same person score about the same on two different occasions?) The reliability measures would be complicated, since one would expect improvement on the second time through.

We would then perform some sort of validity test. Is the test measuring what it is supposed to measure? If the food knowledge test is supposed to predict likely candidates for success in a cooking school, does it actually do so?

Finally, having satisfied ourselves that we had a reliable and valid test, we would then administer the test to a large sample of people (hundreds to thousands of people) randomly selected from the population of people for whom the test was designed (e.g., high school seniors, all adults, etc.).

Ask yourself whether you believe the food test is meaningful. How would you validate it? What might it be used for? What would it correlate with?

FURTHER ACTIVITIES

Sketch out what you think would be an appropriate test for use in predicting success in a particular profession: e.g., fighter pilot, baseball player, or architect. Then ask yourself how you would validate the test.

Answer Sheet

Score one point for each correct answer
(Listed next to each answer are the percentages correct out of 174 students.)

1. potatoes – Germany (83.9%)
2. corn – Mexico (78.7%)
3. sesame oil – China (28.2%)
4. olive oil – Italy (93.7%)
5. soy sauce – China (97.7%)
6. cumin – India or Mexico (78.2%)
7. oregano – Italy (90.2%)
8. curry – India (73.0%)
9. chili – India or Mexico (90.2%)
10. liverwurst – Germany (97.7%)
11. turmeric – India (48.3%)
12. yogurt – India (44.8%)
13. bean curd – China (44.8%)
14. ghee – India (60.3%)
15. sushi – Japan (55.7%)
16. lasagna – Italy (100%)
17. taco – Mexico (98.8%)
18. paella – Spain (40.2%)
19. moussaka – Greece (43.7%)
20. goulash – Hungary (73.6%)
21. sukiyaki – Japan (76.4%)
22. mousse – France (74.7%)
23. sate – Indonesia (8.6%)
24. biryani – India (37.4%)
25. mole – Mexico (14.9%)
26. trifle – England (47.7%)
27. kim chee – Korea (13.2%)
28. champagne – France (80.4%)
29. bread – yeast (97.1%)
30. yogurt – milk (88.5%)
31. raisins – grapes (96.0%)
32. meringue – egg white (74.1%)
33. bacon – pig (99.9%)
34. prunes – plums (77.0%)
35. lox – salmon (66.7%)
36. pickle – cucumber (97.7%)
37. wine – grapes (100%)
38. sauerkraut – cabbage (89.1%)
39. chitterlings – pig or intestine (29.3%)
40. caviar – fish eggs (91.4%)
41. marzipan – almond or sugar (31.0%)
42. guacamole – avocado (48.3%)
43. chicken soup – boiling (96%)
44. bread – baking (100%)
45. scrambled eggs – pan frying (98.3%)
46. pot roast – braising (46.6%)
47. shish kebab – broiling (57.5%)
48. spaghetti – boiling (97.7%)
49. soufflé – baking (83.3%)
50. hash-brown potatoes – pan fry-sautéing (96.6%)
51. collard greens – boiling (55.7%)

CHAPTER 16

Personality

Learning Objectives

1. List the four orientations from which the subject of personality is approached.

ASSESSING PERSONALITY

Structured personality tests

2. Understand the construction and the use of the Minnesota Multiphasic Personality Inventory (MMPI). What is the importance of score profiles and validity scales?
3. Explain why the MMPI isn't a commonly used test for normal people. Name one of the tests that is used instead.
4. Be familiar with the different types of test validity and how various personality tests measure up.
5. Understand why the uniformly small correlations between the psychopathic deviance scale of the MMPI and various behavioral patterns don't invalidate the Pd scale.

Unstructured personality tests

6. Be able to explain the rationale for projective techniques. Describe some of these procedures.
7. List the scoring categories used in the interpretation of Rorschach inkblots, and know what general rules are employed.
8. Be familiar with the differences in interpretation between the Rorschach and the Thematic Apperception Test (TAT) in regard to perceived content.
9. Know why TAT interpretation is impressionistic and global.
10. Summarize the issues and arguments in assessing the validity of the TAT and the Rorschach.

TRAIT THEORY

The search for the right taxonomy

11. Understand the trait approach to personality.
12. Describe Cattell's approach to developing a taxonomy of personality traits. What modifications of Cattell's analysis have been suggested and why?
13. Discuss Eysenck's taxonomy of neuroticism and extroversion-introversion. What personality differences are encompassed by this scheme?

Trait versus situation

14. Explain the importance of cross-situational consistency, or inconsistency, in the argument against trait theory.
15. Discuss the trait theory/situationism debate as another manifestation of the nativist/empiricist controversy.
16. Describe how situationists explain how we see our friends' personalities as consistent.
17. Describe how superficially different expressions of a personality trait contribute to apparent behavioral inconsistency. What are the implications for trait theory?
18. Understand the importance of the interaction between a personality and a situation in personality assessment.
19. Know how Snyder's self-monitoring scale measures behavioral consistency in different situations.
20. Understand why mentally disturbed persons exhibit more cross-situational consistency than normal people.
21. Be able to explain the idea of "person constancy" and why it strikes a happy medium between the concepts of solid stability and complete plasticity of the individual personality.

Traits and biology

22. Define temperament, and describe its effect on a person's personality.

23. Know how stable an individual's temperament is, as demonstrated by Buss and Plomin's temperament scale.

24. Discuss the evidence that personality traits may have a genetic component.

25. Describe how Eysenck compares the introverts and the extroverts in terms of their arousal systems. What research on sensation seeking has Zuckerman done that correlates with Eysenck's findings?

THE PSYCHODYNAMIC APPROACH

26. Contrast the psychodynamic and the trait approaches. Indicate the parallels of each approach to approaches to drama or acting.

Personality structure and development:
The Freudian account

27. Review Freud's ideas that are relevant to the issue of personality, particularly the issue of unconscious conflict.

28. Summarize Freud's view of the stages of psychosexual development.

29. Explain how Freud and his followers generate personality types, such as the anal character. Explain the concepts of fixation and reaction formation.

30. Cite the evidence for both the existence of anal character types and the origin of anal traits in childhood experiences.

Personality and patterns of defense:
psychoanalysis after Freud

31. Describe Karen Horney's views about patterns of neurotic conflict, including mention of basic anxiety and vicious circles.

32. Distinguish between the Freudian position, Karen Horney's position, and the view of the ego psychologists.

33. Explain what coping mechanisms are and how they relate to Freudian defense mechanisms.

34. Understand what longitudinal studies tell us about the importance and consistency of coping patterns.

A BEHAVIORAL APPROACH TO PERSONALITY

35. Contrast the behavioral approach with the psychodynamic approach and trait theory.

Social learning theory

36. Define the approach of social learning theory.

37. Indicate how social learning theorists account for personality differences in terms of different ways of approaching the world.

38. Define attributional style, and note its components. Relate attributional style to depression.

39. Distinguish control and self-control. Describe delay of gratification, and how it is measured in children.

40. Describe the developmental course of delay of gratification and what the early ability to delay gratification predicts about later behavior. Why might there be such a relation?

THE HUMANISTIC APPROACH

The major features of the humanistic movement

41. Describe the basic differences between the humanistic approach and all of the other approaches to personality that have been discussed.

42. Explain the hierarchy of needs, including definitions of deficiency needs and self-actualization.

Evaluating the humanistic approach

43. Discuss the empirical and conceptual problems of the humanistic approach.

44. Indicate the sense in which humanistic psychology is a protest movement. Relate it to other movements of a similar character in history, especially the Romantic movement.

TAKING STOCK

45. Summarize the four basic views of personality presented in this chapter. Evaluate their contribution to a total theory of personality, and describe the analog, in drama, to each of these approaches.

Programmed Exercises

1. The way that people differ in their desires, feelings, and in the expression of these feelings reflects their *personal* *differences*   personality differences

2. In the comic dramas that they performed, the Greeks and Romans thought of the different characters and their respective personalities as *types* . The same characterizations were used in literature.   types

3. Some felt that these stock characters were two dimensional, and that more *rounded* characterizations were needed.   rounded

4. Others were concerned over the *internal* versus *external* forces that caused a character to act as he did.   internal, external

5. These arguments between the different schools of drama and literature are analogous to debates between different psychological theories of personality. The *trait* *theory* holds that personality is best understood by the description and analysis of underlying personality traits.   trait theory

6. Achieving selfhood and actualizing one's own potential would be consistent with the *humanistic* approach to personality.   humanistic

7. The behavioral approach insists that an individual's actions and thoughts are produced by the *situation* that he is in at any given time.   situation

8. According to *psychodynamic* *theory* , the important aspects of personality originate from buried unconscious conflicts and desires.   psychodynamic theory

9. Implicit in the use of personality tests is the assumption that personality patterns are essentially *consistent* over time.   consistent

10. *Personality* tests were developed to enable us to predict people's future behavior.   Personality

ASSESSING PERSONALITY

11. The first personality test was administered to army recruits and was meant to identify *emotionally disturbed* soldiers.   emotionally disturbed

12. The MMPI is termed *multiphasic* because it assesses a number of personality *traits* simultaneously.   multiphasic
        traits

13. The MMPI is scored by comparing the scores on each of the ten major scales to those of the relevant *criterion* *group* .   criterion group

14. The authors of the MMPI emphasize the *discriminatory* power of a question in distinguishing between the criterion group and normal subjects.   discriminatory

15. In interpreting scores on the MMPI, it is necessary to examine score *profiles*, which present the scores on all the scales in graphic form.   profiles

16. In order to detect whether or not subjects are lying on test items or are trying to fake mental illness, the MMPI uses two **validity scales** made up of items no one can honestly deny and of items so bizarre that few would endorse them.

validity scales

17. It is difficult to interpret MMPI scores for **normal** subjects since the criterion groups used to define the scales were composed of **psychiatric** patients.

normal

psychiatric

18. One test which was developed using normal subjects as the criterion group is the **C** **P** **I** **California Psychological Inventory**

California Psychological Inventory

19. The degree to which a test can predict real-world events is called its **predictive validity**

predictive validity

20. Devising and testing hypotheses about the relation between an underlying trait and various behavioral effects comprises **construct validation**

construct validation

21. High scores on the psychopathic deviance scale of the MMPI reflect **aggressiveness**, while low scorers are generally considered **good natured**.

aggressiveness

good natured

22. The use of **projective techniques** was, in part, a protest against the **highly structured** nature of paper-and-pencil techniques.

projective techniques

highly structured

23. One of the concerns of the originators of projective techniques was that a subject could **lie** to **himself** when taking a test like the MMPI.

lie, himself

24. The idea behind projective techniques is that in **structuring** unstructured materials, a subject will reveal deeper facets of his **personality**

structuring

personality

25. The three categories used in scoring Rorschach inkblots are **location**, which concerns the portion of the blot used, **determinants** which denote the attributes of the stimulus that the subject responds to, and **content**, which refers to what the subject sees.

location, determinants

content

26. In interpretations of Rorschach inkblots, use of the entire blot is said to reflect **integrative** thinking, while attention to details suggests **compulsive**

integrative (or conceptual)

compulsiveness (or rigidity)

27. Rorschach responses indicating human movement are interpreted as indicating **imagination** and those dominated by color suggest **emotion**.

imagination

emotionality (or impulsivity)

28. Traditionally, **content** has been less important than the other categories in the interpretation of Rorschach inkblots.

content

29. The **Thematic Apperception Test**, in which subjects tell stories about pictures, places a major emphasis on content.

Thematic Apperception Test (TAT)

30. Contrary to traditional beliefs, Rorschach **content** has been shown to correlate more highly with external criteria than do **global** assessments based on verbatim protocols.

content

global

TRAIT THEORY

31. The major task in determining the proper traits with which to classify personality is the development of a(n) _taxonomy_ of personality difference.

    taxonomy

32. Cattell's taxonomy of personality is based on _language_, using factor analysis to discover how _trait words_ are inter-related.

    language

    trait words

33. According to Eysenck, both _introverts_ and _extroverts_ are un-sociable and withdrawn, but the former's unsociability is not tainted by fear of social activities.

    introverts, neurotics

34. Some psychologists have argued that the reason that many tests, both introspective and projective, are not good predictors of future behavior is that most people exhibit a lack of _cross-situational_ consistency.

    cross-situational

35. _Situationism_ maintains that human behavior is largely determined by the situation a person is in, rather than by the actual, internal traits of the person.

    Situationism

36. Contrary to situationistic claims, some _longitudinal_ studies have shown a fair amount of _consistency_ of personality.

    longitudinal

    consistency

37. Another argument against situationism is that perceived behavioral inconsistency may be more _apparent_ than _real_ since the expression of a constant trait may _vary_ over time.

    apparent, real

    vary

38. When a person's reactions cannot be predicted adequately solely by situation or by _individual differences_, the critical factor may be _interaction_.

    individual differences

    interaction

39. Since cross-situational consistency varies from person to person, it may be regarded as a _trait_ that only some individuals possess.

    trait

40. One can assess how much a person adjusts his behavior to fix a situation by having him complete the _self-monitoring_ scale developed by Mark Snyder.

    self-monitoring

41. _Mentally Disturbed_ persons exhibit more behavioral consistency across situations than do normal persons, due to strong internal factors that affect their responses.

    Mentally disturbed

42. The intuitive belief that most people remain unchanged over time is known as _person constancy_ and is similar to size and shape constancy in perception.

    person constancy

43. It is believed that a person's _temperament_ ultimately originates from his biological makeup.

    temperament

44. Identical twins show more similarity of personality than do fraternal twins, indicating some _heritability_ of personality traits.

    heritability

45. According to Eysenck, introversion corresponds to a high level of _arousal_; thus, persons of this type are actually more awake than others.

    arousal

46. Zuckerman's research on _sensation seeking_ indicates that those people with a higher arousal system (introverts) have higher levels of the neurotransmitter _norepinephrine_ in their brains. Those with lower levels of this neurotransmitter are underaroused, and as a result are likely to seek thrills and take risks.

    sensation seeking

    norepinephrine

THE PSYCHODYNAMIC APPROACH

47. According to the psychodynamic approach, to understand a person is to understand hidden psychological forces, often called _Dynamics_ , that underlie her behavior.

    dynamics

48. The central determinant of personality, for Freud, is _unconscious conflicts_ that arise in _childhood_ and affect later personality.

    unconscious conflicts, childhood

49. According to Freud, the fundamental principle of unconscious conflict is defense against _anxiety_ . A particularly important defense mechanism, which pushes unpleasant thoughts out of consciousness, is called _Repression_

    anxiety

    repression

50. According to Freud, the mouth, anus, and genitals are the focus of pleasure-seeking in childhood. These areas are called _erogenous zones_ .

    erogenous zones

51. Freud claims that in development, there is a successive focus on each of these zones, resulting in the sequence of stages from _oral_ to _anal_ to _phallic_.

    oral, anal, phallic

52. Then, after the genital stage, Freud holds that children go through a _latency period_, in which sexuality lies dormant, followed by the adult situation, described as the _genital_ stage.

    latency period

    genital

53. People who are exceedingly clean and orderly, and who are also stubborn and stingy are thought, in the Freudian scheme, to have experienced a _reaction formation_ at the anal stage, and are said to display the _anal_ _character_.

    reaction formation

    anal character

54. Contrary to the predictions of Freud, people showing anal characteristics do not differ from those who do not show anal characteristics in severity of _toilet training_.

    toilet training

55. The _neo_-_Freudians_ differ from Freud in that they emphasize inner conflicts based on interpersonal as opposed to biological sources.

    neo-Freudians

56. According to Horney, neurotic conflicts are caused by _basic anxiety_ , an all-pervading feeling of being alone and helpless in a hostile world. These conflicts may harden into personality characteristics, because the conflicts create a self-perpetuating _vicious circle_ .

    basic anxiety

    vicious circle

57. In _ego psychology_, there is an emphasis on cultural and interpersonal factors, as well as stress, on the healthy modes of _coping_ with the world.

    ego psychology

    coping

58. A __longitudinal study__ by Vaillant indicates consistency in   longitudinal study

coping patterns, with more __mature__ coping patterns in older   mature
and better-adjusted people.

A BEHAVIORAL APPROACH TO PERSONALITY

59. The behavioral approach is associated with the theoretical position

called __Behaviorism__ It emphasizes control of behavior from the   behaviorism
__situation__   situation (environment)

60. According to __social learning__ theory, personal differences   social learning
can be accounted for in cognitive terms.

61. Some of the cognitive qualities on which people differ are (list   any three of: competencies,

three) __competencies, expectancies,__ and __subject values__   encoding strategies, expectancies,
subjective values,

62. The way that people explain good or bad events that they   self-regulatory systems

experience is called their __attributional style__   attributional style

63. People suffering from depression tend to have an attributional
style that shows a tendency to attribute unfortunate events in

their lives to __global__ , __stable__, and __internal__ causes.   global, stable, internal

64. The ability to refrain from doing some things one wants to do is

called __self - control__.   self-control

65. "Willpower," or the ability to put off desired goals is called by

psychologists, __delay of gratification__   delay of gratification

66. A major feature of successful delay of gratification is __transforming__ transforming (changing)
what is unpleasant into what is pleasant. One mode of accom-
plishing this is __distraction__ during the delay interval.   distraction

67. The more one can delay gratification as a young child, the

__better__ is one's adjustment and competence in adolescence.   better

THE HUMANISTIC APPROACH

68. In contrast to the behavioristic and psychoanalytic approaches to
personality, humanistic psychologists describe themselves as

having a __positive__ view of human motivation.   positive

69. Maslow describes the behaviorists and psychoanalysts as focusing
on physiological needs such as hunger, thirst, and escape from

pain, which Maslow calls __deficiency needs__ .   deficiency needs

70. Maslow places the needs referred to above at the bottom of the

__hierarchy of needs__ . At the top is the desire to realize   hierarchy of needs

oneself to the fullest, called __self - actualization__   self-actualization

71. According to humanistic psychologists, a basic part of one's
subjective experience is one's sense of oneself as both agent and

object, called one's __self - concept__   self-concept

72. According to Rogers, a solid sense of self-worth depends on a

child's feeling of __unconditional positive regard__   unconditional positive regard

73. According to Maslow, satisfaction of lower-level needs and a reasonable sense of self-worth allow for the expression of the desire for *self - actualization*   self-actualization

74. Self-actualized persons are more likely to report profound and deeply felt moments in their lives, called *peak experiences*   peak experiences

75. One problem with the humanistic approach is that there is little *evidence* to support the assertions made about human nature.   evidence

76. Another problem is that, in an important sense, people like Adolf Hitler fit the description of being *self - actualized*   self-actualized

77. In parallel with the Romantic movement, humanistic psychology can be seen as a *protest* movement.   protest

TAKING STOCK

78. The four different approaches to personality represent four different theoretical *perspectives*, each of which may have some validity.   perspectives

79. The four different approaches correspond to four different approaches to the presentation of character in *drama*   drama

Self-Test

1. Personality differences include:
   a. intelligence, ability, and insight.
   b. desires, feelings, and modes of expressing these needs and feelings.
   c. none of the above
   d. both a and b

2. The four orientations to personality are:
   a. trait theory, psychoanalytic theory, attribution theory, behavioral theory.
   b. trait theory, humanistic theory, psychogenic theory, behavioral theory.
   c. psychodynamic theory, humanistic theory, behavioral theory, projective theory.
   d. trait theory, humanistic theory, psychodynamic theory, behavioral theory.

3. Trait theory:
   a. is consonant with the beliefs of Aristophanes.
   b. assumes consistency of personality patterns.
   c. establishes personality prototypes such as the garrulous person, the flatterer, etc.
   d. a and b

4. The first personality and intelligence tests were similar in that both were _____, but differed in that the former was _____ and the latter was _____ .
   a. diagnostic, unstructured, structured
   b. unstructured, descriptive, normative

   c. diagnostic, poorly validated, well-validated
   d. structured, descriptive, diagnostic

5. The California Psychological Inventory (CPI) uses _____ criterion groups.
   a. no
   b. pathological
   c. normal
   d. random

6. When a test can foretell some real-world event, it is said to have:
   a. face validity.
   b. reliability.
   c. predictive validity.
   d. unproven validity.

7. Which of the following illustrates construct validation?
   a. correlating the Nielsen rankings of television shows with the amount of fan mail the stars receive and with the number of articles written about the show
   b. the correct choice of presidential candidates by the Gallup polls
   c. the confirmation of a proposed genetic theory through population studies
   d. the repeated modification and testing of a new car design to ensure safety and good performance

8. Projective techniques differ from tests such as the MMPI and CPI in that the former are more:
   a. structured.
   b. quantitative.
   c. variable.
   d. all of the above
   e. none of the above

9. In structuring unstructured materials, it is expected that a subject:
   a. will reveal his capacity for conceptual organization.
   b. will be relieved of objective test anxiety and will thus perform most effectively and honestly.
   c. will project his deepest feelings and conflicts upon the ambiguous stimulus.
   d. will be distracted from the psychologist's analysis of the subject's voice tone, body language, and gestures in responding.

10. Two examples of projective tests are:
    a. the MMPI and the Thematic Apperception Test (TAT).
    b. the Rorschach and the TAT.
    c. the Rorschach and the CPI.
    d. all of the above

11. The three categories used in interpreting the Rorschach are:
    a. location, negativism, color.
    b. location, content, determinants.
    c. content, impulsiveness, use of white space.
    d. impulsiveness, happiness, truth value.

12. Which of the following is *not* an established piece of evidence against the validity of the Rorschach inkblot test?
    a. the failure of highly intelligent people to use the entire inkblot more than others do
    b. the lack of relation between Rorschach indices and psychiatric diagnosis
    c. the failure of artists to demonstrate a preponderance of human movement in their perceptions
    d. the fact that individual Rorschach indices show little relation to external validity criteria

13. While the TAT has not fared well as a diagnostic tool, it has shown some promise as an indicator of:
    a. intelligence.
    b. motives.
    c. hidden fears.
    d. imagination.

14. A taxonomy is a:
    a. classification system.
    b. rating scale used in psychiatric diagnosis.

c. type of mental disorder.
d. class of stable personality traits.

15. Eysenck has formed a hypothesis that all personalities can be classified on the basis of a rating on two independent scales. They are _____ and _____ .
    a. paranoid, schizophrenic
    b. shy-outgoing, anxiety
    c. neuroticism, extroversion-introversion
    d. psychopathic deviance, extroversion-introversion

16. Walter Mischel has found that children are _____ in their behavior in different circumstances. He saw this as evidence _____ the validity of personality traits.
    a. consistent, for
    b. inconsistent, for
    c. consistent, against
    d. inconsistent, against

17. The concept of situationism is most opposite to the assumptions underlying:
    a. the MMPI and CPI.
    b. the Rorschach and TAT.
    c. all of the above
    d. none of the above

18. Situationists:
    a. deny the existence of individual differences.
    b. believe that social roles play a large part in the situations people get into.
    c. claim that situations themselves are the best predictors of people's reactions.
    d. believe that past situational experiences determine personality traits.

19. In _____ with Mischel, some authors have claimed that there is a higher level of consistency in people's behavior than previously believed. They hypothesize that reactions that appear _____ in gross analysis are really different manifestations of _____ underlying sources.
    a. agreement, dissimilar, different
    b. agreement, dissimilar, the same
    c. disagreement, similar, different
    d. disagreement, dissimilar, the same

20. Studies by Endler and Hunt have looked at person-situation interactions. Their results suggest that the practicality of assigning traits like fear to people:
    a. is useless.
    b. has been experimentally validated.
    c. should be qualified to be more specific to individual circumstances.
    d. is minimal since internal fluctuations in trait strength cause behavior to vary from situation to situation.

21. High self-monitors are:
    a. not adaptable.
    b. inconsistent.
    c. consistent.
    d. rigid.

22. Which of the following people would show behavioral consistency across situations?
    a. the manic-depressive
    b. the schizophrenic
    c. the psychotic
    d. all of the above

23. Person constancy involves the notion that:
    a. all people behave in essentially the same way for a particular situation.
    b. people are not consistent but we perceive them as being that way.
    c. we tend to see a person in only one situation, so we think of him only in that situation.
    d. all of the above
    e. none of the above

24. Introverts differ from extroverts in all of the following ways *except*:
    a. they are solitary.
    b. they are cautious.
    c. they are slow to change.
    d. they have a lower pain threshold.
    e. none of the above

25. Which of the following is true of sensation seekers?
    a. They have underactive norepinephrine systems in their brain.
    b. They are overaroused in certain systems of their brain.
    c. They have a low pain tolerance.
    d. They react more to external stimuli than those who are not sensation seekers.

26. According to Freud, the unconscious conflicts that have a formative effect on personality originate in:
    a. the phallic stage.
    b. the latency period.
    c. childhood.
    d. the psychodynamic approach.
    e. the erogenous zones.

27. An adult who dislikes eating and avoids kissing and smoking would, according to Freud, be described as:
    a. fixated at the oral stage.
    b. showing a reaction formation from the oral stage.
    c. an oral character.
    d. an anal character.

28. Which of the following are integral components of Freudian theory?
    a. psychosexual stages
    b. unconscious conflict
    c. fixation and reaction formation
    d. b and c
    e. all of the above

29. Evidence relating early childhood experience to later personality indicates:
    a. support for the general Freudian view.
    b. little support for the idea that experience in the anal stage affects later personality.
    c. support for the view that the anal stage directly affects later personality development.
    d. a and c
    e. none of the above

30. According to Horney, the vicious circle:
    a. results from neurotic conflict.
    b. is more likely if there is more basic anxiety.
    c. depends on an aggressive personality.
    d. a and b
    e. all of the above

31. Repression : deciding to ignore unpleasant news ::
    a. unconscious defense : conscious defense
    b. inattention : reaction formation
    c. coping : ego psychology
    d. anxiety : conflict
    e. house : bedroom

32. Social learning theorists share with behaviorists a focus on:
    a. learning.
    b. instinctive behavior.
    c. psychodynamic mechanisms.
    d. expectancies and other cognitions.
    e. b and d

33. Some adults prefer $10 now to $12 a week later. This preference illustrates a failure of:
    a. basic anxiety.
    b. global attributional style.
    c. stable attributional style.
    d. delay of gratification.
    e. none of the above

34. Delay of gratification tasks can be mastered by strategies such as:
    a. distracting oneself.
    b. thinking about the reward.
    c. mentally transforming the goal object into another more desirable object.
    d. all of the above
    e. a and c

35. The humanistic approach differs from both the behavioristic and psychoanalytic approaches in all but one of the following ways. Which of the

choices below is *not* a difference between these approaches?

a. emphasis on the positive side of human nature

b. assumption of a hierarchy of needs

c. acknowledgment of the existence of deficiency needs

d. emphasis on self-actualization

e. emphasis on free choice

36. In contrast to the behavioristic approach, the trait, psychoanalytic, and humanistic approaches all:

a. emphasize internal causes of behavior.

b. focus on the conflict between biological and social needs.

c. posit a hierarchy of needs.

d. take a basically statistical approach to personality.

e. emphasize the role of the environment in shaping personality.

37. Self-actualization is:

a. at the top of the need hierarchy.

b. associated with a higher frequency of peak experiences.

c. dependent on satisfaction of lower-level needs.

d. all of the above

e. a and b

38. Unconditional positive regard in the humanistic scheme, and failure to fixate at the oral or anal phases in the psychodynamic scheme, are both:

a. features of personality.

b. contributing factors to adult psychopathology.

c. dependent on repression.

d. influenced by genetic predisposition.

e. conditions for a well-adjusted adult personality.

39. Like the Romantic movement, the humanistic movement can be seen as a protest against:

a. classical conditioning.

b. an overemphasis on culture.

c. a narrow and mechanical approach to human nature.

d. reliance on the scientific approach.

e. c and d

40. Overall, the four approaches to personality each:

a. represent valid alternative perspectives.

b. present views that cannot, ultimately, coexist with all of the others.

c. overemphasize the importance of culture.

d. emphasize reason over feelings.

e. assign a different role to the function of drama.

Answer Key for Self-Test

1. b p. 449	21. b p. 468
2. d p. 450	22. d p. 468
3. b p. 450	23. e p. 469
4. c p. 452	24. e pp. 462, 471
5. c p. 453	25. a p. 472
6. c p. 454	26. c p. 474
7. a p. 454	27. b pp. 474–75
8. e p. 455	28. e pp. 474–75
9. c p. 455	29. b p. 476
10. b p. 455	30. d p. 477
11. b p. 456	31. a p. 479
12. a p. 458	32. a pp. 480–81
13. b p. 459	33. d p. 482
14. a p. 460	34. a p. 483
15. c p. 461	35. c p. 484
16. d p. 464	36. a pp. 480, 484
17. c p. 464	37. d pp. 485–86
18. c p. 464	38. e pp. 475, 486
19. d p. 465	39. e p. 488
20. c p. 467	40. a p. 489

Investigating Psychological Phenomena

CONSTRUCTING A PERSONALITY INVENTORY

Equipment: None
Number of subjects: One, yourself
Time per subject: Forty-five minutes
Time for experimenter: Forty-five minutes

Constructing a test to assess a personality trait is an involved process. It requires the creation of test items and the validation of these items through administration of the test to large groups of subjects. While it would be impossible to illustrate all the steps in this process through a short exercise such as this, it is possible to provide an idea about some of the issues that are involved. That is the purpose of this demonstration.

A first draft of a test for a particular personality trait has been created.* Before reading on, you should take this test. Listed below are twenty-one questions for you to answer. Try to put yourself in each of the following situations and on the answer sheet mark the choice that would best describe your reactions. Limit your replies to the choices given and answer every question.

*We thank Lisa Lange, John Prevost, Barb Merriam, Laurie Tunstall, and Julie Nuse for their permission to use the inventory they prepared as part of a course project supervised by Dr. Charles Morris. We also thank Dr. Morris for kindly supplying the correlational data.

Draft Personality Inventory

	strongly disagree	slightly disagree	slightly agree	strongly agree
1. I am in a crowded bar sitting with some friends. A good-looking individual comes up to me and asks me to dance. I like to dance but I notice that the dance floor is empty and answer no.	1	2	3	4
2. I get an important exam back and I disagree with the grading on one of the problems. But I accept my grade, avoiding a confrontation with the professor.	1	2	3	4
3. I enjoy attending seminars and discussion groups as opposed to large lectures.	1	2	3	4
4. I'm in a restaurant and receive some bad food. Instead of saying something, I stay quiet but leave a small tip.	1	2	3	4
5. My family is moving to another state and I will be attending a new school. I look forward to meeting new people and making new friends.	1	2	3	4
6. I find it easy to liven up a dull occasion.	1	2	3	4
7. I am required to form groups in a class and interact on a subject. The groups are formed but I tend to listen more than offer information.	1	2	3	4
8. If I were in the waiting room of a doctor's office and a stranger sat down next to me, introduced himself, and started asking me questions, I would feel nervous and uncomfortable.	1	2	3	4
9. I can usually enjoy myself at a party even if I know almost no one there.	1	2	3	4
10. A teacher asks questions to which I know the answers, but I never raise my hand for fear that the answers might not be what the teacher is looking for.	1	2	3	4
11. I become uncomfortable and at a loss for words, usually blushing, when I am given a compliment.	1	2	3	4
12. I often find myself taking charge in group situations.	1	2	3	4
13. I prefer being with people and going to parties rather than spending my spare time alone pursuing personal interests or hobbies.	1	2	3	4
14. If someone was smoking a cigarette in a nonsmoking section and the smoke was bothering me, I wouldn't hesitate to ask the person to put out the cigarette.	1	2	3	4
15. I often look back at a situation and think of things I should have done or said.	1	2	3	4
16. I feel proud to be called on to give a toast at a social gathering.	1	2	3	4
17. I would go out of my way to make a stranger feel comfortable in a group in which the people are unfamiliar to him.	1	2	3	4
18. When I've been waiting in line for service for a long time and someone cuts in front of me, I feel angry but don't say anything about it.	1	2	3	4
19. I prefer not to answer the door when I know it's a salesman because I have a hard time getting him to leave once he's inside the door.	1	2	3	4
20. When I've struck up a conversation with the person sitting next to me, a long plane flight seems more enjoyable.	1	2	3	4
21. I consider myself to be a shy person.	1	2	3	4

Now that you have answered the questionnaire, you are probably aware that it is intended to assess shyness. The questions themselves were constructed as candidates that might have something to do with predicting how shy people are. How can one tell if the questionnaire accomplishes its purpose or which questions are the best predictors of shyness?

One possibility is to examine the face validity of each of the questions. Since you have just answered the questions and since you are now aware that its purpose is to test for shyness, you can do this yourself. Examine each question and decide whether you think that it would be a good predictor. That is, does the question ask subjects about a reaction that should depend on how shy the subjects are? Try to pick out the four questions that you think would best predict shyness and the four that would be least relevant. Note, by the way, that the questions are constructed so that for some (items 1, 2, 4, 7, 8, 10, 11, 15, 18, 19, and 21) a high score (e.g., 4) would indicate more shyness, while for the rest, a low score (e.g., 1) would indicate more shyness. This is only done to provide variety; your assessment of each question should be independent of this point.

Questions that would best predict shyness	Questions that would least predict shyness
1. _____	1. _____
2. _____	2. _____
3. _____	3. _____
4. _____	4. _____

Your judgment of the quality of a question is a measure of face validity (that is, the extent to which a question, on the face of it, is a good predictor of shyness), but this is not the only possible measure of validity. Another criterion is to have some independent measure of a subject's shyness and correlate responses to each question with the measure. Presumably, if a question were a good predictor of shyness, it would correlate highly with this measure.

One such measure is a subject's response to question 21. This question directly asks subjects for their own assessment of whether they consider themselves to be shy. In order to determine how well each test question correlates with this self-assessment of shyness, sixty-nine subjects were given this questionnaire and correlations of each question with question 21 were calculated. They are presented in Table 1 below.

TABLE 1

Correlations of Each Question in the Questionnaire with Question 21

A low correlation (a positive or negative value close to 0) indicates that there is little relationship between the answer to that question and the answer to question 21; a high correlation (a value closer to -1 or $+1$) indicates a relationship between responses to that question and responses to question 21. For example, item 10 has a correlation of .42 with item 21. This means that subjects who tend to agree with the statement in question 10 tend to agree also with the statement in question 21. Likewise, subjects who tend to disagree with the statement in question 10, also tend to disagree with the statement in question 21. A negative correlation, such as in question 6, indicates that subjects who tend to agree with the statement in 6 tend to disagree with the statement in 21. Likewise, those who tend to disagree with the statement in 6 tend to agree with the one in 21 (note that even though a correlation is negative, it still means that there is a relationship between the two items in question, but a reverse relationship).

Question:	1	2	3	4	5	6	7	8	9	10
Correlation:	.23	.08	$-.15$	$-.08$	$-.20$	$-.28$	.38	$-.24$	$-.24$	.42

Question:	11	12	13	14	15	16	17	18	19	20
Correlation:	.29	$-.22$	$-.20$	$-.27$	.32	$-.37$	$-.16$	.17	.09	$-.07$

Compare your judgments of question quality against these correlations to see whether the ones you judged as good have either high positive or high negative values; also, check whether the questions you judged as poor have correlations near 0.

Another validity criterion that may be reasonable is the total score on the test. The logic of using this criterion is that individual questions may vary in how well they indicate shyness, but the test *as a whole* may be a much better indicator. If this were so, then it would be sensible to correlate scores on individual questions with those on the whole test to see which questions best predict the total test score. This was done for the same sixty-nine subjects as above; the correlations are presented in Table 2.

TABLE 2

Correlations of Each Question with the Total Test Score

As in Table 1, a low value means little relationship of that question with the total test score, while a higher value (either positive or negative) means that there is some relationship. For example, the correlation of .55 for question 10 indicates that subjects who tend to agree with the statement in item 10 tend to have a high total score on the questionnaire, while subjects who tend to disagree with the statement in 10 tend to score low on the whole questionnaire. Another illustration is the correlation of −.49 for question 5. This means that subjects who tend to disagree with the statement in 5 tend to get a high total score, while subjects who tend to agree with the statement in 5 tend to have a low score.

Question:	1	2	3	4	5	6	7	8	9	10
Correlation:	.45	.41	−.54	.13	−.49	−.44	.46	.42	−.53	.55
Question:	11	12	13	14	15	16	17	18	19	20
Correlation:	.37	−.42	−.35	−.44	.40	−.46	−.27	.35	.25	−.01

Again, see how well your judgments of question quality are related to these correlations. Note also an interesting pattern in the two sets of correlations presented in Tables 1 and 2. Item 10 has both the highest absolute correlation with question 21 and the highest correlation with the total test score. Also, item 7 has very high correlation with both criterion measures. This consistency suggests that these two items may well be good, valid indices of shyness. How did you rate these items? Examine the items themselves to see if you can explain why they might be better than others.

Note also that two items, 4 and 20, have very low correlations with both criterion measures. How did you judge these items? Why do you think they have such low correlations?

If we were to continue to develop a "shyness inventory," we might well try to use other validity criteria as well as the three described above. For example, we might try to use the inventory to predict some behavior that is characteristic of shy people. This would allow us to assess the predictive validity of the test. Whatever the criteria, though, the objective of test construction is to find questions that best predict that which you are trying to assess. This exercise should have given you some insight into the process by which this objective is reached.

Investigating Psychological Phenomena

EXPLANATORY STYLE (ATTRIBUTIONAL STYLE) AND THE CAVE TECHNIQUE: MEASURING A SUBJECT'S EXPLANATORY STYLE

Equipment: None
Number of subjects: None
Time per subject: None
Time for experimenter: 45–60 minutes

This activity introduces you to the measurement of explanatory or attributional styles, a subject discussed in the text as part of the cognitive/behavioral approach to personality. Through this exercise you will learn how to determine a basic component of a person's explanatory or attributional style, the habitual pattern of explanations an individual makes for good and bad events.

Two types of explanatory style have been identified—optimistic and pessimistic. Individuals with a pessimistic explanatory style systematically believe that the causes of bad events are internal ("it's my fault"), stable ("it's going to last forever"), and global ("it's going to undermine everything I do"). In contrast, individuals with an optimistic explanatory style systematically believe that the causes of bad events are external ("it's someone else's fault"), unstable ("it's only temporary"), and specific ("it will only affect some of the things I do") (Schulman, Castellon, and Seligman, 1989). A pessimistic explanatory style has been found to be correlated with depression: Individuals with a pessimistic explanatory style show greater helplessness when confronted with a bad event than do individuals with an optimistic explanatory style (Seligman et al., 1979).

The Attributional Style Questionnaire (ASQ) (Seligman et al., 1979) is one instrument that is used to measure explanatory style. The Content Analysis of Verbatim Explanations (CAVE) (Peterson and Seligman, 1988) is another. The CAVE technique is useful for rating the attributional style of those who are unwilling or unable to take the ASQ and involves rating spoken or written material (e.g., a transcript from a therapy session, a speech, or a page from a diary) along the three causal dimensions—internal vs. external, stable vs. unstable, and global vs. specific (Schulman et al., 1989).

The CAVE technique is a complex two-step process of *extraction* and *rating*. The following is a summary of the information needed to use this technique.

THE EXTRACTION PROCESS

The extraction process involves taking, or "extracting," events and what the subject believes are their causes word for word from written or spoken material. Events can be thoughts or feelings (e.g., "I was afraid"); they can be social (e.g., "I was praised by my employer") or physical (e.g., "I was in a car accident"). They may have occurred in the past, be occurring in the present, or may potentially occur in the future. The "causal attribution" is whatever the subject perceives to be the reason for the event. For example, for the event "I was praised by my employer," some causal attributions might be "the boss was in a good mood that day" or "I've been doing a good job lately."

To be extracted, the event and its (perceived) causes—or the event-attribution unit—must satisfy the following conditions (Schulman et al., 1989):

1. The event must be unambiguously good or bad from the subject's point of view. Events that the subject views as neutral should not be extracted. Event-attribution units that have good *and* bad elements, and events that do not affect the subject, should not be extracted.

2. The subject must express his or her own explanation for that event. Simply agreeing with or quoting another person's (e.g., the therapist's or interviewer's) explanation is unacceptable.

3. There must be a clear causal relationship between the explanation and the event. The explanation of the event should not simply be a justification, description, or definition of the event. The explanation should clearly show what the subject believes was the cause of the event.

It's worth emphasizing that event-attribution units must be extracted using the subject's own words. If a unit does not contain enough information for it to be understood out of context (e.g., the extracted sentence contains a pronoun without an antecedent), any relevant information must be added in brackets.

Second, while the word "because" is often a signal that an explanation is to follow, that word alone is neither necessary nor sufficient for an explanation to be extracted. A causal relationship may exist between an event and an attribution even though "because" is not used. In addition, the word "because" does not always signal a causal relationship. It may serve to qualify a response or may function as an equivalent to the word "but." Under these circumstances, you should not make an extraction.

Exercise 1: Extracting event-attribution units. Use the following transcript from a cancer patient to practice extracting events and their attributions. Don't forget that they must meet the above three conditions. Underline what you think are appropriate event-attribution units in section 1 below. Then check the answers before extracting the remainder of the transcript. Answers and discussion are on pages 224–25.

Interviewer: How was your weekend?

1. *Patient:* Well, I couldn't do anything all weekend because I felt so rotten. The doctor wanted me to get out, but I felt so bad that I just couldn't do anything. I couldn't even do any work around the house. . . . I'm just too sore. I just haven't felt well from the surgery. I may have gotten a virus with the surgery.

Interviewer: What are your feelings about the doctors at this hospital?

2. *Patient:* It has bothered me that I have to keep asking to get information at the hospital about the cancer. Doctors just seem like they don't want to talk to you about your condition, and I feel it's my body and I want to know. Besides that, I'm really quite comfortable with them because they have been so warm and reassuring. I used to feel very nervous around doctors. I used to go to the doctor only when it was something big . . . something I knew I couldn't handle.

Interviewer: How have the chemotherapy treatments been for you?

3. *Patient:* I kind of feel comfortable with the radiation treatments because I have read quite a few articles on radiation over the past few years. In a way, though, chemotherapy just kind of bothers you. . . . I think it's knowing that even while it is getting rid of the cancer cells it can do damage to other cells.

Interviewer: Tell me a little about your husband and your marriage. How have they been affected by your cancer?

4. *Patient:* I've been afraid to talk to my husband about my cancer, lately, because he's been so distant.

Interviewer: I understand that he hasn't come to the hospital with you very often. How do you feel about that?

5. *Patient:* It's been very upsetting that he hasn't come into the hospital with me for my treatments. Yes, I know it's because he drives a truck and this is his busiest time of year. It's funny . . . it's hard for us now, but the first few years of marriage were really the most difficult. For the first few years, being sick and all, I expected him to take more responsibility around the house than he did. It's working out a lot better now that I know what to expect and what not to expect from our marriage.

Interviewer: How are your children handling your latest bout?

6. *Patient:* I hadn't told my oldest son about coming out of remission until a few days ago. He didn't know about it because he lives out of state. I'm really glad that I finally told him because he seemed relieved to know exactly why I've been so down lately. My oldest son and I are very close. I guess it's because we have been through so much together.

Now check your results with the answers on pages 224–25.

THE RATING PROCESS

The second process of the CAVE technique involves rating extracted attributions along the three causal dimensions. We will give you experience with the rating process only on the external vs. internal scale.

The internal vs. external scale. The internal vs. external scale measures the extent to which a cause is attributed to something within or outside the self. A rating of 1 indicates that the attribution is completely external. It is assigned if the individual attributes a cause solely to another person's actions, the difficulty or ease of the task, the time, or the environment. A rating of 7 indicates that the attribution is completely internal. It is assigned if an individual attributes a cause solely to any behavioral, physical, or mental characteristic of the self. Ratings from 2 to 6 are given if the individual attributes the cause to some combination of self and other. Often these are the most difficult to assign, because the difference between adjacent ratings in this range is slight and hard to specify. Generally, however, ratings of 2 or 3 are assigned if the attribution is more external than internal. A rating of 4 is assigned if the attribution is as much external as it is internal. It is also assigned if the unit does not provide enough information to assign another rating. Ratings of 5 or 6 are assigned if the attribution is more internal than external (Schulman et al., 1989).

Examples. Several examples may help to clarify the difference between the ratings.

1	2	3	4	5	6	7
external						internal

Event: I didn't get the job
Attribution: because the company is so discriminatory.

This attribution should receive a rating of 1 on the internal vs. external scale. The individual attributes not getting the job solely to the fact that the company is discriminatory. This is a purely external attribution.

Event: I'm having problems with a friend
Attribution: because she can't accept my perfectionism.

This attribution should receive a rating of 2 or 3 on the internal vs. external scale. The cause is attributed to a combination of self and other: The friend's intolerance *and* the individual's own perfectionism. However, close examination of the phrasing of the attribution reveals that the friend's inability to accept perfectionism is perceived as more responsible for the problems than the perfectionism. Thus, the attribution is more external than internal and merits a rating of 2 or 3 rather than 5 or 6.

Event: We're getting a divorce.
Attribution: We're just not compatible.

This attribution should receive a rating of 4 on the internal vs. external scale. In this context, the use of "we" indicates that the event (divorce) is attributed to the incompatibility of self *and* other. The attribution implies that both individuals have contributed equally to cause the event.

Event: I did well on the test
Attribution: because I studied hard.

This attribution should be rated 7 on the internal vs. external scale. Doing well on the test is attributed solely to the individual's own behavior—studying hard. Thus, the attribution is purely internal.

Event: I just forgot part of my speech and don't even remember what I said.
Attribution: I think it was a combination of being very nervous and very tired.

This attribution should be rated a 5 or 6 on the internal vs. external scale. It is certainly an internal attribution. The subject admits that he forgot the speech because he was nervous and tired. However, the attribution should not receive a 7. The rating would have been a 7 if the subject had phrased the attribution, "It was because I was very nervous and very tired." Instead, the subject states, "I think it was a combination of being very nervous and very tired." In doing so, the subject distances himself somewhat from actually causing the event. Thus, the attribution is slightly less internal than a 7.

Exercise 2: Rating attributions. Rate the attributions from exercise 1 along the internal vs. external scale. Answers and discussion are located on pages 225–26.

ANSWERS TO EXERCISE 1

1a. *Event:* I couldn't do anything all weekend
   Attribution: because I felt so rotten.
1b. *Event:* . . . I just couldn't do anything
   Attribution: I felt so bad. . . .
1c. *Event:* I couldn't even do any work around the house.
   Attribution: I'm just too sore.
1d. *Event:* I just haven't felt well from the surgery.

Attribution: I may have gotten a virus with the surgery.

2a. *Event:* It has bothered me that I have to keep asking to get information at the hospital about the cancer.
   Attribution: Doctors just seem like they don't want to talk to you about your condition, and I feel it's my body and I want to know.
2b. *Event:* I'm really quite comfortable with them [the doctors at this hospital]
   Attribution: because they have been so warm and reassuring.
2c. *Event:* I used to feel very nervous around doctors.
   Attribution: None

This is an unacceptable extraction because the event is not unambiguously good or bad. Also, it is not adequately explained.

2d. *Events:* I used to go to the doctor only when it was something big . . . something I knew I couldn't handle.
   Attribution: None

This is an unacceptable extraction because the subject does not adequately explain the event. Also, the event is not unambiguously good or bad to the subject.

3a. *Event:* I kind of feel comfortable with the radiation treatments
   Attribution: because I have read quite a few articles on radiation over the past few years.
3b. *Event:* Chemotherapy just kind of bothers you.
   Attribution: I think it's knowing that even while it is getting rid of the cancer cells it can do damage to other cells.

4a. *Event:* I've been afraid to talk to my husband about my cancer . . .
   Attribution: because he's been so distant.

5a. *Event:* . . . He [the husband] hasn't come into the hospital with me for my treatments.
   Attribution: . . . He drives a truck and this is his busiest time of year.
5b. *Event:* . . . It's hard for us now.
   Attribution: None

This is an unacceptable extraction because the event is not adequately explained.

5c. *Event:* The first few years of marriage were really the most difficult.
   Attribution: . . . Being sick and all, I expected him to take more responsibility around the house than he did.
5d. *Event:* It's [the marriage is] working out a lot better
   Attribution: now that I know what to expect and not to expect from our marriage.

6a. *Event:* I hadn't told my oldest son about my coming out of remission until a few days ago.

Attribution: None

This is an unacceptable extraction because the event is not unambiguously good or bad to the subject. Also, it is not adequately explained.

6b. *Event:* He [her son] didn't know about it [her coming out of remission]

    Attribution: because he lives out of state.

This is an unacceptable extraction because the event is not unambiguously good or bad from the subject's point of view. Also, the event does not affect the subject.

6c. *Event:* I'm really glad that I finally told him [her son]

    Attribution: because he seemed relieved to know exactly why I've been so down lately.

6d. *Event:* My oldest son and I are very close.

    Attribution: I guess it's because we have been through so much together.

Discussion: Much of this transcript is extractable for two reasons. The first reason is that the subject finds most of the events she discusses in the transcript clearly good or bad. For instance, "he hasn't come into the hospital with me for my treatments" is an acceptable event because it is clearly a negative event for the subject. In fact, the subject admits that the event upsets her. In contrast, the sentence "I used to go to the doctor only when it was something really big . . ." cannot be extracted because the event (going to the doctor) is not unambiguously good or bad from the subject's point of view.

The second reason why much of this transcript is extractable is that the subject eventually explains most of the events she discusses with the interviewer. In other words, she attributes a cause to almost every event. However, there are several exceptions. The sentences "I used to feel very nervous around doctors," "it's hard for us now," and "I hadn't told my oldest son about coming out of remission until a few days ago" are examples of events that should not be extracted. These events are unacceptable because they are not adequately explained by the subject.

ANSWERS TO EXERCISE 2

1a.	7	3b.	3
1b.	7	4a.	1
1c.	7	5a.	1
1d.	2	5c.	5–6
2a.	2	5d.	7
2b.	1	6c.	1
3a.	4–5	6d.	4

Discussion.

Attribution Number(s)	Rating	Explanation
1a, 1b, 1c, and 5d	7	The subject attributes the events solely to physical or mental characteristics of the self.
2b, 4a, 5a, and 6c	1	The subject attributes the events solely to the actions of another person.
1d	2	"Virus" and "surgery" are external causes, but the subject implicates herself in the cause by "having gotten" the virus.
2a	2	The main cause of her problem is external (the doctors), but she implicates herself in the cause by "wanting to know."
3a	4–5	A combination of the subject's reading (internal) and the information of the articles (external) led to her feeling comfortable — emphasis may be on reading though.
3b	3	A combination of the subject's "knowing" and "it" (chemotherapy) is the cause — the emphasis is on the "it."
5c	5–6	The subject stresses that her expectations are responsible for the marital difficulties, though the husband is also partially involved in this process.
6d	4	The cause is mutual — it is as external as it is internal.

(Source: Schulman and Seligman, 1989.)

Since seven of the subject's attributions have a score of 3 or lower and six have a score of 5 or higher, the subject would be rated as slightly more optimistic than pessimistic. Keep in mind, though, that the subject has only been rated on one causal dimension — internal vs. external. It would, of course, be necessary to rate her attributions on the two other causal dimensions — global vs. specific and stable vs. unstable — and to extract and rate additional transcripts, as well as use other measures, to draw any useful conclusions about her explanatory style.

In summary, explanatory style can have a significant effect on health. The more pessimistic a person's explanatory style, the more susceptible that person can be to depression. A growing body of research has also linked a pessimistic explanatory style with suppression of the immune system and an increased vulnerability to certain diseases.

Whether therapy can change a pessimist into an eternal optimist has not yet been proved. Current research is examining whether changes in explanatory style are long-lasting. If explanatory style can be successfully changed, the CAVE technique could be a useful tool in preventing depression and the development of certain diseases.

EXPLANATORY STYLE IN SPORTS

On a lighter note, explanatory style may also be used to predict success or failure in sports. A sports team, like an individual, possesses an explanatory style—either pessimistic or optimistic. A team that habitually blames its losses on lack of talent ("We lost because the team is just no good"), an internal attribution, would have a pessimistic explanatory style. A team that habitually blames its losses on the bad judgment of umpires ("We lost because the umpire made a lousy call"), an external attribution, would have an optimistic explanatory style (Rettew et al., in press).

One study evaluated the explanatory style of twelve National League baseball teams in the 1986 season to find out whether their style would predict their performances in the 1987 season. Event-attribution units were extracted from sports pages and then rated. Teams that had a more internal (thus more pessimistic) explanatory style in 1986 were in fact found to have won fewer games in the 1987 season than teams with more optimistic styles. In fact explanatory style proved to be a better predictor of wins in the 1987 season than had wins in the 1986 season (Rettew, in press). So keep explanatory style in mind when ranking teams in the preseason—you might end up backing an underdog that winds up at the World Series.

References

Peterson, C., and Seligman, M. E. P. 1988. Content analysis of verbatim explanations: The CAVE technique for assessing explanatory style. Unpublished manuscript.

Rettew, D. C. In press. Explanatory style in sports. In Seligman, M. E. P., and Buchanan, G. (Eds.), *Explanatory Style*.

Schulman, P., and Seligman, M. E. P. 1989. Self-administered training in the CAVE technique: Content analysis of verbatim explanations. Unpublished manuscript.

Seligman, M. E. P., Abramson, L. Y., Semmel, A., and von Baeyer, C. 1979. Depressive attributional style. *Journal of Abnormal Psychology* (88): 242–47.

Seligman, M. E. P., Kamen, L. P., and Nolen-Hoeksema, S. E. 1988. Explanatory style across the life-span: Achievement and health. In Heatherington, E. M., Lemer, R. M., and Perlmutter, M. (Eds.), Child development in life-span perspective. Hillsdale, N.J.: Erlbaum, pp. 91–114.

CHAPTER 17

Psychopathology

Learning Objectives

DIFFERENT CONCEPTIONS OF MADNESS

Insanity as demonic possession

1. Give examples from historical sources of the treatment of madness as demonic possession.

Insanity as a disease

2. Describe the history of the treatment of insanity as a disease.
3. Describe the somatogenic view of mental illness, referring to the example of general paresis.
4. Define psychogenic disorders and explain the historical role of hysteria in clarifying the nature of these disorders.

THE PATHOLOGY MODEL

5. Explain the pathology model of mental illness.

Subcategories of the pathology model

6. Briefly describe the medical, psychoanalytic, and learning models as approaches to psychopathology.

Mental disorder as pathology

7. Discuss the sense in which the term pathology can be applied to mental disorders.

Classifying mental disorders

8. Distinguish between symptoms and syndromes.
9. Indicate how mental illnesses are classified, referring to the changes in the latest taxonomy, DSM-III-R.

Explaining disorder: diathesis, stress, and pathology

10. Describe the diathesis-stress explanation of mental illness.
11. List what one has to know in order to explain fully a mental (or bodily) disorder.

SCHIZOPHRENIA

The symptoms

12. Describe the major symptoms of schizophrenia in the areas of thought, social relationships, motivation, and behavior.

Subcategories of schizophrenia

13. Describe the modern emphasis on positive and negative symptoms.

The search for the underlying pathology

14. Show how the assumption of a disorder in focus of activity can explain many of the symptoms of schizophrenia.
15. Describe the dopamine hypothesis and indicate the types of evidence in favor of it. Suggest what types of experiments might prove it.
16. Describe the anatomical deficit theory of schizophrenia. How are the anatomical and neurotransmitter theories related? Describe the two-syndrome hypothesis.

More remote causes of schizophrenia

17. Review the evidence for genetic factors in schizophrenia.
18. Describe the role of environmental effects in schizophrenia, including low social status and family pathology.
19. Evaluate the alternative possibilities that the environmental correlates of schizophrenia are caused by or are causes of schizophrenia.

The pathology model and schizophrenia

20. Review the symptoms, underlying pathology, and remote causes of schizophrenia. Review the evidence for an organic basis for schizophrenia.
21. Apply the diathesis-stress model to schizophrenia.

MOOD DISORDERS

The symptom pattern

22. Distinguish bipolar disorder from major depression. Compare and contrast mania and depression in terms of symptoms.
23. Discuss the relation between suicide and depression.
24. Define seasonal affective disorder.

Organic factors

25. Review the evidence for a genetic involvement in the causation of bipolar disorder.
26. Discuss the biochemical explanation of depression.
27. Understand how the biochemical hypothesis suggests and accounts for the success of drugs in treating depression.

Psychogenic factors

28. Review the evidence for psychogenic factors in depression.
29. Discuss whether mood or cognitive disorders come first in the causation of depression.
30. Describe Beck's cognitive theory of depression.
31. Describe the learned helplessness theory of depression, and summarize the evidence in favor of it that comes from both animal and human research
32. Explain how the idea of despondent attributional style as a cause of depression grew out of the concept of learned helplessness, and review the evidence for this position.
33. Indicate the explanations for the higher incidence of depression in American women, as opposed to men.
34. Indicate the adequacy of each theory of depression to account for the range of symptoms.

Mood disorders and the diathesis-stress conception

35. Apply the diathesis-stress conception to mood disorders.

ANXIETY DISORDERS

36. Define anxiety disorders.

Phobias

37. Describe phobias, and explain how they can be accounted for in terms of conditioning. What problems does the conditioning view have in explaining agoraphobia?

Obsessive-compulsive disorders

38. Describe the symptoms of obsessive-compulsive disorders.

Generalized anxiety disorders

39. Describe generalized anxiety disorders and both conditioning and psychoanalytic explanations for them.

Panic disorder

40. Define panic disorder, and understand how it differs from generalized anxiety disorder. Give some explanations of this disorder.

Anxiety disorders and the pathology model

41. Discuss the extent to which it is necessary to invoke anxiety as a cause of anxiety disorders. Evaluate the alternative that, at least sometimes, the symptom is the disease.
42. Apply the diathesis-stress model to anxiety disorders.

CONVERSIONS AND DISSOCIATIVE DISORDERS

43. Contrast conversion disorders and dissociative disorders with anxiety disorders.

Conversion disorders

44. Describe conversion disorders, and give the psychoanalytic explanation of them.

Dissociative disorders

45. Describe amnesia, fugue state, and multiple personality.

Factors that underlie conversions and dissociative conditions

46. Consider both anxiety defense and play-acting explanations of conversions and dissociative disorders. Evaluate the value of psychoanalytic and conditioning accounts of these disorders and the anxiety disorders.

PSYCHOPHYSIOLOGICAL DISORDERS

47. Define psychophysiological disorders. Note the critical difference between psychophysiological disorders and conversion disorders.

Essential hypertension

48. Know what essential hypertension is, and be able to explain what the role of stress and autonomic arousal in causing it is.

Coronary heart disease

49. Review the role of biological and psychological factors in the causation of coronary heart disease.
50. Describe the Type A personality. What aspects of this personality type seem most associated with coronary heart disease?

The diathesis-stress concept and psychophysiological disorders

51. Apply the diathesis-stress model to psychophysiological disorders and to the issue of which type of disorder (e.g., essential hypertension, peptic ulcer) occurs in an individual.

A CATEGORIZING REVIEW

52. Explain how mental disorders can be classified according to the organic or mental basis of both the symptoms and the underlying pathology.

THE SOCIOLOGICAL CRITIQUE OF THE PATHOLOGY MODEL

What society does to those it calls mad
53. Describe the treatment of institutionalized people.

Whom does society call mad?
54. Describe the consequences of being labeled as mentally ill and of being institutionalized.

Social deviance
55. Discuss the distinctions between criminals and sociopaths.
56. Review the causes of sociopathy.

Some contributions of labeling theory
57. Evaluate the contribution of the sociological viewpoints and labeling theory, in particular, to the understanding of sociopathy and other forms of mental "illness." For what types of "illness" is this approach most convincing?

THE SCOPE OF PSYCHOPATHOLOGY

58. Discuss the problem of defining psychopathology and uncovering common principles underlying it.

Programmed Exercises

DIFFERENT CONCEPTIONS OF MADNESS

1. A dominant early social response to insanity, which resulted in practices as varied as trephining the skull or the burning of witches, was based on the conception of insanity as

   demonic possession   demonic possession

2. Prior to the nineteenth century, people with severe mental illness

   were treated more or less as we currently deal with **criminals**   criminals (or prisoners)

3. The disappearance of the psychotic symptoms of **general paresis**   general paresis (or syphilis)
   following administration of penicillin provides strong evidence for a view of mental illness as a disease.

4. Mental symptoms that can be directly explained by malfunction

   at the organic level are called **somatogenic** Those, like hysteria,   somatogenic
   that are best explained at the psychological level are called

   psychogenic   psychogenic

5. A disorder that is characterized by symptoms that appear to be

   somatic but have no organic basis was once called **hysteria**   hysteria

THE PATHOLOGY MODEL

6. According to the **pathology model**, a particular disease is   pathology model
   considered as the underlying cause of specific mental symptoms.

7. According to the **medical** model, mental illness has an organic   medical
   basis, to be treated with somatic therapies. According to the

   learning model, mental disorders are, in large part, the result   learning
   of maladaptive learning. According to the **psychoanalytic** model,   psychoanalytic
   mental illness results from psychogenic factors, of the sort described by Freud.

8. A **syndrome** is a pattern of symptoms that go together.   syndrome

9. In the most recent classification or taxonomy of mental illness, called DSM-III-R, more emphasis is placed on the description of disorders, rather than on *theories* about their cause.

DSM-III-R

theories

10. According to the *diathesis stress* conception, mental illness results from the interaction between a predisposition and some set of environmental events.

diathesis-stress

11. The analysis of mental disorders in the medical model includes description of remote and immediate *causes*, which lead to the *symptoms* of the disorder.

causes

symptoms

SCHIZOPHRENIA

12. The incidence of schizophrenia is about one American out of every *one hundred*

one hundred

13. Schizophrenic symptoms include disorders in thinking and selective *attention*

attention

14. Schizophrenic persons often lose contact with other people as a result of social *w/drawal* This may lead to progressively worse problems, because they have few opportunities for reality *testing*.

withdrawal

testing

15 Schizophrenic symptoms include elaboration of the private world, such as *delusions* of persecution and hearing voices or other *hallucinations*

delusions

hallucinations

16. Schizophrenics typically show either *apathy* or *inappropriate* affect.

apathy, inappropriate

17. Delusions are typical symptoms in a common form of schizophrenia, *paranoid* schizophrenia.

paranoid

18. A schizophrenic with unusual motor reactions such as remaining motionless for long periods was classified as *catatonic*

catatonic

19. A more modern classification of schizophrenia contrasts abnormal behavior, or *positive* symptoms, with the absence of normal behaviors, or *negative* symptoms.

positive

negative

20. A cognitive theory of schizophrenia holds that many symptoms, especially the disturbances in language and thought, result from an inability to keep things in proper focus. This results in an inability to hold on to one *line* of thought or action.

line (train)

21. One argument for an organic basis for schizophrenia is the effectiveness of a group of drugs called *phenothiazines* in treatment.

phenothiazines

22. A current organic theory of schizophrenia holds that it results from too much brain activity caused by the catecholamine neurotransmitter *dopamine* which may cause the overstimulation characteristic of schizophrenia.

dopamine

23. Anatomical evidence indicates that brain *atrophy* is associated with schizophrenia.

    atrophy (damage)

24. According to the __2__-*syndrome* hypothesis, both anatomical deficits and neurotransmitter excess are causes of schizophrenia. The anatomical deficits are thought to be associated with the

    two-syndrome

    negative symptoms and the neurotransmitter excess with the

    negative

    positive symptoms.

    positive

25. Twin studies indicate that there is a significant *genetic* factor in the causation of schizophrenia.

    genetic (hereditary)

26. Identical twins show a *concordance* of 44 percent for schizophrenia.

    concordance

27. Studies indicate that schizophrenia is much more common in *lower* classes and that class status is both a cause and effect of schizophrenia.

    lower

28. There is evidence that *family* pathology may cause schizophrenia, but there is also evidence that it may be caused by schizophrenia.

    family

29. In accord with the diathesis-stress model, the evidence for a genetic predisposition for schizophrenia corresponds to the

    diathesis while the demonstrated role of environmental events

    diathesis

    corresponds to the *stress* .

    stress

MOOD DISORDERS

30. While schizophrenia can be regarded as essentially a disorder of thought, in disorders such as mania and depression, the dominant

    disturbance is one of *mood* .

    mood

31. The two major types of mood disorders are *bipolar* disorder

    bipolar

    and *major depression*

    major depression

32. *Mania* is the opposite of depression and is characterized, among other things, by endless talking and overabundance of energy.

    Mania

33. Depression is associated with a high rate of *suicide*.

    suicide

34. Depression associated with decreasing amounts of light as winter

    approaches is called *seasonal affective disorder*

    seasonal affective disorder

35. Twin studies indicate a higher role for genetic factors in

    bipolar than in *unipolar* disorders.

    bipolar, unipolar

36. There is evidence that abnormal levels of either of two neuro-transmitters *serotonin* and *norepinephrine* may account for mood disorders. At high levels, these neurotransmitters may lead to

    serotonin, norepinephrine

    mania , while at low levels, they may lead to *depression*

    mania, depression

37. Two major types of antidepressant drugs are _monoamine oxidase inhibitors_ and _tricyclics_. They operate, respectively, by preventing the _breakdown_ of transmitters or by preventing their _reuptake_.

monoamine oxidase inhibitors (MAO), tricyclics

breakdown

reuptake

38. According to a number of psychogenic approaches to depression, the primary disorder is _cognitive_, which leads to changes in _mood_.

cognitive

mood

39. Beck asserts that depression results from a set of negative beliefs, and can be successfully treated with _cognitive_ therapy.

cognitive

40. According to the _learned helplessness_ theory of depression, depression is caused by an expectation that one's actions will have no significant effects.

learned helplessness

41. As a result of the difficulty in explaining symptoms such as self-blame in depression, emphasis on psychological causative factors has changed from learned helplessness to despondent _attributional style_

attributional style

ANXIETY DISORDERS

42. An irrational and intense fear of an object or situation is called a _phobia_.

phobia

43. According to a conditioning view, phobias expand by the process of _generalization_

generalization

44. A fear of open places or places from which one cannot escape is called _agoraphobia_

agoraphobia

45. In _obsessive-compulsive_ disorders, anxiety is produced by persistent internal events (thoughts or wishes).

obsessive-compulsive

46. _Obsessions_ are persistent thoughts. _Compulsions_ are acts performed in an attempt to deal with these thoughts.

Obsessions, Compulsions

47. In phobias, anxiety is focused on a particular object or situation. In _generalized anxiety_ disorders, it is all-pervasive.

generalized anxiety

48. _Panic_ disorder is more acute than generalized anxiety disorder, but like generalized anxiety disorder, it doesn't focus on a particular object or situation.

Panic

49. Some have explained panic disorder as an over-reaction to the bodily symptoms of _fear_.

fear

50. The success of _behavior_ therapy suggests that, in at least some anxiety disorders, the symptom _is_ the disease.

behavior

CONVERSIONS AND DISSOCIATIVE DISORDERS

51. In _conversion_ or _dissociative_ disorders, according to the psychoanalytic view, the primary defense against anxiety is repression or denial.

conversion, dissociative

52. In conversion disorders, the principal symptom is a _somatic_ somatic (bodily)
disorder, such as paralysis.

53. In dissociative disorders, a whole set of mental events are
removed from ordinary _consciousness_. These disorders include consciousness
fugue _state_ and _amnesia_ (cite two types). fugue state, amnesia, or
multiple personality

PSYCHOPHYSIOLOGICAL DISORDERS

54. In _psychophysiological_ disorders, organic damage is caused by psycho- psychophysiological
physiological factors.

55. Chronic elevation of high blood pressure is called
essential hypertension essential hypertension

56. It is believed that hypertension results from continual _sympathetic_ sympathetic
arousal. This may be caused by excessive _stress_. stress

57. The _type_ _A_ personality is associated with increased Type A
risk of coronary heart disease. The component of the personality
most associated with coronary heart disease is _hostility_. hostility

58. In the face of continued stress, some people get peptic ulcers,
some get essential hypertension, some get other psychophysiological disorders, and some show no obvious effects. These
differences may be accounted for in terms of a preexisting diathesis (predisposition,
somatic _diathesis_ susceptibility)

59. Psychophysiological disorders have primarily _organic_ symptoms organic
and primarily _mental_ underlying pathology. mental

THE SOCIOLOGICAL CRITIQUE OF THE PATHOLOGY MODEL

60. According to Szasz and others, at least some of the symptoms of
mental illness result from the fact that a person is given a specific
diagnosis or _label_ of some type of mental illness. label

61. D. L. Rosenhan's study shows that people who lie about having
auditory hallucinations can be diagnosed as schizophrenic and may auditory hallucinations
remain on a mental ward for some weeks, while behaving totally
normally, because of this initial faked symptom.

62. Someone who behaves antisocially without signs of remorse is
called an antisocial personality, or _sociopath_ sociopath

63. Szasz and others have emphasized the stigmatizing effect of
being _labeled_ as mentally ill and the dangers of using _deviance_ labeled, deviance
as a sole criterion for mental illness.

Self-Test

1. Treatment of "mental disorders" in the past by
such procedures as trephination or burning at the
stake is indicative of a conception of these disorders as caused by:

    a. microorganisms.
    b. criminal impulses.
    c. degeneration.
    (d) demonic possession.
    e. medical malpractice.

2. The discovery of a cure for general paresis gave support to the view of mental illness as:
   a. demonic possession.
   b. akin to criminality.
   c. a disease.
   d. somatogenic.
   e. resulting from medical malpractice.

3. If a specific enzyme lack was pinned down as the cause of a previously poorly understood severe mental illness, it would change its classification from _____ to _____ .
   a. psychosis, neurosis
   b. disease, pathology
   c. psychoanalytic, medical
   d. psychogenic, somatogenic
   e. minor, serious

4. Both the medical model and the psychoanalytic model:
   a. emphasize somatogenic disorders.
   b. fail to explain conversion disorders.
   c. are limited versions of the pathology model.
   d. emphasize psychogenic disorders.
   e. emphasize the role of learning.

5. Understanding of a disease includes knowledge of its symptoms, underlying pathology, remote causes, and:
   a. immediate cause.
   b. psychogenicity.
   c. psychoanalytic roots.
   d. deviance.
   e. a and c

6. Certain types of color blindness occur, invariably, if a person inherits a particular gene or pair of genes from his or her parents. This "disorder" does not fit the diathesis-stress model, because:
   a. there is no diathesis.
   b. there is no stress.
   c. both diathesis and stress are present, but either is sufficient for manifestation of the disorder.
   d. both diathesis and stress are present, but they do not interact.
   e. c or d

7. The general idea that schizophrenics have difficulty distinguishing between personal (internal) and external events can be used to explain some of the symptoms of schizophrenia. Which of the following schizophrenic symptoms can be explained in this manner?
   a. delusions
   b. hallucinations
   c. catatonic immobility

   d. a and b
   e. all of the above

8. Delusions differ from hallucinations in that:
   a. delusions are associated with ideas of persecution.
   b. delusions are based on interpretations of real events.
   c. delusions are primarily visual while hallucinations are auditory.
   d. delusions are associated with apathy.
   e. delusions cause social withdrawal.

9. Delusions in paranoid schizophrenics, or bizarre behaviors in catatonic schizophrenics, are examples of:
   a. syndromes.
   b. diatheses.
   c. ideas of reference.
   d. negative symptoms.
   e. positive symptoms.

10. The idea that the fundamental disorder in schizophrenia is a cognitive deficit having to do with failure to keep things in proper focus can explain all but which feature of schizophrenia?
    a. disconnected thought
    b. rhyming associations
    c. social withdrawal (as a consequence of overstimulation)
    d. apathy
    e. c and d

11. Chlorpromazine is a drug in the phenothiazine family and is effective as therapy for schizophrenia. Phenothiazines are known to block the action of dopamine at the synapse. Dopamine is a neurotransmitter. Low levels of dopamine in animals lead to the neglect of stimulation. Taken together, these findings suggest:
    a. that schizophrenia results from an excess of dopamine, leading to overstimulation or overload.
    b. that there is a strong, enzyme-based hereditary deficit in dopamine in schizophrenics.
    c. that schizophrenics have too little dopamine, leading to cognitive and affective symptoms.
    d. that there is probably no direct relation between dopamine levels and schizophrenia.
    e. that drugs should be given simpler names.

12. Penicillin : general paresis :: _____ : schizophrenia
    a. dopamine
    b. brain atrophy
    c. phenothiazines

d. norepinephrine

e. genetics

13. According to the dopamine theory of schizophrenia, a drug that opposes the effect of dopamine would:
  a. be likely to reduce positive symptoms of schizophrenia.
  b. be likely to reduce negative symptoms of schizophrenia.
  c. cause schizophrenic symptoms in normal people.
  d. oppose the effect of phenothiazines.
  e. a and b

14. The two-syndrome hypothesis asserts that:
  a. the positive and negative symptoms of schizophrenia have different causes.
  b. anatomical and neurotransmitter disorders produce different types of schizophrenia.
  c. there are two anatomical deficits underlying schizophrenia.
  d. phenothiazines and dopamine are the two causes of schizophrenia.
  e. a and b

15. The concordance rate among identical twins for schizophrenia is 44 percent, while the comparable figure for fraternal twins is 9 percent. These results suggest that:
  a. genetic factors predominate as causes of schizophrenia.
  b. there is a very weak genetic component in the causation of schizophrenia.
  c. schizophrenia is essentially caused by environmental factors.
  d. the primary cause of schizophrenia is probably lack of a neurotransmitter, rather than a genetic effect.
  e. both genetic and environmental factors play important roles in the causation of schizophrenia.

16. The incidence of schizophrenia is higher in the lower classes. This suggests that:
  a. social class is a causal factor in schizophrenia.
  b. schizophrenics are lower in social class because they are schizophrenic.
  c. schizophrenia does not have a strong organic component.
  d. a and/or b
  e. all of the above

17. There are some reports of poorer mental health in the *adoptive* parents of schizophrenics. This, along with studies of differences in the behaviors of mothers to their schizophrenic and normal children, suggests that:
  a. pathological home environments cause schizophrenia.
  b. schizophrenic children can induce pathological behavior in parents.
  c. there is an organic basis for schizophrenia.
  d. there is a psychogenic basis for schizophrenia.
  e. a and d

18. The pathology model of schizophrenia presented in the text includes all but one of the following assumptions. Which assumption is not included?
  a. Family pathology leads to deficits in the function of brain neurotransmitters.
  b. Some genetic factors contribute to pathology in the function of certain brain neurotransmitters.
  c. Neurotransmitter deficits can lead to inability to focus in time or space.
  d. Inability to focus in time or space can lead to social withdrawal.
  e. Inability to focus in space and time can lead to inappropriate emotions.

19. Manic disorders share with some forms of schizophrenia which of the following symptoms?
  a. hallucinations
  b. social withdrawal
  c. shifting from one subject to another in conversation
  d. blunted affect in response to stimuli that would normally elicit affective responses
  e. enormous amounts of energy

20. A person shows little interest in the world around him. He shows little emotional response and has disconnected thoughts. On this basis, the most likely guess for a diagnosis would be:
  a. mania.
  b. major depression.
  c. bipolar disorder.
  d. schizophrenia.
  e. a or c

21. According to biochemical hypotheses, low levels of norepinephrine or serotonin are causative factors in:
  a. mania.
  b. depression.
  c. schizophrenia.
  d. a and b
  e. a and c

22. All but one of the following provide evidence in favor of the theory that low levels of norepineph-

rine in the brain lead to depression. Which of these findings does not support this theory?

a. Drugs that deplete norepinephrine cause depression in normal subjects.

b. Helplessness training in animals depletes norepinephrine.

c. Drugs which increase the availability of norepinephrine are effective in therapy for depression.

d. Norepinephrine is involved with the systems in the brain that produce arousal and activation.

e. Dopamine, a neurotransmitter related to norepinephrine, is implicated in the causation of schizophrenia.

23. In terms of the biochemical hypothesis, which holds that high levels of norepinephrine (or serotonin) cause mania, which of the following should be an effective therapy for mania?

a. tricyclics

b. MAO inhibitors

c. a drug that increases reuptake of norepinephrine

d. a drug that decreases the rate of breakdown of norepinephrine in the synaptic gap

e. a drug that increases the rate of synthesis of norepinephrine in the synaptic terminals

24. According to Seligman's helplessness views, the low affect of depression results from:

a. low levels of norepinephrine.

b. negative cognitions that produce affective changes.

c. a tendency towards suicidal thoughts.

d. bipolar mood change.

e. self-hatred.

25. Which of the following symptoms of depression is particularly difficult to explain for both the biochemical and psychogenic (learned helplessness) theories?

a. negative affect

b. inactivity

c. responsiveness to antidepressant drugs

d. self-hatred

e. none of the above

26. According to the learned helplessness theory of depression, which of the following would be the most relevant diathesis for depression?

a. depletion of norepinephrine or serotonin

b. past experiences in which a person could not control his/her environment

c. genetic factors

d. parents who gave the person too much responsibility as a child

e. c or d

27. The advantage of the attributional style explanation of depression over learned helplessness is that the former can explain:

a. inactivity.

b. suicidal thoughts.

c. self-blame.

d. global depression.

e. low levels of norepinephrine.

28. Which of the following hypothetical findings would oppose the attributional style explanation of a higher incidence of depression in adult females?

a. equal incidence in both sexes in pre-adolescence

b. equal incidence in both sexes in traditional cultures

c. lower levels of brain norepinephrine in females

d. lower levels of activity in adult females

e. a and b

29. Which of the following lists of disorders is arranged in order of *increasing* importance of psychogenic causative factors?

a. schizophrenia, depression, manic-depressive psychosis

b. schizophrenia, general paresis, phobias

c. phobias, depression, mental retardation

d. general paresis, depression, phobias

e. schizophrenia, phobias, general paresis

30. One effective treatment for specific phobias is to expose the phobic person to weak instances of the phobic object while the subject relaxes. The strength of the stimulus is gradually increased. Under these conditions, many phobias disappear, and no undesirable symptoms seem to replace them. This therapeutic success is an argument in favor of:

a. the conditioning view of phobias.

b. a diathesis-stress model of phobias.

c. a biological basis for agoraphobia.

d. none of the above

e. all of the above

31. A disorder in which anxiety is handled by repetitive and ritualistic acts is called:

a. phobia.

b. fugue state.

c. obsessive-compulsive disorder.

d. conversion hysteria.

e. generalized anxiety disorder.

32. If phobias are often about objects and obsessions are about thoughts, then panic disorder can be said to be about:

a. physiological symptoms.

b. lack of ability to escape.

c. sexual objects.

d. denial of fear.

e. sympathy.

33. Behavior therapists argue that the neurotic (anxiety disorder) symptom _____ the disease.

a. causes

b. is

c. can be separated from

d. is one consequence of the underlying

e. is a reaction to

34. Amnesia, fugue state, and multiple personality are all examples of:

a. obsessive-compulsive disorders.

b. psychoses.

c. conversion disorders.

d. dissociative reactions.

e. none of the above

35. The fundamental distinction between anxiety disorders and conversion or dissociative disorders is that:

a. anxiety disorders are more generalized.

b. anxiety is an explanation only for anxiety disorders.

c. organic factors are much more heavily involved in anxiety disorders.

d. In anxiety disorders, the anxiety is expressed more overtly.

e. a and b

36. Psychoanalysts and behavior therapists would probably agree that anxiety disorders are:

a. indications of an underlying mental disorder.

b. learned.

c. ways of compensating for other problems.

d. all of the above

e. none of the above

37. Hypertension is believed to be caused by:

a. thickening of artery walls.

b. higher sensitivity of artery muscles to stimuli.

c. increased autonomic responsiveness to stressful stimuli.

d. high levels of exposure to emotional stress.

e. all of the above

38. Obesity, smoking, and hostility all have in common the fact that they are all:

a. components of the Type A personality.

b. risk factors for coronary heart disease.

c. associated with a competitive personality.

d. decreased in essential hypertension.

e. a and b

39. If a study found that, under the stress of threat of terrorism for a period of years, a group of 100 people developed a wide variety of psychophysio-logical disorders, including ulcers in some, hypertension in others, and asthma in still others, this would be evidence in favor of:

a. a diathesis factor.

b. a stress factor.

c. a role for neurotransmitters.

d. an organic origin for psychophysiological disorders.

e. therapeutic use of the antibiotic terrormycin.

40. A fundamental difference between a conversion disorder and a psychophysiological disorder is that:

a. treatment of the organic "complaint" is much more likely to be effective in psychophysiological disorders.

b. psychophysiological disorders are much more likely to be accompanied by low levels of neurotransmitters.

c. conversion disorders are mental in origin.

d. anxiety is critically involved in the origin of almost all psychophysiological disorders.

e. psychophysiological disorders always involve the nervous system.

41. In terms of the model of categorization of mental disorders in the text, diabetes : psychophysio-logical disorders :: schizophrenia :

a. general paresis

b. bipolar disorders

c. asthma

d. sociopathy

e. pneumonia

42. According to Szasz, in practice, people are treated as mentally ill simply because they are:

a. self-destructive.

b. suffering some sort of organic disorder.

c. deviant.

d. from another culture.

e. taking drugs.

43. Labeling theory predicts that mental disorder is determined by what the culture labels as a disorder. Which of the following findings argues against this view?

a. Rosenhan's study on being sane in insane places

b. normal occurrence of behaviors in some cultures that are considered deviant in others

c. roughly equal incidence of schizophrenia in different cultures

d. the very high incidence of conversion disorders in Europe early in this century

e. none of the above

44. A person is apprehended after committing a series of crimes. The question is whether he should be treated as a criminal or a sociopath. All but one of the following characteristics suggest that he is a sociopath. Indicate the characteristic that suggests a criminal, rather than sociopath, diagnosis.
   a. He is a loner.
   b. He feels no guilt for the crimes committed.
   c. He is anxious.
   d. He is charming.
   e. He is intelligent.

Answer Key for Self-Test

1. d pp. 493–94	24. b p. 513
2. d p. 496	25. d pp. 512–13
3. d pp. 495–96	26. b p. 513
4. c p. 497	27. c p. 513
5. a p. 500	28. e p. 514
6. b p. 500	29. d pp. 495–96,
7. d pp. 502–3	509–10, 515
8. b p. 503	30. a p. 516
9. e pp. 503–4	31. c p. 516
10. d p. 504	32. a p. 517
11. a p. 505	33. b p. 519
12. c p. 505	34. d pp. 520–21
13. a p. 505	35. d p. 520
14. e p. 505	36. b p. 519
15. e p. 506	37. e pp. 522–23
16. d p. 507	38. b p. 523
17. b p. 507	39. a p. 525
18. a p. 508	40. a p. 522
19. c p. 509	41. d p. 525
20. d pp. 501–3	42. c p. 526
21. b p. 511	43. c pp. 526–27
22. e p. 511	44. c pp. 529–30
23. c pp. 511–12	

Investigating Psychological Phenomena

DEPRESSION AND NEGATIVE EXPERIENCES

Equipment: Stopwatch or watch with second indicator
Number of subjects: One, yourself; you will also need the cooperation of a friend to serve as a timer for about five minutes
Time per subject: Twenty minutes
Time for experimenter: Twenty minutes

Depression is a very common disturbance. It can vary from almost universal "blue" moods to a serious, chronic, and incapacitating disorder. Because at least some of the characteristics of deep (psychotic) depression occur occasionally in most people, it is possible to study depression in a general population. In any population, there seems to be a more or less continuous distribution of people along a dimension running from depression to elation.

Severe depression is characterized by depressed mood, loss of interest in others and normally desirable things (such as food), feelings of hopelessness, helplessness, and worthlessness, and slowed down thought and motor activity. Many of these symptoms appear in mild forms in the general population. It is reasonable to expect that mildly depressed people will show some of the same bases or causes of their symptoms as severely depressed people.

A number of theories of depression are outlined in the text. These include biochemical explanations (e.g., depletion of norepinephrine), and psychological theories emphasizing hopelessness or learned helplessness. In this study we will explore a particularly simple additional theory: People are depressed because bad things happen to them. Clearly, some people get depressed in the face of success and others remain nondepressed following a series of adverse events. Nonetheless, it seems very reasonable that negative experiences would contribute to the causation of depression. We will test the hypothesis that people who are more depressed have had relatively more adverse experiences in the recent past.

A major purpose of this exercise is to illustrate some of the difficulties that arise in the scientific study of psychopathology. More than in previous studies in this study guide, we want to make you aware of the problem of making definitive measurements that clearly support a particular hypothesis. We want you to appreciate the difficulty of research and at the same time realize that progress can be made.

The first problem that we face is this: How do we measure depression? A basic issue that arises is the matter of "subjective" or "objective" measurement. In the case of a mood disorder, one might be inclined to subjective measurement, and indeed, much of the diagnosis of depression is concerned with what people say about how they feel. More objective measurements would involve observation of people (facial expression, level of activity) or having them report on their own activities (how many hours they sleep each night, for example). In this study we look at a totally subjective measure, the subject's rating of his or her own mood. Remember that we are dealing with the range of depression and elation seen in the general population, and not with people actually diagnosed as depressed. In the case of diagnosis, interview and observation by an experienced clinician is involved, sometimes along with administration of a question inventory. We will use only self-ratings of mood and will collect two such ratings: one for the subject's momentary mood (how depressed he or she feels now) and the other for how depressed he has felt, in general, over the past year.

The second problem is this: How do we develop a measure of the incidence of negative and positive events in the recent life of each subject? We will use as our measure the subject's recall of negative and positive events over the past year. There are many problems and alternative interpretations of the results of this procedure. We will discuss them after you have served as a subject in this study.

Fill out the two rating scales below and enter your self-ratings on the answer sheet at the end of this section. Then continue to the recall task.

Rate what you judge to be your mood, right now. Circle the most appropriate number.

Extremely Depressed	Very Depressed	Moderately Depressed	Slightly Depressed	Neither Depressed Nor Happy
9	8	7	6	5

Slightly Happy	Moderately Happy	Very Happy	Extremely Happy	
4	3	2	1	

Rate what you judge to have been your mood, on the average, over the last twelve months.

Extremely Depressed	Very Depressed	Moderately Depressed	Slightly Depressed	Neither Depressed Nor Happy
9	8	7	6	5

Slightly Happy	Moderately Happy	Very Happy	Extremely Happy	
4	3	2	1	

RECALL OF NEGATIVE AND POSITIVE EVENTS

For this measure you will need the assistance of a friend who will time two separate two-minute intervals for you. No one but you will see what you write down.

You will go through two recall tasks, in order. Get a pen or pencil and sit at a table. When you are comfortable, ask a friend to say "Go" when the second hand of a watch crosses 12. When your friend says "go," turn to the next page, read the sentence at the top, and follow the instructions. Ask your friend to say "stop" when two minutes have elapsed. You should then stop the task.

The next time the second hand passes 12 (i.e., a minute after you complete the first part of the task), have your friend time another two minutes. When he or she says "go," turn to the page after the one you had just written on, read the instructions, and follow them for two minutes.

Do not read on until you have completed the above task.

You are asked to perform the following task for exactly two minutes.

Someone will time the two minutes. When he says "go" read the sentence below and follow the instructions. Continue until you hear "stop" at two minutes.

List below all of the negative things that have happened to you in the last twelve months.

_____

_____

_____

_____

_____

_____

_____

_____

_____

_____

_____

_____

_____

_____

_____

_____

_____

_____

_____

_____

_____

_____

_____

_____

_____

_____

You are asked to perform the following task for exactly two minutes.

Someone will time the two minutes. When he says "go" read the sentence below and follow the instructions. Continue until you hear "stop" at two minutes.

List below all of the negative things that have happened to you in the last twelve months.

_____

_____

_____

_____

_____

_____

_____

_____

_____

_____

_____

_____

_____

_____

_____

_____

_____

_____

_____

_____

_____

_____

_____

_____

Add up the number of negative and the number of positive events that you remembered. Put these numbers on the answer sheet at the end of this section. Also enter the difference between the number of negative events and the number of positive events (# negative events minus # positive events), and the total # of events recalled (# negative events plus # positive events).

ANALYSIS OF DATA

We have obtained this same data (depression ratings and event scores) from sixty-four undergraduate students at the University of Michigan. We will present these data here. You will add your own results to theirs, and we will then discuss the results.

MEASURES OF DEPRESSION

We used two measures of depression: Rated mood now and rated mood over the last twelve months. You might expect that momentary and long-term mood would be related but that the two could sometimes be different. That, in fact, is just what our data show. Below is a scatter plot that presents the data from all sixty-four subjects (see the statistical appendix to the text to learn more about scatter plots). Each point on the plot represents the two mood scores for one subject. Enter your own data point.

There is a positive relation between the two measures of depression. All relations described in these results will be expressed as correlation coefficients (see the statistical appendix). A value of $+1.00$ indicates a perfect positive correlation, a value of -1.00 a perfect negative correlation, and a value of 0.00 indicates no relation at all.

Our measure of "mood now" correlates $+.458$ with the measure of "mood over one year."

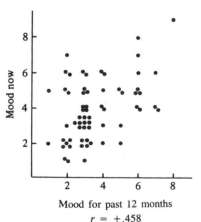

Mood for past 12 months

$r = +.458$

Looking at the scatter plot, you can see that there is some relation between the two mood measures. The general pattern of dots goes from lower left (happy on both scores) to upper right (depressed on both scores). But there are some exceptions. The correlation is positive, but far from perfect. Mark your point on the graph. Does your point fit in with the general pattern, or is it something of an exception? If an exception, can you explain this (e.g., it has been a very good year for you, but something unpleasant just happened to you)?

EVENT SCORES AND DEPRESSION

Before we test the major hypothesis (relatively more negative events in more depressed people), we can examine another prediction that can be made from the symptoms of seriously depressed people. Such people are characterized by a slowing down of action and thought. If this symptom also appears, in milder form, in the low levels of depression in the student population, we would expect a slowdown in memory search, along with other mental events. Therefore, we would expect that more depressed students would recall fewer events, positive or negative. (This type of finding would surely be true in a comparison of seriously depressed hospitalized patients versus "normal" subjects.) We can test for this possibility by computing the correlation between self-rated depression (mood now) and the total number of events recalled (positive plus negative events). Note that because high scores on the depression rating mean more depression and high scores also represent large numbers of events recalled, we would expect a negative correlation: High depression scores go with low event recall scores.

For our sixty-four subjects, the correlation between "mood now" and the total events is $-.052$: There is no evidence of any relation. Enter your score on these two measures in the scatter plot on the next page. You can see by examining the scatter plot that the two measures do not seem to be related. The relations between "mood over one year" and total events is also small: The correlation is $+.135$ (this is very small, but also in the direction opposite to the direction we predicted). There are two possible interpretations of our result. One is that our sample is not representative of the population, and that there actually is a negative depression—total event relation. Given the data we have, there is no reason to believe this. Another interpretation is that there is no relation, but that there might well be such a relation if we looked at severely depressed people as well: That is, the slowdown of mental function may only be marked in severe depression.

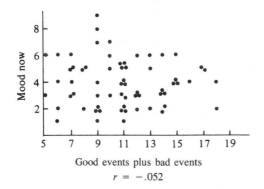

Good events plus bad events
$r = -.052$

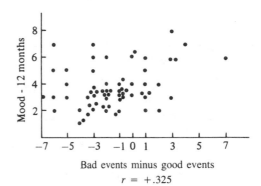

Bad events minus good events
$r = +.325$

We now ask whether increased depression goes with a higher relative incidence of negative events. If this was true, we would expect a positive correlation between either depression score and the difference between number of negative and number of positive events recalled. We present below the scatter plot for both depression scores. Enter your own points on each of these plots. Just by inspecting these scatter plots you should be able to see that there is a positive relation: Higher depression scores *tend* to go with higher negative minus positive event scores. In fact, the correlations are:

Mood now vs negative − positive events
$r = +.460$
Mood over one year vs negative − positive events
$r = +.325$

The relations are not overwhelming, but there is a clear relation. For example the .460 correlation is significant at more than the .001 level: This means that a correlation this high could come about less than one chance in 1000 if there was no relation between mood now and negative − positive events in the population (see the statistical appendix).

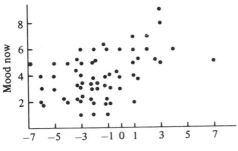

Bad events minus good events
$r = +.460$

DISCUSSION AND COMMENTS

Our hypothesis that in college populations depression as measured by self-rating is positively related to relative recall of recent negative events has been confirmed. We will now discuss a few problems in interpreting these results, in order to make you more aware of the type of thinking that must go into research in general and especially in this area.

First, our measure of events can be interpreted in a number of ways. We did not actually measure the number of positive and negative events that our subjects experienced. We measured their *recall* for these events. A predominance of negative events could mean either that the subject experienced more of them or that the subject selectively remembers them . . . presumably because she is depressed. Remember that correlations show relations, but not causes (see the statistical appendix). Our hypothesis was that negative events cause depression. But the results of our study could be taken to indicate that in a relatively depressed mood, a person is more likely to remember negative events. The fact that the correlation was bigger between negative minus positive events and mood now, as opposed to mood over the last year, suggests that current mood may well influence what one thinks about. Of course, it is also possible that both effects exist: Negative events lead to depression and depression leads to selective memory for negative events. There is some evidence in the literature for both of these effects. Under further activities, we will discuss ways of finding out whether both of these effects actually occur.

Second, even if more negative events do occur in more depressed people, the events may not be a cause of depression. By virtue of being depressed, more negative events may occur to a person. For example, a depressed student will be less active, less inclined to study, and will probably not perform as well as he could in school.

Third, the same event that is evaluated as negative by someone who is depressed may not be considered negative by that same person when she is in a good mood (or by another person in a better mood). Many events may be both positive and negative (e.g., receiving a B in a course when one hoped for an A but did very little work and actually worried about getting a C, or the break-up of a relationship which had been unsatisfactory for some years). Read through your own events and decide how many could be seen as positive or negative.

We have just begun to scratch the surface, but we hope that you can appreciate the fact that a study like this would be just a beginning and that many more studies would have to be done to clarify the relation between negative events and depression. It should also be clear that whatever that relation is, there are many factors that influence depression. After all, the correlations we do have between depression and events are significant, but they are not that high. We might improve the correlations by getting better measures of depression and negative and positive events. But we also know from other studies, including those dealing with levels of catecholamines in the brain and specific types of past experiences (e.g., helplessness), that other factors are involved.

FURTHER ACTIVITIES

Try to think of some ways in which you could pull apart the effects of actual negative experiences and selective recall of them. After you decide on a few methods, read our suggestions below.

One approach is to get a more objective measure of the actual negative and positive events that a person has experienced. It is not practical to follow them around for a year. But one could get a fair measure by giving them a checklist of rather objective events, that are clearly negative or positive. Thus you could ask someone whether, over the past year:

A close relative or friend died
A course was failed
A job was lost
A favorite team had a disappointing season
A close relationship was broken

and so on and, of course, a set of positive events.

One could then compare the negative minus positive recall score to the results of the checklist. What would you administer first to the subjects: the free recall or the checklist? Why? You could try to make up an appropriate checklist for college students. It isn't easy.

A second approach is to test whether depressed people selectively remember negative events. For example, you could write a story that included a number of negative and positive events. It could be read to subjects and one could measure their recall for the story, say one hour later. One could look at whether people who are more depressed remember relatively more of the negative events.

Answer Sheet

(If your instructor collects the data, fill out the report sheet in Appendix B.)

Self-rating of mood now (enter number) _____

Self-rating of mood over last twelve months (enter number) _____

Number of negative events recalled _____

Number of positive events recalled _____

Negative minus positive events _____

Negative plus positive events _____

CHAPTER 18

Treatment of Psychopathology

Learning Objectives

1. Be aware of the two major approaches to the treatment of mental illness.

SOMATIC THERAPIES

Drug therapies

2. Know the major types of psychiatric drugs and their uses. Cite the evidence that such drugs function specifically as antischizophrenic or antidepressant agents.
3. Evaluation of drug therapy is difficult. Be prepared to discuss necessary conditions for proper evaluation. Refer to control groups, the placebo effect, and the double-blind technique in your discussion.
4. Know about the limitations of drug therapy. What are the side effects of drug therapies, both for the patient and for society?

Other somatic therapies

5. Give the rationale for the use of prefrontal lobotomy in the treatment of mental illness. Cite evidence on the effectiveness of this technique.
6. Be aware of the role of electroconvulsive shock treatment. Know when such treatment is warranted.

PSYCHOTHERAPY

7. List the five major types of psychotherapy, and know the theoretical underpinnings of each.

Classical psychoanalysis

8. Describe the investigative techniques used in classical psychoanalysis. Discuss the relevance of transference.

Modern versions of psychoanalysis

9. Know what modern psychoanalysis emphasizes.

Behavior therapy

10. Review the basic assumptions made by behavior therapists. How are these assumptions translated into treatment techniques?
11. Describe the basic assumptions underlying flooding and implosion. What are the differences between these techniques?
12. Describe how systematic desensitization uses response incompatibility to eradicate phobias. What are major differences and similarities between systematic desensitization and flooding?
13. Describe aversion therapy and give examples of its use.
14. Know the major approach used in the application of operant techniques.

Cognitive-behavioral therapies

15. Discuss how cognitive therapies differ from traditional psychoanalysis. What are the major assumptions of cognitive therapy?
16. Be prepared to describe the basic technique used in cognitive therapy.

Humanistic therapies

17. Describe how humanistic therapists approach the topic of mental illness. Characterize Rogerian therapy.
18. Describe the history of existential therapy.

Some common themes

19. Note the common themes underlying the various therapeutic schools. List their major differences.

EVALUATING THERAPEUTIC OUTCOME

20. Cite extraneous factors that might influence the perception of whether a therapy is effective.

Does psychotherapy work?

21. Discuss the evidence concerning the effectiveness of psychotherapy. Describe the role of meta-analysts in answering this question.

22. Know whether there are differences in the effectiveness of the various therapies.

EXTENSIONS OF PSYCHOTHERAPY

23. Discuss how psychotherapy has been extended.

Group therapy

24. Understand the motivations for treating patients in groups.

25. There are various benefits that accrue to group

therapy that do not accrue to individual therapy. List them.

Marital and family therapy

26. The major goal of family therapists is to treat relationships, not individual members of the group. Be prepared to discuss this.

The expansion of therapeutic goals

27. Discuss how the goals of therapy have been expanded since Freud.

A CENTURY OF THERAPY

28. Review the effectiveness of psychotherapy and of somatic therapies.

Programmed Exercises

SOMATIC THERAPIES

1. Historically, proposed treatments for mental illness have fallen into one of two categories. One treats the illness at a(n) _biological_ level, while the other uses a(n) _psychological_ approach.

   biological, psychological

2. Attempting to restore the proper harmony among the bodily humors in order to reestablish the balance between bodily and mental functions was the purpose of early _somatic therapies_ such as bloodletting.

   somatic therapies

3. A schizophrenic patient undergoing drug therapy has the greatest chance of being helped by the drug _chlorpromazine_

   chlorpromazine (Thorazine)

4. It has been suggested that chlorpromazine acts merely as a(n) _sedative_ but the available evidence indicates that chlorpromazine and other antischizophrenic drugs have a _specific_ drug effect.

   sedative

   specific

5. An individual feels extremely depressed most of the time. We would expect one of the _tricyclic_ drugs to be most effective in relieving his symptoms.

   tricyclic

6. Unlike other drug therapies, _lithium_ seems to have preventative powers in the treatment of bipolar disorder.

   lithium

7. Simple "before-and-after" measurements are not adequate for evaluating the effectiveness of a drug because they don't take _spontaneous_ improvement into account.

   spontaneous

8. A set of patients was given sugar pills and told that they were potent pain killers. Many of the patients reported that the "pain killer" was working. This illustrates the effect of a _placebo_ .

   placebo

9. It is hypothesized that a new drug will alleviate symptoms of air
   sickness. One hundred volunteers received an injection of this
   colorless liquid, while another 100 volunteers received an injection of saline solution (a colorless and totally inert liquid). All
   200 subjects took part in a simulated flight. Both subjective and
   objective indices of discomfort were recorded. Neither patient
   nor experimenter knew who received the drug. This study used a
   double - blind technique to guard against any effects of   double-blind
   expectations.

10. The biggest cost associated with drug therapy is the likelihood of
    unpleasant *side effects*.   side effects

11. In a prefrontal lobotomy, the connections between the *thalamus*   thalamus
    and the *frontal* lobes are severed.   frontal

12. Electroconvulsive shock treatment (ECT) is most effective in the
    treatment of *depression*; however, repeated shocks may cause   depression
    brain damage and *amnesia*   brain damage, amnesia

PSYCHOTHERAPY

13. According to the *psychoanalytic* school, neurotic ills stem from   psychoanalytic
    unconscious defenses against unacceptable urges.

14. A patient is asked to say whatever comes into his mind. This
    technique is known as *free association*   free association

15. During a therapy session involving free association a patient
    repeatedly changed the subject or forgot what he was about to
    say. This patient was displaying *resistance* an indication that he   resistance
    was about to remember something that he had previously tried to
    forget.

16. While Freud wanted patients to gain insight into their motives,
    he didn't want these insights to be merely *intellectual emotional*   intellectual, emotional
    involvement is necessary for genuine self-discovery.

17. Freud considered first *catharsis* and then *transference* as the means   catharsis, transference
    for producing emotional involvement.

18. The *neo - Freudian* view emphasizes interpersonal and   neo-Freudian
    cultural factors rather than psychosexual development.

19. Behavior therapists hold that the condition Freud called neurosis
    is caused by maladaptive *learning* which can be corrected   learning
    through *reeducation*   reeducation

20. A straightforward way to remove a classically conditioned
    response is through *extinction*   extinction

21. *Flooding* is the technique in which a patient agrees to be   Flooding
    exposed to a fear-arousing stimulus for some period of time.

22. A version of flooding, called *implosion* therapy, has the patient   implosion
    imagine fear-provoking stimuli of an intense sort.

23. The major goal of behavior therapists in treating phobias is to break the link between the _conditioned_ stimulus and the _fear_ response.

conditioned, fear

24. Sequential tensing and relaxing of the major muscles produces muscular relaxation, which is considered incompatible with a fear response. Pairing the former with fear-evoking stimuli in order to eradicate phobias is part of the _systematic desensitization_ paradigm.

systematic desensitization

25. Since fear-evoking stimuli can seldom be brought into the treatment room, systematic desensitization must depend on the patient's _imagination_ of fear-evoking situations according to a(n) _anxiety hierarchy_

imagination

anxiety hierarchy

26. A man who is afraid of heights is asked to imagine that he is standing on the observation deck at the top of the Empire State Building and leaning over the edge. The therapist is trying to _flood_ the patient with anxiety and _extinguish_ the link between the stimulus and fear response.

flood, extinguish

27. In order to break compulsive fingernail biters of their habit, we coat their nails with a harmless but extremely bitter liquid so that they experience an unpleasant taste each time they bite their nails. This is an example of _aversion_ therapy.

aversion

28. A _token economy_ uses operant reinforcement techniques to change patients' responses. This technique is usually most effective with in-patients.

token economy

29. In contrast to behavior therapists, some therapists dispense with all conditioning techniques and, instead, help the patient acquire more appropriate ways of thinking. This is known as _cognitive_ therapy.

cognitive

30. Unlike other forms of therapy, _humanistic_ therapists deal with the individual at a global level.

humanistic

31. Rogers believes that people often dislike themselves. In his _client - centered_ therapy, an attempt is made to provide a situation in which personal growth can resume.

client-centered

32. Humanistic therapy is characterized by its _nondirective_ nature, in which the therapist avoids advising or interpreting.

nondirective

33. _Existential_ therapy is an attempt to cope with the difficulty of some to see meaning in their lives.

Existential

34. One component of existential therapy is the _encounter_, a meeting of two people who see each other as independent entities.

encounter

35. The major focus of psychoanalysis is _understanding_ of behavior therapy, _doing_; of cognitive therapy, _thinking_; and of humanistic therapy, _feeling_.

understanding

doing, thinking

feeling

36. One common element of all therapists is _emotional defusing_ as the patient is encouraged to rid himself of intense and unrealistic fears.

emotional defusing

37. An important part of therapy helps show the patient how he reacts to others and is called *interpersonal learning* This adds to self-knowledge gained through *insight*.

interpersonal learning

insight

EVALUATING THERAPEUTIC OUTCOME

38. A valuable recent technique for investigating treatment effectiveness is *meta-analysis*, in which a comparison is made between those receiving treatment and those who have not been treated.

meta-analysis

EXTENSIONS OF PSYCHOTHERAPY

39. *Family* therapists are more interested in the relationships within the family as a unit than in the family members as individuals.

Family (Marital)

40. When a set of people get together to help each other manage a common difficulty under the direction of a therapist, this is known as *group* therapy.

group

Self-Test

1. Proposed remedies for mental disorders:
   a. are few.
   b. can be divided into biological and psychological intervention.
   c. all have a high success rate.
   d. all of the above
2. Somatic therapies:
   a. involve getting the patient to imagine other people's feelings.
   b. involve role playing and acting out of fears.
   c. treat mental illness as a physical illness.
   d. none of the above
3. The family of drugs called phenothiazines seems to be effective in reducing symptoms of schizophrenia, including:
   a. withdrawal.
   b. hallucinations.
   c. thought disorder.
   d. all of the above
4. The action of phenothiazines that makes them effective drugs for the treatment of schizophrenia is that they block dopamine receptors. This must mean that schizophrenia could be caused by:
   a. too little dopamine being taken up by receptors at synapses.
   b. too little dopamine being produced at synapses.
   c. too much dopamine being taken up by receptors at synapses.
   d. can't tell from the action of the drugs

5. Evidence that phenothiazines act as more than sedatives includes:
   a. the fact that true sedatives, like phenobarbital, have little calming effect on schizophrenics.
   b. the fact that these drugs have a specific drug effect on symptoms that are particular to schizophrenia.
   c. the fact that these drugs have no effect on anxiety or depression.
   d. all of the above
6. The phenothiazines (especially chlorpromazine) reduce many symptoms of schizophrenia. Below are characterizations of five patients suffering from some form of mental illness. Which patients would be expected to improve with chlorpromazine treatment?
   i. This patient suffers from bizarre thoughts and beliefs.
   ii. This patient is withdrawn and noncommunicative.
   iii. This patient has frequent hallucinations.
   iv. This patient is easily agitated.
   v. This patient is deeply depressed.

   a. all of the above
   b. i, ii, v
   c. ii, iii, v
   d. ii, iv, v
   e. i, ii, iii, iv
7. Depression is best treated (pharmaceutically) by:
   a. one of the tricyclics.

b. chlorpromazine.

c. amphetamines.

d. lithium carbonate.

8. It has been suggested that lithium carbonate may:

 a. be a general cure for most forms of mental illness.

 b. be totally useless, acting only as a placebo.

 c. prevent future episodes of bipolar disorder.

 d. have a general activation and arousal effect rather than a specific treatment effect.

9. Which of the following sources would be convincing evidence that antidepressants do more than just produce euphoria to counteract the depression that they are meant to treat?

 a. if they acted on normal subjects to increase euphoria

 b. if they had specific action on neurotransmitters

 c. if they had an influence on other illnesses such as panic disorder

 d. if they did not produce euphoria in normal subjects

10. A researcher finds that after drinking nothing but milk for three months, three patients (out of nine) report that they no longer suffer from migraine headaches. The researcher proclaims the curative powers of milk. What critical questions cannot be answered due to the absence of a control group?

 a. What is the spontaneous recovery rate without treatment?

 b. How did the milk cure the headaches?

 c. Why were only one-third of the patients cured?

 d. Can this finding be repeated?

11. A motorist takes his car to the garage for a tune-up. Unbeknownst to him, the mechanic is dishonest and tells the motorist that he tuned the car when, in fact, he hadn't. The motorist feels that the car does run better. This is an example of:

 a. the placebo effect.

 b. schizophrenia.

 c. a double blind.

 d. desensitization.

12. A new drug is believed to alleviate the symptoms of bipolar disorder. The drug is tested in the following manner: One group of patients receives the drug in pill form, and another similar group receives a sugar pill. No patient knows which group he is in. A panel of psychiatrists evaluates each patient before and after the treatment period. The panel is not told whether a patient is getting the drug or the sugar pill. This is an example of:

 a. a placebo effect.

 b. simultaneous control.

 c. the double-blind technique.

 d. transference.

13. While drug therapy has produced a drastic decline in institutionalized patients, this has occurred at some cost. Patients on phenothiazine, for example:

 a. experience varying side effects from their drugs.

 b. make only marginal adjustments to the outside world.

 c. must continue to take their drugs after release.

 d. all of the above

14. A treatment which was designed to liberate the patient's thoughts from his pathological emotions, but which produces ambiguous results and which may impair foresight and attention is:

 a. electroconvulsive shock treatment (ECT).

 b. prefrontal lobotomy.

 c. lithium treatment.

 d. catharsis.

15. Electroconvulsive shock treatment (ECT) was originally used to treat schizophrenia but was later found to be more effective in treating:

 a. depression.

 b. mania.

 c. compulsive behavior.

 d. It is still most effective in treating schizophrenia.

16. ECT:

 a. is faster than many antidepressant drugs.

 b. can produce severe memory impairment.

 c. is generally used only after drug therapy has been tried.

 d. all of the above

17. Orthodox (classical) psychoanalysis:

 a. states that illness is a result of unconscious defenses against unacceptable urges.

 b. states that most problems date back to childhood.

 c. was developed by Freud.

 d. all of the above

18. The cure for mental illness can be achieved by _____ according to the classical psychoanalysts.

 a. the victory of reason over passion

 b. a complete suppression of bad memories

 c. a reenactment of the cause of the problem

 d. none of the above

19. When a patient is asked to say whatever comes into his mind, it is believed that sooner or later the

memory relevant to the disorder should appear. This technique is known as:

a. resistance.

b. repression.

c. free association.

d. role playing.

20. Psychoanalysts believe the emotions are a principal part of therapy. One means for bringing emotions into play involves the relationship between the patient and therapist. The patient begins to behave as if the analyst were an important figure in his own life. This is known as:

a. catharsis.

b. transference.

c. resistance.

d. intellectualization.

21. Modern day practitioners of psychoanalysis:

a. emphasize interpersonal factors rather than sexual development.

b. subscribe to neo-Freudian views.

c. focus on the patient's present rather than his past.

d. all of the above

22. Behavior therapists argue that:

a. the theoretical notions of psychoanalysis are untestable.

b. the therapeutic effectiveness of psychoanalysis is unclear.

c. neurosis is caused by maladaptive learning.

d. all of the above

23. The behavior therapist tends to emphasize:

a. giving the patient insight into the origins of his problems.

b. righting improper behavior patterns without regard for underlying causes.

c. curing the patient by a variety of means, including free association.

d. enabling the patient to reach a full realization of his human potentialities.

24. For behavior therapists, fear:

a. is a classically conditioned response.

b. has its roots in early childhood.

c. is a manifestation of emotional traumas.

d. is an operantly conditioned response.

25. Since behavior therapists believe that one of the causes of certain strong fears, such as that of heights, is early classical conditioning, their therapy rests on the principle of:

a. second-order conditioning.

b. extinction.

c. reinforcement.

d. punishment.

26. The technique of flooding makes use of which of the following principles?

a. classical conditioning

b. extinction

c. implosion therapy

d. token economy

27. On which sort of subjects would you expect implosion therapy to have its greatest impact?

a. those with no phobias

b. those with vivid imagery

c. those who have been systematically desensitized

d. those given cognitive therapy

28. In systematic desensitization, the patient first learns muscular relaxation and then constructs an anxiety hierarchy of fear-evoking situations. The next step is:

a. to imagine the least fearful situation while relaxed.

b. to experience the least fearful situation while relaxed.

c. to imagine the most fearful situation and then relax as the conditioned link is extinguished.

d. to give the patient homework assignments involving exposure to fear-evoking stimuli.

29. Systematic desensitization relies on which of the following principles?

a. extinction

b. flooding

c. counterconditioning

d. none of the above

30. A patient who has a morbid fear of elevators is asked to imagine his most fear-producing situation. The therapist must be a proponent of:

a. systematic desensitization.

b. implosion therapy.

c. the placebo effect.

d. none of the above

31. The pairing of an unpleasant stimulus with an undesirable behavior is known as:

a. paired associate learning.

b. cognitive therapy.

c. response-produced anxiety.

d. none of the above

32. There is some question about the lasting effectiveness of aversion therapy because:

a. it doesn't even seem to last while the patient is in the therapist's office.

b. the effects wear off even while the aversive stimulus is still applied after some time has passed.

c. without the aversive stimulus, the lasting effects seem to fade.

d. it has been shown to be an ineffective treatment for alcoholism.

33. Token economies

a. are ineffective with in-patients.

b. are a form of instrumental conditioning.

c. are a form of classical conditioning.

d. are based on the use of extinction.

34. A therapist confronts a depressed patient with the irrationality of his belief that he cannot get a good job because he thinks he is incompetent despite evidence to the contrary. This therapist is most likely to be a proponent of:

a. modeling.

b. cognitive therapy.

c. desensitization.

d. could be any of the above

35. Cognitive therapies:

a. focus on the patient's beliefs and attitudes rather than his behavior.

b. are not primarily concerned with the patient's history.

c. do not rely heavily on behavior modification.

d. all of the above

36. One of the features on which cognitive therapies concentrate is:

a. the behaviors exhibited by patients.

b. the automatic thoughts that patients seem to have.

c. the irrationality of beliefs that patients have.

d. more than one of the above

37. In contrast to traditional psychoanalysis or behavior therapy, humanistic therapists:

a. are interested in causes rather than effects.

b. deal with only one symptom at a time.

c. treat the individual at a global level.

d. believe that neuroses are a product of society.

38. The view that many emotional disorders result from a belief that everything is pointless characterizes the school of the:

a. psychoanalysts.

b. nihilists.

c. existential therapists.

d. all of the above to some degree

39. In contrast to pharmaceutical approaches to mental illness, psychotherapy:

a. is much more effective.

b. involves interpersonal interaction.

c. is more relevant to the nature of psychopathology.

d. none of the above

40. It seems as if the different forms of psychotherapy concentrate on different aspects of the problem. In particular:

a. cognitive therapy concentrates on the patient's thoughts.

b. psychoanalysis concentrates on the patient's understanding of his past.

c. humanistic therapy concentrates on the patient's feelings.

d. all of the above

41. Psychoanalysis can be summarized by the word "unconscious" in the same way that behavior therapy can be represented by "conditioning." What word best summarizes humanistic therapy?

a. cause

b. feeling

c. directive

d. rational

42. All of the following are common to the various therapeutic schools except:

a. interpersonal learning.

b. insight.

c. emotional defusing.

d. therapy as an all-or-none process.

43. One of the differences between family therapy and classic psychoanalysis is:

a. family therapists deal with a group of individuals, not just one.

b. family therapists concentrate on relationships, not individual mental health.

c. family therapists don't concentrate on the developmental history of each individual.

d. all of the above

44. If psychotherapy's only effect is nonspecific,

a. it may nevertheless have value in providing a shoulder to lean on.

b. it will have proved largely an ineffective course of treatment.

c. it will then, by definition, be just a placebo effect.

d. it will be more effective than if its effect had been specific.

Answer Key for Self-Test

1. b p. 534
2. c p. 534
3. d p. 535
4. c p. 535
5. d pp. 535–36
6. e p. 535
7. a p. 536
8. c p. 536

Investigating Psychological Phenomena

DEMONSTRATION OF ROLE PLAYING

Equipment: Nòne
Number of subjects: Yourself and one other
Time per subject: Thirty minutes
Time for experimenter: Thirty minutes

Role playing is one technique used by therapists to educate their patients about various aspects of interpersonal relations. This technique requires at least two people to assume the roles of individuals other than themselves in a particular social situation. In so doing, the hope of the treatment is that the participating individuals will gain some insight about the feelings, emotions, and cognitions of the persons whose roles are being played.

Although the technique sounds simple enough in principle, in actual practice it is a bit risky. As the following quote illustrates, role playing participants frequently lapse back into their own personalities and have to be reminded about their role playing activities.

[The therapist] says "Tom, do you really care for me?" Tom says "I would say to her that I do, but she'd complain." Therapist: "Don't tell me what you *would* do. I'm Jane. Talk to me. Tom, do you really care for me?" Tom (turning away, looking slightly disgusted): "Yes." Therapist (still as Jane): "You don't say it like you mean it." Tom: "Yeah, that's what she says, and I usually . . ." Therapist (interrupting): "You're again telling me *about* what you'd say. I'm Jane. Tom, you don't say it like you mean

it." Tom: "It's very hard for me to answer her when she says that." Therapist: "OK, I'm Jane. Tell me how you feel." Tom: "Jane, when you do that it really turns me off. Maybe if you didn't ask me so often I'd be able to say it spontaneously without feeling like a puppet . . . (then, in a tone that indicates he is now talking to the therapist as therapist) Gee, I wonder what would happen if I really said that to her" (Wachtel, 1977, pp. 234–35).

You can try role playing on your own to discover some of its features. Solicit the participation of a fellow student of the opposite sex from your introductory psychology class and set up the following situation.

The two of you are married and have just graduated from college. Each of you has very well-defined career plans, and you have each been skillful and lucky enough to have been offered very attractive first jobs that fit precisely the career lines that you have planned. The problem is that your job offers are in cities 1,000 miles apart. How do you decide what to do?

You should go through two sessions: first, have a discussion about this problem with your partner with each of you playing yourselves. Write down each of your responses on paper. Second, switch roles and try having the discussion again. In each case, put yourselves in the other's situation. Again, write your responses on paper.

After you have finished playing both roles, talk about differences in the conversations that resulted from your playing the male versus the female role. Compare the transcripts of each session. Did this help you gain a different perspective on the problem?

At this point, you might want to try another role-playing exercise in which the two roles are quite different from one another. This will allow you to take two very different perspectives on a scene. Try out the following scene:

One of you should assume the role of an instructor for a course you are both taking (perhaps introductory psychology), while the other plays the role of a student. The issue is that the student has scored poorly on the midterm examination, but he feels that at least part of the reason for his poor performance is that he was graded unfairly by the instructor. In addition, the student was faced with taking four midterm exams within three days, so his performance was bound to suffer. Now imagine that the student has come in to talk with the instructor about these issues. The person playing the role of the instructor should really try to assume the personality and attitudes of the real instructor in the course as much as possible. After you have acted out a scene, switch roles. This time, to add some variety, have the student role be one of a very aggressive student who is determined not to leave the instructor's office without a change of grade. Again, after each scene, write down your impressions so that you can later discuss and evaluate them.

Having finished this scenario, think about some of the following questions: Was it more difficult to as-sume the role of the instructor or student? Was it difficult to stay in character without lapses? What insights have you gained about instructor-student rela-tionships? Would this be a useful exercise for students and instructors to try in general? How was this role-playing exercise different from the first one?

Statistics: The Collection, Organization, and Interpretation of Data

Learning Objectives

1. Review what the topic of statistics is about. Know when statistical tests are needed in psychological research.

DESCRIBING THE DATA

2. Define scaling. Why is it important to understand the types of number scales?

Categorical and ordinal scales
3. Understand what categorical and ordinal scales are. Be able to describe the arithmetic operations permitted with each. Give examples of these scales.

Interval scales
4. Cite the important feature of an interval scale. Give examples.

Ratio scales
5. Know what defines a ratio scale. Give some examples of ratio scales.
6. Discuss how interval and ratio scales differ. What arithmetic operation is permitted with ratio scales?

COLLECTING THE DATA

The experiment
7. List the essential ingredients of an experiment.
8. Know what the difference between independent and dependent variables is.

Observational studies
9. Discuss how observational studies differ from experiments and how they are similar.

10. Review the advantages and disadvantages of observational studies.

The case study
11. Discuss the role of the case study in psychological research. Know when it is to be preferred over other methods.

SELECTING THE SUBJECTS

Sample and population
12. Be able to explain the difference between a sample and a population. Know when you would choose a sample.

Random and stratified samples
13. Understand some of the factors that must be taken into account in sampling.
14. Discuss the merits of random versus stratified sampling.

Sampling responses
15. Explain why one must be careful in sampling responses.

ORGANIZING THE DATA: DESCRIPTIVE STATISTICS

Frequency distribution
16. Describe how a frequency distribution is created from the raw scores in an experiment. To get practice in constructing a frequency distribution, plot one for the following heights (in inches) of males in a small class: 72, 72, 68, 66, 74, 73, 69, 69, 70, 67, 66, 73, 72.

Measures of central tendency

17. Know what a measure of central tendency is and why it is useful. Describe the three measures of central tendency that are commonly used. Calculate these three quantities for the scores given above.

Measures of variability

18. Describe what the range of a group of scores is, and describe why the range has limited utility. What is the range for the scores given above?

19. Understand what the variance of a set of scores is. Why is it a useful measure of variability? Calculate the variance and standard deviation of the scores given above.

Converting scores to compare them

20. Know how percentile ranks are calculated and how they permit comparison of scores obtained from different tasks.

21. Define z-score. Why is it useful for comparing scores from two distributions?

22. Explain how z-scores and percentile ranks are similar.

The normal distribution

23. Give the characteristics of a normal distribution.

24. Be able to convert a z-score into a rank for a variable that has a normal distribution.

25. Understand the principle that can explain when a variable will be distributed normally. To do this you should roughly understand how a repeated binomial event will approximate a normal distribution.

DESCRIBING THE RELATION BETWEEN TWO VARIABLES: CORRELATION

Positive and negative correlation

26. Understand what positive and negative correlation is.

27. Describe how a scatter plot is constructed. What does it show? What does a line-of-best-fit have to do with a scatter plot?

The correlation coefficient

28. Understand what various values of r mean.

29. Know how a correlation coefficient is computed. Understand the logic of this computation, as well.

Interpreting and misinterpreting correlations

30. Give examples of cases for which a correlation cannot be interpreted in terms of one variable causing changes in another. What is the danger in interpreting correlations in terms of cause-effect?

INTERPRETING DATA:
INFERENTIAL STATISTICS

Accounting for variability

31. Know what accounting for variance means.

32. Understand how variance is accounted for in actual experiments, such as the examples given in the text.

33. Know how to account for variance in correlational data.

Hypothesis testing

34. Know what null and alternative hypotheses are. How do critical ratios allow us to rule out one of these hypotheses?

35. Discuss the trade-off involved in the decision about where to set the cutoff for the critical ratio.

36. Be able to describe how hypotheses about differences between means can be tested using a critical ratio.

37. Understand the relationship between a sample mean and a population mean.

38. Define standard error, and know what role it plays in testing hypotheses about sample means.

39. Be sure to follow the statistical analysis of the imagery experiment presented in the text.

40. Explain what it means to be reasonably confident that the mean of the population will fall within a specified interval.

Some implications of statistical inference

41. Explain how statistical conclusions are probabilistic. How does this affect these conclusions both about population means, and about individuals?

42. Explain why statistical conclusions should be conservatively drawn.

43. Based on your knowledge of how to compute a critical ratio, describe how sample size affects a statistical conclusion. When may statistical and psychological significance differ?

Programmed Exercises

1. The collection, organization, and interpretation of numerical data

   comprise the topic of _____ .   statistics

DESCRIBING THE DATA

2. When all subjects in a group perform differently, or when the same subject performs differently on different occasions, we say

   that the data contain _____ .   variability

3. Differences among subjects _____ groups and _____   between, within
   groups are the two sources of variability that are analyzed by
   statistical methods.

4. The assignment of numbers to events is called _____ .   scaling

5. The type of _____ that numbers represent is defined by   scale
   which arithmetic operations are permitted on those numbers.

6. The assignment of the gears in a car to the categories first,

   second, and third involves the use of a _____ scale.   categorical (nominal)

7. If you ask someone to rank four cola drinks from most to least

   preferred, you would be using an _____ scale.   ordinal

8. The Fahrenheit scale of temperature is an _____ scale as   interval
   indicated by the fact that the difference between 30° and 35°
   equals the difference between 75° and 80°.

9. The scale of length in feet is a _____ scale; thus, we can say ratio
   that a board of 4 feet is twice as long as a board of 2 feet.

COLLECTING THE DATA

10. If an experimenter were interested in the effect of instructions-to-
    image on memory performance, he might run an experiment with

    an _____ group given imagery instructions, and a _____   experimental, control
    group given standard memory instructions.

11. In the experiment referred to in question 10, the type of instruction

    is the _____ variable, and a measure of recall performance is   independent

    the _____ variable.   dependent

12. An _____ _____ of the effects of city versus suburban   observational study
    living on rates of schizophrenia would involve selecting schizo-
    phrenic patients who had lived in urban or suburban environments.

13. The study of a particular aphasic subject intensively to reveal
    features of language behavior involves the use of a

    _____ _____ approach.   case study

SELECTING THE SUBJECTS

14. Psychologists are interested in drawing conclusions about

    _____ of subjects, but since it is frequently impractical to   populations

    test large numbers of people, they tend to test _____ , then   samples
    generalize their conclusions.

15. A _____ sample is said to be unrepresentative of a population.   biased

16. A procedure for selecting subjects in which all individuals are

    equally likely to be selected is called a _____ _____ .   random sample

17. _____ _____ is a technique for selecting subjects in which one tries to represent certain subgroups of a population in proportion to their size.   Stratified sampling

ORGANIZING THE DATA: DESCRIPTIVE STATISTICS

18. A _____ _____ of birthweight could be represented by a   frequency distribution

_____ , a graph of the numbers of people in a sample who   histogram
are born at various weights in the range to be studied.

19. There are three major measures of central tendency, the

_____ , _____ , and _____ .   mean, median, mode

20. The distribution of reaction times in an experiment is likely to be

_____ , since there will be none below 0, many short ones,   skewed
and fewer and fewer long ones.

21. The _____ is a measure of variation that is defined as the   range
difference between the highest and lowest scores.

22. The _____ is a measure of variation that takes account of   variance
each score's deviation from the mean. Its square root is called

the _____ _____ .   standard deviation

23. The _____ _____ of a score is the percentage of scores   percentile rank
that lie below it.

24. A _____ _____ expresses scores in terms of units of   z-score (standard score)
standard deviations from a mean.

25. The heights of females in a population form a

_____ _____ , one in which there are equal frequencies   normal distribution
of heights on both sides of the mean.

DESCRIBING THE RELATION BETWEEN TWO VARIABLES: CORRELATION

26. If two dependent variables are related to one another, they are

said to be _____ .   correlated

27. If we ranked the top ten runners in the world so that the top
runner was ranked 1 and the last runner was ranked 10, and if
we based these ranks on time to run the 1500 meter race, there

would by definition be a _____ correlation between rank and   positive
time.

28. On the average, the faster one can complete each item on an
aptitude test, the higher one's score assuming that one doesn't

sacrifice accuracy. There is thus a _____ correlation between   negative
time per item and test score.

29. Plotting two dependent variables, one on the abscissa and one on
the ordinate, yields a graph that shows the relationship between

the variables. This is called a _____ _____ .   scatter plot

30. A line fit to the points of the graph described in question 29 is

called a _____-_____-_____-_____ .   line-of-best-fit

31. A _____ _____ of −1 indicates that there is a perfect _____ correlation between two variables.

correlation coefficient

negative

INTERPRETING DATA: INFERENTIAL STATISTICS

32. We say that we have _____ variance when we can attribute some of the variability in a set of scores to a particular factor.

explained (accounted for)

33. Squaring a correlation coefficient yields a proportion of _____ which is explained.

variance

34. For the experiment described in question 10, the _____ hypothesis is that there is no difference between the groups,

null

while the _____ hypothesis is that the group with imagery instructions will recall more items.

alternative

35. The _____ _____ of a test statistic is usually set at 2 so that the probability of choosing the alternative hypothesis when the null hypothesis is, in fact, correct is quite small (one chance in twenty).

critical ratio

36. The standard deviation of a distribution of sample means is called the _____ _____ .

standard error

37. The _____ _____ is the range within which we can be fairly confident the actual population mean will fall.

confidence interval

38. There are three important characteristics of statistical conclusions. They are affected by sample _____ , they are _____ , and they are _____ .

size, probabilistic

conservative

Self-Test

1. If there are 100 questions on a test, with each question worth one point, then the set of scores from 0 to 100 constitutes:
   a. a nominal scale.
   b. an ordinal scale.
   c. an interval scale.
   d. a ratio scale.

2. If we wanted to investigate the effect of cigarette smoking by mothers on birth defects in their children, we would likely:
   a. perform an experiment.
   b. use correlations.
   c. perform an observational study.
   d. use a case study approach.

3. An experimenter is interested in determining the effects of caffeine on sleeping behavior. He selects two groups of subjects to test his hypothesis that caffeine causes sleeplessness. Group 1 drinks regular coffee before bedtime, while group 2 drinks decaffeinated coffee. The experimenter then measures the amount of time it takes subjects to fall asleep (as measured by an electroencephalogram). In this experiment:
   a. amount of sleep is the dependent variable and caffeine is the independent variable.
   b. amount of sleep is the independent variable and caffeine is the dependent variable.
   c. both are independent variables.
   d. both are dependent variables.

4. In the description of question 3:
   a. group 1 is the control group; group 2 is the experimental group.
   b. group 1 is the experimental group; group 2 is the control group.
   c. both groups are experimental; the experimenter has failed to include a control.
   d. neither group is experimental; this is an observational study.

5. If we test a randomly selected group of college students and then generalize our results to all college students, then:
   a. we are using a stratified sampling procedure.
   b. we are making inappropriate inferences.

c. we would need to correlate the results of our sample.

d. we are testing a sample in order to draw conclusions about a population.

6. Suppose we wanted to know the size of the memory span (how many items a subject could hold in short-term memory) for all students in a particular school. To do this, we place all the names of all the students in a hat and draw out 100 for testing. This procedure is known as:

a. stratified sampling.

b. biased sampling.

c. random sampling.

d. skewed sampling.

7. If, in question 6, we had samples by grade in school, then we would have employed the technique of:

a. stratified sampling.

b. biased sampling.

c. random sampling.

d. skewed sampling.

8. The results of an examination are graphed so that each score is listed in order on the abscissa, and the number of students receiving that score is plotted on the ordinate. Such a graph:

a. is a frequency distribution.

b. is a histogram of the scores.

c. is not a scattergram.

d. could be a normal distribution.

e. all of the above

9. Suppose the graph in question 8 turned out to look like the graph below. From this we could conclude that:

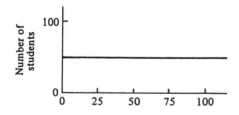

a. the mean is greater than the median.

b. the mode is 50.

c. the variance is 0.

d. the test was statistically significant.

e. none of the above

10. Suppose the graph in question 8 turned out to look like the graph at the top of the next column. From this we could conclude that:

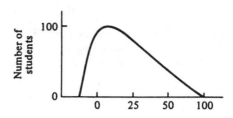

a. the distribution is normal.

b. the median is lower than the mean.

c. the students with a score of 75 are in the 75th percentile.

d. the mode is 100.

e. none of the above

11. For the following five scores, 1, 2, 3, 4, 5:

a. the median is 3.

b. the mean is 3.

c. the variance is 2.

d. all of the above

e. a and b but not c

12. Variability : central tendency : variance :

a. correlation

b. z-score

c. mean

d. standard deviation

13. All of the following could be measures of variation in a set of scores except:

a. mean − median.

b. highest score − lowest score.

c. sum of (each score − mean)^2.

d. average of highest two scores − average of lowest two scores.

14. Consider two examinations: On one, the mean is 50, the standard deviation is 5, and your score is 65. On the other, the mean is 50, the standard deviation is 2, and your score is 60. Which of the following is true?

a. Your percentile rank is higher on the second test.

b. Your z-score is higher on the second test.

c. You can meaningfully compare your z-scores on the two tests.

d. You cannot meaningfully compare your raw scores on the two tests.

e. all of the above

15. If a set of scores on an exam has a mean of 75 and a standard deviation of 10, then:

a. the distribution must be normal.

b. the distribution must be symmetric.

c. a score of 50 corresponds to a z-score of −2.5.

d. a z-score of 1.0 equals a test score of 75.

16. If SAT scores have a mean of 500 and a standard deviation of 100, and if IQ scores have a mean of 100 and a standard deviation of 15, then with an SAT score of 650 and an IQ score of 115:
    a. the z-score for IQ will be higher than the z-score for SAT.
    b. the percentile score for IQ will be higher than the percentile score for SAT.
    c. both of the above
    d. the percentile score for IQ will be 84.
    e. the scores on the two tests will not be comparable since the tests differ.

17. If we found a correlation coefficient of −.88 between reaction time and performance on a test of motor skill, we could conclude that:
    a. a high score on the test of motor skill predicts a fast reaction time.
    b. a high score on the test of motor skill predicts a slow reaction time.
    c. motor skill causes people to have faster reaction times.
    d. reaction time and motor skill are largely unrelated.

18. In the scatter plot shown below:
    a. there is no relationship between x and y.
    b. the correlation coefficient is statistically significant.
    c. the correlation coefficient is close to 0.
    d. variable x is the independent variable.

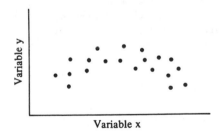

Variable x

19. If a line-of-best-fit for a scatter plot were flat, then:
    a. the correlation would be 1.
    b. the correlation would be 0.
    c. the correlation would not be significant.
    d. we know nothing about the correlation until we calculate it.

20. Which of the following correlation coefficients shows the strongest inverse relationship between variables x and y?
    a. .82
    b. −.74
    c. 0
    d. −1.14

21. If the correlation between a parent's and his children's scores on a test of motor skills were .70, then we would know that:
    a. seventy percent of the variability of the children's score is accounted for by the parents' scores.
    b. seventy percent of the variability in the parents' scores is accounted for by the children's scores.
    c. children's motor skills are caused by the skills of their parents.
    d. none of the above

22. An experiment is performed to determine whether eating breakfast improves one's test performance. Two groups are given tests, one group after eating a good breakfast, one after no breakfast. Consider the following hypothesis. Eating breakfast has no effect on test performance. This hypothesis:
    a. can only be evaluated probabilistically.
    b. is called the "alternative" hypothesis.
    c. cannot be evaluated in this experiment.
    d. is assessed by examining within-subject variability.

23. In the experiment of question 22 which of the following would be necessary in order for us to believe that eating breakfast enhances test performance?
    a. The sample must be normal.
    b. The sample must be statistically significant.
    c. The between-subject variance must be larger than the within-subject variance.
    d. all of the above
    e. none of the above

24. Suppose you were to discover a hospital in which there were 8 new births each day, and you wished to test the hypothesis that this hospital had more births per day than the average hospital of its size. To do this we would need to know:
    a. the correlations among births at all the hospitals in question.
    b. the mean, standard deviation, and number of hospitals in the comparison group.
    c. only the standard error of the births in the comparison group.
    d. none of the above

25. Two hospitals report an average of 8 births per day with a standard deviation of 10 births. For hospital A, this average was computed over 25 days; for hospital B, it was computed over 400 days. The standard errors of births in these hospitals:
    a. are equal.
    b. are 2 in hospital A and .5 in hospital B.

c. are not comparable because of the difference in number of days.

d. none of the above

26. If a sample mean is 20, its standard deviation is
30, and the number of subjects in the sample is
9, then:

a. you can be fairly confident that the sample
is normal.

b. a subject with a score of 25 is in the fifth
percentile.

c. a score of 17 would be equal to a z-score
of 1.

d. you can be fairly sure that the population
from which this sample was drawn has a
mean greater than 0.

27. Suppose you're trying to predict whether a Republican or Democratic candidate will win a particular
senatorial race. You conduct a poll of the relevant
voters and discover that 53% would vote for the
Republican and 47% for the Democrat. Who do
you think will win?

a. You can be reasonably confident that the
Republican will win.

b. You can be reasonably confident that the
Democrat will win.

c. Given the polling data, it's not clear who
will win.

d. There isn't enough information to make a
prediction one way or the other.

Answer Key for Self-Test

1. d pp. A3–A4
2. c p. A5
3. a p. A4
4. b p. A4
5. d p. A6
6. c p. A6
7. a p. A6
8. e pp. A7–A13
9. e pp. A7–A10, A21
10. b p. A8
11. d pp. A8, A10
12. c pp. A8–A10
13. a pp. A8–A10
14. e pp. A11–A12
15. c pp. A11–A12
16. d pp. A12–A13
17. a pp. A15–A16
18. c pp. A14–A15
19. b p. A15
20. b pp. A15–A16
21. d pp. A16–A18
22. a p. A25
23. c pp. A22–A23
24. b pp. A23–A24
25. b pp. A23–A24
26. d p. A24
27. d p. A25

Investigating Psychological Phenomena

APPLYING STATISTICAL CONCEPTS

Equipment: None
Number of subjects: None
Time per subject: None
Time for experimenter: 45 minutes

This exercise provides an opportunity for you to
apply some of the statistical concepts described in the
text. Reconsider the experiment described on p. A4 of
the text in which subjects are tested for recall performance on lists of twenty words with and without instructions to form images. Imagine that twenty subjects
had been run in this experiment – the ten described in
the text plus ten others. The data of all these subjects
are presented in Table 1 below. In the first column
are the recall scores with imagery instructions; the
second column contains recall scores when no imagery
instructions were provided; the third column is the
difference between the first two, the amount of improvement. Finally, the fourth column contains the
results of a test of imagery ability that was given to
each of the subjects in this hypothetical experiment
(scores on this test could range from 0 to 40). Using
the data in this table, perform the following tabulations
and analyses.

TABLE 1

Subject	Score with imagery	Score without imagery	Improvement	Test of imagery ability
Alphonse	20	5	15	30
Betsy	24	9	15	26
Cheryl	20	5	15	27
Davis	18	9	9	21
Earl	22	6	16	33
Fred	19	11	8	26
Germaine	20	8	12	32
Hortense	19	11	8	38
Imogene	17	7	10	30
Jerry	21	9	12	27
Kerry	17	8	9	29
Linda	20	16	4	24
Moe	20	10	10	26
Nicolas	16	12	4	22
Orry	24	7	17	36
Penelope	22	9	13	32
Quarton	25	21	4	23
Ronald	21	14	7	26
Steven	19	12	7	24
Terry	23	13	10	28

1. Create frequency histograms of the recall data on the two unlabeled sets of axes below. The left graph is for the recall scores with imagery instructions, and the right is for recall scores without imagery instructions. Note that you must decide what specific values to place on each axis for each graph.

Frequency histograms

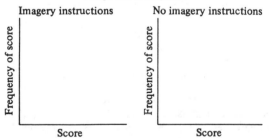

Imagery instructions   No imagery instructions

2. Calculate the mean, median, and mode of each of the distributions whose scores you have plotted above.

3. Calculate the range and standard deviation of each of these distributions.

4. Analyze the improvement scores to test the hypothesis that imagery instructions lead to better recall performance than no imagery instructions. To do this, you must compute a critical ratio that evaluates the sample mean of the improvement scores against the

population mean for the null hypothesis (no improvement). Is this critical ratio larger than 2.0? If so, how do we interpret the improvement scores?

5. Examine the relationship between the improvement scores and performance on the test of imagery ability in two ways. First, create a scatter plot on the axes presented below. Second, compute a correlation coefficient between these sets of scores. Is there a relation between the variables? How would you interpret this relation psychologically?

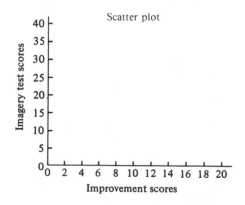

Scatter plot

Now that you have completed your analyses, you should turn to the next page to examine the correct answers and compare them to your own answers.

Answers to Statistical Exercise

1.

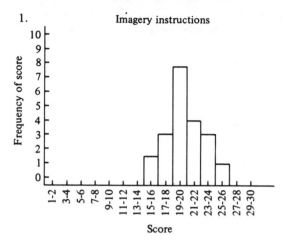

2. Imagery instructions
   Mean = 20.35
   Median = 20
   Mode = 20
   No imagery instructions
   Mean = 10.10
   Median = 9
   Mode = 9

3. Imagery instructions
   Range = 9
   Standard deviation = 2.46
   No imagery instructions
   Range = 16
   Standard deviation = 3.89

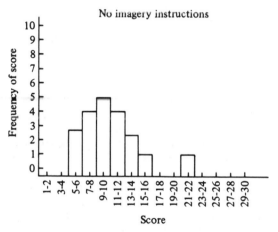

4. Critical ratio =
$$\frac{\text{sample mean} - \text{population mean by null hypothesis}}{\text{standard error of the mean}}$$

standard error of the mean

$$= \frac{\text{standard deviation}}{\sqrt{N}}$$

$$= \frac{4.05}{\sqrt{20}}$$

$$= .91$$

$$\text{critical ratio} = \frac{10.25 - 0}{.91}$$
$$= 11.26$$

This critical ratio is much larger than 2.0; therefore we may conclude that there is a statistically significant improvement in recall scores comparing no imagery to imagery instructions.

5. Scatter plot

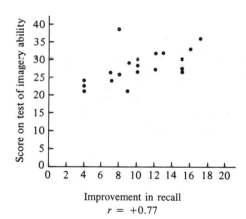

Improvement in recall
$$r = +0.77$$

The correlation coefficient, r, is $+0.77$.

Both the scatter plot and the correlation coefficient indicate that there is substantial relationship between the variables. We might propose the following hypothesis to account for this relationship. Subjects with a better imagery ability are better able to form mental images in the memory task and thus perform better. Our hypothesis must remain tentative, however, since we are not permitted to draw cause-effect conclusions from correlational data.

APPENDIX B

On the following pages you will find the report sheets for several of the experiments in the preceding chapters. If your instructor wants to collect the data for these experiments, use these report sheets. You can cut them out and hand them in to your instructor.

Chapter 2

REPORT SHEET – HEART RATE

Data from Three Subjects (A, B, and C)

Instruction and time	A	B	C
"Begin and Relax"			
00:00–0:30			
0:45–1:15			
"Increase, physical activity"			
1:30–2:00			
2:15–2:45			
"Relax"			
3:00–3:30			
3:45–4:15			
"Increase, mental"			
4:30–5:00			
5:15–5:45			
"Relax"			
6:00–6:30			
6:45–7:15			

List for each subject the basic situation that they imagined in the "increase" minutes.

	Physical	Mental
A	_____	_____
B	_____	_____
C	_____	_____

Chapter 1

REPORT SHEET – NERVE IMPULSE

Practice Trial 1 ankle = Time in seconds*

Part I Trial 1 ankle = _____

Trial 2 ankle = _____

Trial 3 ankle = _____

Trial 4 ankle = _____

Trial 5 ankle = _____

Part II Trial 1 upper arm = _____

Trial 2 upper arm = _____

Trial 3 upper arm = _____

Trial 4 upper arm = _____

Trial 5 upper arm = _____

Test

Part III Trial 1 ankle time = _____

$\div$ 25 = _____ (a)

Trial 2 upper arm time = _____

$\div$ 25 = _____ (b)

Trial 3 upper arm time = _____

$\div$ 25 = _____ (c)

Trial 4 ankle time = _____

$\div$ 25 = _____ (d)

$\dfrac{a + d}{2}$ = _____ (average ankle time)

$\dfrac{b + c}{2}$ = _____ (average upper arm time)

Average ankle time − average upper arm time = _____ (difference 1)

(1) Distance of ankle to base of the neck (for third tallest person) = _____

(2) Distance of upper arm to base of the neck (for third tallest person) = _____

Distance 1 − distance 2 = _____ (difference 2)

$\dfrac{\text{difference 2}}{\text{difference 1}}$ = _____ (speed of nerve impulse)

*Record time accurate to .1 second.

Chapter 3

REPORT SHEET – LEARNED TASTE AVERSIONS

Number of subjects questioned _____

Number of subjects with aversions _____

Number of subjects who confirm Garcia's

notions _____

Summarize the results from all of your subjects below. You decide which questions are relevant to each feature of learned taste aversion, and summarize your results with respect to each of the features listed below.

BELONGINGNESS Relevant questions (Nos.)

_____

_____

_____

ONE TRIAL LEARNING Relevant questions (Nos.)

_____

_____

_____

LONG CS-US INTERVAL Relevant questions (Nos.)

_____

_____

_____

NOVELTY EFFECT Relevant questions (Nos.)

_____

_____

_____

"IRRATIONALITY" Relevant questions (Nos.)

_____

_____

_____

OTHER INTERESTING RESULTS:

_____

_____

_____

Chapter 3

REPORT SHEET – MAZE LEARNING

Trial	Time	Number of errors
1	_____	_____
2	_____	_____
3		_____
4	_____	_____
5	_____	_____

(using paper
with cut-out hole)

Chapter 4

REPORT SHEET – MEASURING BRIGHTNESS CONTRAST

Background values:	1	3	4	5	7	10
matching value 1:	_____	_____	_____	_____	_____	_____
matching value 2:	_____	_____	_____	_____	_____	_____
matching value 3:	_____	_____	_____	_____	_____	_____
Total matching value:	_____	_____	_____	_____	_____	_____
Average matching value:	_____	_____	_____	_____	_____	_____

Chapter 6

REPORT SHEET – IMAGERY INSTRUCTIONS

Answer sheet for list 1

1. _____
2. _____
3. _____
4. _____
5. _____
6. _____
7. _____
8. _____
9. _____
10. _____
11. _____
12. _____
13. _____
14. _____
15. _____
16. _____
17. _____
18. _____
19. _____
20. _____

Answer sheet for list 2

1. _____
2. _____
3. _____
4. _____
5. _____
6. _____
7. _____
8. _____
9. _____
10. _____
11. _____
12. _____
13. _____
14. _____
15. _____
16. _____
17. _____
18. _____
19. _____
20. _____

Chapter 8

REPORT SHEET – IMPLICIT LEARNING

1. _____   9. _____   17. _____
2. _____   10. _____   18. _____
3. _____   11. _____   19. _____
4. _____   12. _____   20. _____
5. _____   13. _____   21. _____
6. _____   14. _____   22. _____
7. _____   15. _____   23. _____
8. _____   16. _____   24. _____

Subject's statement of rule: _____

_____

_____

_____

_____

_____

_____

_____

_____

Number of correct responses out of 24: _____

Chapter 9

REPORT SHEET – PERSONAL SPACE

1 person elevator	Number of cases with subjects in predicted place (7 or 9)	_____/15
2 person elevator	Number of cases with subjects in predicted place (7 and 9)	_____/15
2 person elevator	Number of cases with subjects in noncontiguous squares	_____/15

Chapter 7

REPORT SHEET

Experiment 1

Color patch list

List 1 _____ sec. _____ errors

List 3 _____ sec. _____ errors

List 5 _____ sec. _____ errors

List 7 _____ sec. _____ errors

List 9 _____ sec. _____ errors

Average = _____ sec.

Total errors = _____

Letter string list

List 2 _____ sec. _____ errors

List 4 _____ sec. _____ errors

List 6 _____ sec. _____ errors

List 8 _____ sec. _____ errors

List 10 _____ sec. _____ errors

Average = _____ sec.

Total errors = _____

Experiment 2

Neutral words

List 1 _____ sec. _____ errors

List 3 _____ sec. _____ errors

List 5 _____ sec. _____ errors

List 7 _____ sec. _____ errors

List 9 _____ sec. _____ errors

Average = _____ sec.

Total errors = _____

Color words

List 2 _____ sec. _____ errors

List 4 _____ sec. _____ errors

List 6 _____ sec. _____ errors

List 8 _____ sec. _____ errors

List 10 _____ sec. _____ errors

Average = _____ sec.

Total errors = _____

Experiment 3

Neutral words

List 1 _____ sec. _____ errors

List 3 _____ sec. _____ errors

List 5 _____ sec. _____ errors

List 7 _____ sec. _____ errors

List 9 _____ sec. _____ errors

Average = _____ sec.

Total errors = _____

Color referent words

List 2 _____ sec. _____ errors

List 4 _____ sec. _____ errors

List 6 _____ sec. _____ errors

List 8 _____ sec. _____ errors

List 10 _____ sec. _____ errors

Average = _____ sec.

Total errors = _____

Chapter 7

REPORT SHEET – THE STROOP EFFECT

Experiment 1

Color patch list

List 1 _____ sec. _____ errors

List 3 _____ sec. _____ errors

List 5 _____ sec. _____ errors

List 7 _____ sec. _____ errors

List 9 _____ sec. _____ errors

Average = _____ sec.

Total errors = _____

Letter string list

List 2 _____ sec. _____ errors

List 4 _____ sec. _____ errors

List 6 _____ sec. _____ errors

List 8 _____ sec. _____ errors

List 10 _____ sec. _____ errors

Average = _____ sec.

Total errors = _____

Experiment 2

Neutral words

List 1 _____ sec. _____ errors

List 3 _____ sec. _____ errors

List 5 _____ sec. _____ errors

List 7 _____ sec. _____ errors

List 9 _____ sec. _____ errors

Average = _____ sec.

Total errors = _____

Color words

List 2 _____ sec. _____ errors

List 4 _____ sec. _____ errors

List 6 _____ sec. _____ errors

List 8 _____ sec. _____ errors

List 10 _____ sec. _____ errors

Average = _____ sec.

Total errors = _____

Experiment 3

Neutral words

List 1 _____ sec. _____ errors

List 3 _____ sec. _____ errors

List 5 _____ sec. _____ errors

List 7 _____ sec. _____ errors

List 9 _____ sec. _____ errors

Average = _____ sec.

Total errors = _____

Color referent words

List 2 _____ sec. _____ errors

List 4 _____ sec. _____ errors

List 6 _____ sec. _____ errors

List 8 _____ sec. _____ errors

List 10 _____ sec. _____ errors

Average = _____ sec.

Total errors = _____

Chapter 11

REPORT SHEET–IMPRESSIONS

	Percent of subjects checking favorable adjective at left			
	Asch's Data		Your Data	
Adjective Pair	group A (24 students)	group B (34 students)	group A (__ students)	group B (__ students)
generous	24	10		
wise	18	17		
happy	32	5		
good-natured	18	0		
humorous	52	21		
sociable	56	27		
popular	35	14		
reliable	84	91		
good-looking	74	35		
serious	97	100		
restrained	64	9		
honest	80	79		

Chapter 13

REPORT SHEET–CONSERVATION OF NUMBER

1. More blue _____
   More red _____
   Both equal _____
2. More blue _____
   More red _____
   Both equal _____
3. More blue _____
   More red _____
   Both equal _____
4. More blue _____
   More red _____
   Both equal _____

5. More blue _____
   More red _____
   Both equal _____
6. More blue _____
   More red _____
   Both equal _____
7. More blue _____
   More red _____
   Both equal _____
8. More blue _____
   More red _____
   Both equal _____

Chapter 17

REPORT SHEET–DEPRESSION

Self-rating of mood now (enter number) _____

Self-rating of mood over last twelve months
(enter number) _____

Number of negative events recalled _____

Number of positive events recalled _____

Negative minus positive events _____

Negative plus positive events _____

Chapter 14

REPORT SHEET—SEX DIFFERENCES

	Your data* (combined with classmate's data)			
	Males		Females	
Item	#	%	#	%
1. Killing cockroach	_____	_____	_____	_____
2. Queen Anne's lace (correct answer: flower)	_____	_____	_____	_____
3. Using word "shit" (less than 5 times)	_____	_____	_____	_____
4. Sew clothes	_____	_____	_____	_____
5. Intercourse only after spiritual love	_____	_____	_____	_____
6. Nude in locker room	_____	_____	_____	_____
7. Crying frequently (very often, often, or only with good reason)	_____	_____	_____	_____
8. Feel like smashing things	_____	_____	_____	_____
9. Chest measurement	_____	_____	_____	_____
10. Change tire	_____	_____	_____	_____
11. Playing radio	_____	_____	_____	_____
12. Prefer dominance in relationship	_____	_____	_____	_____
13. Overweight	_____	_____	_____	_____
14. Washing hair when depressed	_____	_____	_____	_____
15. Sleep in nude	_____	_____	_____	_____
16. Closest parent (mother)	_____	_____	_____	_____
17. Keep room neat	_____	_____	_____	_____

*Tabulate your results below in the following way. For the "yes" or "no" questions (e.g., item 1), add up the number of subjects who answered "yes." Then calculate what percentage answered "yes." For the "true" or "false" questions (e.g., item 8), record those who answer "true." For other items (e.g. item 2), add up the number of subjects whose answers are the same as those indicated in parentheses under "Item" (e.g., item 2—flower).

List the femaleness scores of all of your subjects:

Males: _____ _____ _____ _____ _____ _____ _____ _____ _____ _____

          _____ _____ _____ _____ _____ _____ _____ _____ _____ _____

Females: _____ _____ _____ _____ _____ _____ _____ _____ _____ _____

          _____ _____ _____ _____ _____ _____ _____ _____ _____ _____

Copyrights and Acknowledgments

Grateful acknowledgment is made to: F. Garb, A. Stunkard, and the *American Journal of Psychiatry* to adapt from Garb and Stunkard. "Taste aversions in man," *American Journal of Psychiatry* 131 (1974): 1204–1207; W. Epstein, I. Rock, and the *American Journal of Psychology* to adapt from Epstein, W., and Rock, I., "Perceptual set as an artifact of recency," *American Journal of Psychology* 73 (1960):214–228; J. R. Stroop and the *Journal of Experimental Psychology* to adapt from J. R. Stroop, "Studies in interference in serial verbal reactions," *Journal of Experimental Psychology* 18 (1935):643–662; A. S. Reber and the *Journal of Verbal Learning and Verbal Behavior* to adapt from A. S. Reber, "Implicit learning of artificial grammars," *Journal of Verbal Learning and Verbal Behavior* 6 (1967):858–863; S. E. Asch and the *Journal of Abnormal and Social Psychology* to adapt from S. E. Asch, "Forming impressions of personality," *Journal of Abnormal and Social Psychology* 41 (1946):258–290.

Illustrations

Page 3 Bugelski, B. R. and Alampay, D. A., "The role of frequency in developing perceptual sets," *Canadian Journal of Psychology* 15 (1961):205–211. Adapted by permission of the Canadian Psychological Association.

Page 12 *bottom* and page 29 Keeton, W. T., *Biological science*, 4th edition. New York: W. W. Norton & Company, Inc., 1986. Copyright © 1986, 1980, 1979, 1972, 1967 by W. W. Norton & Company, Inc.

Page 15 Hodgkin, A. L., and Huxley, A. F. "Action potentials recorded from inside nerve fibers," *Nature* 144 (1939):710–11. Adapted by permission.

Page 28 Nisbett, R. E., "Taste, deprivation and weight determinants of eating behavior," *Journal of Personality and Social Psychology* 10 (1968):107–116. Copyright 1968 by the American Psychological Association. Reprinted by permission.

Page 30 Harlow, H. F., "Learning and satiation of response in intrinsically motivated complex puzzle performance in monkeys," *Journal of Comparative and Physiological Psychology* 43 (1950):289–294.

Page 39 Reproduced by permission of the publishers from Köhler, W., *The mentality of apes*, London, England: Routledge & Kegan Paul Ltd., 1976.

Page 41 *bottom* Pavlov, I. P., *Lectures on conditioned reflexes*, vol. 1. New York: International Publishers, Co., Inc. 1928. Adapted by permission of International Publishers Co., Inc.

Page 43 From Spooner, A., and Kellogg, W. N., "The backward conditioning curve," *American Journal of Psychology* 60 (1947): 321–334. Copyright © 1947 by The University of Illinois Press. Reprinted by permission of the publisher.

Page 70 Gombrich, E. H., *Meditations on a hobby horse*. Oxford, England: Phaidon Press, 1963.

Page 72 From James J. Gibson, *The perception of the visible world*. Boston, Mass: Houghton Mifflin Co., 1950.

Page 73 Photograph by William Vandivert. From *Scientific American*, April 1960. Reprinted with permission of William Vandivert and *Scientific American*.